Plea Bargaining's Triumph

Plea Bargaining's Triumph

A HISTORY OF PLEA BARGAINING
IN AMERICA

GEORGE FISHER

Stanford University Press
Stanford, California

Stanford University Press
Stanford, California
© 2003 by the Board of Trustees of the
Leland Stanford Junior University
All rights reserved

Reprinted by permission of the Yale Law Journal
Company and William S. Hein Company from the *Yale
Law Journal*, vol. 109, pp. 857–1086.

Printed in the United States of America
on acid-free, archival-quality paper

Library of Congress Cataloging-in-Publication Data

Fisher, George, 1959–
    Plea bargaining's triumph : a history of plea bargain-
ing in America / George Fisher.
        p.   cm.
Includes bibliographical references and index.
    ISBN 0-8047-4459-9 (alk. paper) : ISBN 0-8047-5135-8 (pbk. : alk. paper)
    1. Plea bargaining—United States—History. I. Title.
    KF9654 .F57 2003
    347.73'72—dc21 2002012185

Typeset by BookMatters in 10/14 Sabon

Original Printing 2003

Last figure below indicates year of this printing:
12   11   10   09   08   07   06   05   04

For Mom and Dick

Contents

Figures and Tables

Acknowledgments

In the making of this book I gathered many debts. Among the biggest are those I owe to the archivists, librarians, and research assistants who helped collect the far-flung records and documents that form the core of my empirical study. I am grateful in particular to Michael Comeau, Janis Duffy, Bill Milhomme, and the reference staff of the Massachusetts Archives, whose patience outlasted my seemingly endless visits to Columbia Point. Mike Haire and John Reardon of the records management team at the Massachusetts Trial Court gave me access to their Worcester records facility and guided me through its maze. And Andrew Gurthet, Dave Bridgman, and Sonia Moss of the Stanford Law School Library never let me feel disadvantaged by the three thousand miles that separated me from most of my sources.

I relied to an enormous extent on a small army of devoted and talented research assistants. Over the years these included Blake Hurst, Tami Swiger, Alexis Haller, Phil Coppinger, Dan Levin, Josh Greenberg, Tyler Fuller, Zoe Scharff, and Steve Mansell. Craig Estes contributed indispensable help managing the case database. And many members of the *Yale Law Journal* gave scrupulous attention to an earlier version of this work. In particular, Maritza Okata, James Sing, and David Lam edited with insight and precision.

Many of my colleagues and friends have read all or part of earlier drafts and have offered me their guidance and insights. Among these are Al Alschuler, Stephanos Bibas, Miriam Conrad, Dick Craswell, Ted Ferdinand, Dan Freed, Lawrence Friedman, Tom Green, Tom Grey, Don Herzog, Adam Hirsch, Susan Klein, Marc Miller, Chet Mirsky, Bill Simon, Avi Soifer, Mary Vogel, Lloyd Weinreb, and Bob Weisberg. They did not all agree with me, but they all helped make this book better than it was.

Plea Bargaining's Triumph

Prologue

There is no glory in plea bargaining. In place of a noble clash for truth, plea bargaining gives us a skulking truce. Opposing lawyers shrink from battle, and the jury's empty box signals the system's disappointment. But though its victory merits no fanfare, plea bargaining has triumphed. Bloodlessly and clandestinely, it has swept across the penal landscape and driven our vanquished jury into small pockets of resistance. Plea bargaining may be, as some chroniclers claim, the invading barbarian. But it has won all the same.

The battle has been lost for some time. It was lost at least by the time prominent observers of the 1920s first lamented our "vanishing jury," and in some places it was lost decades before then. In the years since the jury succumbed in a war few knew it was waging, advancing waves of who-lost-the-jury scholarship have tried to retrace the path of defeat. Much of this work has charged that the ever-weightier burden of modern jury trials overbore the system, which surrendered to the plea bargain's efficiency to avert collapse. Another, newer collection of studies looks beyond the courtroom to spy out broader social forces that aided plea bargaining's cause. But in the breadth of their scope, these studies overlook the first principle of conflict: Victory goes to the powerful. And so, although we can find many worthy accounts of why the jury fell, we must ask instead why plea bargaining triumphed.

Like most of history's victors, plea bargaining won in great part because it served the interests of the powerful. In the battlefield of the criminal courts, the kind of power that mattered most was the authority to dictate sentences, which judges had and prosecutors generally lacked. To track the course of plea bargaining's rise, we must discover how prosecutors secured the power to make it happen and why judges, who always had the power, began to see plea bargaining as in their interest. In this account of plea bargaining's rise, legislators will play a large role because their power to allocate sentencing authority between prosecutor and judge tilted the terms of battle. And criminal defendants, who nominally held an absolute power to plead or not to plead but who often found themselves hopelessly undefended, must play a real if complicated part.

This is not a social history of plea bargaining's rise, if by that is meant a story that highlights the play of social forces and minimizes the role of human actors. Although recent scholars have put forth appealing accounts of the electoral pressure of new immigrants or the analogical force of new industry in the creation of "assembly-line justice," these theories stand without evidence or fall beside the point. Plea bargaining's triumph was manifestly the work of those courtroom actors who stood to gain from it. To the extent that external actors, especially legislators, played a conscious role in the struggle, they mainly took sides with the ultimately defeated jury trial. And to the extent that broader social forces such as immigration and industrialization influenced the outcome of the conflict, they did so by increasing the criminal caseload on the one hand and the civil caseload on the other, thereby altering the interests and options of prosecutors and judges.

And yet in one striking way, the story of plea bargaining's rise is bigger than the actors who made it happen. Once it took hold, plea bargaining possessed a power of its own. That power derived ultimately from the individual power of those whose interests plea bargaining served. In its collective form that power made plea bargaining a dominant force in the evolution of modern American criminal procedure. Plea bargaining's influence sometimes appears on the face of the historical record. This is most true in the case of probation, one of the most enduring nineteenth-century contributions to our penal mechanisms. I will argue that the birth of probation was in some part, and perhaps in large part, the work of prosecutors who sought a new way to expand their power to bargain for pleas. Once in place, probation grew in symbiosis with plea bargaining and in time became one of the most useful tools of lawyers cutting deals.

Plea bargaining's role in shaping other procedural institutions appears more subtly in the historical record. But there is an unmistakable correlation between those procedural changes that have survived and thrived and those that have aided plea bargaining's cause. The pattern compels a conclusion that plea bargaining has so fast a grip on the mechanism of justice that antagonistic institutions cannot survive. The demise of the indeterminate sentence, for example, one of the most promising of the late nineteenth century's progressive brainchildren, bears the mark of plea bargaining's malice. A true indeterminate sentence, in which only prison officials and parole boards could set the length of criminal sentences, would have stripped both judges and prosecutors of the power to bargain over the length of terms and would have hobbled the plea-bargaining regime. But though widely promoted, true indeterminate sentences never emerged, and even the half-measure that we have come to know as parole found its development stunted when it threatened the dominance of plea bargaining.

The rise of probation and the fall of indeterminate sentencing are but two of plea bargaining's victories. Before canvassing the rest, we need to follow the course of plea bargaining's ascent to learn the source of its strength.

THE SETTING

I trace these events as they unfolded in America. Although the earliest instances of plea bargaining may well have happened elsewhere,[1] and although plea bargaining in time would spread across the common law world and beyond, it triumphed here first. Within America, I focus on Massachusetts. Massachusetts is the birthplace of probation, and though I had little suspicion when I set out that plea bargaining and probation would prove so closely linked, it seemed likely that such innovations would find a common home. Moreover, Massachusetts was among the states that acted most vigorously in the nineteenth century to suppress the sale of alcohol, and there was reason to suspect that enforcement of liquor laws played a part in plea bargaining's early rise.[2]

Within Massachusetts, I focus mainly on its largest county—Middle-sex—which spreads south and east from the New Hampshire border to Boston's western edge, sweeping in the pioneering mill town of Lowell, the hamlets of Lexington and Concord, and cosmopolitan Cambridge.[3] Middlesex County's diversity avoids the possible distortions of Boston's idiosyncrasies, one of which was a distinct lack of enthusiasm in enforc-ing the state's liquor laws.[4] Moreover, Middlesex was the practicing ground of Asahel Huntington, perhaps the first prosecutor in history to be called up on charges of plea bargaining. And Middlesex is where I practiced as a prosecutor, an experience that left me familiar with the ways of its courts and perhaps more aware of the ways things have changed.

Within Middlesex County, I look most closely at the middle tier of the county's judicial system, which had jurisdiction over all but the most seri-ous crimes. A succession of courts occupied this middle tier during the nineteenth century—the Court of General Sessions of the Peace through 1803, the Court of Common Pleas from 1804 until 1859, and the Superior Court after 1859.[5] At the four annual sittings of the Court of General Sessions of the Peace, local justices of the peace presided jointly over jury trials.[6] At both the Court of Common Pleas and the Superior Court, jury trials took place before professional judges who rode circuit throughout the state, sitting in each county three or four times a year and ensuring some statewide uniformity of practice.[7] These middle-tier courts promise to be better sites for this study than the courts of the lower tier. The bottom tier of the state's judiciary lacked two institutions—jury and prosecutor—whose role in the criminal system looms far too large for us to think that much can be explained without them.[8]

My examination of the upper tier, occupied by the Supreme Judicial Court, will not range far because the criminal trial jurisdiction of that court was quite narrow and grew narrower as the nineteenth century wore on. Like judges of the middle tier, justices of the high court rode cir-cuit across the state to preside over criminal jury trials.[9] At the century's start, their jurisdiction included an array of serious crimes, but soon shrank to include only capital crimes, a category that, in turn, dwindled by mid-century to include only murder. In 1891 the Supreme Judicial Court lost even murder trials to the courts of the middle tier.[10]

Because it rarely handled more than a few criminal trials a year, the Supreme Judicial Court would not serve well as a focus for a study of plea bargaining's rise. Still, it is important to include its business in this study, not only to assure that the practices I observed in the middle tier were not somehow peculiar to less serious criminal cases, but also to take advantage of the sometimes superior records of Supreme Judicial Court business and of the deeper insights they afford. As we will see, the rise of plea bargaining before the Supreme Judicial Court tracked roughly the same course as in the courts of the middle tier. Though it began perhaps a little later, plea bargaining in capital cases soon caught up with and at times overtook the development of plea bargaining in the middle tier. More importantly, the same dynamic was at work in both tiers: The powers and interests of individual courtroom actors appear to explain the course of plea bargaining's rise.

The records of the middle-tier courts for the years before 1859 have survived in almost full form, and those for the years since have suffered only minor losses and deletions. I have found no important gap in the records of the Supreme Judicial Court.[11] Complete as they may be, these records are hardly expressive of what went on in the courts of nineteenth-century Massachusetts and are maddeningly silent about the motivations behind most guilty pleas. The clerk's vacant formulas usually erased the tracks of any express agreement by prosecutor or judge to grant the defendant a concession in exchange for a plea.

In most cases, therefore, we must use other methods to distinguish those defendants who pled guilty out of remorse for their crimes or to shorten their engagements in court from those who did so as part of a *plea bargain*, expecting to win some concession in exchange. We must employ still other devices to distinguish *explicit* plea bargains, in which the parties spoke out loud the terms of their exchange, from *implicit* bargains, in which the defendant pled guilty for an unpromised but hoped-for reward. My sampling of more than 4,000 cases often permits statistical conclusions about the frequency and nature of plea bargaining even when individual case reports are mute.[12] And newspapers and other contemporary sources can help decipher the clerk's cryptic codes. These sources also make plain that the lessons of Middlesex County apply generally throughout Massachusetts and, with allowances for statutory and regional variances, in several other jurisdictions as well.

THREE WAVES

This is hardly the first account of plea bargaining's early rise. It follows instead in the wake of three waves of historical scholarship. Each of these has advanced understanding, yet each has left the essential dynamic of plea bargaining's success largely unrevealed.

The first wave, in the 1920s and early 1930s, marked the true age of plea bargaining's discovery. In a series of privately and publicly funded surveys of the operations of the criminal justice system in various American jurisdictions, small bands of law professors and elite lawyers quite literally discovered that plea bargaining had overrun the nation's courts.[13] In a sense, this first wave of plea bargaining scholarship was historical only by accident. After setting out to describe the justice system as it was, the authors discovered that the system they expected to find already was a relic of the past.

Several of these system-wide surveys—notably the 1922 Cleveland study edited by Harvard's Roscoe Pound and Felix Frankfurter and the 1931 Wickersham Commission report on the federal criminal justice system—have grown famous in their own right. Yet the two scholars who gave the most enduring voice to this first age of discovery wrote in the far less exalted pages of one of the nation's fledgling law journals. On the first page of the first issue of the *Southern California Law Review*, Dean Justin Miller of the University of Southern California Law School exposed "The Compromise of Criminal Cases."[14] Writing in the same pages a year later, Columbia's Raymond Moley lamented "The Vanishing Jury."[15]

Though Miller and Moley both drew on the findings of the various system-wide surveys, their studies stand as the first attempts to define in detail the contours and origins of plea bargaining. Their common tone of muted alarm reflects their rarefied academic perches. Miller opened with the declaration that "[i]n theory there should be no compromises of criminal cases." But in practice, "the condonation and compromise of criminal cases is frequent and the methods of evading the clear purpose of the written law are varied."[16] Moley led with the striking finding that of 13,117 felony prosecutions begun in Chicago in 1926, only 209 ended in convictions by a jury.[17] He declared that the worst aspect of the already dominant plea-bargaining regime was its invisibility. "The very difficulty with which the facts concerning this practice have been unearthed," he wrote, "shows how easy it has been for prosecutors to indulge in this sort of compromise without exciting public interest."[18]

Like the earliest masters of certain schools of art and architecture, Miller and Moley set standards that later authors often have failed to match. Both tethered their theories of plea bargaining's origins to reams of assembled facts. Miller's empirical method reflected his background as a California county prosecutor.[19] He asked prosecutors throughout the state about the methods and prevalence of case compromises in their districts. Then he collated their responses into a painstaking taxonomy of compromise. For each of more than a dozen species and subspecies (not all of which would constitute plea bargaining today), he cited studies and quoted long passages from prosecutors' replies to his inquiries.[20] When he determined at last to suggest why compromise was so common, he said little more than what every prosecutor already knew: The number of acts made criminal, such as alcohol sales and driving offenses, had expanded greatly;[21] courts had failed to keep pace with ballooning caseloads; and the mounting public burden of increased jury service had exhausted public patience.[22] These factors merely describe different facets of the general problem of growing workloads. Miller therefore has some claim to being the first theorist to declare caseload pressure the cause of plea bargaining.

Moley's justly more famous study mimicked Miller's in its fidelity to fact. But whereas Miller's work constitutes history only in the primary-source sense that it recorded the conditions of its day, Moley also delivered a true history of plea bargaining's past. And whereas Miller built his taxonomy of compromise on a database of prosecutorial anecdotes, Moley relied only rarely on anecdotes, preferring instead to track plea bargaining's statistical footprint. Even today, Moley's article stands among the few truly useful statistical histories of plea bargaining. Despite occasional criticism of his methods,[23] two of his discoveries are among the most important unearthed by any historian of plea bargaining—that plea bargaining in New York began its long rise in the first half of the nineteenth century and that it reached near-modern proportions by century's end.

Moley also can claim a place among plea bargaining's most sophisticated theorists. Like Miller and others who took part in the age of discovery, he attributed much of plea bargaining's success to the force of caseload pressure.[24] And like every plea-bargaining theorist of every age, he saw that prosecutors value the practice both for its efficiency and for the easy victories it hands them. But Moley reached further than most in exploring other interests plea bargaining served. He explained how the secrecy of the process permitted prosecutors to claim stunning conviction rates without disclosing how rarely they risked losing at trial. And he saw that judges found refuge in the security plea bargaining afforded against reversal on appeal.[25] True, Moley had blind spots. Even as he explained why judges should like plea bargaining, he wrongly predicted that judges would, if given the power, act to frustrate plea bargaining's advance.[26] This mistake stemmed from another: Because Moley never thought to ask where prosecutors found the power to plea bargain, he never discovered the essential role judges played in plea bargaining's rise.

Four decades passed after Miller and Moley's age of discovery before a second wave of historical studies came into view. Unlike the works of the first wave, most of these studies of the 1970s resisted any simple story based on caseload pressure. Here we can see how the theories of the first wave were perhaps a product of their time. Locked in a titanic struggle against alcohol running, the nation's courts sank beneath the sheer weight of liquor cases. Hence the Wickersham Commission's 1931 report echoed Miller and Moley in blaming plea bargaining on caseload pressure. By 1930 prosecutions under the federal Prohibition Act had grown to eight times the volume of all federal prosecutions in 1914. In many urban jurisdictions, the commission noted, "the enforcement agencies maintain that the only practicable way of meeting this situation . . . is for the United States Attorneys to make bargains with defendants."[27]

But by the 1970s, with memories of prohibition fading and plea bargaining still very much on the scene, new historians of the practice sought other explanations for its rise. Milton Heumann led this second wave with "A Note on Plea Bargaining and Case Pressure," an empirical attack on the old theory.[28] Heumann's method was, as he acknowledged, rough. To determine whether guilty plea rates correlated with caseload pressure, he simply compared guilty plea levels in Connecticut's various counties with each county's caseload, using caseload as a surrogate for caseload pressure.[29] But caseload pressure is, of course, a function of caseload *and* staffing—the busiest court in the state can have the lowest caseload pressure if it has enough judges and prosecutors. Yet Heumann made no adjustment for the number of judges and prosecutors assigned to each court.

Heumann's otherwise careful study nonetheless helped dislodge the old fixation on caseload pressure and opened the gates to a flood of new theories of plea bargaining's rise. Amid the profusion that followed, the two accounts that gained greatest currency enjoyed near-complete freedom from empirical testing. In the first, the brilliantly rhetorical "Torture and Plea Bargaining," John Langbein argued that plea bargaining arose because trial rules had grown so complex as to make the jury trial an "absolutely unworkable" way to resolve most criminal disputes.[30] On this score and others, Langbein compared plea bargaining with the judicial torture of medieval Europe, which triumphed after the old system of proof had grown top-heavy with protective procedures.[31]

In one sense Langbein's theory did not stray far from old notions of caseload pressure. The significance of cumbersome trial procedures was that cases took too long to try. But unlike caseload pressure, a relatively easy phenomenon to measure over time, the complexity of trial procedures eludes easy measuring. Langbein is surely right to claim that trials in eighteenth-century England moved far faster than in today's America.[32] But neither Langbein nor Albert Alschuler, who later endorsed his theory,[33] made any attempt to document the pace of trials in nineteenth-century America, the essential setting of any account of plea bargaining's rise.

I undertake that task in Chapter 5. As I report there, Langbein's theory is not wholly without foundation. True, I saw little evidence of increasing trial length throughout most of the nineteenth century, when plea bargaining took hold as the dominant means of resolving criminal cases. But I did find that murder trials grew suddenly longer toward the very end of the century, just as plea bargains in murder cases grew suddenly more common. So we should retain Langbein's theory as a complement to older accounts of caseload pressure. Though it surely cannot explain the long course of plea bargaining's rise, it perhaps can shed light on certain moments of unusual growth.

Lawrence Friedman and Robert Percival introduced the second dominant theory of the second wave in *Roots of Justice*, a broad-ranging study of criminal justice in California's Alameda County between 1870 and 1910. Friedman and Percival looked to the role that increasingly sophisticated policing and evidence-gathering techniques may have played in the development of plea bargaining.[34] "In [an earlier policing] system run by amateurs," they argue, "with no technology of detection or proof, a trial was perhaps as good a way as any to strain the guilty from the innocent." But once professional police and full-time prosecutors, aided by the new "police science" of fingerprinting and blood tests, came on the scene, "it could no longer be assumed that trial by jury . . . was the normal way to handle a criminal case. After all, police and prosecutors had already 'tried' the defendant. Why not leave it to them?"[35]

Like Langbein's theory of top-heavy trial procedures, Friedman and Percival's view has the virtue of common sense. People surely might have seen no point in trying a defendant already proved guilty by forensic evidence. But Friedman and Percival must rest on common sense alone. Richly detailed in other respects, their study neither documents a greater use of scientific evidence in Alameda cases as the century wore on nor demonstrates in any other jurisdiction a link between the rise of sophisticated police techniques and increased plea bargaining.[36] And though the authors took pains to note a distinct shift in the method of bargaining cases over the forty years of their study—a shift I discuss somewhat later—they did not suggest how new policing techniques could explain the change.[37]

After *Roots of Justice* appeared in 1981, there was a second, shorter lull in historical scholarship on plea bargaining. A third wave, emerging at decade's end, brought book-length treatments by Mary Vogel and Theodore Ferdinand and a shorter study by Mike McConville and

Chester Mirsky.[38] These works proceed from three common premises. The authors agree, first of all, that any reliable conclusion about the forces giving rise to plea bargaining must rest on painstaking analysis of a great many actual cases. They agree as well that this empirical undertaking must be both macroscopic and microscopic—it must embrace both statistical overviews and individual case histories. And they agree that this analysis cannot confine itself to the courts, but must reach out and take account of larger political and social realities, including community attitudes toward plea bargaining.

In the chapters ahead I mimic the methodological rigor of the third wave, amassing and analyzing thousands of Middlesex County cases while dissecting the individual details of many dozens. I do not, however, follow the studies of this era to their socially rooted conclusions. In time I examine each of these works in detail. For now, it is enough to say that while any study of so broad a phenomenon as plea bargaining must attend to the larger social setting, we are unlikely to find the root causes of so court-focused a practice anywhere outside the courtroom. So, although I adopt the methods of the third wave, I more often take the court-centered, caseload-conscious view of the first wave.

In the end, all three scholarly waves have overlooked certain critical dynamics that helped shaped plea bargaining's course. Almost every study of every era has worked from the assumption that prosecutors always had a unilateral power to plea bargain, but did not always have reason to use it. In fact the opposite has been true: Virtually from the beginning, public prosecutors have preferred plea bargains to trials, but often have lacked the power to make plea bargains happen. In casually assuming that prosecutors could bargain if they wanted to, these studies have overlooked the essential role judges played in plea bargaining's triumph. Even Moley, who saw the allure plea bargaining could hold for judges, assigned this factor far too little weight.

Having failed to see that plea bargaining had become the darling of both prosecutors and judges, these studies missed the consequences of such favor. Any institution that holds the affection of both of the system's major players will amass a staying power of its own. Hence plea bargaining has not merely endured, but has grown to be the dominant institution of American criminal justice.

THE ROAD AHEAD

This account of the rise of plea bargaining begins in the opening decade of the nineteenth century. One could begin earlier, as there is solid evidence of plea bargaining in earlier centuries, but that evidence is of isolated, episodic plea bargaining, whereas this is the story of plea bargaining's triumph as a systemic regime. Told chronologically, the story divides fairly neatly into two parts. During the first three-quarters or so of the nineteenth century, plea bargaining in Massachusetts advanced mainly in the realm of liquor law prosecutions and murder cases, where for reasons I explore, prosecutors had the power to negotiate pleas without any participation by the judge. These early deals took the form of *charge bargaining*—in exchange for the defendant's plea to one or more of several charges, the prosecutor dropped other charges or (in the case of murder) reduced the charge to a lesser offense. In the last quarter of the century, as judges converted to the cause of plea bargaining, it most often took the form of *sentence bargaining*, in which the defendant's plea won a reduced sentence. Backed by judges as well as prosecutors, plea bargaining now broke the narrow hold of liquor and murder prosecutions and conquered the entire penal territory—so that by century's close, guilty pleas accounted for some eighty-seven percent of criminal adjudications in Middlesex County.[39]

As useful as this simple chronology may be, at times I stray from the rather clean story line it provides. My aim is to highlight how the changing powers and interests of each courtroom actor played dominant roles in shaping the course of change. These two ways of telling the story—chronologically and by focusing on individual actors—are not always at odds. I begin with the role of prosecutors, whose influence emerged most clearly in the liquor law prosecutions of the century's first half, and I conclude with judges, whose changing behavior in the last quarter of the century assured plea bargaining's triumph. At times, though, the focus on individual actors has required me to leap ahead or fall back.

So I begin with prosecutors. That prosecutors consume three chapters of this nine-chapter study is not because their power to bargain was greatest of all. In fact, judges held the largest share of the power to dictate sentences and therefore to plea bargain. Rather, I linger on the prosecutor's role precisely because the prosecutor managed to elude the judge's control only rarely—and then only by virtue of extraordinary legislative grant or procedural ingenuity.

In Chapter 1, I address the first of these extraordinary legislative grants, made in the context of liquor law prosecutions and, with some differences, in murder cases. My research in Middlesex County confirms earlier findings of a strikingly high rate of plea bargaining in Massachusetts liquor prosecutions in the early nineteenth century. Various good theories might explain a link between liquor cases and plea bargaining, but the evidence overwhelmingly points to one—that the liquor law's distinctive penalty scheme, which assigned a fixed fine to almost every offense, deprived the judge of almost all sentencing discretion and put the prosecutor in a position to manipulate sentences by manipulating charges. Similarly, in capital cases, the prosecutor had the power to spare defendants mandatory death by permitting them to plead guilty to a lesser charge. Prosecutors quickly exploited these narrow grants of sentencing authority and put in place a very modern practice of charge bargaining for pleas.

Explaining the source of prosecutorial power to plea bargain is the hard part—it is easy to see why prosecutors wanted to plea bargain. Prosecutors of the nineteenth century, like prosecutors today, plea bargained to ease their crushing workloads, made heavier in the nineteenth century by their part-time status, their utter lack of staff, and a caseload explosion perhaps set off by newly founded police forces and massive immigration. And of course, they plea bargained to avoid the risk that wanton juries would spurn their painstakingly assembled cases. Given such clear incentives, the task of explaining the rise of prosecutorial plea bargaining in liquor and capital cases should have been complete at the end of Chapter 1—for as soon as prosecutors had the power to plea bargain, they surely would have used it. But because several scholars have dismissed the importance of caseload pressure in explaining the rise of plea bargaining, I must take up that issue in Chapter 2. I must also consider why judges were not partners in this early rise of plea bargaining. For if they had been, plea bargaining would not have been limited to liquor and murder cases—in which prosecutors had the power to plea bargain on their own—but could have extended across the criminal docket.

In Chapter 3, I step briefly out of the courthouse and into the State House. Massachusetts legislators reacted sourly when they discovered how prosecutors were using the power unwittingly bestowed on them by the liquor law's rigid penalty scheme. At mid-century the legislature eliminated this power and very nearly succeeded in snuffing out prosecutorial plea bargaining in liquor cases. The legislature did not, however, disturb prosecutors' power to conduct charge bargaining in murder cases, for there had been relatively few such bargains by mid-century. The result was that during the third quarter of the nineteenth century, plea bargaining advanced more dramatically in murder cases than in any other category. Even in liquor cases, the legislature's efforts to eradicate prosecutorial charge bargaining failed. After losing formal power to manipulate sentences in liquor cases, prosecutors retreated to the more covert and informal tactic of placing cases "on file." This procedural maneuver, often done in exchange for a defendant's guilty plea, allowed prosecutors to elude altogether the legislature's sentencing provisions. The primitive device of *on-file plea bargaining* evolved directly into what we know today as probation. By the end of the century, probation had become one of plea bargaining's most dependable foot soldiers.

Turning from the prosecutor's role in early plea bargaining to that of other actors, I move on in Chapter 4 to consider the part played by defendants. It is not hard to see why defendants, given the chance, would plead guilty for a measure of leniency. It is far less clear why their behavior on this score might change over time. Middlesex court records disclose that during the first half of the nineteenth century, decades before plea bargaining began its dramatic ascent, there had been a long decline in the proportion of nonliquor cases that ended in a plea. I argue that the guilty pleas defendants often offered at the beginning of the century were not plea bargains made in exchange for leniency, but rather the hopeless gestures of defendants who lacked lawyers and who properly saw that they had little chance of winning if they went to trial on their own. The gradual increase in the number of defendants who chose trial during the first part of the century therefore may mean that more and more defendants had counsel.

Then, in the third quarter of the century, a sudden assault on the power of defendants to take their cases to trial may have reversed this course and helped speed the rise of plea bargaining. Until the 1860s, criminal defendants throughout America lacked the right to testify at their own trials. In 1866, Massachusetts became only the third state to permit defendants to testify in their defense under oath. The vast majority of states followed suit by the end of the century. The legislators who passed these defendant-testimony laws no doubt aimed to help defendants by granting them the power to swear to their innocence even as they retained the absolute right to stay silent if they chose. Yet these laws had the probably unintended effect of discouraging defendants with criminal records from going to trial at all. Seasoned criminals knew that if they took the stand to claim their innocence, the rules then permitted prosecutors to undermine defendants' credibility by telling the jury about their past convictions—in most cases destroying any real chance of acquittal. Yet if they failed to testify, defendants believed, juries would convict them for their silence. Together with the growing practice of probation, defendant-testimony laws confronted every defendant with a good reason to plea bargain. The new laws helped persuade accomplished criminals to plead guilty, while the promise of probation, which was available almost exclusively to first offenders who pled guilty, served as an incentive for everyone else.

The combined willingness of all prosecutors and many defendants to bargain for pleas was not enough, however, for the practice to thrive outside the narrow context of liquor and murder cases. The statutory penalty structure for most crimes gave Massachusetts judges such great discretion in sentencing that the prosecutor typically could not guarantee a low enough sentence to win the defendant's plea. Plea bargaining's sweeping triumph during the last quarter of the nineteenth century therefore suggests that judges had entered plea bargaining's ranks. I argue in Chapter 5 that a caseload explosion on the civil side of Massachusetts courthouses helped force this change of judicial heart on the criminal side, for in Massachusetts, as in most American jurisdictions, the same judges sat on both civil and criminal cases. The industrial boom of the last part of the nineteenth century—and especially the spread of railroads and street cars—spawned a whole new strain of personal injury litigation that, case for case, absorbed far more time than the contractual nonpayment cases that once had filled the civil dockets. The figures in Massachusetts are clear: As judges devoted a hugely increasing proportion of their time to the civil caseload, they devoted a shrinking proportion to the criminal caseload, and they resolved more and more criminal cases by guilty plea.

By century's end, all three of the courtroom's major actors—prosecutor, defendant, and judge—had found reasons to favor the plea bargaining regime. For prosecutor and judge, who together held most of the power that mattered, the spread of plea bargaining did not merely deliver marvelously efficient relief from a suffocating workload. It also spared the prosecutor the risk of loss and the judge the risk of reversal, and thereby protected the professional reputation of each. In fact, by erasing the possibility of either factual or legal error in the proceedings, plea bargains protected the reputation and hence the legitimacy of the system as a whole. Seen in this light, as a function of the interests of prosecutor, defendant, judge, and the system itself, plea bargaining's triumph seems inevitable. And yet other historians of plea bargaining have attached little or no importance to this dynamic of powers and interests. I devote Chapter 6 to their competing accounts of plea bargaining's progress. In particular, I examine Mary Vogel's study of plea bargaining in nineteenth-century Boston and Mike McConville and Chester Mirsky's New York-based account. Their appealingly rich arguments that plea bargaining emerged in response to the social and political tensions of the day challenge my own, more courtroom-centered approach. I explain why I believe their theories must give way to the facts at hand.

Yet my own recounting of plea bargaining's rise to dominance would offer little if it explained events in one smallish northeastern state and nowhere else. So in Chapter 7, I look outside Massachusetts and ask whether the variables of power and interest that spurred plea bargaining's march there can account for its advance elsewhere. In England, New York, and California, the evidence suggests that they can.

I move on in Chapter 8 to explore the power that plea bargaining as an institution has amassed by serving the interests of power so well. The power of the various actors who stood to gain from plea bargaining became, in a sense, plea bargaining's power. This collective, systemic interest in plea bargaining promoted the rise of those institutions of criminal procedure that helped plea bargaining and hindered those that stood in its way. In the nineteenth century, plea bargaining fostered probation's rise and thereby created a hugely versatile plea-bargaining tool. In the late nineteenth and early twentieth centuries, plea bargaining helped stave off the indeterminate sentence, which had threatened to halt plea bargaining's progress. And in the twentieth century, plea bargaining played a surprisingly direct role in assisting the creation of public defenders' offices. In turn, these organizations for defense of the poor assured that in a majority of criminal cases, the defense lawyer would share the prosecutor's and judge's interests in maximizing systemic efficiency—and hence in plea bargaining. These examples of plea bargaining's influence over other institutions of criminal procedure are merely case studies within a larger trend. In fact, it is hard to think of a single enduring development in criminal procedure in the last 150 years that has not aided plea bargaining's cause.

Finally, in Chapter 9, I examine how the power to plea bargain has evolved since the late twentieth century. Before the advent of modern sentencing guidelines, both prosecutor and judge held some power to bargain without the other's cooperation. The result of their mutually independent bargaining strength was a certain balance of power, which to some degree protected defendants from abuses of power by either official. Today, sentencing guidelines have recast whole chunks of the criminal code in the mold of the old Massachusetts liquor laws. By assigning a fixed and narrow penalty range to almost every definable offense, sentencing guidelines often empower prosecutors to dictate a defendant's sentence by manipulating the charges. Guidelines have unsettled the old balance of bargaining power among prosecutor, judge, and defendant by ensuring that the prosecutor, who always had the strongest interest in plea bargaining, now has almost unilateral power to deal.

And so in time we arrive again at the Massachusetts liquor laws, where I now begin.

1

Liquor Laws, Murder Cases, and the Prosecutor's Power to Charge

In 1807 Samuel Dana took office as the first Middlesex County attorney.[1] His main forum would be the Court of Common Pleas, which occupied the middle tier of the Massachusetts criminal judicial enterprise. Dana did not launch his young office with honor. After a run-in with the three presiding judges at the December 1808 sitting of the court, an indignant Dana responded with something less than the decorum of the day. "I too often perceive," he advised the judges in a letter of complaint, "an unbecoming impetuosity, and snarling manner, ill suited to the soft ermine of justice."[2]

Two months later a legislative committee reported on Dana's conduct and announced charges against him. Dana's affront to the court was not the worst of his alleged wrongs. He had to explain as well why he had represented a crime victim in a civil suit even as he prosecuted the case's criminal counterpart.[3] Such arrangements put prosecutors in a position to leverage their official power for private gain. The law therefore barred prosecutors, "during the pendency of [any] prosecution, [from being] concerned, as counsel or attorney for either party, in any civil action depending on the same facts."[4]

The list of charges went on. Dana, the committee alleged, had billed the court for services to crime victims that seemed to fall within his official duties. When Dana listed these services among the costs owed by the court, he neglected to say the money was for him.[5] Here, too, Dana seemed to find himself on the wrong side of the law. No public prosecutor was to "receive any fee or reward . . . for services in any prosecution, to which it shall be his official duty to attend."[6] When the judges pointedly asked about these costs, Dana "observed that it was well known that [crime victims] were often obliged to get the professional assistance of lawyers." He did not point out, however, that he was the lawyer in question.[7]

Against each of these well-founded charges, Dana mounted a pathetic and lawyerly defense. Of his impudent letter to the judges, he simply noted that "however incautiously it may be expressed, . . . it contained my real opinion as to the correctness of their proceeding in the case."[8] On the charge that he had prosecuted a case while handling a related civil suit, Dana had more to say. He claimed that he did not actually conduct the civil suit. Rather his law partner, William M. Richardson, had done so. Normally this defense would be no defense at all, as most partners pool revenues in some fashion. So Dana added that Richardson had handled the case "not on the partnership account, but on that of Mr. Richardson individually."[9] Yet Dana might well have profited indirectly from his partner's revenues, even if those funds somehow stayed separate from the rest.

Finally, there was the matter of Dana's billing the court for his services to crime victims. True, Dana allowed, the law forbade him to collect for "prosecution" services that fell within his "official duty." But these services, he said, were merely "professional" and not "official." And although they were "founded upon the issue of the prosecution," they were "not a part of the prosecution."[10] This last claim sliced very finely, for the services in question—helping crime victims collect from court the costs they incurred in bringing charges—followed quite naturally from the prosecutions themselves. As for his failure to tell the court that the money was for him, Dana protested, "The question was not asked; nor was any inquiry or observation made, which sug[g]ested to me an idea that the court considered it material to whom the sum was paid."[11]

Concluding his defense with an aggressive flourish, Dana accused the legislative committee of adopting "a mode of proceeding . . . certainly calculated, to wound an innocent reputation, to gratify personal malice and party prejudice, and to answer electioneering ends."[12] Sadly, no source I have found discloses the legislature's verdict on the affair. It appears in any event that by the end of 1809 Dana was out of office, for the same "snarling" judges had appointed another in his place.[13] Yet Dana won the last hand. When the legislature reorganized the Court of Common Pleas in 1811, those judges lost their seats, and Dana became the new court's chief.[14]

CHARGE BARGAINING IN LIQUOR CASES

For our purposes, Dana's most important legacy lies not in his spat with the judges, but in another aspect of the December 1808 sitting of the Court of Common Pleas, the sitting that gave rise to his troubles.[15] We find in the records of that term the case of Josiah Stevens of Tyngsborough, who faced prosecution under the state's 1787 liquor license law, which required that alcohol retailers be licensed.[16] The Stevens prosecution was one of Dana's first liquor cases and only the third liquor case to come before the Court of Common Pleas in Middlesex County since that court first started hearing criminal matters in 1804.[17] Dana had drawn up a four-count indictment against Stevens. Count one charged him with being a "common seller" of alcohol, counts two and three with making particular unlicensed sales, and count four with selling alcohol and permitting the buyer to drink on Stevens's premises. The court's clerk narrated the outcome: "[T]he said Josiah [Stevens] says he will not contend with the Commonwealth. And Samuel Dana Esquire Atty. for the Commonwealth in this behalf says that in consequence of the defts. plea aforesaid he will not prosecute the first third and fourth counts against him any further."[18] In other words, Dana and Stevens had struck a deal: In exchange for the defendant's plea of no contest, Dana dropped three of the four counts of the indictment. On the remaining count, Stevens paid a fine of $6.67 and $47.12 for the costs of prosecution.[19]

Dana prosecuted only one additional liquor case during the rest of his brief tenure as county attorney. In March 1809, he brought a four-count indictment against Nathan Corey, a husbandman of Stow. Count one charged Corey with being a common seller of alcohol, and counts two, three, and four with making particular unlicensed sales. The clerk's account of the result varies from that in *Stevens* only in that Dana lived up to his part of the bargain first: "Samuel Dana Esquire Attorney for the Commonwealth in this behalf says that he will no further prosecute the said Nathan Corey upon the first second and fourth counts in said indictment and thereupon the said Nathan Corey by leave of Court says he will not contend with the Government as to the third count in said indictment."[20] Corey paid a fine of seven dollars together with $19.73 in costs.[21]

These are by no means the earliest pleas of guilty or no contest I discovered in my search of the Middlesex court records. In fact, a surprisingly high percentage of cases in the earliest years of my study ended in such pleas. In the Court of General Sessions of the Peace, which heard criminal cases before criminal jurisdiction passed to the Court of Common Pleas in 1804,[22] seventy-three percent of adjudicated cases in 1789–1790 ended in a plea,[23] and sixty-six percent of those in 1799–1800.[24] In 1809, when Nathan Corey stood before the Court of Common Pleas, fifty-eight percent of adjudicated cases ended by plea.[25] These were not merely liquor cases, but included both felony and misdemeanor cases from across the broad jurisdiction of the middle-tier courts. But *Stevens* and *Corey* are two of only three cases in those years that appear on the face of the records as *clear plea bargains*.[26] That is, these are the only cases in which the clerk's account discloses a concession made in exchange for the defendant's plea. Throughout this study, I use the term *clear plea bargain* to refer to those cases in which the record makes it clear that the defendant won a concession by offering a plea. By contrast, I use the expression *guilty plea* to refer to cases in which the defendant pled guilty but the record reveals no compensating concession. Sometimes we can look behind the silent record of a simple "plea" to discover the terms of a "bargain," but this is a matter we will take up in time.

The Charge Bargaining Technique

Although *Stevens* and *Corey* are among the earliest clear plea bargains to emerge in my survey, they are of a remarkably sophisticated cut. We cannot know Dana's thoughts as he sought these four-count indictments, but today we would say that a prosecutor who brought several charges in the hope of gaining leverage in plea negotiations had "over-charged" the case. Dana may have had other motives for charging these cases as he did,[27] but given the four-count indictments, he was in a position to threaten the defendants with multiple penalties and then to reward their pleas of no contest by dropping three of the four counts. Stevens and Corey chose not to plead plainly "guilty" to the remaining count of the indictment. Rather, they would "not contend with the Commonwealth," and by means of these pleas of nolo contendere, they spared themselves any admission of fault while giving the court the power to convict and sentence them.[28] To winnow the excess charges, Dana employed the nolle prosequi, or nol pros, which the Supreme Judicial Court only recently had declared to be an exclusively prosecutorial device.[29] Gadget for gadget— multiple-count indictments, nolo pleas, and nol prosses—these early plea bargains rival some of the best work of modern plea practitioners. And yet they emerged here, only a year into the tenure of the first county attorney, an almost primordial instinct of the prosecutorial soul.

Sophisticated as these pleas may have been, it is not immediately obvious why they worked. Why should Stevens and Corey have pled guilty, even to a single charge, if the presiding judges had the power to punish them severely for the one remaining violation? True, one's exposure is always greater having been convicted on four counts than on one, but many defendants might prefer to keep their right to seek an acquittal from a jury rather than to trade it for an uncertain reward. They might even flatter themselves with the hope that if they went to trial and lost, the judges still would not punish them severely. And conversely, why should Dana have dropped three charges and risked the possibility that the judges would, on the one remaining count, impose an overly lenient sentence? Had the judges been partners in these plea bargains and had they made their sentencing intentions clear, then any such reservation on Dana's or the defendants' part would have dissolved. But the record discloses no reason to think the judges took part in the deal.

In fact, neither Dana nor the defendants needed to worry that the judges might disappoint their expectations in the bargain, because the judges simply had no power to do so. The liquor law's penalty structure left them too little discretion. On a conviction of being a "common seller," as charged in count one of both indictments, the law prescribed a fine of exactly twenty pounds.[30] Twenty pounds was a good deal of money, amounting at the exchange rates of the day to almost sixty-seven dollars,[31] or more than the total in fines and costs paid by either defendant. The common-seller count therefore gave Dana real strength in any plea negotiation. If the defendants had risked trial and lost on that count, the court would have had no choice but to impose the statutory fine. On the other hand, once Dana nol prossed the count in exchange for a plea, the court lacked any power to impose the fine.

Although the license law prescribed a specific fine for almost every offense the law defined,[32] it did grant judges some sentencing discretion. In cases of single unlicensed sales, the law provided for a fine of between two and six pounds.[33] Despite the uncertainty that this flexible sentencing range injected into the outcome, Dana and the defendants still could agree in advance on the exact penalty the defendants would pay. That is because another statute gave Dana the power to determine the costs of prosecution, which the defendant had to pay.[34] Costs often were several times greater than the statutory fines. Dana's discretion to set costs therefore was more than sufficient to offset any uncertainty about the judges' fines.

By depriving judges of almost all sentencing discretion in liquor law cases, the legislature had assured that prosecutors could—by over-charging, selectively nol prossing, and manipulating the amount of costs—dictate the defendant's sentence. That is, the legislature had empowered prosecutors to engage in charge bargaining without fear that the court's noncooperation might unsettle the terms of the bargain. In no other statute of consequence to the daily practice of the middle-tier courts had the legislature bestowed such power on the prosecutor. Excepting only very serious crimes that carried mandatory life or death sentences, none of the typical common law offenses called for a minimum sentence. The penalty for petty larceny was zero to one year or a fine of zero to three hundred dollars; for grand larceny, it was zero to five years or zero to six hundred dollars; for breaking into a shop at night, it was zero to twenty years; for forging a bank bill or unarmed robbery, it was zero to life.[35]

In nonliquor cases, therefore, the prosecutor could not credibly threaten defendants with certain and steep punishment if they went to trial and lost, because the court's potential leniency had no bounds. True, the prosecutor had some power to limit the defendant's maximum exposure. At least after 1838, he could use a partial nol pros to reduce a charge of grand larceny to petty larceny and thereby guarantee defendants who pled guilty a maximum one-year sentence.[36] But the records I surveyed in the earlier half of my study rarely disclose such behavior. We may presume that simply reducing the maximum exposure when the lowered maximum still involved substantial prison time usually was not sufficient to induce a defendant to plead. It is, therefore, no surprise that of the forty-nine clear plea bargains disclosed in the record books of the middle-tier courts during the years I studied between 1789 and 1849, thirty-three—or fully two-thirds—took place in liquor cases.[37] Put differently, clear plea bargains took place in twenty-four percent of adjudicated liquor cases, but in fewer than three percent of all other adjudicated cases.[38]

As the figures in note 38 show, however, Dana's tactic in *Stevens* and *Corey* did not become a favorite of Middlesex prosecutors until sometime in the 1840s. Asahel Stearns, who succeeded Dana as county attorney and held the office for some two decades,[39] took a somewhat less aggressive tack in liquor cases. In 1824, for example, Stearns indicted twelve persons for violations of the liquor law. In three of these cases, he alleged multiple counts and exacted a plea bargain on the *Stevens-Corey* model. But in each of the remaining nine cases, he charged a single count of unlawful sale.[40] The defendants in all nine cases readily pled either guilty or no contest, apparently regarding their seven-dollar fines and modest costs as preferable to an expensive trial. In 1829, the next year I studied, Stearns resolved eight out of nine liquor cases in this manner.

I do not consider these cases to be clear plea bargains because the record discloses no concession made in exchange for the defendant's plea. They may be examples of implicit plea bargains, however, in which the defendant offered a plea expecting that some concession would be made.[41] After all, the law empowered Stearns to set the costs of prosecution, and a trial no doubt would have inflated those costs. Stearns tried only two liquor cases in the years I studied, only one of which ended in a conviction. (Prosecutors assessed costs only against convicted defendants.) In that case, from 1820, he charged his defeated opponent costs of $39.85.[42] In the other liquor case that arose in the same term of the court, the defendant pled no contest, and Stearns put costs at just $23.21.[43]

An assault-and-battery case Stearns prosecuted in 1814 makes even plainer how useful a plea-bargaining tool the cost-setting power could be. Archibald McIntire and William Fletcher were codefendants in the case. McIntire pled guilty while Fletcher went to trial and lost. Although the court fined each man five dollars, Stearns spurned such even-handedness. He put McIntire's costs at $4.76 and Fletcher's at $39.53.[44]

There is some reason to think that those liquor defendants who pled guilty or no contest in 1824 and 1829 had in mind the amount of costs Stearns might assess, for the records show a striking regularity in those amounts. Of the nine defendants from 1824 who pled either guilty or no contest and won no obvious concession, six were assessed costs of $13.77, two costs of $14.77, and one costs of $14.97. Of the eight defendants in this category from 1829, three were assessed costs of $11.49 and two costs of $18.14.[45] There is little reason to think that Stearns manipulated the amount of costs to induce defendants to plead. Rather, the most likely explanation for assessing different defendants the same, very specific figures is that Stearns pooled the costs of prosecuting liquor cases from a particular town and divided them among all the liquor defendants from that town who offered a plea.[46] This practice assured that defendants could know in advance the amount of costs they faced if they offered a plea. The record books disclose that in 1824 six of the nine defendants just mentioned had lawyers—and all but one of them the same lawyer—who no doubt could have helped the clients predict the consequences of their pleas.[47]

The power to set the costs of prosecution was perhaps a more potent plea-bargaining tool in liquor cases than in others. By custom, if not by law, prosecutors rarely assessed costs when a convict was sent to prison.[48] Because the liquor law did not call for imprisonment except on a second or third offense during the first half of the century,[49] costs were an almost invariable part of the disposition. And as a proportion of the total penalty, costs loomed large in liquor cases, in which the customary fine for making a single unlicensed sale was seven dollars, and costs were consistently more. In all events, Stearns was able to use cost-setting and, to a lesser extent, Dana's multiple-charge tactic as well as other strategies to win pleas from twenty-four of the thirty-three liquor defendants he prosecuted in the years I studied. He went to trial only twice and nol prossed charges without winning pleas in seven cases. In contrast, of 224 *non*liquor cases that Stearns prosecuted in these years, he resolved only eighty-one by plea (and only four by clear plea bargains), took sixty-three to trial, and abandoned prosecution by entering nol prosses in most of the rest.

Advancing the Technology of Charge Bargaining

If Asahel Huntington, who succeeded Stearns in about 1832, proved to be even more resourceful in managing his liquor caseload, it was perhaps because he had to be (see Table 1.1). In 1834, the first year I studied of Huntington's tenure, he prosecuted ninety-five cases of all types, more than double the forty-one cases Stearns handled in 1829. And that was just in Middlesex County. An 1832 statute had split the state into districts, so Huntington took on the new title of district attorney and assumed an enlarged realm that included Essex County, Middlesex's smaller but still substantial neighbor.

Within two years, Huntington had begun to formulate his signature contribution to plea-bargaining technology: the preprinted, multicount liquor-indictment form. He deployed several primitive versions of this device in 1834. In the case of Samuel Elliot, he used a preprinted indictment form that alleged four counts of making single unlicensed alcohol sales. Huntington filled in Elliot's name, the relevant dates and places, and other information peculiar to Elliot's offense. His use of a preprinted form suggests that far from tailoring the charges to Elliot's specific acts, Huntington had embraced a routine practice of charging multiple counts of unlicensed sales. Facing this four-count indictment, Elliot chose to plead no contest on two counts in exchange for Huntington's nol pros of the other two.[50] In the case of Amos Adams, Huntington pasted together two of these four-count forms. Adams pled guilty to count one, and Huntington nol prossed counts two through eight.[51] In several other cases, Huntington used a preprinted form that alleged one count of being a common seller and one count of making a single sale, to which he often appended an additional, handwritten single-sale count.[52]

Huntington's multicount liquor forms grew more sophisticated with time. Figure 1.1 reproduces one such form from 1843. In the first of five counts, it charges the defendants, Henry and Albert Sprague of Cambridge, with being common sellers of alcohol. Count two alleges a

1.1.

The First County and District Attorneys of Middlesex

YEARS OF SERVICE	COUNTY OR DISTRICT ATTORNEY
1807–1809, 1811	Samuel Dana
1811–1813	Timothy Fuller
1809–1811, 1813–1832	Asahel Stearns
ca. 1832–1845	Asahel Huntington
1845–1847	Albert H. Nelson
1848–1855	Charles Russell Train

SOURCES: William Davis supplied the date of Dana's appointment. See Davis, *Bench and Bar*, vol. 2, 33. The succession of Dana, Fuller, and Stearns is confusing. Court records show Asahel Stearns was appointed Middlesex County attorney in 1809. But Dana apparently was reappointed as county attorney on September 3, 1811, and was succeeded by Timothy Fuller on November 20 of the same year. Stearns apparently did not retake the office until August 20, 1813. I have described the legislation surrounding these appointments in greater detail in note 13 in this chapter.

Charles Warren reported that Stearns served until 1832. See Warren, *History of the Harvard Law School*, vol. 1, 313. I have found no source giving the dates of Huntington's service. He was certainly in place as of 1834 (see Middlesex Ct. C.P. R. Book 263 [March 1834]).

It appears that Albert H. Nelson took office as district attorney in December 1845. The *Lowell Courier* noted his appointment on December 10, 1845 ("Albert H. Nelson, Esq.," *Lowell Daily Courier*, December 10, 1845, 2). Nelson made his last appearance in the Court of Common Pleas Record Books in the October 1847 session; Train made his first in February 1848 (Middlesex Ct. C.P. R. Book [Feb. 1848], on file with the Massachusetts Archives; Middlesex Ct. C.P. R. Book [Oct. 1847], on file with the Massachusetts Archives). For Train's end-date, see Davis, *History of the Judiciary*, 289.

single sale, and counts three through five allege being an unlicensed retailer.[53] As revised in the state's 1836 code, the license law punished the first of these offenses by a fine of exactly one hundred dollars and each of the last four by fines of exactly twenty dollars.[54] A defendant who dared risk trial on such an indictment and lost could not hope for leniency, for the judge had no discretion in sentencing whatsoever. This was the sad discovery of Daniel McCrillis, who in 1849 was convicted of four counts, fined $160.00, and assessed costs of $88.05.[55] Those defendants who chose instead to fight another day and who pled to one or more of the twenty-dollar counts fared far better. They regularly secured nol prosses on at least the first and most expensive count and paid moderate costs of

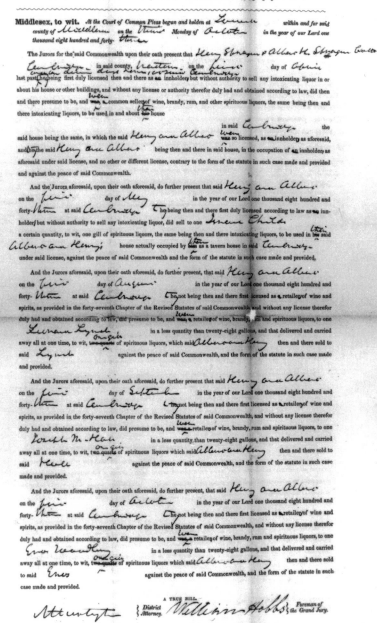

Figure 1.1. Huntington's multicount liquor form. Indictment form from *Commonwealth v. Henry Sprague & Albert H. Sprague*, Middlesex Ct. C.P. R. Book 423 (Oct. 1843), on file with the Massachusetts Archives.

between twenty and forty dollars.[56] Huntington had complete discretion to reward defendants in this way. As the Supreme Judicial Court wrote in 1838, "[I]t is perfectly clear that a *nolle prosequi* may be entered [before trial] at the pleasure of the prosecuting officer. . . . The Court has no right to interfere . . . ."[57]

However useful Huntington's multicount forms and liberal nol prossing practices may have been in managing his liquor caseload, their virtues did not immediately appear to the legislators who discovered his doings sometime in 1843 or early 1844. A House investigating committee summoned Huntington to respond to two sets of charges. The first alleged simple graft—that Huntington had received fines and court costs from defendants and failed to pay the whole amount over to the state.[58] The second alleged "mal-administration . . . [i]n taking less than might have been required on the discharge of indictments found and not tried."[59] The original complaint by Representative Cyrus Washburn of Lynn, in Essex County (within Huntington's district), was slightly more pointed: It specifically alleged that Huntington "has been guilty of malpractice . . . by receiving of Defendants . . . sums of money much less than that which the statute laws fix[] . . . and thereby discharging the said Defendants on his own responsibility without a trial."[60] These charges, the committee noted, "all relate to [Huntington's] official administration of the laws of the Commonwealth, against selling spirituous liquors without license."[61] It appears the committee was reacting in part to the September 1842 sitting of the Court of Common Pleas in Essex County, at which Huntington managed to dispose of all eighteen of his liquor cases without a trial.[62]

Shocked to find plea bargaining going on in the Commonwealth's courts, the committee demanded that Huntington appear and explain himself. He denied the allegations of graft, and the committee ultimately deemed those charges unsupported.[63] As for the charges of malpractice by plea bargaining, Huntington stoutly admitted that they "were true in fact," and "he claimed the right under the laws of the Commonwealth" to do exactly as the committee alleged.[64] Then he offered the legislators a plea-bargaining primer for use in liquor license cases, which began with his acknowledgment of the practice of multiple charging:

[W]henever a number of penalties had been demanded in different counts of the same indictment, and the defendant came forward and proposed an adjustment, [Huntington's] usual course had been—

1st. To require the party to enter a plea of nolo contendere.
2d. To enter into an agreement to abstain from future sales of liquors without license.
3d. To pay at least one penalty to the Commonwealth, and all costs which had then accrued. And
4th. That the indictment should then stand continued as security that the defendant would fulfill his agreement, and to be further prosecuted in case the defendant still continued in his course of a willful violation of the laws.[65]

I will return to the significance of steps two and four of this method in Chapter 3, when I take up the origins of prosecutorial probation. In steps one and three, Huntington merely adopted and institutionalized the plea-bargaining approach Dana had put to use in 1808.

Huntington contended that in light of his crushing workload, this procedure was "most conducive to the public interest."[66] The legislature had eliminated the office of attorney general in 1843,[67] leaving the various district attorneys saddled with "the entire direction and management of all prosecutions and suits in behalf of the Commonwealth."[68] And there was nothing sneaky about his plea-bargaining tactics: "It was very distinctly in evidence," the committee allowed, "that this course was taken openly and publicly . . . and impartially applied to all; that it was known to the Courts, the Bar, the County Commissioners, and all other persons who had occasion to take any interest in the administration of this department of the law."[69] In the end, Huntington wholly won over the committee, whose report overflowed with his "extraordinary zeal and untiring industry"; his "intelligence, integrity, fidelity and ability"; his "arduous and exhausting" and "severe and long continued exertions"; and his devotion "even to the peril of his life"—for Huntington had been sick from overwork—"to the discharge of his official duties."[70] The committee was barely less florid in its praise of Huntington's method of plea bargaining in liquor cases, which it said "tend[ed] more than any other course in the class of cases to which it was applied, to attain the just end of all punishment, the prevention of the offence, the reformation of the offender."[71]

Despite the committee's vindication, announced in January 1845, Huntington departed from office later the same year because (it was said) "of the inadequacy of [his] salary."[72] His successor perhaps took courage in the legislature's lavish endorsement of Huntington's tactics, for he dispatched his liquor cases in an even more brazenly public manner. Hence we find this notice concerning district attorney Albert Nelson in the *Lowell Journal* of April 2, 1847:

> LICENSE CASES. The Newburyport Advertiser says that Mr. Nelson, Attorney for the Essex and Middlesex district, states that at the *present* term, it is his intention when the parties complained of plead guilty, and enter into recognizance to observe the law, *not* to press for the fines which are incurred, but simply to exact the costs of Court. At the next term, however, he announces that no more settlements of cases will be made; but that full fines will be exacted in every case where the parties are convicted.[73]

In Chapter 3, I describe how it was that Nelson could promise not to exact fines against defendants who pled guilty under a statute that mandated fines. For now, the significance of this mid-century announcement of a district attorney's fire sale in liquor license cases is Nelson's manifest confidence in his own power to make such promises without concern about possible interference from the court.

Charles Russell Train, who followed Nelson into office in 1848,[74] proved to be the most enthusiastic of Middlesex's early plea-bargaining practitioners. Train quickly mastered the plea bargainer's art and deployed the Dana–*Stevens*–*Corey* model of charge bargaining and Huntington's preprinted, multicount liquor-indictment forms with unprecedented regularity. In 1849, Train charged multiple counts in eighty-nine percent of his liquor indictments and managed to resolve twenty of fifty-six adjudicated liquor cases with clear plea bargains. All but one were built upon multicount indictments, the district attorney's nol pros of selected counts, and the defendant's plea of guilty to the rest.[75]

CHARGE BARGAINING IN MURDER CASES

Train was the fifth in a chain of Middlesex prosecutors (beginning with Dana and running through Stearns, Huntington, and Nelson) to exploit an extraordinary power to craft deals in liquor cases. He appears to have been the first Middlesex prosecutor to make use of an analogous, if less precise, power to cut deals in capital cases. I mentioned earlier that the legislature abolished the office of attorney general in 1843.[76] For six years, before the legislature reinstated the office,[77] the various district attorneys took on the task of trying capital cases before the Supreme Judicial Court. During their six years before the high court, Middlesex prosecutors conducted three capital trials. In his only murder trial, Huntington won a manslaughter verdict and a seven-year prison sentence.[78] One of Nelson's two trials ended in a conviction and death sentence,[79] the other in a verdict of not guilty by reason of insanity.[80]

The Nature of Murder Bargains

Train had a single capital case before the court—in October 1848—and he avoided trial with a plea-bargaining technique much like the one he used in liquor cases before the Court of Common Pleas. Barney Goulding stood charged with murdering his wife, Ellen, by beating her in the head.[81] He pled not guilty at his arraignment and claimed his right to a jury trial. Under a Massachusetts law that granted counsel to capital defendants, the court assigned two prominent members of the Middlesex bar to defend him—Theodore H. Sweetser and Benjamin F. Butler.[82] Though Butler later earned fame as a Union general and governor of Massachusetts, he and his cocounsel apparently decided that in this case, the better part of valor was to plead their client out. The clerk recorded the result: "And afterward in this same term the said Barney Goulding, otherwise called Barnett Goulding, retracts his [not guilty] plea above pleaded, and says he is guilty of manslaughter. And Charles R. Train, Esquire, attorney for the Commonwealth in this behalf, says, he will no further prosecute this indictment as to the malice aforethought, and the charge of murder."[83] On his manslaughter conviction, the court sentenced Goulding to two years in the house of correction.[84]

Had Goulding insisted on trial and been convicted of murder, he would have faced the mandatory penalty of death. The legislature did not divide murder into degrees until 1858, and until then all murder remained capital. Train's generosity in nol prossing the malice component of the murder indictment, hence reducing the charge to manslaughter, shrank

Goulding's possible sentence to a prison term of between zero and twenty years. As I noted a moment ago, the judge sentenced Goulding near the bottom of that range.

Train's was not the first clear plea bargain in a capital case in Massachusetts, though it does appear to have been among the first. As early as 1804, the Supreme Judicial Court, sitting in its capacity as a trial court, accepted a guilty plea in a murder case. That plea was far from a bargain, however, as it merely secured the defendant's compulsory execution—perhaps explaining the court's insistence that the defendant reconsider before the court would record his plea.[85] The earliest clear plea bargains I have found in capital cases did not take place until 1841.[86]

That year, Attorney General James Austin negotiated two such bargains before the Supreme Judicial Court. In one, a murder case, the bargain took much the same form as in Train's *Goulding* case.[87] In the second, charging rape, the defendant pled guilty to assault with intent to rape. Austin then nol prossed "the other and further part of the indictment"—that is, so much of the indictment as charged an actual rape.[88] Rape, like murder, carried a mandatory death sentence, while assault with intent to rape carried any term of years up to life in prison. In this case the judge sentenced the defendant to five years. Rape soon ceased to be a capital offense—by 1852 murder was virtually the only crime still deemed capital—and every other charge bargain I encountered in a capital case involved murder.[89]

Beyond those conducted by Train and Austin, one other capital charge bargain took place during the 1840s—this one in a murder case prosecuted by the district attorney of the Southern District, John H. Clifford, in 1845.[90] Together, the four charge bargains by these three prosecutors accounted for ten percent of all adjudicated capital cases in my survey of Supreme Judicial Court business in the 1840s.[91] In the 1850s, when Clifford, now attorney general, handled most of the state's murder prosecutions,[92] seventeen percent of adjudicated capital cases ended in charge bargains of this sort.

The trend turned sharply upward in the 1860s. Twenty-five of fifty-three murder cases—or forty-seven percent—ended in charge bargains. Although the rate of charge bargaining retreated somewhat to forty-three percent in the 1870s and thirty-five percent in the 1880s, during the 1890s

1.2.

Clear Plea Bargains in Murder Cases Before the Supreme Judicial Court

DECADE	NUMBER OF ADJUDICATED MURDER CASES	NUMBER OF CLEAR PLEA BARGAINS	BARGAINS AS % OF TOTAL
1840s	41	4	10
1850s	42	7	17
1860s	53	25	47
1870s	77	33	43
1880s	51	18	35
1890s	67	41	61

SOURCES: Annual Reports of the Attorney General; Sup. Jud. Ct. R. Books. Figures from 1849 through the end of the century, with the exception of 1853, are based on the attorney general's annual summaries of his work and therefore should include all murder prosecutions. As the attorney general either did not exist or produced no summary of cases from 1840 to 1848 or in 1853, figures for those years are based on a study of the Supreme Judicial Court's record books for its sittings in Suffolk, Middlesex, Bristol, Hampden, Norfolk, and Worcester counties. From 1851 onward, murder accounted for all capital cases. In the earlier years, rape, arson, burglary, and armed robbery also appeared on the Supreme Judicial Court's dockets, but the only clear plea bargain involving any crime other than murder was the rape case noted earlier in the text (see this chapter, notes 88 and 89 and accompanying text).

a record sixty-one percent of murder cases ended in charge bargains (see Table 1.2).[93] In contrast, the rate of charge bargaining in all other non-liquor prosecutions never exceeded eleven percent of adjudicated cases in any one year,[94] and across all years stood at just three percent.[95]

Three Puzzles

At least three moments in this chronology of plea bargaining in murder cases seem to require some explanation: Why, first of all, did bargains in capital cases emerge in 1841 and not earlier? Why did they advance so dramatically in the 1860s? And why, after some slackening, did they advance even more dramatically in the 1890s? The last question is best left until Chapter 5, when the discussion moves into the last quarter of the century. I take up the first two questions now.

At one level, it is surprising to learn that plea bargaining in capital cases emerged as early as 1841. It is true that scattered instances of plea bargaining, even in serious cases, crop up quite early in the historical record. I consider these in more detail in Chapter 7. But Austin's 1841 charge bargains were not two scattered instances, but rather the beginning of a regular practice of charge bargaining in murder cases. Within three decades, such bargains would account for nearly half of all murder cases, and they would remain a prominent force through the balance of the century. This timetable challenges the views of those historians who have argued that American courts resisted plea bargaining and discouraged its rise until at least the late nineteenth or even early twentieth century.[96]

Still, in the context of my arguments here, 1841 seems rather late for charge bargains to emerge in capital cases. After all, charge bargains in liquor cases appeared in Middlesex County as early as 1808, only one year after the appointment of the first county prosecutor, and they took place in some of the very first liquor cases heard by the Court of Common Pleas.[97] These early deals seem to have been the product of a nearly instantaneous reaction of two chemical ingredients—the existence of a public prosecutor and the prosecutor's power to bargain, conferred by the liquor law's rigid penalty scheme. Yet if prosecutors had such power in capital cases, then why was this reaction so delayed?

There are, in fact, several reasons to expect that charge bargains might have proved rarer in murder cases than in liquor cases. Perhaps the most obvious is that prosecutors might have felt that justice and public opinion demanded a full measure of punishment in murder cases. Trading the mandatory death penalty assigned to murder for the uncertain zero-to-twenty-year prison term assigned to manslaughter might have offended basic prosecutorial instincts. It is also possible that the attorney general, who worked full time, felt less caseload pressure than did the part-time county prosecutors who handled liquor prosecutions—an issue I take up more fully in Chapter 2. But such arguments suggest only that charge bargains in capital cases should have been comparatively rare, whereas my research has turned up none before 1841.[98]

A possible solution to the mystery lies in the peculiar procedural form of charge bargains in capital cases. In liquor cases, as consideration for the defendant's plea to one of several counts of an indictment, the prosecutor would nol pros the remaining counts. Murder cases, in contrast, generally involved but a single offense, so there was no option to nol pros whole counts of the indictment. Moreover, as any single count charging murder was enough to assure the defendant's execution, nol prossing selected counts (in the rare multiple-murder cases) would create no incentive for a plea. Instead, the prosecutor's consideration for the defendant's plea took the form of a *partial nol pros* that effectively reduced the charge. In Train's 1848 murder case, for example, after the defendant pled guilty to manslaughter, Train said "he will no further prosecute this indictment as to the malice aforethought, and the charge of murder."[99] Similarly, in his 1841 rape case, Attorney General Austin responded to the defendant's plea of guilty of assault with intent to rape by "certif[ying] . . . that he will prosecute on the other and further part of the indictment"—that is, so much of the indictment as charged rape—"no further."[100]

Only three years earlier, in 1838, Austin had asked the Supreme Judicial Court to ratify his power to nol pros part of a single-count indictment.[101] The court declared, "If the attorney general may enter a *nolle prosequi* as to the whole of an indictment, or of a count, so he may do it as to any distinct and substantive part of it."[102] Although the court maintained that earlier cases, "if they are law, are decisive of" the legality of partial nol prosses,[103] those earlier cases gave only shaky authority for the practice. In two of the three cases cited by the court, both from 1805, the Supreme Judicial Court itself had recommended that the prosecutor enter a partial nol pros to eliminate a possibly defective part of the indictment.[104] Capital charge bargains, in contrast, involved the attorney general's independent use of a partial nol pros, undertaken without the court's guidance. Moreover, these two cases did not actually consider the legality of the partial nol pros, as the defendants apparently had contested only the sufficiency of the indictment.

The third case, from 1828, provided useful commentary on the question of partial nol prosses, but no useful law. The court wrote that in the usual case, entering a partial nol pros, at least after conviction, "could be of no prejudice to the defendant."[105] The court ruled, however, that entering a partial nol pros in the particular circumstances of that case was unfair to the defendant, and it granted him a new trial as a result.[106] Only in 1838, then, did the Supreme Judicial Court for the first time uphold the attorney general's unilateral power to nol pros part of an indictment.[107] It is true that a later treatise writer would cite the 1828 case as authority for the prosecutor's power to enter a partial nol pros,[108] but the Supreme Judicial Court, in later years, appears always to have relied on the 1838 case, though it sometimes cited one of the earlier cases as well.[109]

After securing this affirmation of his powers in 1838, Austin put it to use in carrying out capital charge bargains as early as 1841. There is, therefore, no sharp disjunction between the early history of charge bargaining in liquor cases and its early history in capital cases. In both contexts, charge bargaining appeared almost as soon as a public prosecutor found he had the power to make it happen.

The second puzzling moment in the chronology of capital charge bargains—the sudden surge during the 1860s—also finds at least partial explanation in the prosecutor's expanding bundle of charging powers. In 1858, the legislature separated the crime of murder into first and second degrees,[110] in one stroke granting prosecutors more precise control over sentencing and more versatility in charge bargaining. Until 1858, plea bargains in murder cases could take only one form: the prosecutor's agreement to reduce the charge to manslaughter in exchange for the defendant's guilty plea. Unlike the nice calibration of sentences that prosecutors could manipulate in liquor cases through multiple charging and selective nol prossing, the penalty scheme in murder was a clumsy tool in their hands. By reducing the charge from murder to manslaughter, the prosecutor could spare the defendant the mandatory death penalty assigned to murder and guarantee him instead a prison term of from zero to twenty years. The prosecutor could not, however, dictate where within this wide-open range the judge would set sentence. No doubt many conscientious prosecutors shunned such deals because the offender's crime, although perhaps not warranting death, deserved far more than the two years given Barney Goulding for killing his wife.

The legislature's separation of murder into degrees helped allay such qualms. After 1858, in exchange for the defendant's guilty plea, a prosecutor could agree to reduce a first-degree murder charge to second degree. The consequence was to replace a mandatory death sentence with mandatory life in prison.[111] The attorney general struck the first two such deals in 1863,[112] and six others followed before the end of the decade. Together they accounted for just under one-third of all plea bargains in murder cases in the 1860s. Although these second-degree deals cannot by themselves account for the striking increase in plea-bargained murder cases in the 1860s, they surely contributed to the rise. When I take up incentives facing defendants in Chapter 4, I consider other reasons for the sharp rise of the 1860s. Still, guilty pleas to second-degree murder proved throughout the rest of the century to be a critical part of the prosecutor's arsenal, consistently outnumbering guilty pleas to manslaughter as a means to resolve murder cases.[113]

Despite the gulf that would seem to divide a liquor law violation that carried a mandatory hundred-dollar fine from a murder charge that carried mandatory death, these two crimes share a common subplot in the story of plea bargaining's rise. In each case, the legislature's assignment of a mandatory minimum penalty—almost unique within the Massachusetts criminal universe—gave prosecutors the power to charge bargain. By using their nol pros power to reduce either the number of charges (in liquor cases) or the gravity of the charge (in murder cases), prosecutors could promise defendants a clear and certain concession in exchange for their guilty pleas. Liquor defendants could save money and accused murderers could save their lives. It is no wonder, then, that liquor and murder cases together accounted for the great majority of the clear plea bargains that took place in Massachusetts courts in the first two-thirds of the nineteenth century. The source of prosecutors' power to charge bargain in these cases is clear. It is time now to ask why prosecutors wanted to use it.

2

The Prosecutor's Motives in Plea Bargaining

As Asahel Huntington told his critics, one reason prosecutors plea bargained was to manage their massive caseloads. Huntington spoke from experience, for as Figure 2.1 shows, an unprecedented wave of cases began crashing upon him during his unlucky tenure. I noted earlier that the Middlesex County caseload jumped dramatically from forty-one cases in 1829, as Stearns's tenure closed, to ninety-five cases in 1834, soon after Huntington's opened. After a lull of only 42 cases in 1839, Huntington's caseload bounced back to 101 in 1843. In the next six years—as Huntington rounded out his years in office, Nelson came and went, and Train entered the scene—the caseload leapt to 443.[1] Although the trend turned upward again toward the end of the century, the Middlesex district attorney never again in our time frame encountered a caseload calamity of this magnitude. Across the Charles River in Boston, the Suffolk County prosecutor faced a similar shock to the system.[2]

CASELOAD PRESSURE: CAUSES AND EFFECTS

The Dynamics

The caseload boom of the 1840s no doubt owed something to the sheer growth of crime that came with an exploding population. Between 1820

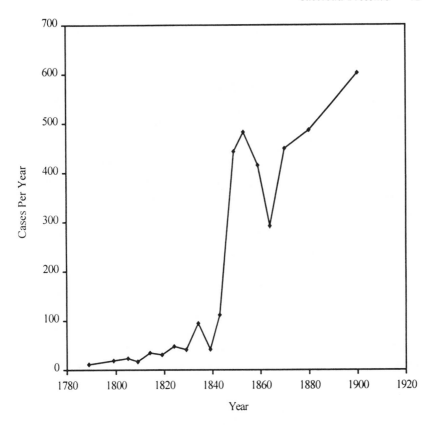

Figure 2.1. Criminal caseload: Middlesex County Superior Court and its predecessor courts.

and 1840, the population of Middlesex grew by more than two-thirds.[3] Perhaps—though this is not clear—improved policing produced more arrests.[4] At least in the realm of the liquor laws, more energetic enforcement seems to have led to more prosecutions.[5] The legislature caused a good deal of the caseload increase with its decision in 1832 to extend the jurisdiction of the Court of Common Pleas to all noncapital crimes, many of which the Supreme Judicial Court had heard before.[6] And caseload grew because more defendants exercised their right to appeal from lower tribunals to the Court of Common Pleas.[7] More defendants were coming to court with lawyers, perhaps explaining why more were so bold as to claim an appeal.[8]

Daunting as it surely was, the spiking caseload depicted in Figure 2.1 does not fully capture the pressures Huntington and his successors faced. The graph does not reflect the addition of Essex County to the district attorney's duties between 1832 and 1848,[9] or the absence of an attorney general during the legislature's unwise experiment with austerity between 1843 and 1849, which shifted responsibility for prosecution of the most serious cases onto the district attorneys' shoulders.[10] A local newspaper referred to the abolition of the attorney general as "nothing less than wanton cruelty" to the state's district attorneys.[11] And so far as the record shows, Huntington and his successors handled their caseloads with no assistance, not even so much as a clerk to help draft their indictments.[12] Little wonder that on leaving office in October 1845, Huntington resorted to nol prossing 252 Middlesex cases outright, perhaps to avoid saddling his successor, Albert Nelson, with his backlog.[13]

Even before the caseload boom of the Huntington years, Massachusetts prosecutors had strong reason to embrace the efficient promise of plea bargaining. Like most public prosecutors in nineteenth-century America, they worked part-time, drew (at best) part-time salaries, and therefore held more than one job. Hence Samuel Dana, who claimed he earned no salary at all as county attorney,[14] also served as president of the Massachusetts Senate during the first two years of his tenure.[15] Asahel Stearns not only served in Congress while he was district attorney, he spent twelve years as the founding and sole full-time professor of the Harvard Law School.[16] Prosecutors with less exalted second jobs felt even more pressure to resolve their criminal cases quickly. Most supplemented their incomes with a civil law practice.[17] Because the Court of Common Pleas heard civil and criminal cases at the same session, these lawyers could do no civil business until their criminal work was done.

Many district attorneys simply rushed through their criminal cases to get on with the business of making money, as one explained to the legislature in 1844:

> The call for my attendance upon the grand jury, occasions a very frequent interference with my engagements in civil cases, and a consequent pecuniary loss to myself. . . . The practice to which [Samuel D. Parker, district attorney of Suffolk County,] alludes, of making extra

exertions in order to dispatch the business before the grand jury, is, I believe, common to all the prosecuting officers. I endeavor, if possible, to have the grand jury dismissed on the morning of the second day, and I generally succeed. To accomplish this, it is often necessary to continue the sessions of the grand jury until late in the evening, and the night is mostly spent in drawing indictments. I know of no combination of bodily and mental labor equal to that to which the prosecuting officers subject themselves on such occasions.[18]

The pressure to plea bargain was therefore part and parcel of part-time prosecuting: No matter how many criminal cases a district attorney handled, he could make more money if he handled them with dispatch.[19] More than a century later, Albert Alschuler found this dynamic still at work. In the 1960s he discovered to his surprise that part-time prosecutors in a downstate Illinois county plea bargained a larger proportion of their cases than did full-time prosecutors in Chicago.[20]

The incentives to get through one's cases grew particularly intense in the 1840s as caseloads leapt higher. In 1843, by the same stroke with which the legislature wiped out the office of the attorney general, it salted prosecutorial wounds with a thirty-percent pay cut.[21] The result was a storm of protest from prosecutors and their supporters, who deluged the legislature with accounts of their overwork. One district attorney calculated that his new seven-hundred–dollar salary worked out to eighty-eight cents a case.[22] Another detailed the burdens of following the court on circuit within his district:

I reside in Greenfield. I have to travel twenty miles to attend the courts at Northampton, forty miles to go to Springfield, and something more than fifty miles by the most direct rout[e] to reach Lenox. There is no rail-road communication except in passing from Springfield to Pittsfield. As the public means of communication between Greenfield and Lenox are very inconvenient, and the season when the courts are held often renders it hazardous to travel with a private conveyance, I frequently go and return by the way of Springfield—which makes the distance travelled about one hundred miles.[23]

A third sounded themes from Dickens:

[U]nremitted professional labors, night and day, with no vacation and no assistance, and perpetual confinement daily and all day, in badly ventilated court-rooms, will break down the best constitution . . . . If [relief] cannot be obtained, I must retire from an office too onerous to be borne by one unassisted individual.[24]

As for Huntington, a Middlesex County newspaper said his "inadequate and niggardly" salary was sad thanks for his "fidelity to his arduous duties."[25] A Middlesex legislator told his colleagues that if they "[p]ut the case of Attorney Huntington to the people of Middlesex county, . . . nine-tenths of the people would say that he should have at least $1000 a year salary."[26] Admitting its errors, the legislature restored the district attorneys' salaries in 1845,[27] and in 1849 it reinstated the office of attorney general.[28]

Perhaps from pure necessity, and perhaps from necessity tinged with pique at the legislature's offenses, prosecutors appear to have accelerated their plea-bargaining practices in the 1840s. That is when the pattern of multiple charging that Huntington built upon his preprinted indictment forms first drew the legislature's attention and when Albert Nelson boldly publicized the terms by which he would deal. It is when Charles Russell Train, who felt the full force of the caseload wave, began to plea bargain his liquor cases with unprecedented frequency. And it is when Train and two other pioneering prosecutors first struck plea bargains in capital cases.

That is not to say that caseload pressure is sufficient for prosecutors to engage in plea bargaining. On the contrary, without the power to make meaningful concessions to defendants, prosecutors normally cannot induce them to plead. The nearly total lack of prosecutorial power to constrain the judge's sentencing discretion in nonliquor cases other than murder probably explains the almost complete absence of clear plea bargains in such cases during the first two-thirds of the nineteenth century. Nor is a big caseload a necessary condition of prosecutorial plea bargaining. Especially when prosecutors were part-time workers, as most American prosecutors were in this period, there was always some pecuniary incentive to reduce their criminal workload, however small their workload was. But as I believe the Middlesex experience of the 1840s helps to show, an increasing caseload obviously does *increase* pressure on prosecutors to plea bargain.

Doubting the Role of Caseload Pressure

I do not join the ranks of recent plea-bargaining scholars who reject "the myth of caseload pressure" told and retold by scholars of the generation before.[29] Two of the new generation of scholars, Mary Vogel and Theodore Ferdinand, have based their research in Boston courts in the nineteenth century, and their arguments against the influence of caseload pressure therefore seem directly contrary to my own analysis. I will consider their work in some depth, both on this narrow question of caseload pressure and, somewhat later, on the larger question of the impulses behind the rise of plea bargaining.

Mary Vogel's work on the emergence of plea bargaining in Boston has sought to expose "The Myth of Caseload Pressure."[30] Yet her evidence of caseload pressure and guilty plea rates actually supports a conclusion that the two were strongly and causally related.[31] Vogel's contrary opinion that caseload was unimportant to the growth of plea bargaining arises, I believe, not from her evidence, which shows caseload and guilty pleas rising roughly in tandem, but rather from the way she charts these trends.

In Figure 2.2, I have reproduced Vogel's diagram plotting the increase of guilty plea rates and caseload between 1830 and 1920.[32] On the basis of this diagram, Vogel concludes that "the surge of guilty pleas, which heralded the rise of plea bargaining during the 1830s, 1840s, and 1850s, preceded rather than followed the marked increase in caseload seen after the 1840s," suggesting that caseload pressure could not have brought on the rise of plea bargaining.[33] But the chronological ordering of the two trends is an unintended illusion of the graph's design. The graph plots both trends—caseload and guilty plea rate—in terms of percentage increases over the year before. Both lines therefore start at zero in 1830 and climb promptly upward. Between 1830 and 1840, the guilty plea line rises rather sharply (perhaps because the guilty plea rate *genuinely* began near zero),[34] while the caseload line rises modestly. This incongruence, if we should call it that, shifts the line representing caseload to the right and makes it *look* chronologically behind the guilty plea line. In fact, during the next period, 1840 to 1850, both lines rise sharply in nearly equal measure and then, between 1850 and 1860, both lines rise modestly in roughly equal measure.

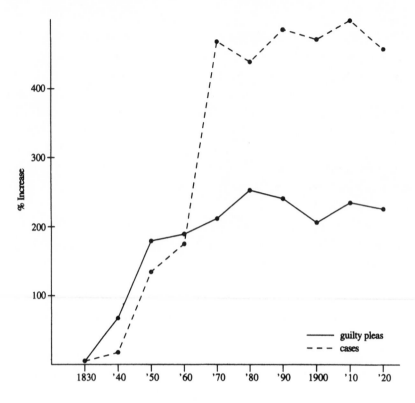

Figure 2.2. Vogel's diagram: Guilty plea rates and caseload pressure.

Between 1860 and 1870, the caseload line takes a dramatic leap upward, while the guilty plea rate rises only modestly. But here we encounter another illusion of the graph's design: The graph apparently compares caseload with the guilty plea *rate*.[35] That is, guilty pleas are expressed as a percentage of all cases. Because caseload can (in theory) expand indefinitely whereas the guilty plea rate cannot exceed one hundred percent, the increase of the guilty plea rate simply cannot keep up with an exploding caseload. It appears that between 1860 and 1870, caseload increased by a factor of two or three,[36] while the guilty plea rate increased from about forty-five percent to sixty or sixty-five percent.[37]

That is, both figures rose substantially, even if one rose more dramatically than the other. It is true that the two trends plotted on Vogel's diagram moved in opposite directions between 1870 and 1880 and between 1880 and 1890, but these instances were both exceptional—occurring only twice in the nine time periods shown—and modest, in the sense that neither trend was moving sharply.

Like Vogel, Theodore Ferdinand produces better evidence of a link between caseload pressure and the rise of plea bargaining than he allows. His study of the Boston Municipal Court, a jury forum nearly identical in form and function to the Court of Common Pleas,[38] shows that caseload held steady or even declined through the first third of the century. Caseload then began spiking in 1836 and more than tripled by 1844.[39] Meanwhile, Ferdinand says, plea bargaining took rise in the late 1830s and early 1840s.[40]

Ferdinand then hesitates to link these two trends in a causal way: "Whether plea bargaining was a response to burgeoning caseloads," he says, "is debatable."[41] Yet the reason for his reticence seems wrong. Ferdinand concludes that plea bargaining in this era was "restricted to vice or regulatory" offenses—two categories that either overlapped with the liquor law or had generally similar penalty schemes.[42] He hesitates to link rising caseloads with rising numbers of guilty pleas because in vice and regulatory offenses, "the sharpest increases [in caseload] were experienced *after* plea bargaining took hold."[43] But Ferdinand's concern that the rise of plea bargaining in vice and regulatory offenses did not mirror the rise in caseload *in those same offenses* mistakes the mechanism that linked caseload pressure with plea bargaining. Caseload pressure *generally* increased prosecutors' incentives to plea bargain. Once prosecutors felt a general incentive to lighten their workload, they struck plea bargains whenever they had the power to do so—that is, whenever rigid penalty schemes permitted them to manipulate sentences by manipulating charges. There is no reason to expect that the category of cases in which prosecutors found that power—a category I label liquor law violations and Ferdinand labels vice and regulatory offenses—should also happen to be the category that grew the fastest.

THE ALLURE OF EASY VICTORIES

Though Vogel and Ferdinand may be skeptics on the role of caseload pressure, neither they nor any other plea-bargaining scholar question a second powerful motive behind the prosecutorial impulse to plea bargain: Plea bargaining handed prosecutors quick, certain, and comparatively effortless victories. Vogel notes that in 1832 the Massachusetts legislature required local prosecutors to report the outcomes of the cases they handled. She surmises, no doubt rightly, that each prosecutor hoped to appear as successful as his peers—a hope made more urgent when the office of district attorney became elective in 1856.[44] In 1844, District Attorney John H. Clifford of the southern district, who went on to become attorney general and governor, made a point of telling the legislature that he had handled 523 cases in the previous year and that "[t]he number of *acquittals* by the verdicts of juries [was just] *four.*"[45] Neither here nor in a similar boast made elsewhere did Clifford trouble his audience with the number of trials he risked in amassing so striking a record of success.[46]

The same feature of county prosecutors' annual reports to the legislature that makes them almost useless to historians of plea bargaining made them supremely useful to prosecutors who aimed to impress—for these reports rarely distinguished between convictions after trial and convictions by plea.[47] In his original plea bargaining exposé of 1928, Raymond Moley saw the significance of such ambiguity:

> What is much more important to the prosecutor is the fact that in such records as most prosecutors make of the work which they have performed, a plea of guilty of any sort is counted as a conviction, and when he goes before the voters for re-election he can talk in large terms about securing convictions when, in reality, these "convictions" include all sorts of compromises. The district attorney's "record," as he usually interprets it to the public, rests upon the ratio of convictions to acquittals and means as much to him as a batting average means to a baseball player.
>
> The extent to which this actual, although not formal, misrepresentation of records is indulged in is indicated by the fact that in practically every state where there are any records at all, the convictions upon plea are lumped with convictions by jury.[48]

For all the outside world knew, a prosecutor with a strikingly high rate of convictions was simply a supremely effective trial lawyer.

But the political usefulness of a strong record of convictions can explain only a general desire among prosecutors to plea bargain. It cannot explain why this desire first found form in liquor cases.

WHY PLEA BARGAIN IN LIQUOR CASES?

I agree with Ferdinand that plea bargaining in Massachusetts first took root in cases involving alcohol, but we part ways at the underlying question of prosecutorial motives. Why did prosecutors choose liquor (and murder) cases as the medium in which to mold the future? I note murder cases in parentheses because Ferdinand, like Vogel, did not extend his research into the Supreme Judicial Court and so could not report early evidence of charge bargaining in murder cases. This discussion therefore speaks mainly of liquor cases, though lessons learned in murder cases inevitably intrude.

My own explanation of plea bargaining's early dominance in liquor cases is brief: Prosecutors plea bargained in liquor cases because they could. Among all of the most commonly prosecuted crimes, only in liquor cases did the statutory penalty scheme so tightly bind the judge's hands in sentencing, enabling prosecutors to dictate sentences by manipulating charges. Not even in murder cases did prosecutors have such complete sentencing power, for when a defendant pled guilty to manslaughter in the course of a prosecutorial charge bargain, the judge's sentencing discretion spanned a full twenty years.

The peculiar power that prosecutors held in liquor cases stands in sharp relief against the ineptitude they showed when attempting to charge bargain in nonliquor cases other than murder. In 1852, for reasons I will discuss shortly, Massachusetts prosecutors lost their power to charge bargain in liquor cases. The record books of the Court of Common Pleas for the next year show that Charles Russell Train handled 482 cases, but secured a clear plea bargain of the sort we have seen in liquor cases only once. In a two-count forgery indictment, District Attorney Train nol prossed one count after the defendant pled guilty.[49]

When Isaac Morse succeeded Train in 1855,[50] he apparently resolved to find new territory on which to establish a charge-bargaining regime. He settled on breaking-and-entering cases. Of thirty-nine indictments Morse sought in 1859 for either breaking and entering or theft from a building, he alleged separate counts for committing the crime by nighttime and by daytime in all but four of them.[51] In contrast, in none of the fifty-two cases of this sort that Train had prosecuted in 1849 and 1853— the two years of his tenure that I studied—did he allege separate nighttime and daytime counts.[52]

Despite Morse's cleverness in positioning these cases for charge bargaining, only four of the thirty-nine ended in the sort of charge bargain that he apparently had in mind—with his nol prossing one of the two counts in exchange for the defendant's guilty plea to the other.[53] It is no surprise that the tactic was so feeble. The maximum penalty for breaking and entering in the nighttime was twenty years. For breaking and entering in the daytime, it was five years.[54] But the judge's sentence in the thirty-five cases that ended in guilty findings exceeded five years only twice and never exceeded ten years.[55] Because there was no minimum punishment assigned to either count and because judges were not much inclined to approach the maximum, Morse conferred little apparent benefit by nol prossing one count.[56]

In fact, as the defendant could not logically be guilty of both a nighttime and a daytime break, the jury usually convicted the defendant on only one count. When the jury did return a general verdict of guilty, Morse often nol prossed one of the two counts.[57] It is little wonder, then, that charge bargaining in breaking-and-entering cases worked only with unrepresented defendants. Although the defendant had counsel in thirteen of these thirty-nine cases, the four charge-bargained cases were not among them.[58] Lacking the kind of control over the sentencing decision that could make a charge bargain meaningful, Morse succeeded in deploying the tactic against only a few defendants—and they were the most poorly informed.

WHY JUDGES DECLINED TO TAKE PART

A difficult question lurks behind Morse's failure to broaden the frontiers of charge bargaining. I have argued that charge bargaining worked only in liquor and murder cases because only in those cases was the penalty scheme rigid enough to allow prosecutors *on their own* to guarantee sentencing concessions to those defendants who pled guilty. But why did prosecutors have to act on their own? The kind of sentencing power that rigid penalty schemes gave prosecutors mattered only if judges were not partners in plea bargaining. Had judges cooperated in plea bargaining, prosecutors could have bargained in almost any sort of case, even those with wide-open penalty structures. Before I turn to Ferdinand's competing theory about why plea bargaining arose most prominently in liquor cases, therefore, I need to consider why judges proved so reluctant to join forces with prosecutors in striking deals in all other cases.

Proving Judges' Reticence

Two bodies of evidence make it clear that through at least the first half—and probably the first three-quarters—of the nineteenth century, judges generally withheld their cooperation from plea bargaining. The first concerns the liquor laws themselves. In 1852, when Massachusetts followed Maine in enacting statewide liquor prohibition, the legislature provided that in cases arising under the new law, "a *nolle prosequi* shall not be entered by the prosecuting officer, except with the concurrence of the court."[59] Apparently, the legislature had reconsidered its 1845 vindication of Asahel Huntington's charge-bargaining practices and reverted to its original, hostile posture. The impact on prosecutorial charge bargaining was immediate and devastating. In 1849, the last year I studied before the law change, Charles Russell Train resolved twenty of fifty-six adjudicated liquor cases with clear plea bargains. In all but one of these, he charged multiple counts, the defendant pled guilty on one or more counts, and Train nol prossed the balance. That year Train sought multiple counts in eighty-nine percent of his liquor indictments—evidence of a concerted plan to gain leverage in anticipation of a plea bargain.[60]

By 1853, having been stripped of his unilateral power to enter nol prosses in liquor cases, Train had abandoned his plan entirely. Not only did he not engage in a single plea bargain on the old model, it appears he did not seek a single multicount liquor indictment.[61] As a result, of twenty-four liquor cases adjudicated in 1853, twenty-one ended in trials. Only three ended in plea bargains, and all of these involved the somewhat covert plea-bargaining technique of placing the cases on file, which I take up in the next chapter. By 1859, the volume of adjudicated liquor cases had grown, perhaps as authorities got used to the new law, but the pattern of disposition stayed much the same. Forty-three of the sixty-two adjudicated liquor cases ended in trials;[62] three ended in simple guilty pleas with no evidence of a concession;[63] and all sixteen plea bargains took the on-file form.

Having once acted to kill prosecutorial charge bargaining, the legislature was vigilant against its resurrection. When lawmakers reenacted the state's liquor prohibition law in 1855 and 1869, they took care to retain the nol pros ban.[64] Prosecutorial charge bargaining in liquor cases never recovered. In fact, virtually the *only* plea bargains that survived in liquor cases after 1852 were of the on-file variety. Only 4 of the 602 liquor cases in the years I studied between 1853 and 1910 ended in a plea bargain of the sort Train had used so extensively in 1849.[65]

It would be hard to attribute the sudden death of multiple-count plea bargaining in liquor cases to any other aspect of the 1852 prohibition law than its elimination of the nol pros as a prosecutorial prerogative. The new law left in place the mandatory penalty scheme that had made the old license law so conducive to plea bargaining: Being a common seller, for example, still carried a mandatory $100 fine, and making a single sale carried a fixed fine of ten dollars.[66] If the 1852 law effectively killed charge bargaining in liquor cases, it must have been because judges disapproved of the practice. The law did not ban nol prosses outright, but banned them "except with the concurrence of the court." That charge bargaining in liquor cases died compels one conclusion: Judges withheld their concurrence.

The second body of evidence of judicial resistance to plea bargaining concerns the resolution of *non*liquor cases in the first third of the century. The records of the Court of Common Pleas show that from 1789—the earliest year I studied—through 1829, between forty-eight percent and seventy-two percent of adjudicated nonliquor cases ended in pleas of guilty

2.1.

Proportion of Adjudicated Nonliquor Cases
Ending in Pleas of Guilty or No Contest

YEAR	PERCENT OF CASES
1789–1790	71
1799–1800	63
1805–1806	59
1809–1810	48
1814–1815	53
1819–1820	59
1824	56
1829	72

SOURCES: Middlesex Ct. C.P. R. Books, on file with the
Massachusetts Archives.

or no contest (see Table 2.1). Despite these very high plea rates (which
soon fell dramatically for reasons I take up in Chapter 4), there is no evidence that plea *bargaining* was going on. That is, there is no evidence that
these defendants won some understood concession for their pleas. Court
records reflect a near-total absence of the sort of charge bargains I examined in Chapter 1, in which the clerk's record made the terms of the deal
clear. Outside the liquor law context, only four such bargains appear in the
fourteen years I studied between 1789 and 1829.[67] Because the penalty
scheme in nonliquor cases left wide discretion in the judge's hands, the
prosecutor could not dictate the sentence by manipulating charges—so
any effective plea bargain required the judge's participation. The lack of
charge bargaining in nonliquor cases, then, is some evidence that judges
were not yet allies in prosecutors' plea-bargaining designs.

There is, moreover, no evidence of *sentence* bargaining in nonliquor
cases during these early years. A numerical analysis of sentencing patterns
discloses no sign of a well-understood practice of granting lighter sentences
to those defendants who pled guilty. True, any such analysis is risky in this
context. Each case has many unknown sentencing variables, including the
defendant's background, the specific details of the crime, and the judge's
habits and moods. More importantly, even if one had a large enough sam-

2.2.

Sentence According to Mode of Conviction in Theft Cases:
Middlesex Court of Common Pleas, 1809–1829

	AFTER PLEA	AFTER TRIAL
Number of Cases	26	17
Avg. Value of Stolen Goods	$14	$14
% Prison	88	88
Avg. Term (months)	2.5	1.8
% Fine	12	18
Avg. Fine	$13	$20
% Assessed Costs	23	18
Avg. Costs	$23	$41

SOURCE: Middlesex Ct. C.P. R. Books.

ple to smooth out such variations, a systematic bias still might slant the outcome: Those defendants who faced the heaviest sentences might have been more likely to go to trial, so even absent any form of plea bargaining, sentences might have been heavier after trial than after a plea. This risk of bias means that a pattern of higher sentences after trial would not necessarily indicate the presence of plea bargaining; but the *absence* of such a pattern probably would be evidence of the absence of plea bargaining.

Simple theft was the only nonliquor crime to appear during the early years of this study often enough to permit numerical analysis.[68] Before 1809, the punishment of thieves generally involved whippings, restitution, and sale into servitude, often as alternatives to one another or to incarceration.[69] Rather than try to compare lashes and bondage with more modern punishments of prison time and fines, I have chosen to examine only those theft cases from 1809 or later and have excluded the few cases in those years that still authorized servitude. In the eight years I studied between 1809 and 1829, forty-three cases of simple theft ended in convictions and sentences of either time or fines. Fortunately, indictments in theft cases almost always attached an exact dollar figure to the goods stolen, so we have some way to judge whether the more serious cases tended to go to trial.

Table 2.2 records my findings. As it happened, the average value of the goods stolen was very nearly the same—$14.02 for cases ending in a plea and $14.08 for those ending in a conviction after trial. And in fact, the likelihood that the defendant would go to prison was the same in both sets of cases—eighty-eight percent. But those accused thieves who pled guilty tended to suffer *heavier* sentences than those who went to trial and lost— on average drawing 2.5 months as opposed to only 1.8 months.

Explaining Judges' Reticence

I believe this evidence, together with that presented over the last several pages, is enough to show that judges in the early nineteenth century generally were not partners in plea bargaining. Prosecutors therefore had to bargain where they could—in liquor cases. In Chapter 4, I explore what moved so many defendants in the first third of the century to plead guilty in other kinds of cases when they won no apparent concession in exchange. For now, the important question is why no concession was forthcoming. Why didn't judges reward defendants for their guilty pleas? And why didn't they at least go along with prosecutors' attempts, after 1852, to enter nol prosses in liquor cases?

The first and most fundamental reason is that judges lacked prosecutors' incentives to plea bargain: They neither faced the same workload pressure nor found the same advantage in the certain (prosecutorial) victory of a plea. Their workload pressure was lower in part because they earned full-time salaries. In 1821 the legislature set salaries at $2,100 for the chief justice of the Court of Common Pleas and $1,800 for each of the associate judges,[70] as compared to the $1,000 that Asahel Huntington earned[71] until the legislature reduced his salary to $700 in 1843.[72] (As one index of a livable wage, in 1849 a prominent lawyer called a salary of $2,500 for the state's attorney general "a good one.")[73] Although there seems to have been no law that barred judges from receiving outside income,[74] I have seen almost no evidence that any judge carried on a law practice or other trade.[75] It is true that four of the five judges of the Court of Common Pleas resigned their posts in indignation after the legislature reduced their salaries to $1,700 in 1843.[76] But four new judges quickly took their spots,[77] and by 1867, associate judges of the Superior Court were drawing $4,200,[78] while the Middlesex district attorney languished at $1,200.[79]

Still, I do not suggest that huge caseload increases, especially those of the 1840s, did not burden judges. That the legislature expanded the Court of Common Pleas from four judges to seven between 1843 and 1851 makes it plain that all parties thought there was stress on the court.[80] But because judges drew full-time salaries and apparently sought no livelihood elsewhere, they lacked prosecutors' financial incentives to dispose of cases as quickly as possible. For them, a day spent trying criminal cases was not a day's civil income lost.

Moreover, the judges profited from the sheer overwork of the district attorneys: A part-time unassisted prosecutor could charge and try only so many cases and therefore could put only so much pressure on a judge. Yet the Middlesex district attorney's salary did not begin to resemble a full-time salary until 1872, when the legislature raised it to $2,000,[81] and I have seen no hint of an assistant district attorney in Middlesex before 1875.[82] When the district attorneys found themselves unable to manage their caseloads, they simply cleaned out their backlog by entering nol prosses en masse.[83] And if judges were therefore somewhat protected from the caseload pressures that plagued prosecutors, they felt perhaps not at all the prosecutor's second incentive to plea bargain—that it meant a clear victory.

Lacking clear incentives to plea bargain, judges may have found themselves more troubled than prosecutors by a principled objection to the practice. In the great majority of cases, the legislature had entrusted judges with very broad sentencing discretion entirely free from review. Once a judge chose a sentence of between zero and twenty years for manslaughter,[84] for example, no higher court could adjust the sentence, nor could any authority short of the governor release the defendant from his term.[85] The notion of taking part in a plea bargain must have deeply offended any judge who fully felt the weight of this burden. No judge could promise in good conscience to impose a particular sentence when ignorant of the facts most critical to the choice of sentence—the details of the crime and the defendant's character and criminal history. And the judge had no unbiased source of this information.

In this light, it is easy to understand a Michigan judge's affronted response to a defense lawyer who asked in 1883 whether the judge would impose a certain sentence if the defendant pled guilty: "I informed him," reported the judge, "that it would be time enough for me to determine

what the sentence should be after the [defendant] was convicted."[86]
There seems to have been a widespread if not uniform nineteenth-century
practice of holding a sentencing hearing, perhaps involving witnesses,
even after a defendant pled guilty.[87] Such a hearing could enable judges to
pass a conscientiously well-informed sentence, but could not become an
aid in plea bargaining. Because the hearing *followed* conviction, it could
not help the judge determine what concession he should offer if the defendant chose to plead guilty.

If, as is likely, sentencing power became a symbol of judges' great
authority and esteem, then they must have bristled at prosecutors who
usurped any part of it. Yet plea bargaining typically involves sharing sentencing authority with prosecutors, who help negotiate the sentences.
Here we stray from an objection founded on principle to one based on
pride. I have seen no expression of judicial attitudes toward prosecutorial plea bargaining during the first half of the nineteenth century, when
the practice first emerged. But toward the end of the century, at a time
when one might have thought judges were reconciled to the phenomenon,
they bitterly voiced their resentment. In 1897 the Rhode Island Supreme
Court considered a nuisance case in which the prosecutor had entered a
nol pros on condition of the defendant's payment of one hundred dollars
plus costs. "We are aware," the court wrote,

> that the custom has obtained, to a considerable extent, for the attor-
> ney-general to compromise or settle this class of cases, as well as cases
> arising under the liquor law, upon the payment of a certain sum of
> money to the State by the defendant; but the practice is a vicious one,
> and meets with our entire disapproval. There is no law authorizing a
> sentence or any legal substitute therefor by consent of parties, without
> the imposition thereof by the court.[88]

In 1913 a former chief justice of Maine's Supreme Judicial Court put
in still harsher terms his opinion of the way prosecutors deployed their
nol pros powers:

> A reprehensible practice . . . is said (and I fear with some truth) to have
> obtained in some counties for the prosecuting officer, even after con-
> viction sometimes, to grant a *nolle prosequi* in consideration of the
> defendant's paying into the county treasury such sum of money as the
> officer may fix upon . . . . [This practice] is a plain, inexcusable usurpa-

tion of a power entrusted to the courts, the power of determining what the penalty should be within the limits fixed by the legislature.[89]

The author wondered at the effrontery of prosecutors who imagined "that they are better judges than the court of what is an adequate penalty for the offense."[90]

Plea bargaining in the early and mid-nineteenth century therefore encountered at least three obstacles to judicial acceptance: It served judges' needs less well than those of prosecutors; it confronted judges' principled aversion to discharging their awesome duty to sentence without full information; and it wounded some judges' pride of power. As a result, prosecutors could plea bargain only when they could do so on their own, without judicial cooperation—and that meant only in liquor crimes and capital offenses. But as I have said, Ferdinand arrives at a different explanation of the early rise of plea bargaining in liquor cases. It is time now to take up his evidence.

The Role of Absent Victims and Savvy Defendants

Ferdinand's massive survey of the court records of Boston, like my more modest study of Middlesex, produced solid evidence of a special relationship between liquor license cases and plea bargaining in the first half of the nineteenth century.[91] Just over half of the liquor law cases in his sample ended in guilty pleas, as compared to only twenty-six percent of typical common law crimes such as larceny and felony assault.[92] Moreover, the rate of guilty pleas in liquor cases increased greatly in the 1840s.[93] Although Ferdinand's statistics do not separate simple guilty pleas from clear plea bargains, as I use the term, he does report a vigorous practice of multiple charging and suggests anecdotally that the tactic was a favorite in liquor cases.[94] Hence, he tells us of restaurateur Peter Bent Brigham. Brigham's name survives on a Boston hospital, but in humbler days in the 1840s, he came repeatedly to court to face a raft of liquor law charges. Each time he pled guilty to one count and paid his modest fine.[95]

In other ways, Ferdinand's account of the early rise of plea bargaining differs from mine. He argues, for example, that Boston constables "invented" plea bargaining in the 1830s as a natural spin-off of the negotiations they conducted with criminals for information about other crimes or for the return of stolen goods. The prosecutor, who "could readily appreciate [plea bargaining's] many advantages, and . . . was in a position to implement it quickly," then expanded the practice that the constables had devised.[96]

The notion that Boston constables invented plea bargaining in the 1830s must confront earlier evidence of plea bargaining in Middlesex and elsewhere. After all, Samuel Dana hit upon a very elaborate form of plea bargaining in 1808; Asahel Stearns used Dana's model in the 1820s; and by 1834, around the time Ferdinand credits Boston constables with inventing the practice, Asahel Huntington had refined it with his preprinted, multicount indictment forms. As we will see in Chapter 7, plea bargaining had appeared in scattered other places long before its invention in Boston. That two parties might trade concessions in order to trade gains surely was not a new concept, and it took little inspiration to extend such familiar tactics to the criminal courts.

It did, however, take power. Unless the prosecutor could guarantee a sentencing concession in exchange for the defendant's plea, no bargain was likely to happen. Yet Ferdinand does not examine how it was that prosecutors were "in a position to implement" plea bargaining in liquor cases. In seeking to explain the early connection between plea bargaining and liquor cases,[97] he does not speak of the license law's rigid penalty scheme or the unusual power to craft charge bargains that it bestowed upon prosecutors. Instead he looks largely to the absence of a victim in liquor cases and to the presence of savvy, business-wise defendants. These factors have some appeal in setting liquor cases apart from most others, but perhaps less than at first appears.

Ferdinand sees two reasons why victimless crimes might have made fertile ground for plea bargaining. The less important, which he notes only in passing, is that there was no injured party to agitate for complete vindication of justice and to resist any proposed plea bargain.[98] Ferdinand does not lean hard on this argument, perhaps because he realizes that liquor crimes were not entirely victimless. Townspeople often made angry demands that prosecutors rid them of their corner tavern-keeper.[99] And although Ferdinand does not look at the work of the Supreme Judicial Court and does not write of plea bargaining in capital cases, he surely would not claim that murder cases lacked victims, though they were a source of vigorous plea bargaining in the middle of the century.

Ferdinand puts more weight on the argument that victimless crimes could end up in court only if the authorities actively went out to investigate. "[T]he investigating official," he notes, "was someone who could also begin negotiations."[100] Yet Ferdinand offers no evidence that liquor prosecutions inevitably arose from official action, and there is some reason to think that official instigation was more the exception than the rule.[101] Moreover, investigating officials "who could also begin negotiations"[102] probably were involved in the arrests of many sorts of nonliquor defendants, such as burglary suspects, who nonetheless rarely pled guilty.[103]

As for savvy defendants, Ferdinand argues that those accused of liquor crimes "were often businessmen . . . [who] recognized the waste in seriously contesting minor charges that carried little stigma" and who were therefore ready to negotiate.[104] Ferdinand surely is right that unless defendants saw a comparative advantage in pleas over trials, no bargain could take place. And he may be right that tradespeople were somewhat quicker than others to see the value of a good deal. But I suspect that Ferdinand carries this argument too far when he suggests that it does much to explain why liquor laws came first in plea bargaining's chronicles. He does not consider how burglars and robbers, for example, streetwise in so many ways, could have been dull to the benefits a plea bargain could promise. And of course, both jailmates and defense counsel might have helped less savvy defendants see the value of a good bargain.[105]

I will not press these points, however, because the lack of individual victims in liquor cases and liquor defendants' frequent status as tradespeople probably did accelerate, if not cause, the progress of plea bargaining in liquor cases. The real shortcoming of Ferdinand's theory of the evolution of plea bargaining is that its powers of explanation expire almost precisely at mid-century, when his study ends. Just two years into the second half of the century, the legislature withdrew the prosecutor's power to enter nol prosses in liquor cases and killed prosecutorial charge bargaining. Whatever may have been the role of absent victims and savvy defendants in facilitating charge bargaining in liquor cases, these factors were not enough to keep the practice alive. In nineteenth-century liquor cases, the prosecutor's unilateral power to nol pros was apparently a necessary condition for charge bargaining to take place.

And despite Ferdinand's arguments about absent victims and savvy defendants, the prosecutor's ability to use his nol pros power to shape the defendant's sentence was also apparently a sufficient condition for charge bargaining to take place. The history of charge bargaining in murder cases suggests as much. Murder was hardly a victimless crime, and the victim's friends and family no doubt pressed for quick and vigorous prosecution. Nor were murder defendants particularly savvy. Although they almost always had counsel appointed free by the state, they lacked the commercial sophistication of liquor dealers. Yet even as charge bargaining in liquor cases disappeared altogether after the legislature withdrew the prosecutor's nol pros power in 1852, charge bargaining in murder cases showed huge gains. The legislature's action had applied only to liquor cases, and prosecutors in capital cases continued unhindered in their practice of entering partial nol prosses in exchange for the defendant's plea to a lesser charge.

Now we must examine the only form of prosecutorial plea bargaining, outside this rarefied context of murder cases, to survive the legislature's mid-century assault on nol prosses in liquor cases. No longer able to charge bargain in liquor cases and lacking judicial support for the sort of broad-based sentence bargaining that would emerge later, prosecutors kept plea bargaining alive as an underground resistance movement sustained by their power to put cases quietly on file. In its versatility, on-file plea bargaining belies Ferdinand's claims about the victimless nature of liquor crimes and the sophistication of liquor defendants. These features perhaps made some cases more attractive targets for plea bargaining, but just as they were not sufficient to keep alive prosecutorial charge bargaining in liquor cases, so they were not necessary to successful on-file plea bargaining. For on-file plea bargaining—from its first appearance in the second quarter of the nineteenth century through its solitary survival in the dark third quarter to its triumphant emergence in the fourth— never was limited to victimless cases or those cases that involved more savvy defendants. Rather, it spread throughout the lower reaches of the Massachusetts criminal docket.

3

On-File Plea Bargaining and the Rise of Probation

Prosecutorial charge bargaining in liquor cases died with the legislature's ban on unilateral prosecutorial nol prosses in 1852. Three years later, the legislature turned the screws even tighter on liquor dealers by attaching a mandatory term of confinement to every offense arising under the liquor prohibition law.[1] The combined effect was that many more liquor cases went to trial. In 1849 only eighteen of seventy-eight liquor cases—or twenty-three percent—went to trial. By 1859, the numbers looked very different. Forty-three out of 107 liquor cases—or forty percent—were tried. Still, the striking thing is not how sharply the trial rate grew, but how small it remained. After all, the law seemed to permit defendants no escape from a liquor indictment except acquittal after trial. So what happened to the sixty-four liquor cases in 1859 that did not go to trial?

A citizen of Middlesex County who chose to investigate liquor law enforcement in the courts in 1859 would have had difficulty even recognizing this as the proper question to ask. A careful review of the record book for the Superior Court and the Court of Common Pleas (the former court succeeded the latter in 1859)[2] would have disclosed only sixty-six liquor cases—forty that went to trial and twenty-six others that ended in guilty pleas (and prison terms) or nol prosses (approved by the court) or dismissals.³ But at various places in this handsome, oversized volume, the citizen might have spied a cryptic heading: "The following Indictments & Complaints . . . the Attorney for the Commonwealth in this behalf orders on file."⁴

The list that followed would not have resolved confusion—it was just a series of names without charges, case numbers, or places of origin. Hoping to find out more, the citizen might have turned in two directions. If the clerk of courts permitted inspection of the file papers for each case, the citizen would have found the charges as well as an account of each case's progress through the court, but the process of inspection would have been plodding. File papers were just that—the loose papers associated with each case, including the charging documents and witness subpoenas, usually folded together and filed according to case number. The curious citizen who chose to review the file papers for several dozen cases would have had to locate the papers for each case and review them, one set at a time.

The alternative was to ask for access to the clerk's docket book. Unlike the record book, intended for both posterity and public inspection,⁵ the docket book apparently was for the clerk's eyes only—both the handwriting and the abbreviations ward off intruders. But with patience, the citizen would have found the answer: In addition to those sixty-six liquor law cases clearly identified in the 1859 record book, there were another forty-one in the docket book, most listed simply as "L.L."—and all but a few placed "on file."⁶ Mixed in with them were another 122 nonliquor cases, most similarly placed on file.

On the whole, the docket book does not disclose why these cases ended up on file, though an occasional note advised that the "Deft. left"⁷ or the principal witness has "gone west."⁸ But in fifteen liquor cases in 1859, the book adds an important procedural detail—that before the case was put on file, the defendant had pled guilty. Hence, in *Commonwealth v. Ann Donovan*, the clerk wrote, "Plea in Court below retracted & now pleads guilty. [O]n file."⁹ Donovan's case and others like it are the focus of my interest here. When I refer to the *on-file mechanism*, I mean those cases that were placed on file after the defendant's plea of guilty or no contest. Later in this chapter I explain why I think this procedure deserves the name *on-file plea bargaining*.

THE ORIGINS OF PROBATION

Donovan's case bears no notation concerning either the mandatory fine or the mandatory prison term that conviction under the liquor law carried. Apparently, the act of placing the case on file stayed execution of the sentence. Although *Donovan* is silent about what happened from that point on, the record in other cases, including many nonliquor cases, adds more, as in a "misdemeanor" prosecution of James Quinlan and John Callahan: "Plea severally guilty—Callahan recogd. on file on probation."[10] Defendant Callahan apparently gave or promised the court an unspecified sum of money as surety for his future appearance or good behavior—that is, he "recog[nize]d" (or entered into a recognizance) for his future good behavior—and was then placed on probation.

These are not the earliest cases to call to mind modern probation, nor did such cases emerge first in Middlesex County. As F. W. Grinnell argued early in the last century,[11] the story of probation's rise should begin with the prosecution of Jerusha Chase in Boston in 1830.[12] And indeed, *Chase* may be the first reported instance of the on-file mechanism at work. In February 1830, Jerusha Chase appeared in the Boston Municipal Court to face a charge of stealing from a residence. The clerk recorded the result: "Feb. 8. Defendant retracts her [not guilty] plea and pleads guilty and recognized in the sum of two hundred dollars with Benjamin Salmon, trader, and Daniel Chase, Cordwainer of Marblehead, to come when sent for and in the meantime to keep the peace."[13] The judge released Chase and charged her two sponsors—Benjamin Salmon and Daniel Chase—to guarantee her good behavior at risk of forfeiting two hundred dollars should they fail. The case itself was placed "on file" (a fact recorded elsewhere) and would stay there as long as Chase remained on good behavior.[14] Though Chase's conviction then lay dormant, the prosecutor had the power to revive it if Chase's behavior later turned worse.

I cannot say exactly when the procedure at work in *Chase* found its way into Middlesex County. Before 1844, the county's criminal docket books contained no information other than what appeared in the record books. As I noted earlier, the record books never disclosed much about the on-file mechanism other than the fact of its existence; before 1849 they did not disclose even that.[15] But beginning with the 1844 docket

book, one can find something very much like the on-file mechanism vigorously in use. The docket book lists seventy-six cases in which the
defendant pled either no contest or (occasionally) guilty. Although almost
all of these involved violations of the liquor law that called for mandatory
fines, the book notes no fines. Instead, it says that the cases were continued—and then continued again. Eventually, the district attorney nol
prossed several of the cases, thereby canceling the fines.[16]

The docket book for 1847 makes it clear that *most* such cases were
destined to end in nol prosses. Twenty-four defendants pled either guilty
or (occasionally) no contest to a violation of the liquor law in the
February session of the Court of Common Pleas. All of these cases were
continued to the June session and then again to the October session. At
the October session, district attorney Albert Nelson nol prossed the
whole slate of cases without demanding a single fine. Nelson's frequent
use of this mechanism sheds light on his 1847 announcement promising
that those liquor defendants who pled guilty at the next session of court
would escape with no fine.[17] That announcement required that defendants "enter into recognizance to observe the law."[18] Although the
Middlesex clerk rarely noted such recognizances in 1847, the clerk in
Essex County, where Nelson also prosecuted, regularly did so.[19] And in
one Essex liquor case in 1847, opposite the clerk's notation that the
defendant pled guilty, Nelson himself scrawled on the file papers, "Deft
to be sentenced if he sells after Sept. 28 1847."[20]

This procedure of permitting the defendant to plead to a liquor charge,
continuing the case for two or more court sessions, and then ultimately
entering a nol pros fell somewhat short of the true on-file mechanism.[21]
Placing a case on file continued it indefinitely and never called on the district attorney to exercise his nol pros powers.[22] But this somewhat more
primitive procedure resembled the on-file mechanism both in permitting
defendants who had pled guilty or no contest to escape a mandatory
penalty and in giving the district attorney some control over the defendant's future behavior.

By the end of 1847, the true "on file" system, so called, had arrived in
Middlesex County.[23] At first it was rarely used. But in 1849, during
Charles Russell Train's second year in office, the on-file mechanism sud-
denly became a major and fairly regular component of the district attor-

ney's work in Middlesex. In the June term of that year, Train placed 108 cases on file. In thirty-two of these, the defendant pled guilty or no contest before Train filed the case.

Train did not immediately make broad use of this procedure in liquor cases. In the June 1849 term, he placed only five liquor cases on file after pleas, while he conducted charge bargains in nine such cases. But he placed a striking total of twenty-seven nonliquor cases on file after pleas, as against only two charge bargains. Most of these nonliquor cases involved crimes at the low end of the criminal ladder: There were eleven victimless sex offenses, three larcenies, three minor assault crimes, two nuisances, and one charge of obstructing an officer. A few crimes stood a rung or two higher: Four cases, all involving the same defendant, alleged counterfeiting and one charged felonious assault.[24]

We should not be surprised at Train's sudden, aggressive use of the on-file mechanism. We saw earlier that his 1849 caseload was more than four times as great as Huntington's 1843 burden and that Train responded in part by wielding his power to charge bargain in liquor cases with even more zeal than his predecessors.[25] Having proved so eager and adept when charge bargaining, Train readily saw the potential of the on-file mechanism for ending cases quickly and well.

Three years later, when the legislature set out to squelch charge bargaining in liquor cases by banning prosecutorial nol prosses, Train had an alternative at the ready. The on-file mechanism was peculiarly adapted to his dilemma. Because placing a case on file postponed it indefinitely, the prosecutor never needed to exercise his now-banned nol pros power. And because cases placed on file were not technically "disposed," the clerk did not fully record them in the official record books. The difficulty of discerning what happened to these cases proved quite convenient to Train, his successors in Middlesex, and his counterparts across the state, for it helped prosecutors evade the legislature's evident wish to end deals in liquor cases.

FORESHADOWING THE LINK WITH MODERN PROBATION

All this would be but a curious historical footnote if the on-file manner of resolving cases had grown up and died in the nineteenth century. But this story of what Ferdinand calls "informal probation" proves to be of real moment.[26] For putting cases on file *was* probation. It was not merely an ideological forebear of the system of probation that first found expression in a Massachusetts statute of 1878.[27] It was, as a matter of court procedure, the selfsame thing. *Penologically*, probation grew more advanced over time as probation officers came into being, but *procedurally*, the on-file mechanism was the same practice Massachusetts later exported to the nation and the world under the label "probation."

For our purposes, the significance of this identity of probation and the on-file mechanism turns on two additional facts. First, prosecutors had in most cases a unilateral (if not exclusive) power to place cases on file. And second, as we have seen prosecutors do in other contexts, they converted their power to the purposes of plea bargaining. By using probation as an instrument of plea bargaining, prosecutors gave this most famous of nineteenth-century contributions to criminal procedure much of its initial vigor.

This argument that probation grew up in symbiosis with prosecutorial plea bargaining rests in turn on a third claim: that the on-file mechanism gave prosecutors all the power they needed to invent a new form of plea bargaining. Tracing the source and the extent of this power will demand painstaking scrutiny of statutes and cases. Here the very tedium of the work is part of the story. I argued earlier that nineteenth-century prosecutors had a built-in interest in plea bargaining. But they achieved the power to satisfy that interest only rarely—either by extraordinary legislative grant or by procedural ingenuity. In Chapter 1, I explored the consequences of the extraordinary grant of power that the legislature unwittingly made by attaching rigid penalty schemes to liquor laws and capital offenses and by leaving unchecked the prosecutor's power to nol pros. In the investigation I now begin, I will try to expose the ingenuity of Massachusetts prosecutors in turning a small procedural device—the simple formality of moving (or not moving) for sentence—into the on-file form of plea bargaining.

As intricate as this examination of prosecutorial powers is, I do not mean to suggest that the particular array of powers that prosecutors discovered in the on-file mechanism was essential to prosecutorial plea bargaining.[28] Rather, I believe that most nineteenth-century prosecutors would have devised a means to plea bargain given any sufficiently broad constellation of powers. In this sense, Massachusetts is just a case study. Later I examine how prosecutors in other places used the particular powers available to them to develop distinct plea-bargaining techniques. For now, we must explore how Massachusetts prosecutors crafted a covert plea-bargaining regime from the various vagaries of Massachusetts practice. In the process, we may see how prosecutors raised up probation as a sibling of plea bargaining and shaped it to do plea bargaining's bidding.

THE PROSECUTOR'S POWERS AND ON-FILE PLEA BARGAINING

Jerusha Chase's business before the Boston Municipal Court on February 8, 1830, began with a guilty plea: "Defendant retracts her plea [of not guilty] and pleads guilty."[29] Her business ended with a generous result: Instead of imposing sentence, the court released her into the custody of her companions on a promise, backed by a pledge of cash, of her future good behavior. Her case was then placed on file. But can we call this an *on-file plea bargain*? Who, if anyone, promised Chase that if she pled guilty, her case would be placed on file—or from whom did she expect this result? These questions raise another: Who had the power to grant Chase this result?

The evidence is strong that *Chase* was in fact a plea bargain and that Jerusha Chase's bargaining partner was not the judge, but rather her prosecutor—James Austin, the Suffolk County Attorney.[30] We have met Austin before. In 1841, having risen to the post of attorney general, he engineered the first capital charge bargains that I encountered in Massachusetts.[31] The prosecutorial charge bargaining described in Chapter 1 conveys some idea of the powers Austin would have wanted and needed to craft an on-file plea bargain. In liquor and murder cases, prosecutors needed two sorts of power to mount a vigorous charge-bargaining practice: the power to protect defendants against unpleasant surprise at the judge's hands during sentencing and a corresponding power to protect themselves from the judge's undue leniency. The question now is whether prosecutors found these powers in the on-file mechanism.

The Power to Protect Defendants from Judicial Severity

In liquor cases, the prosecutor's power to promise the defendant a specific sentence in exchange for the defendant's guilty plea derived from the liquor law's fixed penalty scheme and the prosecutor's unreviewable power (before 1852) to nol pros additional counts of the indictment. In murder cases, the prosecutor's power to reduce the charge to manslaughter and thereby lift the threat of death accomplished the same purpose. Although the prosecutor could not promise the defendant a specific sentence within the zero-to-twenty-year range provided for manslaughter, the prosecutor could promise "not death" and "not more than twenty years"—surely enough to convince many defendants to plead guilty. If the on-file mechanism proved a source of prosecutorial plea bargaining, then it must in a similar way have given prosecutors the power to limit the sentence the judge could impose.

The Power to Put Cases on File. In search of this prosecutorial power to limit sentence, I set out to discover which courtroom actor—prosecutor or judge—had the power to put cases on file. Like so many other questions I asked in the course of this study, this question proved to be the wrong one. It turns out that the power to place cases on file is only a cover for the power that matters: the power to stay sentence. But though misguided, my question did not prove fruitless. I went in search of the power to place cases "on file" because that was the discourse of the day. And just as I was deceived about where the relevant power lay, so it appears some contemporaries were too. For while the power to place cases on file migrated into judges' hands, where some no doubt thought it should be, the power that really mattered remained in most cases and for a long time firmly in the prosecutor's grip.

On the issue of who held the power to place cases on file, the record and docket books of the Middlesex courts tell an intriguingly garbled story. I quoted earlier from the record book for 1859, which states flatly that "the Attorney for the Commonwealth . . . orders [these cases] on file."[32] A few years earlier, in 1853, the clerk was even more pointed: "The following Indictments and Complaints, Charles R Train Esquire, Attorney for the Commonwealth in this behalf, orders to be placed on file."[33] But going forward from 1859, we find more mixed meanings. Between 1860 and 1876, the clerk often attributed the on-file list to the district attorney (seventeen times) and less often to the court (eight times). But with interesting frequency, the clerk simply neglected to say who had ordered that the standard list of cases be placed on file: Seventeen times in these years, the clerk wrote, "The following Indictments and Complaints, to wit," and then listed dozens of names— but never finished his sentence.[34] Docket books for these years make it clear that the listed cases were placed "on file," but do not say by whom.[35] Then, from 1877 on, the clerk wrote clearly and consistently that the listed cases were, "by order of the Court, placed on file."[36] This variance across the decades is not the only confusion encountered. In 1859, for example, some of the cases that appear in the record book as having been ordered on file by the district attorney appear in the docket book as having been ordered on file by the court.[37]

Perhaps Ferdinand saw the same sort of confusion in Boston, for he concludes simply that the decision to put a case on file "may be initiated by the judge as well as the prosecutor" and that "[u]nfortunately, it was not possible to differentiate the prosecutor's [decisions] from those of the judge."[38] I think the best conclusion to draw from this jumble is that the power to place cases on file shifted haltingly over the third quarter of the century from the prosecutor to the judge. It is also possible that the clerk himself did not always know who had placed cases on file, or even that the clerk did know but thought (perhaps because it was impolitic to attribute too much power to the prosecutor) that it was better not to say.

Statutes are not much more useful than court records in this search. With some unintended humor, the Supreme Judicial Court wrote in 1874 in *Commonwealth v. Dowdican's Bail* that "this practice [of putting cases on file] has been recognized by statute. Sts. 1865, *c.* 223; 1869, *c.* 415, § 60."[39] One catches the irony only after looking up the two statutes that supposedly "recognized" the on-file practice. The 1865 citation traces to An Act to Prevent Evasions of the Provisions of Section Fifty-Eight of the Eighty-Sixth Chapter of the General Statutes—that is, an act to prevent evasions of the legislature's ban on prosecutorial nol prosses in liquor cases. The law provided that no liquor case "shall be laid on file or disposed of except by trial" without the court's approval.[40] The legislature had enacted this *anti*-filing ordinance after a series of witnesses told a Senate committee that prosecutors were placing cases on file to get around the nol pros ban.[41] And the court's 1869 citation led to the legislature's reenactment of this same anti-filing law.[42]

From the court's reference and from these two statutes, we learn two important facts, each suggested by negative inference. First, by listing as the only statutory authority for the practice of placing cases on file two laws that greatly restricted this power, the Supreme Judicial Court implied that formerly there had been a practice without statutory authority. Second, by making a point of writing and then reenacting a law that barred placing liquor cases on file without the court's consent, the legislature implied that formerly prosecutors had put liquor cases on file without the court's consent.

The legislature perhaps came to the conclusion that prosecutors were unilaterally placing cases on file as a result of the 1865 hearings on enforcement of the liquor laws that had led to the Act to Prevent Evasions.[43] Among the witnesses at the hearings was George P. Sanger, district attorney of Boston's Suffolk County, who said that until his office recently discontinued the practice, "it was thought, if we collected the costs, and placed the case on file, it was better, after a verdict of guilty," than to press for sentence.[44] Whether based on Sanger's admission that "we" placed cases on file or on some other evidence, several members of the committee that heard his testimony wrote in their report that "witnesses said that attorneys evaded the prohibitory law by . . . *placing cases on file.*" The report then added that such "attorneys act upon the same principle as the liquor dealers, whom they try to shield, and prostitute their honorable profession to a connivance with vice, regardless of justice and humanity."[45]

By directing such harsh language at lawyers and by enacting soon afterward a law to prevent prosecutors from putting liquor cases on file without the court's consent, legislators seemed to declare their belief that prosecutors were placing cases on file. It is unclear whether the Act to Prevent Evasions succeeded in stopping prosecutors from filing liquor cases. On the one hand, Middlesex Superior Court record books show a marked disruption of on-file plea bargaining in liquor cases. In the two terms of court I studied in 1864—the last year before the law change—I observed eleven on-file plea bargains in liquor cases. I saw only one in the single term of court I studied in 1870.[46] And in 1900, the last year I studied in depth, only 12 of 225 on-file plea bargains took place in liquor cases.[47] On the other hand, some evidence suggests that judges in neighboring Suffolk County readily consented to prosecutors' requests to place liquor cases on file.[48] We need not resolve this uncertainty, for even while the nominal power to place cases on file appeared to be shifting toward the judge, the real power lay elsewhere.

The language of placing cases "on file" appears so prominently in the court's docket books that I was blinded at first to the right question, though it should have been clear all along. For this study of plea bargaining's rise is not much concerned with those cases that ended up on file because a defendant or witness left town. Rather, we want to know about those cases in which the defendant pled guilty and then, just when the judge normally would have passed sentence, someone instead put the case on file. In these cases, the important question is not who placed the case on file—that is merely the mechanism that held the case in abeyance while sentence was stayed—but rather who stayed the sentence. And the surprising answer to this question is that the prosecutor did.

The Power to Stay Sentence.   To track the prosecutor's power to stay sentence, we have to go back to 1830 and the case of Jerusha Chase. The trial judge, Peter Oxenbridge Thacher, wrote that after Chase pled guilty, "sentence would have been pronounced, . . . but upon the application of her friends, and with the consent of the attorney of the commonwealth, [the defendant] was permitted, upon her recognizance for her appearance in this court whenever she should be called for, to go at large."[49] Thacher has been quite vague about the distribution of the power to stay Chase's sentence: Her "friends" applied for the stay; the prosecutor "consent[ed]" to it; and it "was permitted"—presumably by the court.[50]

Compare, now, the reporter's headnote to the case, which appears on the page before the judge's summary and most likely was written in the early 1840s: The "defendant pleaded guilty to an indictment, and the prosecuting officer did not move for sentence, but laid the indictment on file, and the defendant was permitted to go at large."[51] The reporter helpfully has alerted us that the procedure Thacher described was actually the "on file" mechanism—something Thacher confirmed in noting that the "indictment has been suffered to sleep upon the files of the court."[52] And the reporter clearly named the prosecutor as the actor who filed the case. More importantly, the reporter suggested that "mov[ing] for sentence" and "la[ying] the indictment on file" were mutually exclusive—that is, placing a case on file is what a prosecutor did instead of moving for sentence.[53]

The question now is whether the prosecutor's failure to move for sentence actually barred the judge from passing sentence. If not, then the prosecutor's promise to withhold his motion would have enticed very few defendants to plead guilty. We have seen already some hints that the prosecutor in fact could block judicial sentencing. Recall that in 1847 District Attorney Albert Nelson announced "that at the *present* term, it is his intention when the parties complained of plead guilty [in liquor license cases], and enter into recognizance to observe the law, *not* to press for the fines which are incurred, but simply to exact the costs of Court."[54] As fines were mandatory under the liquor license law, Nelson's failure to "press for the fines" must have relieved the judge of the obligation to pass sentence,[55] though we cannot yet be sure that it barred the judge from sentencing. Similarly, when the legislative committee I mentioned met in 1865 to consider enforcement of the liquor laws, it asked whether the district attorneys had failed "to bring the convicts to sentence, or to enforce the sentence."[56] The prohibition law at the time called for mandatory confinement, so again the district attorney's failure to move for sentence must have released the judge from the law's directives. But did it *prevent* the judge from passing sentence?

One hint that it did is a remark made almost in passing by the Supreme Judicial Court in 1838: "After a verdict of guilty is rendered, the defendant is to be sentenced on motion of the attorney general; and we have no doubt of his authority to enter a *nolle prosequi* after verdict."[57] The court implied that the prosecutor had full discretion to choose between passing sentence and forgoing it and that the prosecutor had to move for sentence before the trial court could pass sentence. But we find some evidence that the trial court could act on its own in prosecutor Charles Russell Train's brief submitted to the Supreme Judicial Court in *Dowdican's Bail*. Arguing in 1874 in his new role as Massachusetts attorney general, Train wrote that an order to place a case on file left "it in the power of the court, at any time . . . , to take the case from the files, and have it proceed to judgment."[58] He made no mention of an intervening motion by the prosecutor. But because the prosecutor in this case *had* brought the relevant motion, Train's omission seems insignificant. In any event, the high court itself wrote that it was "within the power of the [trial] court at any time, *upon the motion of either party*, to bring the case forward and pass lawful order or judgment therein."[59] This language leaves rather little doubt that a trial court would have no power to remove a case from the files without a motion from the prosecutor (or from the defendant, though it is hard to imagine why a defendant would move for sentence).

It turns out that we have to travel another quarter-century forward to find more conclusive evidence on the point. In 1899 a southern Massachusetts district attorney, Robert Harris, submitted his report to the Plymouth County Commissioners. In remarking on the awesome responsibility of sentencing, Harris wrote, "The District Attorney has a large judicial discretion. He can decline to ask for sentence, or he can ask for it, and until he asks that sentence be imposed, the court can do nothing."[60]

A shrewd reader might appraise Harris's claim of power warily, as it surely served his interests. But in two rulings during the next few decades, the Supreme Judicial Court affirmed that the prosecutor had all the power Harris claimed. In the later of the two, *Commonwealth v. Kossowan* of 1929,[61] the court mildly chastised a trial judge for not passing sentence despite an 1895 law declaring that "[o]n conviction of any offense not punishable by death, sentence shall be imposed."[62] "The reasons why sentence was not promptly imposed do not appear," the court wrote.[63] "Manifestly the case was not filed or prosecution suspended. The case of *Commonwealth v. Carver* is not pertinent."[64] If we turn now to *Carver*, we may expect to find an exception to the statutory command that the trial judge pass sentence upon conviction. In that 1916 case, a jury had convicted the defendant on two indictments, one alleging forgery and one larceny. The trial judge did not pass sentence on the forgery indictment. "The reason for this," the high court wrote, "presumably is that . . . this case was placed on file."[65] Declining to review the defendant's claims of error in the forgery case, the court concluded that "the exceptions taken in that case are not properly before us. There has been merely a suspension of active proceedings in the case, and as yet no final disposition. Unless and until the prosecuting attorney shall move for sentence there is no occasion to pass upon the conduct of the forgery trial."[66]

It is impossible, I think, to escape the combined force of Harris's claim and the court's statements in *Kossowan* and *Carver*. Even after an 1895 law required judges to pass sentence upon conviction, Harris still could claim that "until [the district attorney] asks that sentence be imposed, the court can do nothing,"[67] and the high court could declare that "[u]nless and until the prosecuting attorney shall move for sentence there is no occasion" for a case to be finally disposed.[68] Moreover, a 1926 commentator on Massachusetts law complained that "[a]nother loophole that should be closed up is one which permits the District Attorney to delay presenting a person to the court for sentence who has been convicted."[69] It is true that this evidence emerges late in our story. Absent contrary evidence, however, the most reasonable conclusion is that the prosecutor's power to bar sentence by failing to move for sentence was more secure *before* the 1895 law than after. This power would explain Nelson's confident 1847 promise of a fine-free disposition for liquor defendants who pled guilty, as well as the legislative committee's 1865 complaint that district attorneys had failed "to enforce the sentence" demanded by the liquor law.[70] Note how unimportant the question I posed at the outset of this search now seems: A defendant who wanted to negotiate a plea bargain with the prosecutor would not have cared whether the prosecutor or the judge had the power to place her case on file. She would have cared only that the prosecutor had the power to assure that the defendant would not be sentenced.

Drawing this confusion of sources together, we may take stock of the prosecutor's power to bar sentence once the defendant had been found guilty—and therefore of his power to ensure that the case would be placed on file. In liquor cases after 1865, the Act to Prevent Evasions disturbed this power in ways that are difficult to disentangle. In earlier liquor cases and in cases involving any other charge, the prosecutor's power was largely a function of his complete discretion to move or not to move for sentence. Because the court could not pass sentence until the prosecutor so moved, the prosecutor had a unilateral power to prevent the imposition of sentence, leaving no other option than to file the case. So our search for the first half of the bundle of powers needed for prosecutorial plea bargaining is complete. In prosecutorial charge bargaining, the prosecutor could guarantee liquor defendants a particular fine and murder defendants a sentence other than death. In on-file plea bargaining, the prosecutor could promise the defendant no sentence at all.

Reassessing Chase. We may now return to Jerusha Chase. As I said at the outset, the court clerk recorded Chase's guilty plea and noted as well that she recognized with sureties in the sum of two hundred dollars. If we add to this the news supplied by the headnote to Judge Thacher's opinion— that the prosecutor refrained from moving for sentence and the case therefore was placed on file—we can reconstruct the course of events that probably lay behind these accounts.[71] First, Jerusha Chase pled guilty in exchange for the prosecutor's promise that he would not move for sentence. Second, because the judge could not pass sentence without the prosecutor's motion, the case was placed on file. And third, Chase was permitted to go after she and her sureties pledged two hundred dollars to guarantee that she would "come when sent for and in the meantime . . . keep the peace."[72]

It is true that the records do not say in so many words that Chase struck a deal with the prosecutor. To get from the information that the defendant pled guilty and the prosecutor failed to move for sentence to the conclusion that she pled guilty in exchange for his promise, I must make an inferential leap, but a short one. It is possible that the defendant pled guilty out of remorse or for some other reason and not because the prosecutor promised leniency, and it is possible that the prosecutor refrained from moving for sentence as a simple matter of good (and generous) prosecutorial judgment after the defendant had pled guilty, but the combined probability of these two events is rather small.

Moreover, there are at least two pieces of circumstantial evidence suggesting that cases that look like *Chase* on the face of the record actually involved an explicit deal between prosecutor and defendant. The more powerful is District Attorney Nelson's 1847 announcement that "at the *present* term," he would "*not* . . . press for the fines" for those defendants who pled guilty in liquor license cases.[73] It is hard to escape the implication of Nelson's announcement that, behind the clerk's reticent notes of cases placed on file after the defendant's plea, there lay an explicit agreement between prosecutor and defendant. The second piece of circumstantial evidence is the surge in use of the on-file technique that took place in Middlesex under District Attorney Train's watch in 1849.[74] It is hard to imagine that so prolific a plea-bargaining pioneer as Train, who not only raised charge bargaining in liquor cases to a new order of magnitude but also negotiated Middlesex County's first charge bargain in a murder case, should have overlooked the potential for plea bargaining in the on-file mechanism.

The Prosecutor's Power to Protect Himself from Judicial Leniency

We must search now for the second sort of power essential to successful prosecutorial plea bargaining—the prosecutor's power to protect himself from the judge's generous whims. Again, the forms of charge bargaining explored in Chapter 1 make the importance of this power clear. The prosecutor's worry in charge bargaining was that after he had nol prossed several counts of an indictment, the judge would hand the defendant too lenient a sentence on the remaining counts. The liquor law's rigid penalty scheme guarded against this result by requiring the judge to impose a particular fine. The prosecutor's inability to guard against an inappropriately light sentence on a manslaughter conviction perhaps limited charge bargaining in murder cases and and could explain why pleas to second-degree murder, which carried mandatory life in prison, proved in the end the more popular option.

In on-file plea bargaining, the prosecutor faced no immediate risk of unfair dealing at the judge's hands because the judge had no immediate role. By failing to move for sentence, the prosecutor left the judge nothing to do except (perhaps) the ministerial task of placing the case on file. The judge's chance to undermine the prosecutor's position in on-file plea bargains came later. And so we come to the second half of the bargain the prosecutor reached with Jerusha Chase—her agreement "to keep the peace."[75]

Triggering Imposition of Sentence. Chase returned to court in 1831 under indictment for a new larceny. Although a jury acquitted her of the second crime, prosecutor Austin apparently believed strongly in her guilt. He concluded that she had violated her pledge to keep the peace and therefore moved that she be sentenced on the original indictment.[76] Now we reach the point at which the judge could have frustrated the prosecutor's well-laid plans either by refusing to pass sentence or by passing a light one. After all, the prosecutor until now had shown the defendant great leniency in allowing her to walk free without facing sentence. On-file plea bargains would have held small allure for a responsible prosecutor if he had been vulnerable to judicial refusal to act when, following the defendant's later breach of the peace, he decided to call in the case for sentence.

The question, then, is whether the prosecutor's *unilateral* power to stay sentence was also an *exclusive* power: If the district attorney moved for sentence, could the court nevertheless place the case on file? And if the district attorney moved to take a case from the files and have sentence pronounced, could the court refuse? Judge Thacher's opinion in *Chase* suggested that the answer to both questions was no.

We already have seen some hint of this result in Thacher's statement that he had permitted the defendant to go at large "with the consent of the attorney of the commonwealth."[77] When Thacher turned to the question squarely before him—whether prosecutor Austin had the power to return to court and demand that Chase be sentenced on her original conviction—he first equivocated, but then by stages grew clear and direct. His first approach to the problem left considerable ambiguity about whether the court could refuse a prosecutor's request for sentencing: "I cannot doubt the court may, on motion, have the party brought in and sentenced at any subsequent period."[78] But his next sentence appears to erase the court's discretion in the matter: "For what was the duty of the court to do at any one time, cannot cease to be its duty by delay."[79] And a page later, Thacher implied in striking language that the prosecutor's discretion was complete: "[Chase's sentence] has been delayed from tenderness and humanity, and not because it had ceased to be the right of the government to claim the judgment."[80]

The Supreme Judicial Court approved Thacher's reasoning, but in an unreported opinion.[81] Apparently, the court did not again take up the matter of filed cases until *Dowdican's Bail* in 1874. That case, like *Chase*, examined the prosecutor's power to remove a case from the files after the defendant was charged with a later offense. As in *Chase*, the court began by remarking on the power to file the case in the first instance. "It has long been a common practice in this Commonwealth," the court wrote, "after verdict of guilty in a criminal case," for the trial court to "order" the case on file "with the consent of the defendant and of the attorney for the Commonwealth."[82] We have now seen this reference to the prosecutor's "consent" twice in the same context. It is fair to conclude that his consent was a precondition to placing a case on file, at least after a guilty verdict or guilty plea gave the prosecutor the right to move for sentence.

The *Dowdican's Bail* court did not, however, adopt Judge Thacher's pointed declaration that the prosecutor had the power to have a case taken from the files and to have sentence pronounced. As we have seen already, the court noted only that it was "within the power of the court at any time, upon the motion of either party, to bring the case forward and pass . . . judgment therein."[83] From this we may conclude that the court had no power to remove a case from the files without a motion from the prosecutor. We may also conclude that the prosecutor could bring such a motion no matter how long the case had sat on file.[84] But we cannot be sure that if the prosecutor brought a motion, the court had to grant it.

I have found just one other reference that might help trace the boundary of the prosecutor's power to prevent a judge from placing (or from leaving) a case on file. In 1917 F. W. Grinnell wrote that "doubt . . . has been expressed in Massachusetts" about whether a judge could place a case on file if the district attorney moved for sentence.[85] He then argued that "the doubt has been resolved" and that "it is the established practice of the state . . . that the District Attorney is not entitled to insist upon sentence."[86]

Grinnell apparently based this conclusion on *Commonwealth v. Macey*, an unreported decision of a Massachusetts Superior Court trial judge. The judge had ruled in favor of his own power to continue a rape case without sentence even after the jury had convicted the defendant and the district attorney had moved for sentence.[87] But *Macey* was decided sometime after 1898,[88] and a statute of that year may have given judges grounds to construe their powers in this area more generously.[89] Even if *Macey* is representative of the state of affairs after 1898—and we cannot be sure that it is—we still should give it fairly small weight in assessing who held the power to stay sentence during the bulk of the nineteenth century.

Once again drawing our confusion of sources together, we may measure the reach of the prosecutor's power to demand that a case be taken from the files and sentence imposed. There seems to be no dispute that timing was not an issue—that is, the prosecutor could move for sentence at any time in the future. If he did, the court was then required to impose sentence (so held *Chase*, 1831); or *might* have been required to impose sentence (*Dowdican's Bail*, 1874); or was not required to impose sentence (*Macey*, after 1898). And if the prosecutor in the first instance moved for sentence upon conviction, the court had no power to place the case on file instead (*Chase*, 1831, and *Dowdican's Bail*, 1874)—or indeed had this power (*Macey*, after 1898).

These conclusions suggest that the answer to our underlying inquiry— whether the on-file mechanism gave prosecutors the power to protect themselves against undue judicial leniency—changed as the century wore on. Early in the century, Judge Thacher's holdings that imposing sentence "cannot cease to be [the court's] duty by delay" and that sentence was "delayed from tenderness and humanity, and not because it had ceased to be the right of the government to claim the judgment" protected prosecutors from judicial refusal to act.[90] Later in the century, prosecutors had reason to feel more vulnerable to the risk of unjustified judicial generosity.

Assessing the Prosecutor's Sentencing Power. But even in the early years, the prosecutor's right to demand judgment generally did not include the right to demand a particular judgment. Except in liquor cases and those few others in which the law fixed a mandatory penalty, the judge, called on to pass sentence, could impose a lenient one. This risk of judicial leniency perhaps discouraged prosecutors from using on-file plea bargaining in more serious cases. Of course, even if prosecutors had been assured of judicial severity when they brought the defendant in for sentencing, they still would have been slow to engage in on-file plea bargaining in serious cases. That is because in the first instance, on-file plea bargaining let the defendant walk free. Prosecutors who took to heart their duty to protect the public—or, after 1856, those concerned about their reelection—would not have engaged in on-file plea bargaining with the more serious criminals before the court.

Yet on-file plea bargaining was not as feeble a tool against criminals as the modern practice usually known as "pretrial probation." A defendant who accepts pretrial probation today places herself under the court's supervision before trial *without pleading guilty or no contest*. Typically, the court, the defendant, and the prosecutor agree that if the defendant abides by the law and adheres to any other condition imposed by the court for a specified period, the court will dismiss the charges—and in the meantime the case is simply held in abeyance.

In on-file plea bargaining, as I use the term, the defendant always entered a plea of guilty or no contest *before* the case was placed on file. At the Senate's 1865 hearings on enforcement of the liquor law, the assistant clerk of courts for Worcester County advised the committee that "[i]t is always made a condition to promise to go out of the [liquor-selling] business, before placing a case on file, and there is always a conviction by plea of guilty, or by a verdict."[91] The distinction between this procedure and modern pretrial probation is crucial: If a defendant placed on pretrial probation commits a later offense, the prosecutor still must convict her of the original charge before the court can impose punishment on that charge. In on-file plea bargaining, as we saw in *Chase*, if the defendant committed a later offense or broke her deal with the prosecutor in some other way, the prosecutor could move for sentence without further ceremony. As the Suffolk County district attorney told the same Senate committee, "if the guilty person offended again, he could be and was invariably sentenced to imprisonment."[92] On-file plea bargaining therefore gave the prosecutor a far stronger hand in controlling the defendant's future behavior.

It is true that as the century wore on, prosecutors' power to claim judgment on the defendant's conviction grew less certain. Judges apparently felt freer to reject prosecutors' demands that a case be taken from the files and sentence imposed. This trend might have discouraged on-file plea bargaining had it not been for another judicial change in attitude. During the last quarter of the century, judges grew more friendly toward plea bargaining and less likely to act in ways that would discourage it. In Chapter 5, I consider the reasons for the judges' change of heart. The next section explores one result.

The Shared Roles of Prosecutor and Judge

From the beginning, defendants who went to trial and lost almost never won the reward of a filed case. In 1849, the first year I studied closely after the appearance of the on-file mechanism in Middlesex County, thirty-seven defendants who had pled guilty or no contest walked out of court with their cases filed. Only two defendants who lost at trial had such luck. In succeeding decades, the story was much the same. In the years I studied between 1853 and 1890,[93] 166 cases were placed on file after pleas of guilty or no contest—but only thirteen after convictions at trial. During most of those years, prosecutors apparently held the balance of power in awarding the on-file mechanism. They seem to have used this power to encourage pleas by withholding case-filing from defendants who troubled them with trials. By the end of the century, as we have seen, judges may have assumed more power to file cases. If so, then it appears they were just as ready as prosecutors to use the on-file mechanism to encourage defendants to plead guilty. In 1900, when 225 cases were placed on file after pleas of guilty or no contest (accounting for forty-one percent of all adjudicated cases), only six cases were placed on file after defendants wagered trial and lost.

Here we seem to have another piece of circumstantial evidence that those cases in which the defendant pled guilty and the case was placed on file involved a clear deal in which the defendant pled guilty in exchange for having her case placed on file. Yet the numbers reported in the last paragraph confront us with two ambiguities. They cannot tell us whether the defendant was negotiating with the prosecutor or with the judge. And they cannot tell us whether any deals that took place were spoken or unspoken. After all, when a course of practice was this clear, it simply might have been understood by all parties. Defendants might have pled guilty because they knew that doing so was their only real hope of having their cases placed on file.

One piece of evidence seems to resolve both ambiguities. In 1886 John Maloney pled guilty to a liquor-related charge in the district court—the lower trial court—where no prosecutor represented the state.[94] The trial court then continued the case indefinitely for sentence on payment of costs by the defendant.[95] When the court later imposed sentence against the defendant—perhaps because he had violated the terms of his release—he appealed. In the course of its ruling, the Supreme Judicial Court compared the case to *Dowdican's Bail*, which had originated in the superior court:

> The postponement [of Maloney's case, granted after the defendant's guilty plea,] was not, and was not intended to be, a continuance, but an end of the prosecution, unless the magistrate should see cause at some future time to notify the defendant that sentence was to be pronounced. It was obviously an arrangement between the trial justice and the defendant, *like that sometimes made in the higher courts between the prosecuting officer and a defendant, with the approval of the court, by which, on payment of costs by the defendant, an indictment or complaint is "placed on file."*[96]

By "an arrangement," the court appears to have meant a plea bargain, though a genteel one. And in this passage, the Supreme Judicial Court made it clear that in the "higher courts"—that is, the superior courts, which then occupied the middle tier of the state's judiciary—"the prosecuting officer and a defendant" struck these bargains.

PROBATION'S BASE-BORN STATUS

At least from the days of *Jerusha Chase*, prosecutors had embraced the on-file mechanism and converted it to a form of prosecutorial plea bargaining. Now it is time to ask whether "on-file plea bargaining" could as aptly be called "probation." In this inquiry, the significance of the dual powers I examined in the last section becomes clear. Prosecutors' unilateral (and sometimes exclusive) power to stay sentence constituted their power to plea bargain—it is what enabled them to promise sentencing concessions without fear of interference from the judge. Prosecutors' exclusive (and sometimes unilateral) power to take cases from the files and demand imposition of sentence is what gave this particular practice the name probation.

A modern observer would have no difficulty seeing that Jerusha Chase, as she left court on February 8, 1830, was on something like probation. Having pled guilty to her crime, she nonetheless walked free, and "no sentence will ever be pronounced against [her]," Judge Thacher wrote, "if

[she] shall behave [herself] well afterwards, and avoid any further violation of the law."[97] Should she, on the other hand, break the law again, she may be "brought in and sentenced at any subsequent period."[98] Some thirty-five years later, in testimony before the Senate committee investigating enforcement of the liquor law, the Suffolk County district attorney explained the consequences of putting a case on file in similar terms: "[I]f the guilty person offended again, he could be and was invariably sentenced to imprisonment."[99] Another decade after that, Charles Russell Train defended the practice of putting cases on file by pointing to its probationary benefits. In his brief to the Supreme Judicial Court in *Dowdican's Bail*, he noted that "[t]he defendant, in all cases where sentence was thus delayed . . . was put on his good behavior, and under bonds, as it were, to live honestly."[100] And when defendants "have misbehaved themselves, they have been sentenced on the original complaint or indictment."[101]

The Surety's Role and John Augustus

Our modern observer might find it somewhat puzzling that the defendant's "bonds" were secured not by a court probation officer, who today acts as "surety" without its financial connotations, but rather by private parties. Jerusha Chase, for example, "recognized in the sum of two hundred dollars with Benjamin Salmon, trader, and Daniel Chase, Cordwainer of Marblehead,"[102] either of whom would have been liable to pay the bond should she have failed to come to court when called for or to keep the peace. And any spark of recognition might fade away when our observer saw the prosecutor's heavy hand in what is now very much the court's business. At least in these early years, few or none were admitted to probation without the prosecutor's favor of withholding a motion for sentence. And all who were on probation, such as Chase and Dowdican, knew that their free time tolled when the prosecutor demanded his due. Yet this same practice emerged by the end of the century under the name probation and claimed fame as the state's singular contribution to American criminal procedure.

To see that the on-file mechanism did not merely resemble probation or foretell it, but rather *was* probation by another name, we have to focus on the role of the sureties who guaranteed the defendant's good behavior while she was on probation and her future appearance should the court call for her. Jerusha Chase's sureties staked two hundred dollars on their faith in her future conduct.[103] But what of defendants who lacked friends of such means? Here we encounter the role of John Augustus, Boston bootmaker and penal reformer, named by himself and others the father of probation.[104] Augustus was in the Boston Police Court one morning in 1841 when he hit upon the philanthropic formula that would occupy his life. He would play the role of surety to indigent defendants whose cases were placed on file during a "season of probation."[105]

Augustus therefore added nothing new to the court system's procedural repertoire, which was in place at least since the time of *Chase*. He merely filled an existing procedural role on behalf of the poor. His enduring contribution was to play that role with insight and to good effect. To decide whether particular defendants were "promising subjects for probation,"[106] Augustus inquired into their reputations and the influences of their peers. While they were on probation, he made sure they were schooled or employed, and he gave "an impartial report to the court, whenever they should desire it."[107] That the district attorney's opposition to his work "gradually and rapidly" gave way is little surprise, for Augustus's vision of the reformatory purpose of probation did not include contests about guilt.[108] "[N]ine out of ten of [those for whom I stood surety] who were guilty have by my advice, pleaded guilty," he wrote, "and thus saved the Commonwealth the expense of a trial in each case."[109]

Just as Augustus contributed no procedural innovation to the existing practice of probation, so the 1878 Massachusetts law that introduced the word "probation" into American criminal codes did little more than perpetuate his role.[110] The act authorized Boston's mayor to appoint a probation officer. It charged this officer with the duty to investigate defendants; to recommend "the placing on probation of such persons as may reasonably be expected to be reformed without punishment"; and to assist those placed on probation so as "to prevent their again offending."[111] Consuming barely more than a page of text, the act never bothered to define probation. With one narrow exception that I will consider shortly, it neither conferred any power nor imposed any procedure on any courtroom actor. As F. W. Grinnell wrote in 1917, the act merely provided new officers to assist in a "well-established and well-recognized and approved existing usage."[112]

On-File Plea Bargaining and Probation: Shared Identities

In fact, almost a decade after the act's passage, the Supreme Judicial Court explicitly merged the concept of "probation" with the old and familiar on-file mechanism. In 1887 in *Commonwealth v. Maloney*, which I quoted some pages back, the court noted that middle-tier trial courts were in the practice "of putting a prisoner convicted before them on probation by indefinitely holding the conviction over him, . . . by putting an indictment on file." The court then added, "When such power is given by statute, it is carefully guarded. See Pub. Sts. c. 212, §§ 74–81; St. 1885, c. 359."[113] Again, the court's statutory citations are significant. The first refers to the body of law governing probation officers.[114] The second refers to the 1885 reenactment of the Act to Prevent Evasions, which barred placing liquor cases on file without the court's approval.[115] The court's language, linked with these two citations, makes it manifestly clear that the court regarded the on-file mechanism to be the equivalent of probation.

Even as late as 1903, the Supreme Judicial Court expressly linked "probation" with placing a case on file. "The defendant pleaded guilty in the Superior Court," the court wrote, "and having entered into the usual recognizance with the probation officer, as surety, he was placed on probation and the complaint against him was filed."[116] It seems that the mechanics of probation had not evolved much since *Chase*, except that now a public probation officer played the role of surety once taken by "Benjamin Salmon, trader, and Daniel Chase, Cordwainer of Marblehead."[117] And just as Jerusha Chase lost her freedom when the prosecutor moved for sentence on the original indictment, so did the defendant in the case just quoted:

> Later in the sitting the district attorney moved for sentence, and at the hearing thereon the judge found that the defendant had not kept the conditions of an oral agreement made between him and the Commonwealth, and under which he had been placed on probation, and that sentence ought to be imposed.[118]

The near-complete identity of the "old" on-file mechanism and the "new" system of probation is apparent also in the record-keeping practices of Middlesex court clerks. As early as 1859, the clerk's docket book entries often collapsed the concepts with the simple notation, "on file on probation."[119] And as late as 1900, the clerk *exclusively* employed the "on file" formula. Although the record and docket books for that year list 212 cases as placed "on file" after a guilty finding and therefore functionally involving probation, the word "probation" appears not once. In 1903, cases that appear in the record book as being placed "on file" appear in the docket book as involving "probation."[120] By 1910, the clerk had split the usual list of cases placed "on file" into two lists—one headed "on file," which presumably included those cases placed on file because a defendant or witness was missing, and the other headed "on probation."[121] Underneath the typewritten words, "on probation," which identified the second list, someone added in a neat script, "On file."[122]

Parsing Prosecutorial and Judicial Power

But in one respect, the clerk's continued use of the term "on file" perhaps overstated the extent to which the procedures of probation remained frozen in time. A fair amount of evidence suggests that by the end of the century, the judge had more power than before to place a case on probation in the face of the district attorney's opposition. I have presented some of this evidence already: Over time, the clerk became more likely to write that "the Court" (rather than the prosecutor) had placed cases on file, and court rulings became less certain about whether the prosecutor's motion for sentence could compel the court to pass sentence.[123] In addition, the probation statutes of the last quarter of the century tipped the balance of probationary power toward the court. Hence the 1878 act referred to "offenders placed on probation by the court";[124] an 1880 act that extended this earlier law statewide said that "the court may permit the accused to be placed upon probation, upon such terms as it may deem best";[125] an act of 1891 gave lower-court justices the power to appoint probation officers, a power formerly vested in city officials, and said the court "may place [a convict] in the care of said probation officer for such time and upon such conditions as may seem proper";[126] and an act of 1898 extended similar powers to superior-court judges.[127]

One can make too much of this apparent power shift. After all, the critical power sustaining on-file plea bargaining was the prosecutor's capacity to protect defendants from being sentenced by the court, which enabled him to extend a meaningful promise of leniency toward those defendants who pled guilty.[128] Well into the twentieth century, it remained clear that without the prosecutor's motion, the court could not pass sentence.[129] It is true that the 1878 act creating a Boston probation officer cast this general proposition briefly in doubt. The act appeared to give the probation officer the power to move for sentence before the court:

> Any person placed upon probation upon the recommendation of such officer may be re-arrested by him upon approval of the chief of police . . . and again brought before the court; and the court may thereupon proceed to sentence. . . . [130]

But this grant of power was both limited and temporary. It was limited in that it applied only in Boston. In 1880, when the legislature established probation officers for the rest of the state, it omitted any such provision.[131] And in 1891, the legislature apparently nullified even the Boston probation officer's power to trigger sentencing. It repealed the earlier probation laws, enacted a single probation statute to govern statewide, and again omitted any grant of power of the sort suggested in the 1878 act.[132]

Moreover, despite the Supreme Judicial Court's 1908 observation that "the principles which lie at the foundation of the [probation] legislation . . . seem to leave the whole matter in the control of the court,"[133] there is some fairly weighty evidence that in practice the prosecutor retained substantial control. I quoted earlier from an 1899 report of Robert Harris, district attorney for the state's southern district.[134] Harris wrote the report specifically to explain "his doings" under the 1898 probation act, which seemed to place control over probation in the court's hands. "[T]he superior court may appoint probation officers," the Act declared, and the "court may place upon probation, under any of said probation officers, any person charged with a criminal offence."[135]

In the face of the act's broad grant of power to the court, Harris brashly claimed control over the county's probation system. "In 1898," he wrote, "I applied for the appointment of a probation officer, and my application was granted by his Honor, Mr. Justice Sherman."[136]

Remarkably, Harris continued in the first person: "I was fortunate in having at hand the man I selected [as probation officer]," but "I made some mistakes, and placed some on probation who should not have been so treated."[137] That a superior-court judge so readily delivered up to the prosecutor the powers granted under the 1898 act is a strong hint that the power of probation up till then had lain in prosecutorial hands. The judge, it seems, had little inclination to assume the chores that new power brought.

But parsing power in this way perhaps has little point in the context of turn-of-the-century probation. We have seen already that 225 of the 231 persons placed on probation in Middlesex in 1900 had pled guilty,[138] so even if the judge had the power to impose probation over the prosecutor's objection, he was using probation as an instrument of plea bargaining no less than was the prosecutor. As I show in Chapter 5, by 1900 judges had become enthusiastic plea bargainers even outside the probation context. In California, where a 1903 probation statute gave judges both legal and actual power to decide which defendants received probation,[139] probation served as a plea-bargaining tool as clearly as it did in Middlesex. Lawrence Friedman and Robert Percival report in their study of Alameda County that thirty-one of thirty-two defendants who were placed on probation in their sample had pled guilty.[140] So predictable was the court's practice that one defendant told a judge, "I pleaded guilty because you can't try to get probation otherwise."[141] Probation, the authors conclude, "gave the guilty plea a powerful thrust."[142]

Assessing Probation's Origins

It may be that by the end of the nineteenth century, the practice of probation in Massachusetts and California and probably many places in between had become so predictable that the power of probation as an instrument of plea bargaining was largely implicit—that is, no defendant needed to be told that a guilty plea was the purchase price of the hope of probation. Friedman and Percival surely suspect as much.[143] But as I hope this account of probation's upbringing in the state of its birth makes clear, probation's origins were coarser than that. From its first appearance in the opening third of the nineteenth century, probation grew in the guise of on-file plea bargaining under the tutelage of prosecutors who often made quite plain the terms by which they would deal.

I do not suggest that probation never would have evolved had it not been an instrument of prosecutorial plea bargaining. Probation served the system well in many ways, not least by relieving prison overcrowding and providing an appropriately mild punishment for first offenders, especially those who could not pay fines. My arguments are both far narrower and somewhat broader. The narrower argument impelled our recent descent into the morass of Massachusetts practice: Prosecutors were ready to exploit the power to plea bargain wherever they could find it. Massachusetts practice tossed them an unlikely scrap of power in barring judges from passing sentence until the prosecutor ceremonially moved for sentence. With this scrap, together with invention and industry, prosecutors built the covert regime of on-file plea bargaining.

The broader argument looks at probation's rise as the first of several proofs of the larger power of plea bargaining as an institution. By the last quarter of the nineteenth century, plea bargaining had become a valued tool not only of prosecutors, but of judges as well. Serving the interests of all those with real power, plea bargaining became a dominant institution by winning their protection. Prosecutors and judges nurtured plea bargaining by promoting other procedural forms, such as probation, that helped plea bargaining thrive.

I return to the power of plea bargaining in Chapter 8. In the next two chapters, I shift the focus from prosecutors and probation to defendants and judges to examine how the powers and interests of those two actors helped shape the course of plea bargaining.

4

The Defendant's Power to Plead

As clear as their interest in plea bargaining may have been, prosecutors' power to bargain was well hidden. Tracking it has absorbed a good many pages. In contrast, criminal defendants had both a clear incentive and a clear capacity to plea bargain. Their incentive lay in the difference between the severe sentence that loomed should the jury convict at trial and the more lenient sentence promised by the prosecutor or judge in exchange for a plea. At first glance, the intensity of a defendant's desire to plead appears to have been a simple function of the power and inclination of the prosecutor or judge to widen this difference. And defendants' power to plead was even clearer and more constant: As the holders of the right to a jury trial, they held the power to waive it. Even when a defendant pled guilty to a capital charge and thereby assured his own execution, the "court ha[d] no power absolutely to refuse" his plea.[1]

We therefore might be tempted to dismiss defendants as mathematical constants to be factored out of our plea-bargaining equation, freeing us to focus instead on the variables of prosecutor and judge. But the evidence stubbornly insists that defendants' desire to plea bargain was not constant after all. Defendants' fundamental preference for the mildest punishment possible remained in place, of course. But their power to win at trial—or at least their perception of that power—rose in one period and fell in the next. And as their hopes of walking free after trial first brightened and then faded, their willingness to plead guilty diminished and grew.

Two changes in trial practice loomed largest in altering defendants' views of their power to win at trial. One took place during the first half of the nineteenth century, when more and more defendants came to court with counsel. Lawyers probably raised these defendants' chances of victory at trial and dulled their enthusiasm to plead. During the second half of the century, defendants suddenly won the right to testify in their own defense. This development, almost surely intended to help defendants, in reality may have narrowed their odds of victory and helped convince them that a good bargain was their best hope. Unfortunately, because defendants left behind sparse records of their thoughts and fears, reconstructing their motives may demand that we take long steps between widely spaced flagstones of evidence.

THE POWER OF REPRESENTATION

The court records of Middlesex County disclose this surprising news: At the very outset of the nineteenth century, about two-thirds of the cases that came before the courts of the middle tier ended in guilty pleas. Figure 4.1 shows the proportion of adjudicated nonliquor cases that ended in a plea of guilty or no contest in the Court of General Sessions of the Peace, the Court of Common Pleas, and the Superior Court.[2] These three courts succeeded one another in occupying the middle tier. Each during its era had jurisdiction to try many or most noncapital offenses. From an initial high of seventy-one percent in 1789–1790, the rate of pleas fell sharply if not steadily until it reached a low of twenty-six percent in 1834. Guilty pleas remained comparatively rare until the late 1870s, when they began their long upswing toward the full-fledged plea-bargaining regime that closed the century.

The strikingly high rate of guilty pleas at the outset of the nineteenth century defies most scholarship, which suggests not only that guilty pleas were rare before the middle of the nineteenth century, but that courts refused or were reluctant to accept them.[3] But it appears that this reluctance was limited largely to capital cases. As a Massachusetts defense

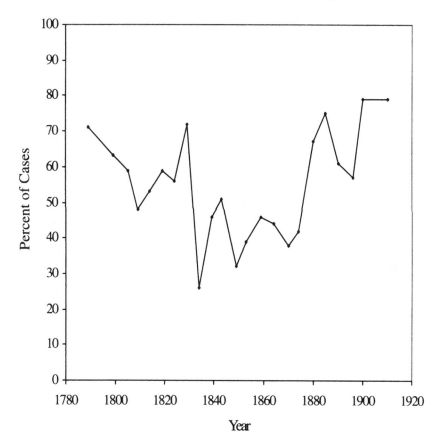

Figure 4.1. Proportion of cases ending in a plea of guilty or no contest (adjudicated nonliquor, nonfiled cases only): Middlesex County Superior Court and its predecessor courts.

lawyer argued in 1866 while seeking to undo a guilty plea in a capital case, such a plea "is suicide, commited under the color of law."[4] The Supreme Judicial Court rejected this argument and ratified the defendant's death sentence, but did acknowledge that courts receive "a confession of guilt in a capital cause" with "great reluctance."[5] In 1877 a former Massachusetts judge and governor wrote that although courts readily accepted guilty pleas in most cases, "in Massachusetts . . . the court will not receive a plea of guilty to an indictment for murder until after a full advisement of the prisoner of the consequences of such a plea."[6] In fact, guilty pleas to capital charges—with no reduction to a noncapital offense—were rare. In Massachusetts I found only five such pleas throughout the century.[7]

Such concerns about judicial suicide had no weight in noncapital cases. As the Ohio Supreme Court wrote in 1892, there is no reason to expect that an old notion that courts should resist a defendant's desire to plead guilty, which "had its origin at a period in the history of the law of England when offenses that would now be regarded as comparatively trivial, were, upon conviction, visited with death," should have much impact in a noncapital American court of a later age.[8] Perhaps we should not be surprised, therefore, by the very high rates of guilty pleas in the noncapital middle-tier courts of Middlesex County.

Yet the news is surprising for another reason: Even as the rate of guilty pleas was falling in the first third of the century, the caseload of the middle-tier courts was rising, sometimes sharply. At the very moment the rate of guilty pleas fell to its 1834 low, the court's caseload leapt from forty-one cases in 1829 to ninety-five cases in 1834.[9] Lower plea rates and larger caseloads translated into what must have been a shocking increase in the number of trials—from six trials of all sorts in 1829 to forty-six in 1834. And as Figure 4.2 shows, the number of trials continued unevenly upward.

I argued in Chapter 2 that caseload pressure helped motivate prosecutors to develop their charge-bargaining techniques in liquor cases. As Chapter 5 shows, caseload pressure helped win judges over to plea bargaining's cause in the latter part of the century. Still, it is not entirely paradoxical that rising caseload pressure did not translate into increased plea bargaining in the first third of the century. I have excluded liquor cases from Figure 4.1 to avoid the distorting impact of the prosecutor's unusual power to charge bargain in liquor cases. In other cases, as I argued in Chapter 1,[10] prosecutors simply lacked the power to escape a rising caseload by plea bargaining.[11] As for judges, during the first decades of the nineteenth century they not only lacked the peculiar incentives of prosecutors to plea bargain but also had principled and pride-based objections to the practice.[12]

The real paradox emerges from these last two facts: If prosecutors lacked the power to plea bargain and if judges lacked the interest, then

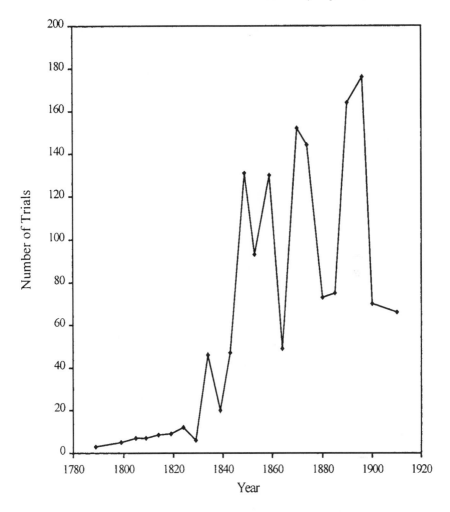

Figure 4.2. Number of trials: Middlesex County Superior Court and its predecessor courts.

why did so many defendants plead guilty in the first decades of the nine-teenth century? These pleas were not, after all, plea *bargains* that involved a concession made in exchange for the defendant's plea—my analysis of sentencing patterns in Chapter 2 showed as much. To explain these pleas, I suggest we shift our focus from prosecutor and judge and ask what might have persuaded defendants to plead guilty even when they could expect no concession in return.

I believe the answer may lie in the role of defense counsel. If very few defendants came to court with counsel in 1789 and an increasing proportion did so thereafter, that alone could explain the high rate of guilty pleas at the outset of the century and the drop in guilty pleas over the next three decades. Before fleshing out this hypothesis, I should expose its weakest part: None of my evidence discloses how many defendants brought counsel to court in the first part of the nineteenth century. The record books of the middle-tier courts in Middlesex County almost never noted counsel, and the docket books began to do so only in 1844. I have found no other study that reports the rate of counsel appearances in any Massachusetts court in the early nineteenth century or before.[13] We must make do, therefore, with the evidence at hand.

Evidence of Representation Rates

The docket books of 1844 and later supply the only direct evidence of the prevalence of counsel in Middlesex courts. At least at first glance, this information lends only mild support to my hypothesis that representation by counsel was rising over the first decades of the century. In 1844 fifty-one percent of defendants came to court with counsel, a number that advanced modestly to sixty percent by 1849 (see Table 4.1). Thereafter, the rate of representation varied within fairly narrow bounds throughout the balance of the century, never again hitting the 1849 high of sixty percent, but also never dropping past the 1880 low of forty-one percent.

Yet there are at least two reasons to believe the rate of representation was growing through the first third of the century. The first is that an ocean away, at London's Old Bailey court, the rate of representation seems to have risen sharply from less than ten percent in 1815 to just shy of fifty percent, or about the same rate as in Middlesex County, in 1855.[14] The second is the suddenness of the transformation that took place in Middlesex County between 1829 and 1834, when the caseload of the Court of Common Pleas more than doubled at the same time that the rate of pleas fell by almost two-thirds. The most likely explanation for the leap in caseload is an 1832 statute that transferred the bulk of the Supreme Judicial Court's criminal trial jurisdiction to the Court of Common

4.1.

Proportion of Defendants with Counsel: Middlesex
Court of Common Pleas and Superior Court

YEAR	PERCENTAGE OF DEFENDANTS
1844	51
1849	60
1853	54
1859	52
1864	54
1870	58
1880	41
1900	46

SOURCES: Middlesex Ct. C.P. R. Books; Middlesex Ct. C.P.
Docket Books; Middlesex Super. Ct. R. Books; Middlesex Super. Ct.
Docket Books.

Pleas.[15] We can expect that along with more serious cases, this transfer of jurisdiction brought with it the lawyers who used to handle those cases before the Supreme Judicial Court.

Unfortunately, that court's record and docket books, like those of the Court of Common Pleas, do not disclose the proportion of defendants who had counsel in these early years. But the gravity of both the tribunal and the crimes charged makes it seem likely that cases heard before the Supreme Judicial Court typically involved defense counsel. In capital cases, the court appointed free counsel. When charged with other crimes that called for long sentences, defendants may have felt it worthwhile to spend their own funds.[16]

The Likely Impact of More Lawyers

If it is true that cases transferred from the Supreme Judicial Court to the Court of Common Pleas brought with them a new contingent of defense counsel, then these lawyers probably carried along a culture in which trials were more the norm and guilty pleas more the exception. For although the rate of pleas in the Supreme Judicial Court exceeded one-half in 1799

4.2.

Proportion of Adjudicated Defendants Who Chose Trial over Plea:
Middlesex Court of Common Pleas and Superior Court

YEAR	% WITH COUNSEL	% WITHOUT COUNSEL
1844	64	39
1849	58	43
1853	77	48
1859	68	45
1864	36	29
1870	53	49
1880	26	21
1900	14	13

SOURCES: Middlesex Ct. C.P. R. Books; Middlesex Ct. C.P. Docket Books; Middlesex Super. Ct. R. Books; Middlesex Super. Ct. Docket Books.

and one-third in 1824, it generally was much lower than in the Court of Common Pleas. It stood at just ten percent in 1829, the last year I studied before the jurisdiction shift, when the rate of pleas in the Court of Common Pleas was a remarkable seventy-two percent.[17]

Of course, a higher rate of trials in the upper court could be due less to the presence of lawyers than to the seriousness of the crimes tried there and the unlikelihood that a defendant would plead guilty in the face of a long prison term. But statistics from the Court of Common Pleas in 1844 and later, when the court's docket books permit us to see the presence of lawyers, suggest that counsel did influence the defendant's choice between trial and plea. Especially in the middle of the century, as Table 4.2 shows, defendants with lawyers were a good deal more likely to choose trial than were defendants without lawyers.[18] If we add to this fact three others, we can arrive at a theory about why a rising rate of representation in the Court of Common Pleas in the first decades of the nineteenth century might have produced not only a falling rate of guilty pleas, but also strong pressure to develop a plea-bargaining regime.

The first additional fact is that defendants who chose trials were consistently more likely to win if they had lawyers—and in most years, they

4.3.

Influence of Counsel on Trial Victory Rate:
Middlesex Court of Common Pleas and Superior Court

	PERCENTAGE OF DEFENDANTS WHO WON ACQUITTALS OR HUNG JURIES	
YEAR	% WITH COUNSEL	% WITHOUT COUNSEL
1844	17	15
1849	48	13
1853	44	22
1859	49	25
1864	54	43
1870	38	20
1880	40	8
1900	59	38

SOURCES: Middlesex Ct. C.P. R. Books; Middlesex Ct. C.P. Docket Books; Middlesex Super. Ct. R. Books; Middlesex Super. Ct. Docket Books.

were far more likely to win (Table 4.3). The second is that defendants who chose instead to plead guilty were usually more likely to get clear plea bargains—either charge bargains or on-file plea bargains—if they had lawyers (Table 4.4). And finally, defendants with lawyers were therefore far less likely to plead guilty without an apparent concession, as opposed to either plea bargaining or going to trial, than were defendants without lawyers (Table 4.5). Friedman and Percival found this pattern repeated decades later and a continent away in California's Alameda County.[19]

A theory of the early years now emerges that helps to explain what came later. Defendants without lawyers, who (I assume) accounted for the great majority of defendants at the beginning of this period, correctly saw that their chances of winning at trial were quite poor—generally no better than twenty-five percent and in some years worse.[20] Lacking the shrewdness to press for a sentencing concession in exchange for their guilty pleas, these unrepresented defendants simply pled to the charges they faced,[21] hoping, perhaps without reason, that the judge might show

4.4.

Proportion of Defendants Offering Pleas Who Won Clear Plea Bargains:
Middlesex Court of Common Pleas and Superior Court

YEAR	% WITH COUNSEL	% WITHOUT COUNSEL
1844	18	23
1849	66	31
1853	33	42
1859	64	31
1864	57	51
1870	36	19
1880	36	33
1900	55	53

SOURCES: Middlesex Ct. C.P. R. Books; Middlesex Ct. C.P. Docket Books; Middlesex Super. Ct. R. Books; Middlesex Super. Ct. Docket Books.

leniency as a reward for their pleas. As defendants grew more likely to have counsel, they saw their chances of winning at trial increase to more than forty percent in most years and to more than fifty percent in some. At that point, they had less regard for the option of throwing themselves on the court's mercy, and their counsel advised them instead to demand some sort of guaranteed concession in exchange for their pleas. Meanwhile, prosecutors chafed at their increasing trial loads. What was worse, the cases that they were most likely to lose because of the opposition of defense counsel were for the same reason the most time-consuming to try. As Boston's prosecutor complained in 1844, "The labor of the trials is increased by the increased attendance of very eminent counsel in the defences."[22] Prosecutors badly wanted more cases to plead out, yet they had a hard time persuading defendants with counsel to plead guilty without guaranteeing them something in return.

Of course, the power of middle-tier prosecutors to grant meaningful concessions extended only to charge bargaining in liquor cases (which happened to have a substantially higher rate of counsel representation than other cases)[23] and to their promise not to move for sentence in the course of on-file plea bargains. In 1852 prosecutors lost their power to

4.5.

Proportion of Adjudicated Defendants Who Pled Without Apparent
Concession: Middlesex Court of Common Pleas and Superior Court

YEAR	% WITH COUNSEL	% WITHOUT COUNSEL
1844	30	47
1849	15	39
1853	15	30
1859	12	38
1864	27	35
1870	30	41
1880	47	53
1900	39	41

SOURCES: Middlesex Ct. C.P. R. Books; Middlesex Ct. C.P. Docket Books; Middlesex Super. Ct. R. Books; Middlesex Super. Ct. Docket Books.

charge bargain in liquor cases when the legislature banned nol prosses without the court's approval.[24] Because on-file plea bargaining involved letting the defendant go in the first instance, that option was inappropriate for the more serious cases on the docket. So despite the great pressure put on prosecutors by the large number of trials in the middle decades of the century, the rate of guilty pleas remained low for some time.

Applying the Analysis to Capital Cases

The records of capital pleas before the Supreme Judicial Court reveal a similar dynamic of interests and constrained options at work. I noted in Chapter 1 that it was unclear until 1838 whether prosecutors had the power to enter partial nol prosses. Until then, prosecutors could not be certain that it was lawful to reduce a charge of murder to manslaughter or a charge of rape to assault with intent to rape.[25] No such reduction appears in the records before 1841. It is hardly surprising, therefore, that virtually every capital defendant went to trial, for pleading guilty to a capital charge such as murder or rape simply guaranteed death.[26]

It is more surprising that even after capital charge bargains appeared in 1841, they remained rather rare for two decades, accounting for only

ten percent of adjudicated capital cases in the 1840s and seventeen percent in the 1850s (see Table 1.2, p.35). One possible reason for their lin-
gering scarcity emerges from an examination of the results at capital trials. It appears that in the 1830s and 1840s, the attorney general had a
dismal record of success. In the 1830s, there were more than three times
as many acquittals or hung juries as capital convictions, and in the 1840s,
almost twice as many (see Table 4.6). With so great a chance of escaping
conviction altogether and so small a chance of going to the gallows
(shrunk even further by occasional commutations), a typical defendant
might well have spurned a guilty plea to take his chances at trial.

The situation changed dramatically in the 1850s. Suddenly, capital
defendants were almost twice as likely to be convicted of some form of
murder as to escape conviction altogether. And suddenly, a manslaughter
plea must have seemed a far more desirable outcome. What brought
about this change in fortunes is not clear. Certainly the option of returning a second-degree murder conviction, available in 1858 and later, must
have reduced the number of hung juries and manslaughter convictions.
Improved policing (the Boston Police Department appointed its first
detectives in 1846)[27] and resulting improvements in evidence gathering
may have helped as well. In any event, these ratios remained largely in
place throughout the rest of the century: The chances of a murder conviction were always substantially greater than the combined odds of an
acquittal or a hung jury.

Although we might not expect the rate of guilty pleas to respond
immediately to outcomes at trial, we would expect to see such a response
within a few years. Defense counsel, present in every capital case, must
have warned clients of the unlikelihood of winning at trial when advising
them whether to strike a deal. So perhaps as a result of the attorney general's improved performance at trial, the proportion of charge bargains in
capital cases grew dramatically. It jumped to forty-seven percent of adjudicated murder cases in the 1860s and then hovered between thirty-five
percent and sixty-one percent for the balance of the century.

In the courts of the middle tier, however, the rate of guilty pleas
remained low through most of the middle third of the nineteenth century.
Stripped of the power to charge bargain in liquor cases and lacking it in
other cases, prosecutors could not promise the kind of sentencing con-

4.6.

Outcomes of Capital Trials Before the Supreme Judicial Court

YEARS	NUMBER OF TRIALS	PERCENT CONVICTED OF CAPITAL OFFENSE	PERCENT CONVICTED OF SECOND-DEGREE MURDER	PERCENT ACQUITTALS OR HUNG JURIES	PERCENT CHARGE BARGAINS
1820–1829	16	38	N/A	31	0
1830–1839	45	20	N/A	64	0
1840–1849	37	27	N/A	49	10
1850–1859	35	40	11	29	17
1860–1869	28	39	14	32	47
1870–1879	45	31	24	27	43
1880–1889	34	24	41	24	35
1890–1899	27	33	26	37	61

SOURCES: Annual Reports of the Attorney General; Sup. Jud. Ct. R. Books; Sup. Jud. Ct. Docket Books. Figures for 1820–1832, 1840–1848, and 1853 are based on surveys of the court's business. See Chapter 1, Table 1.2 and notes 86, 91. Because this table does not reflect manslaughter convictions, trial outcomes do not total one hundred percent. And because the table lists trial outcomes as a percentage *of trials* and lists charge bargains as a percentage *of adjudicated cases*, the totals for each year exceed one hundred percent.

cessions that would entice defendants to plead guilty. Yet during the last quarter of the century, the rate of guilty pleas grew strikingly. Two causes may have been at work. The first was the legislature's decision to let defendants testify at trial, which had the ironic result of persuading some defendants that trial was hopeless and that a guilty plea—even one that purchased no promised concession—was their only option. Second, the weight of an unremitting trial load began to press upon judges, who had far broader powers than prosecutors to make concessions. This latter development is the focus of the next chapter. The former I take up now.

THE IMPACT OF DEFENDANT-TESTIMONY LAWS

The Dilemma of Choice

In 1866 Massachusetts became the third state in the nation to grant criminal defendants the right to testify in their own behalf.[28] The next year, Judge Seth Ames of the superior court scoffed at the idea that the new law would help defendants. Ames, who would rise to the Supreme Judicial Court in 1869,[29] argued that the law left the defendant with two unpleasant alternatives. First, he could choose silence and face almost inevitable conviction. True, the law declared that the defendant could testify "at his own request, but not otherwise" and guaranteed that "neglect or refusal to testify shall not create any presumption against" him.[30] But Ames called these "fallacious and idle" words.[31] "[T]he jurors all know that the defendant has the privilege (as it is called) of making himself a witness if he sees fit; and they also know that he would if he dared."[32] His silence "will, and inevitably must, create a presumption against him, even if every page of the statute-book contained a provision that it should not. The statutes might as well prohibit the tide from rising . . . ."[33] In short, if the defendant "should decline to make himself a witness, the jury would convict him without leaving their seats."[34] And so this law *permitting* defendants to testify "will inevitably *compel* the defendant to testify, and will have substantially the same effect as if it did not go through the mockery of saying that he might testify if he pleased."[35]

Yet if the defendant did as he must and took the stand, he faced a second unpleasant alternative: Those defendants who had criminal records would be "torn to pieces by cross-examination."[36] That is because the law of evidence allowed lawyers to cast doubt on the truthfulness of opposing witnesses by showing they had been convicted of a crime.[37] In the days when defendants could not testify, they rarely had to fear that their past convictions could become evidence against them. But having gained the right to testify, they found themselves subject to the same rules of impeachment that confronted all other witnesses.[38] Ames himself, sitting as a trial judge shortly after Massachusetts enacted its defendant-testimony law, admitted evidence that a testifying defendant previously had pled guilty to forgery.[39] Ruling on appeal in that case, the Supreme Judicial Court wrote that "[t]he defendant . . . offered himself as a witness, and the rules of evidence affecting the competency or credibility of witnesses were all applicable to him in that character."[40]

Others of Ames's day saw the dilemma he saw. In 1869, only months after New York had given criminal defendants the right to testify, the *New York Times* wrote that "[t]he moment they become witnesses they subject themselves, like other witnesses, to the cross-examination of the District-Attorney, which may extend to their whole past career, and is sure to bring out facts that prejudice their case." The author then asked the obvious question: Why should the guilty take the stand?

> The truth is, if they do not take the stand, a strong presumption of their guilt is inevitable in the minds of the jury; for although the law expressly declares that the failure on the part of the prisoner to avail himself of its privilege, shall not work any presumption against him, yet, as was very pointedly stated by Mayor Hall in discussing the law, "the proviso is like all other attempts to legislate against moral convictions—an abortion."

In a tone that almost exactly echoed Ames, the author continued, "Juries *will* draw an inference unfavorable to the man who refuses to take the stand and declare his innocence . . . although the law declares they shall not." And so he concluded, "Thus the guilty man is placed between two fires . . ."[41]

The law of evidence no longer lumps together criminal defendants and ordinary witnesses. Courts now recognize that a testifying defendant who is impeached with his past crimes suffers a risk that confronts no other witness. Juries may regard the defendant's past crimes as evidence not merely that he is a liar—the purpose for which they are admitted—but also that he is a thief (or rapist or murderer) and convict him on that basis. Most evidence codes therefore restrict impeachment of defendants with past crimes, though they by no means forbid the practice.[42]

But those defendants who chose to testify in nineteenth-century Massachusetts enjoyed no such special protection. In 1867 the Supreme Judicial Court reviewed a trial judge's ruling admitting evidence of the defendant's past crimes "to affect his credibility as a witness, but for no other purpose."[43] The defendant's counsel complained on appeal "that it is a subtlety beyond the capacity of jurors" to confine such evidence to its impeachment value rather than "regarding it as affecting his character generally."[44] To this the high court curtly replied: "By availing himself of the privilege [to testify, the defendant] assumed the character of a witness, and subjected himself to the liabilities incident to that position. The statute does not exempt him from cross-examination, and impeachment as a witness; and there is no reason why he should be exempt from it."[45] In 1889 the Supreme Judicial Court even permitted the defendant in a liquor-selling case to be impeached with evidence of a past liquor-selling conviction, despite a real risk that the jury would convict her simply because she had committed the same crime before.[46]

The Upshot of the Dilemma

Ames did not venture to predict the consequences of a law that gave accomplished criminals the options of being convicted on their silence or convicted on their testimony. The task of explaining the law's full impact fell to a New York prosecutor of a later generation who wrote with the benefit of four decades' experience with these statutes. Arthur Train, son of Middlesex prosecutor Charles Russell Train,[47] was serving as an assistant district attorney in Manhattan in 1906 when he wrote *The Prisoner at the Bar*, the first of his series of chatty commentaries on the state of criminal justice. Train confirmed, first of all, the two horns of Ames's dilemma. On the one hand, those defendants who "do not testify . . . will probably pay the usual penalty":[48]

> Three jurors out of five will convict any man who is unwilling to offer an explanation of the charge against him. How they reconcile this with their oath it would be hard to understand, if they were accustomed to obey it literally in other respects. The writer has heard more

than one talesman say, in discussing a verdict, "Of course we couldn't take it against him, but we *knew* he was guilty because he was afraid to testify."[49]

On the other hand, those who do testify, if they have criminal pasts, "are more than likely to be convicted 'on their records'":[50]

> The professional criminal usually has a "record" and he knows full well that in view of his past history, if there be any sort of a case against him, his own defence, however eloquent or ingenious, will go for nothing. An affirmative answer to the simple question, "Have you ever been convicted?" is, in three cases out of five, equivalent to a plea of guilty.[51]

In fact, Train wrote, even defendants who remained silent were likely to be convicted on their records: An experienced juror "discovers that the district attorney cannot prove the prison record . . . of the defendant unless the latter subjects himself to cross-examination by taking the witness-stand, and hence is likely to suspect that any defendant who does not testify is an ex-convict."[52]

The consequence of the defendant's predicament, Train concluded, was "that the jury in the ordinary run of criminal cases passes upon the guilt or innocence of very few professional criminals."[53] Instead, a defendant with a criminal past, who therefore has the choice of being convicted on his silence or convicted on his record, "generally throws up his hands and stolidly takes his medicine"—and "dickers for the lowest plea he can get."[54] And "when the jury disband at the conclusion of the term with the thanks of the court, they have seen few professional criminals, save for a fleeting glance as one or two are led to the bar to admit their guilt."[55] The upshot was that a law that purported to grant defendants a new right to testify at trial instead deprived those defendants who had criminal records of the right to any meaningful trial, and left them with little alternative but to seek the best plea bargain they could get.

What Ames anticipated and Train witnessed was not peculiar to their part of the country. By the turn of the century, every state but Georgia permitted defendants to testify.[56] In California, which passed a defendant-testimony law in 1866 just ahead of Massachusetts,[57] Friedman and Percival saw an unexpected second dimension to the link between defendant-testimony laws and defendants' incentives to plead out. They quote a judge at a 1910 sentencing hearing congratulating a defendant on his good sense in pleading guilty: "You can rest assured if you had gone on the witness stand and told some perjured tale about this affair, you would have received a heavier sentence."[58]

This rationalization brilliantly expands the versatility of defendant-testimony laws as a spur to plea bargaining. For it grants those judges who pretend to shun plea bargaining of a crasser sort a noble basis for rewarding the defendant's plea. Moreover, it gives judges an appropriately principled reason to punish defendants for wasting the court's time with a trial. After all, the jury's guilty verdict normally conveys its judgment that the defendant, if she testified, lied.[59]

The *New York Times* saw as much when it commented on New York's new defendant-testimony law in 1869. The paper reported the lament of criminal defense lawyers that their clients often "make such bungling work in telling their story . . . that their perjury becomes patent to all." Then "when they come to be sentenced the Court does not scruple to give them the extreme penalty of the law, and give as a reason for [such] severity that they have added to the crime with which they were charged that of perjury."[60] This attitude among sentencing judges created an Ames-like dilemma not just for those defendants who had criminal histories that might be grounds for impeachment, but for all defendants. All defendants risked being convicted for their silence, and when tried before judges intent on penalizing them for their perjury, all defendants risked being punished for their speech.

In short, defendant-testimony laws probably led many defendants to regard their odds of winning at trial poorly. And these laws may have led defendants to fear that if they went to trial, testified, and lost, the judge would punish them for their apparent perjury. As a result, many defendants perhaps shrank from trial altogether and grew more willing to bargain for deals they once might have shunned. In fact, in the hope that their pleas would win the judge's favor, defendants may have grown more willing to plead guilty even without a promised concession.

Of course, other developments also might have moved defendants to believe that their chances at trial were hopeless. Some scholars have argued that the rising efficiency of the police generated more evidence and tighter cases. This suggestion is sound enough in theory and may be true, but I have seen no contemporary commentary that good police work was making it harder for defendants to win at trial. In any event, Train's report makes it clear that at least some defendants who might have chosen trial under the old regime (in which the law uniformly barred them from testifying) declined trial under the new.

There is no reason to expect that this effect would be immediate. The dynamic Train described turned on juror expectations. Because jurors expected defendants to testify, a defendant could not afford to sit quietly through his trial. Juror expectations presumably did not change overnight. Only after jurors had internalized the new order, in which defendants could take the stand, would they become suspicious of those defendants who stayed silent. So the result in Massachusetts might be just about what we would expect. The dramatic conversion to a plea-bargaining regime, shown in Figure 4.1, started about a decade after defendants first began to take the witness stand.

The Dynamic of Change

That defendant-testimony laws proved to be of such convenient assistance to plea bargaining's cause was not, I think, a matter of design. These laws were the culmination of a long legal evolution—one that wiped out a whole series of old common law rules that barred the testimony of certain classes of persons.[61] They were not the brainchildren of nineteenth-century prosecutors or judges intent on squeezing defendants into passing up their trial right. Even as bitter a critic of the new laws as Seth Ames failed to mention that the dilemma he set out with such insight would produce more pleas of guilty. There is no evidence in the early history of defendant-testimony laws that their backers promoted them either openly or otherwise as instruments of plea bargaining.

But neither do I think that the quick and durable success of laws that happened to encourage plea bargaining was pure good (or ill) fortune. We now have traced two of the nineteenth century's greatest innovations in criminal procedure—probation and defendant-testimony laws—to plea bargaining's doorstep. Of these, only probation took form in some measure as the *work* of a plea-bargaining regime, but both proved strong allies in the cause.

What's more, they proved to be coordinated allies. Although defendant-testimony laws helped persuade all defendants to plead guilty, they worked best against defendants with criminal pasts. And although few jurisdictions barred probation for defendants with criminal pasts, it quickly developed in Massachusetts and elsewhere that few repeat offenders got probation. As early as 1852, John Augustus, Boston's pioneering unofficial probation officer, noted that he had "confined [his] efforts mainly to those who were indicted for their first offence."[62] Boston's (and the nation's) first official probation officer, Edward H. Savage, wrote in his annual report for 1880 that 341 of the 376 probation cases he had completed that year involved first offenders.[63] Some states in fact limited probation to first offenders by law.[64]

I will wait until Chapter 8 to explore the evolutionary principles that could explain the spread and staying power of institutions that so handily promoted plea bargaining's cause. For now it is enough to realize that, going into the last quarter of the nineteenth century, two of the three major courtroom actors had strong incentives to plea bargain. They lacked only the power. Prosecutors had lost the power to charge bargain once afforded them by the peculiar penalty structure of the liquor laws. Their power to put defendants on probation by means of on-file plea bargains could not reasonably extend to the more serious crimes on the docket. And murder cases, in which prosecutors retained the power to charge bargain and used it extensively, made up only a tiny fraction of the docket. Criminal defendants, who had complete power to fulfill their end of any bargain by pleading guilty, had no power to ensure a reward for their pleas. The full development and final victory of plea bargaining as a systemic regime therefore awaited the judge's helping hand. Judges held most of the power to sentence, but until the last quarter of the nineteenth century, they stayed far from the plea-bargaining fray. The interests of plea bargaining, it seems, had not yet touched their own.

5
Judges and the Power to Sentence

In our journey through the first three-quarters of the nineteenth century, we have stumbled over no evidence that judges commonly lent their aid in plea bargaining. The great proportion of defendants who pled guilty at the beginning of the century do not seem to have done so in exchange for a reward promised by—or perhaps even expected from—the judge or anyone else. Their sentences appear to have been no lighter than those of defendants who wagered trial and lost. Perhaps they pled guilty in the hopeless realization that without lawyers, they had small chance of prevailing at trial.[1] If so, then rising numbers of lawyers in the early decades of the century stanched this flow of unrewarded pleas. The result, as it appeared in Figure 4.1 (p. 93), was that through the middle third of the nineteenth century, the rate of guilty pleas reached its lowest point in my century-long survey.

Though prosecutors suffered under the crushing caseloads of the 1840s and 1850s, they could do little to lighten their loads, for their power to plea bargain had strict bounds. Working with what pockets of power they had, they devised two forms of plea bargaining and conducted each with little or no judicial assistance. In liquor and murder cases they took advantage of the law's peculiarly rigid penalty scheme and their initially unsupervised nol pros power to initiate charge-bargaining regimes. During the legislature's 1844 investigation into his bargaining practices, Asahel Huntington laid before the committee his sophisticated practice of multiple charging and selective nol prossing. That judges played no substantial role in this scheme must have been clear to the legislators, for when they set out to restrict such deals in the 1852 liquor prohibition act, they declared that "a *nolle prosequi* shall not be entered by the prosecuting officer [in liquor cases], *except with the concurrence of the court.*"[2] It seems legislators were right to think prosecutors the problem, for in 1853, court records disclose no multiple charging in liquor cases and no more charge bargains.[3] Judges apparently withheld their "concurrence" from charge bargaining in liquor cases.

Stripped of the unilateral power to charge bargain, prosecutors retreated to the second form of plea bargaining permitted by their limited powers. By promising to withhold a motion to sentence in exchange for the defendant's plea, they engaged in on-file plea bargaining in a broad range of cases. In liquor cases, the legislature again moved to defeat the tactic by making judges partners in the prosecutors' power. By declaring that "[n]o [liquor] case . . . shall be laid on file . . . unless . . . upon the certificate of the presiding magistrate or judge,"[4] the 1865 "Act to Prevent Evasions" largely ended on-file plea bargaining in liquor cases. For most of the latter half of the nineteenth century, therefore, the only forms of clear plea bargaining that appear more than occasionally on the records and dockets of Middlesex County are those in which the legislature left the prosecutors' unilateral power to deal unmolested: charge bargains in murder cases and on-file plea bargains in nonliquor cases.

Not all plea bargains, of course, appear on the record books as clear plea bargains, in which the clerk disclosed the concession granted for the defendant's plea. There might have been many defendants who had quiet assurances of lighter sentences should they plead guilty and many others who had real, though unspoken, reasons to believe that their plea would reap a lenient reward from the judge. The long-depressed plea rates of the middle third of the century, however, suggest that judges did not commonly dispense such rewards.

Then, beginning in the 1870s, the rate of guilty pleas turned first mildly and then sharply upward. After a modest retreat in the 1890s, the rate turned upward again and in 1900 reached its highest point in our period. It stayed constant in 1910, the last year I studied in depth. The conclusion is hard to escape that judges had begun to engage in sentence bargaining. We cannot attribute the enormous growth in guilty pleas to a change in the power or preferences of prosecutors. No new law either restored their power to charge bargain in liquor cases or created in other broad categories of crime the kind of rigid penalty scheme that first gave prosecutors that power in liquor and murder cases. In 1890 charge bargains still accounted for only four percent of all guilty pleas, and the twenty-seven charge bargains I found in 1900 amounted to only six percent of all pleas.[5]

Nor did anything so drastically alter defendants' options or incentives that it could explain the huge rise in guilty pleas at century's end. As the proportion of defendants with counsel held fairly steady through the last four decades of the century,[6] there is little reason to think that a growing proportion of defendants pled guilty out of sheer hopelessness.[7] It is likely that a fair number of guilty pleas grew out of the 1866 defendant-testimony law, which diminished the power of defendants with criminal pasts to take a winning case to trial and might have prompted them to plead guilty without a guaranteed concession. But the booming increase in guilty pleas during the last quarter of the century must have been due to more. By 1900 the proportion of adjudicated cases resolved by plea had grown simply too large (eighty-seven percent) for us to believe that so many defendants pled guilty without a real and rather certain reward.[8]

In fact, sentencing patterns suggest that judges rewarded defendants for their pleas. Table 5.1 reports the sentencing data for four of the most frequently prosecuted crimes in the last two decades of the century. Only in theft cases was the benefit to those who pled guilty less than dramatic. In breaking-and-entering cases, defendants who went to trial and lost spent on average about twice as long in prison as those who pled guilty. In assault-and-battery cases, those who lost after trial were almost three times as likely to go to prison as those who pled guilty. And in liquor cases, not only were those who lost after trial more than three times as likely to go to prison, but they also paid far more in fines and costs. I have excluded from these calculations all cases that were placed on file after the defendant's guilty plea because I want to isolate the judge's role in sentencing, and it is unclear in these decades how the judge and prosecutor divided the power to place cases on file.[9] The number of on-file plea bargains in these years was quite large—had I included them, the "sentencing" advantage to defendants who pled guilty would have appeared even starker.[10]

I think these figures reflect more than the impulsive generosity of judges who were gratified to see defendants admit their guilt. Rather, they are strong evidence that by the last quarter of the century, judges had become full partners in a thriving practice of sentence bargaining. But why would a judiciary that had once shunned taking part in prosecutorial plea bargaining now take up plea bargaining with enthusiasm? In Chapter 2, I suggested that there were at least three obstacles to judicial acceptance of plea bargaining. First, judges lacked the major incentives that drove prosecutors to bargain—the prosecutors' crushing workloads and their taste for effortless convictions. Second, judges objected on principle to the idea of passing sentence without full information about the defendant's crime and background. And third, proud judges took offense at having to share sentencing power with prosecutors. Yet by century's end, a form of plea bargaining that seemed to demand judicial complicity was thriving. Some things must have changed.

I argue in the next three sections that some things did change—and changed in a way that gave judges a real incentive to plea bargain, weakened their principled resistance to bargaining, and protected their pride from prosecutorial invasion of their sentencing power. The new incentive came from an exploding civil caseload, brought about by a revolution in transportation and industry and a resulting wave of tort actions of unprecedented number and complexity. Judges' principled objections gave way as newly commissioned probation officers investigated defendants' crimes and backgrounds and gave judges enough information to make reasoned sentencing decisions after a plea—and as newly appointed parole boards relieved judges of the responsibility of setting defendants' sentences with precision. Judicial pride found refuge in the development of sentencing mechanisms that let prosecutors make promises during plea bargaining without taking sentencing power (or at least without taking it overtly) from judicial hands.

5.1.

Sentence According to Mode of Conviction: Middlesex Superior Court, 1880–1900

	BREAKING AND ENTERING[a]		SIMPLE THEFT		ASSAULT AND BATTERY		LIQUOR CRIMES[b]	
	PLEA	TRIAL	PLEA	TRIAL	PLEA	TRIAL	PLEA	TRIAL
Number	66	20	38	10	38	13	84	30
Avg. Value of Stolen Goods	$39	$42	$78	$346	—	—	—	—
% Prison	100	100	89	100	21	62	15	53
Avg. Term (months)[c]	18.7	38.5	10.7	12.8	5.8	5.5	3.6	3.4
% Fine	0	0	11	0	79	46	99	100
Avg. Fine	—	—	$28	—	$20	$21	$67	$106
Avg. Costs[d]	—	—	—	—	$17	$21	$22	$50

SOURCES: Middlesex Super. Ct. R. Books (Oct. 1880, June 1885, Feb. 1890, Oct. 1896, 1900).

[a] I have excluded breaking and entering a residence because it is substantially more serious than other breaking-and-entering crimes.

[b] For purposes of this table, liquor crimes include keeping liquor with intent to sell, making unlicensed sales, and maintaining a liquor nuisance. In this time frame, the first two of these were punishable by a fine of between fifty and five hundred dollars or imprisonment of between one and six months or both. See Act of Apr. 5, 1875, ch. 99, §§ 1, 13, 1875 Mass. Acts 664, 664, 668. Maintaining a liquor nuisance was punishable by a fine of between fifty and one hundred dollars and imprisonment of between three and twelve months. See Mass. Rev. Laws ch. 101, § 7 (1902).

[c] "Avg. Term" refers to the average term of confinement of those defendants sentenced to serve time. I have excluded from this calculation those defendants sentenced to an indefinite time at the Massachusetts reformatory or a juvenile facility. See Chapter 8, notes 27, 29–31, and accompanying text, where I discuss the Massachusetts reformatory. When the judge specified a minimum and maximum term in state prison, I calculated a sentence midway between the minimum and maximum.

[d] Costs were very rarely assessed when the defendant served time. No costs were assessed in 1896 or 1900. See Middlesex Super. Ct. R. Books (1896, 1900).

INCENTIVES: JUDGES' CASELOAD PRESSURE

On October 14, 1885, a Salem lawyer named Charles Thompson made a note in his diary: "This P.M. news came that I am appointed or *nominated to judgeship of Superior Ct.* Several called to congratulate me."[11] Eight days later, with the anomalous expedition of a slower age, Thompson could write that he had been "to Boston & was qualified by Governor Geo D Robinson as Associate Justice of the Superior Court."[12] Four days after that, our fifty-eight-year-old judicial novice was on the road: "Went to Pittsfield & held Court for a fortnight."[13] From Pittsfield, Thompson went to Greenfield,[14] and from Greenfield, apparently, to Boston, where he held court until the night before Christmas.[15] For the next two years, before his diary came to a close, Thompson set down in staccato half-sentences his frenetic zigzags across the state, now and then stopping to punctuate, "Have been very busy"—"[v]ery busy indeed"— "a number of cases not disposed of."[16]

Knowing only this much, we could not say that Thompson had a harder time of it than his predecessors on the Court of Common Pleas. They, too, rode circuit, and although Thompson occasionally resorted to horseback,[17] he at least normally could take the train. Moreover, there is plenty of evidence that judges in earlier times sometimes left for their next sitting before completing the calendar at the last stop.[18] Nor can I argue that the ever-mounting criminal caseload of the last quarter of the century, when judges appear to have gone over to plea bargaining's cause, weighed more heavily upon them than before. Table 5.2 shows that through the last half of the century, the number of criminal cases per judge in Middlesex County never again got so high as in 1849. It is true that as the district attorney began to draw a full-time salary and then to take on assistants,[19] his office was able to bring a higher proportion of all cases before the court for its attention. But even when I exclude all those cases that the district attorney presumably handled on his own or that took up little of the court's time (those ending in complete nol prosses, whether or not upon payment of costs, those placed on file without a guilty finding, and those in which the defendant failed to appear), the middle of the century remains the worst period I have studied in terms of criminal cases per judge.

5.2.

Criminal Cases per Judge: Middlesex Court of Common Pleas and Superior Court

YEAR	TOTAL CASES	NUMBER OF JUDGES	NUMBER OF CASES PER JUDGE	NUMBER OF CASES BROUGHT BEFORE A JUDGE	NUMBER PER JUDGE
1824	48	4	12	39	10
1829	41	4	10	27	7
1834	95	4	24	65	16
1839	42	4	11	36	9
1843–1844[a]	112	5	22	93	19
1849	443	6	74	271	45
1853	482	7	69	319	46
1859	415	10	42	257	26
1864[b]	292	10	29	159	16
1870[b]	449	10	45	309	31
1880[b]	486	11	44	330	30
1900	602	18	33	546	30

SOURCES: Middlesex Ct. C.P. R. Books; Middlesex Ct. C.P. Docket Books; Middlesex Super. Ct. R. Books; Middlesex Super. Ct. Docket Books. See also Act of Apr. 5, 1859, ch. 196, § 7, 1859 Mass. Acts 339, 341, which set the number of superior court judges at nine; Davis, *History of the Judiciary*, 243–44, which supplies the number of judges through 1859; Dimond, *Superior Court*, 75, 77, 93, 97, which supplies the number of judges from 1859 through 1900. Middlesex was one of fourteen counties in the state. To get a real idea of how many cases each judge handled per year, one would have to repeat this analysis in each of the others. As Middlesex is large and diverse, there is no reason to think that its patterns of change were unlike those in Massachusetts as a whole.

[a] Average per year.

[b] Calculated from totals for one or two of the three annual sessions (see Appendix A).

Longer Trials?

Of course, cases per judge would be a poor measure of judicial caseload pressure if the burden of each case had been growing over time. John Langbein has argued that the increasing complexity of the law of evidence and "the lawyerization of the trial . . . made jury trial so complicated and time-consuming that they rendered it unworkable as the routine dispositive procedure" and forced the system to turn instead to plea bargaining.[20]

The argument has enormous commonsense appeal. And in fact, my evidence suggests that increasing trial length may have played a part in the surge of plea bargaining in murder cases in the 1890s. But this evidence is uncertain, and there is little or no evidence of a broader connection between trial length and plea bargaining that can help explain plea bargaining's nineteenth-century rise.

We should begin the hunt for such evidence in the upper tier, as the records of Supreme Judicial Court business give us a somewhat surer footing for conclusions. The annual reports of the attorney general, which commenced in 1832 and continued with occasional interruptions throughout the century, often noted the number of days consumed by each trial before the high court.[21] Table 5.3 reports the average length of murder trials during the last two-thirds of the century.[22] Two striking facts emerge from this table, one opposing Langbein's thesis, one apparently supporting it. The first is the absence of any substantial increase in trial length between the 1830s, the last decade in which the records reveal no charge bargaining, and the 1860s, when almost half of all adjudicated murder cases ended in charge bargains. In fact, in the 1860s, the average trial length fell to its lowest point in the years of this study. Then, as the length of trials rose slightly in the next two decades, the proportion of charge bargains *fell*.

Langbein's thesis finds support in the data from the 1890s, when both trial length and the proportion of charge bargains increased dramatically. But a complicating factor clouds this scene. In 1891 the legislature transferred jurisdiction over murder trials from the Supreme Judicial Court to the superior courts.[23] As we saw in Figure 4.1, the overall rate of guilty pleas in Middlesex Superior Court increased sharply during the last quarter of the century. If we exclude on-file plea bargains, which substantially increased the guilty plea rate but never took place in murder cases, sixty-one percent of adjudicated nonliquor cases in superior court ended in guilty pleas in 1890 and seventy-nine percent in 1900. Given the dynamic of powers and interests that prevailed in the superior court and that I believe gave rise to the habit and culture of plea bargaining in that court, we might expect to find that once this court took custody of murder cases, the rate of plea bargains in such cases would creep toward the overall average. A charge-bargaining rate of sixty-one percent in murder cases during this decade therefore might be just about what we would

5.3.

Average Length of Massachusetts Murder Trials

YEARS	NUMBER OF CAPITAL TRIALS	NUMBER OF MURDER TRIALS WITH RECORDED LENGTHS	AVERAGE LENGTH OF MURDER TRIALS (DAYS)	% OF ADJUCATED CAPITAL CASES ENDING IN CHARGE BARGAINS
1832–1839	45	15	3.2	0
1840–1849	37	2	4.0	10
1850–1859	35	11	3.5	17
1860–1869	28	28	3.0	47
1870–1879	45	32	3.8	43
1880–1889	34	23	4.1	35
1890–1899	27	16	6.6	61

SOURCE: Annual Reports of the Attorney General.

NOTE: For my method of calculating the length of trials, see note 21 in this chapter. For an explanation of the incomplete records of the 1840s and 1850s, see Chapter 1, note 91 and Table 1.2.

expect. And this result might have followed even had there been no change in the length of murder trials.

If we look now at the work of the superior court and court of common pleas, it is hard to discern any broad support for the thesis that increasing trial length led to the rise of plea bargaining. It is true that one prosecutor complained in the 1840s that "[t]he labor of the trials is increased by the increased attendance of very eminent counsel in the defences."[24] But it is also true that court records reveal no clear trend toward substantially longer trials in the last quarter of the nineteenth century, when the guilty plea rate in the courts of the middle tier grew tremendously. Perhaps that is because the proportion of defendants with counsel—the particular concern of the prosecutor just quoted—stayed fairly steady over the same time span.[25]

The Middlesex court clerk did not record the length of individual trials in the nineteenth century. The data at hand, however, can give us some sense of the average length. Table 5.4 reports the number of days consumed by each criminal session of the middle-tier courts in Middlesex

5.4.

Trials per Day and Other Cases per Day: Middlesex Court of
Common Pleas and Superior Court

YEAR	JUDGE-DAYS	TRIALS	TRIALS PER JUDGE-DAY	OTHER CASES	OTHER CASES PER JUDGE-DAY
1839[a]	17	12	0.7	14	0.8
1843–1844[b]	117	94	0.8	130	1.1
1849	79	131	1.7	312	3.9
1853	54	93	1.7	389	7.2
1859	78	130	1.7	285	3.7
1864[a]	34	38	1.1	187	5.5
1870[a]	33	62	1.9	121	3.7
1880[a]	19	21	1.1	119	6.3
1885[a]	26	24	0.9	c	—
1890[a]	34	58	1.7	c	—
1896[a]	29	60	2.1	c	—
1900	44	70	1.6	532	12.1
1910	111	66	0.6	c	—

SOURCES: Middlesex Ct. C.P. R. Books; Middlesex Ct. C.P. Docket Books; Middlesex Super. Ct. R. Books; Middlesex Super. Ct. Docket Books.

[a] Totals for one or two of the three annual sessions (see Appendix A).
[b] Two-year totals.
[c] Not measured.

County and the number of cases tried per day.[26] Because the Middlesex Court of Common Pleas did not begin to hold separate criminal and civil sessions until June 1839, I have no earlier data. The low figures for trials per day in the earliest years (indicating long trials) probably mean that there were certain "fixed costs" at each session of the court—routine business that consumed court time but is not reflected in the number of cases disposed. When the sessions of the court were short, as they were early on, they therefore appear to have been less efficient. And just as trials were probably faster than they appear in the earliest years, they were probably faster than they appear in the later years as well. In the later years, most sessions of the court had to process a good number of cases that did *not* go to trial—after all, the vast majority of cases ended in guilty pleas—but those cases still absorbed some of the court's time.[27]

There is little here to suggest a sharp rise in trial length at the close of the century. The pace of trials in 1900, when the rate of guilty pleas reached its end-of-century high, just about equaled the pace in 1849, when the guilty plea rate reached almost its lowest point.[28] The best indication of a trend toward longer trials emerged *after* the turn of the twentieth century. The relatively slow trials of 1910 perhaps foreshadowed the longer trials of our day, but they cannot explain the plea-bargaining boom that marked the last decades of the nineteenth century. By 1900, the rate of guilty pleas had reached a plateau and stood essentially unchanged in 1910.[29]

The Civil Caseload Explosion

At bottom, I do not believe criminal caseload pressure was the moving force behind the late-century judicial conversion to plea bargaining.[30] To that extent I agree with Vogel and Ferdinand and others who have sought to debunk the long-accepted wisdom that rising caseload pressure brought on plea bargaining.[31] But the received wisdom turns out to be largely right—it simply focused on the wrong side of the courthouse. The crucial caseload pressure came not from criminal courtrooms but from their civil counterparts, a factor all studies of this era have left out.[32]

Figure 5.1 depicts judicial workload in its most irreducible form: the number of judge-workdays consumed each year by the criminal and civil business of the middle-tier courts.[33] The lowest line, representing the total number of workdays per judge, shows that after the caseload depression of the Civil War had offset the highs of the late 1840s, judges were able to limit the share of their time devoted to Middlesex County business[34] to about twenty days per judge per year throughout the last several decades of the century. The widening gap between the steeply rising line representing the civil workload and the jaggedly steady line representing the criminal workload makes it clear that judges maintained their overall workload only by devoting a smaller and smaller proportion of their time to criminal business. The greatly increasing efficiency of the judicial workday on the criminal side—rising from 3.3 cases per day in 1859 to 12.4 cases per day in 1900—therefore served not to increase judges' leisure, but to increase the attention they paid to their civil caseloads.[35]

The civil caseload phenomenon pictured in Figure 5.1 was neither a

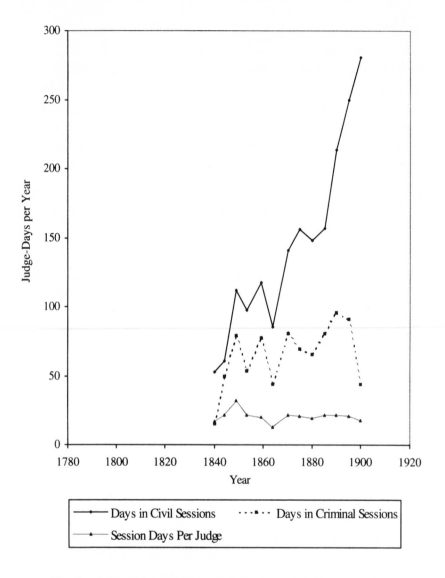

Figure 5.1. Length of criminal and civil sessions: Middlesex Court of Common Pleas and Superior Court.

passing phase nor a Middlesex peculiarity.[36] It represents instead one of the great transformations of American law.[37] It did not respond simply to the booming population growth of the era, but rather to the suddenly expanding mechanization of production and transportation. It is a measure of the human carnage wrought by massive but still-primitive machinery deployed by industrialists and railroad barons bent on profit and untethered by government safety regulations.[38]

Between 1880 and 1900, the number of negligence suits filed in Boston jumped from about 120 to about 3,300.[39] As personal injury tort suits began to crowd out the nonpayment contract disputes that had been the staple of the court's civil diet,[40] a kind of time-intensive litigation that turned on past events and cumbersome eyewitness testimony displaced the quick and orderly paper-based litigation of earlier times.[41] And as lawyers tempted by large contingency fees began to sling shots at the State Street law firms that defended the railroads, streetcars, and textile mills,[42] the ravaging civil warfare so familiar today spread from courthouse to courthouse, and lawyers multiplied faster than the population.[43]

The Impact on Plea Bargaining

But if the numbers represented in Figure 5.1 are clear, their lesson is less so. Why should judges who faced an explosion in civil litigation have chosen to acquiesce and take part in a prosecutorial invention that served to limit only their criminal workload? I believe the answer is that judges, like prosecutors, plea bargained because they could. Overworked prosecutors of the first three-quarters of the century charge bargained in liquor and murder cases because rigid penalty schemes gave them the leverage they needed. So, too, overworked judges of the last quarter of the century turned to plea bargaining for relief from their out-of-control civil caseloads, because they had far greater power to coerce pleas on the criminal side than to induce settlements on the civil side.

In a criminal case, after all, the judge could make the defendant a hard-to-refuse offer. He could promise the defendant a lenient sentence for her plea, and he could threaten a harsher sentence should she choose trial and lose. In the great majority of cases, the judge's nearly wide-open sentencing discretion gave him the power to make good on both promise and threat, mediated only by the defendant's power to win acquittal from a jury.

In a civil case, in contrast, the judge's power to promise a palatable outcome to a party who agreed to settle extended only so far as his ability to persuade the opposing party to go along. Likewise, his power to threaten an unhappy outcome to a party who risked trial and lost reached little further than his capacity to influence the jury to deliver an unfavorable monetary award. It is true that the doctrine of remittitur gave judges the power to order a new trial unless a victorious plaintiff agreed to give up whatever portion of a jury's award the judge thought excessive.[44] But Massachusetts law did not recognize additur in nineteenth-century tort cases, so judges could wield no similar power against defendants in personal injury actions.[45] And even remittitur was not an unbounded power to reduce damages, analogous to the sentencing power in criminal cases, but rather an indirect power to threaten a new trial unless the plaintiff accepted the reduced judgment.

Though civil settlements surely were growing over our period—from 15.7% of cases in 1865 to 28.4% in 1895 to 41.9% in 1905—no study I have seen attempts to discern the judge's role in this increase.[46] Even if judges perhaps had the means to coerce settlement in some civil cases, they obviously did not succeed in keeping their civil workload within bounds.[47] The spiking line in Figure 5.1 representing their civil workload shows how essential it was that judges use what means they had to encourage pleas on the criminal side.

Exactly how judges in criminal cases communicated their desire for pleas and conveyed their promises and threats to criminal defendants is something I will take up in a few pages. For now, the important point is that on the criminal side—and the criminal side only—both the judges' promises and their threats had the force to work their purpose.

PRINCIPLES: THE EFFECTS OF PROBATION AND PAROLE

Even if judges had come to feel the caseload pressure long felt by prosecutors, a principled judge nonetheless might have refused to commit himself to a particular sentence without first hearing all the information normally supplied by a trial or sentencing hearing. By the last part of the century, however, such principled resistance had less foundation than before. The most significant reason was the legislature's creation of public probation officers as a reliable and arguably impartial source of information about the defendant's background and alleged offense.[48]

Probation's Role

The 1878 act that authorized a probation officer for Suffolk County charged that person with the "duty . . . to attend the sessions of the courts of criminal jurisdiction, . . . to investigate the cases of persons charged with or convicted of crimes and misdemeanors, and to recommend to such courts the placing on probation of such persons as may reasonably be expected to be reformed without punishment."[49] The 1880 act extending probation officers to the rest of the state required them "to carefully inquire into the character and offence of every person arrested for crime." It assigned them "the special duty . . . to inform the court, so far as is possible, whether a person on trial has previously been convicted of any crime."[50] Supplied with this information about the defendant's crime, character, and record, even a conscientious judge could settle on a sentence without the court proceedings that once disclosed the same information.

From the beginning, probation officers fulfilled the duties assigned them by these acts to gather information and relay it to the court. Boston's first public probation officer, Edward H. Savage, reported in 1881 on his investigatory activities the year before: "I have visited the City Prison every morning, taken a list of the names, and offences of those in custody, and the names of arresting officers, seen the prisoners at their cells, then repaired to the court, had interviews with officers and others interested, in order to be prepared to take action in any case that seemed to demand attention."[51] Several years later, Savage elaborated: "[I]t becomes the important duty of the [probation] officer to make a thorough investigation into the reputation and true character of the offender. It is not enough to learn what people say; but the officer should have a personal interview with the prisoner, study his disposition, his intentions, his constitutional make-up, and, as far as possible, learn the probabilities of reform."[52] Savage said he repeated this investigatory course for 698 defendants in 1879 and for more than 3,000 in 1882 and in several succeeding years.[53]

Of course, none of this well-collected information could have helped a judge reach an appropriate sentence unless the probation officer passed it on. And although both the 1878 and the 1880 acts gave probation officers the duty to "recommend" to the courts which defendants should be placed on probation—and no doubt envisioned that probation officers would convey the results of their investigations at that time—neither statute made it clear whether probation officers could make those reports *before* conviction.[54] It would have done little to assist plea bargaining if the judge heard the needed information only after a trial or guilty plea. The 1880 law's imposition of a "special duty [on] each probation officer to inform the court . . . whether *a person on trial* has previously been convicted of any crime" surely seems to require a report before conviction.[55] But a 1916 probation manual declared it to be "doubtful if even . . . [this provision] authorizes such information to be given prior to a determination of guilt."[56] The manual adds that "[w]ith this doubtful exception, the probation officer's duty in cases before the court begins after conviction."[57]

Yet the probation manual perhaps protests too much. Why instruct probation officers to withhold information from the court unless there was pressure on them to disclose it? An English observer's 1899 report to the House of Commons on the activity of Boston's probation officers seems to confirm suspicions. The observer quoted from a "statement of the methods employed in carrying out his duties [that] was prepared for me by Mr. Keefe, the Chief Probat[ion] Officer," and that was "confirmed" by the presiding judge of the Boston courts:

> The probation officer visits the prison daily at 7 o'clock, a.m., talks with each prisoner, ascertaining the facts of his connection with the offence charged, his address, his former record (if any) and any information of benefit to the prisoner, keeping in mind the good of the Commonwealth.
>
> The records of drunkenness are looked over, former arrests recorded *and given to the presiding Judge for reference when the prisoner is called.*
>
> The assistant probation officers (in the cases of drunkenness) visit the homes each morning, *reporting to the Judge, when the prisoner is called, facts ascertained at the homes.* If the prisoner provides for his family and has steady work, . . . [he] is usually placed on probation. . . .

. . .

... In many cases the Judge cannot get at the true facts when the case is presented to the Court *and depends upon the probation officer's investigation in deciding the case.*[58]

Contrary to the probation manual's admonitions, probation officers apparently disclosed a great deal of information to the court before conviction—information that might have gone far to ease the qualms of conscientious judges who thought it wrong to pass sentence with less than full information. Perhaps, therefore, we have come upon another way, beyond encouraging first offenders to plead guilty, in which probation assisted the rise of plea bargaining.

PAROLE'S ROLE

The nineteenth century's other distinctive contribution to penal practices also may have eased judges' principled objections to plea bargaining. In 1870 a prominent meeting in Cincinnati of the American Prison Association, chaired by future President Rutherford B. Hayes, launched the indeterminate sentencing movement in America.[59] The *reality* of the indeterminate sentence, had it ever taken hold in its truest form, would have done much to wreck the plea-bargaining regime. If the judge had no other role than to dispatch the defendant to prison and if other authorities determined the date of release, then the only meaningful promise the judge could make in exchange for the defendant's guilty plea would have been to put the defendant on probation rather than send him to prison. Plea bargaining would not have died in such a setting—we already have seen that defendants often pled guilty to win a chance at probation—but neither would it have flourished, for no conscientious judge could promise to spare serious criminals from serving any time at all.

In Chapter 8, I return to this clash between plea bargaining and the indeterminate sentence to show how the plea-bargaining regime succeeded in putting down this challenge to its forward march. Now, though, it is important to see what sustenance plea bargaining drew from the *principles* of the indeterminate sentence. For even as the true indeterminate sentence fell to history's dust heap,[60] the concept survived in corrupted forms, and its theoretical underpinnings proved more lasting than the institution itself.

Those underpinnings were quite simple. First, punishment should look to the future and not the past. That is, the critical concern in arriving at a just sentence was not what the defendant had done, but when it would be safe again to release him upon the community.[61] The second underpinning followed from the first. Because the judge, even after trial, knew little more about the defendant's capacity for reform than what one could learn from a study of his past behavior, the judge was distinctly unqualified to pass a fixed sentence. "It is absurd," wrote a former Massachusetts prison commissioner and a leading advocate of the indeterminate sentence in 1899, "to suppose that any judge can tell in 1900 whether a criminal will or will not be fit to return to the community in 1905."[62]

No doubt the claim that judges were incompetent to fix the right sentence aroused judges' indignation.[63] Making matters worse, state legislatures began to carve away at judicial sentencing authority. Massachusetts helped lead the trend. In 1857 and 1858, long before the Cincinnati Congress, the legislature provided for "statutory good time"—a fixed reduction from the judge's sentence that convicts could earn by their good behavior in prison.[64] In 1880 the legislature granted probation officers the power to recommend the release of any misdemeanant with less than six months left to serve—and authorized the district attorney, in place of the judge, to approve the release under this act of any person sentenced in superior court.[65] An 1884 law permitted the prison commissioners to release virtually any convict they deemed "reformed."[66] The legislature created its first almost-genuine indeterminate sentence in 1886, but since judges could use this sentencing option or not as they pleased, the balance of sentencing power did not shift much.[67] Finally, by acts of 1894 and 1895, the legislature put in place the parole regime that most of us know today as the "indeterminate sentence," which required judges to set minimum and maximum terms when they sent a convict to state prison and gave prison authorities the power to choose a release date between those bounds.[68]

The same English observer I quoted earlier expressed his astonishment at American parole laws, which "violate[d] the fundamental principle that . . . the sentence of the court shall be the final arbitrament of the case."[69] He surmised that these laws sprang in part from a "want of respect for, and confidence in, the State's Judiciary."[70] It is hard to imagine that American judges missed the slight these laws implied. To the extent the gravity of their sentencing power ever had held them back from casting it among the lots of the gaming table, the considered judgment of legislators that the judges' word should not be the last must have weakened their resistance. And the knowledge that another authority would later adjust the sentences of the court must have made it seem at least a little less important to get those sentences exactly right.

Hence both probation and the indeterminate sentence eased judges' principled objections to engaging in plea bargaining. Even as probation officers supplied information that let judges set an appropriate sentence without hearing evidence, the principles of indeterminate sentencing released judges from the obligation to set that sentence with precision. With their moral guard down and with alarming civil caseloads pressing them to cut deals where they could, judges perhaps gave in to temptation and dealt.

PRIDE: THE PLEA-WITHDRAWAL RULE

But how—that is, by what mechanism—did judges deal? How did they communicate to defendants the reward tendered in exchange for their pleas? Several possibilities present themselves.

Implicit Plea Bargaining

For those observers who find any scent of judicial coercion to plead guilty repellant, the least offensive option is "implicit" bargaining. In an implicit-bargaining regime, defendants simply guess, perhaps based on the judge's past practice, that his sentence will be more lenient after a plea than after trial. For an implicit-bargaining regime to account for the very high percentages of guilty pleas that prevailed in the last decades of the nineteenth century, judges must have sentenced in highly predictable ways. After all, without some sound assurance of a reward, so many defendants would not have pled guilty.

Very occasionally, the records do reveal the sort of stark sentencing patterns that might have supported a broad implicit-bargaining regime. The February 1890 session of the Middlesex Superior Court presents perhaps the best example I have seen. Of the twenty defendants who pled guilty to breaking and entering, eight received three-year sentences, and all the rest received less time or no time at all. Of the six defendants convicted of that crime after trial, only one received less than three years (twenty-four months), one got exactly three years, and the four others got substantially more.[71] It seems possible that the court generally adhered to an understood practice that imposed a three-year cap for breaking-and-entering defendants who pled guilty and a three-year floor for such defendants who demanded trial and lost.[72]

But although the last decades of the century were marked by very high rates of guilty pleas across most categories of crime, I have not seen stark sentencing patterns generally. In 1900, for example, fifty-four out of fifty-seven persons charged with breaking and entering pled guilty.[73] Sentences for those who pled guilty ranged from simple filing and probation (thirty cases) to indeterminate sentences in the Massachusetts reformatory or reform school (eleven cases) to house-of-correction time averaging twelve months (thirteen cases). Of the three defendants who lost after trial, one found his case placed on file; one was sentenced to an indeterminate term at the Massachusetts reformatory; and one received twenty months in the house of correction. These results, more typical than the fairly clear pattern I saw in February 1890, suggest that something besides implicit bargaining was at work in persuading so many defendants to plead guilty.

Explicit Promises and Threats

That additional mechanism might have included an explicit promise by the judge to impose a certain sentence if the defendant pled guilty. Perhaps it included as well an explicit threat to impose a certain—or ominously uncertain—higher sentence should the defendant lose after trial. That judges today in many jurisdictions, including Middlesex, bargain directly with defendants or their counsel is beyond dispute.[74] But although there is some evidence of judicial plea bargaining in the late nineteenth century, it is both thin and geographically far-flung. In 1880, for example, the Missouri Supreme Court reported that a trial judge had spoken with the defendant's lawyers and had led them to believe "that if the defendant would plead guilty, he would receive the lowest punishment allowed by law."[75] Similarly, the Michigan Supreme Court in 1884 condemned a trial judge's "imprudent" statement to defense counsel "that, if the respondent should plead guilty, I should view his case as one meriting less punishment than I should feel disposed to impose should he be convicted after a trial by jury."[76] Even in that case, the trial judge insisted that he had uttered the offending words only after firmly rejecting several earlier appeals by the defendant's representatives to predict what he would do in the event of a plea.[77] And in Maine in the 1890s, there is evidence that the justices of the Supreme Judicial Court, who still sat as local trial judges, permitted liquor dealers to avoid further prosecution under the state's prohibition law if they came into court once a year and paid a fine plus costs.[78]

The absence of much other evidence of explicit judicial plea bargaining does not mean that the practice did not take place elsewhere, perhaps even in Massachusetts. The condemnation of the Missouri and Michigan high courts would have encouraged judges to conceal the signs of such deals, just as they do today.[79] Still, lacking all evidence of such goings-on in Massachusetts, not only in court records but also in newspapers and other contemporary sources, I think it best to conclude that explicit judicial plea bargaining did not play a great role in the surge of guilty plea rates that marked Middlesex County court business in the last decades of the nineteenth century.

Accepting the Parties' Recommendation

A third pleading mechanism perhaps proved more potent than implicit plea bargaining in encouraging defendants to plead and yet spared judges the demeaning and disfavored role of hawking a deal. In the simpler version of this deceptively simple technique, the judge merely acceded to the sentencing recommendation of the parties. Although I have no precisely contemporaneous evidence of this process at work, a description given to a committee of the Massachusetts Legislature in 1923 by a former assistant district attorney makes the practice sound well-worn:

> [T]he district attorney and his assistants call in police officers and government witnesses and get their stories. Then defendants' counsel are heard, and then, unless a trial is absolutely unescapable, a crime is disposed of by agreement between counsel and the judge is asked to rubber-stamp the agreement with his O.K. If there is the slightest doubt that he will do so the case goes off the list to await the time when a

judge will be presiding who is not likely to be so independent. . . . The judge has, of course, the power to upset any agreed disposition that comes before him and to make his own full and independent investigation into the case and to use his own judgment, but if he does so he uses up much precious time and embarrasses the district attorney exceedingly. Any judge who has had experience with the administration of the criminal law is likely to follow unhesitatingly the recommendations of a district attorney whose judgment he trusts . . . . [80]

To modern ears, this plea-bargaining technique may sound so simplistic and obvious as hardly to merit the label "technique."[81] Yet its sheer simplicity masks its brilliance. It neatly disposed of four impediments to judicial plea bargaining. First, because all of the haggling over terms took place between counsel and out of the judge's presence, this technique did not dirty judicial hands or sully judicial principle. Second, because the defendant's ability to predict the judge's sentence turned on exactly one aspect of the judge's sentencing practice—whether he did or did not habitually follow the parties' sentencing recommendations—this technique gave defendants far more assurance of a particular sentence in exchange for their pleas than did implicit plea bargaining. As the passage just quoted suggests, lawyers quickly learned which judges presented even "the slightest doubt" that they would go along—and learned to wait for a judge "who [was] not likely to be so independent." Third, unlike prosecutorial charge bargaining of the sort that took place in the liquor cases of the first half-century, this technique did not deprive judges of any of their cherished sentencing power—and therefore posed no threat to their pride. As the prosecutor said, "The judge has, of course, the power to upset any agreed disposition that comes before him . . . ."[82]

Finally, this technique usually protected prosecutors from judicial whimsy. I argued earlier that one disincentive to charge bargaining in murder cases was the prosecutor's lack of dexterity in formulating a precise sentence. It is unlikely that prosecutors happily traded the mandatory death penalty assigned to first-degree murder for the zero-to-twenty-year prison term assigned to manslaughter unless they had some assurance as to where within this range the court's sentence would fall. And yet if the defendant refused to plead to the mandatory life penalty assigned to second-degree murder, there was no other option. A judge's rigid habit of following the parties' sentencing recommendations would have eased the prosecutor's mind.

Something like this appears to have been at work in the 1892 murder prosecution of Raffaele Scorpio. The attorney general reported that the defendant's guilty plea to manslaughter "was accepted on condition that the maximum penalty would be taken without objection." The defendant indeed received a twenty-year term.[83] Although the attorney general's use of the passive voice made it unclear who—prosecutor or judge—"accepted [the plea] on condition" of the maximum sentence, there is little doubt he meant the prosecutor. Although in the last decades of the century, the attorney general tended to write his reports in the passive voice, in earlier decades he regularly noted that "I" accepted the defendant's guilty plea.[84]

For all its brilliance, the technique of simply ratifying the parties' sentencing recommendations suffered from real shortcomings. Under this regime, risk-averse defendants would refuse to plead unless they felt assured that the judge was among those who always "rubber-stamp[ed] the agreement." Any judge who fell outside this group must have faced a stream of litigants who wished only to postpone their business until the judge moved on to another jurisdiction. But to preserve his reputation as one who went along with agreements, the judge had to go along almost all the time. So despite the formal reservation of sentencing power in judges' hands, judges might have felt that the district attorney had stripped them of that power. As the prosecutor just quoted said, "It must irk to be a rubber-stamp."[85] And even if the judge had reconciled himself to this role, some defendants must have felt too mistrustful of his intentions to relinquish their trial right for anything less than a guaranteed concession. At bottom, this system offered the defendant no assurance against unpleasant surprise should the judge decide to disappoint all parties' expectations.

THE MAGIC OF PLEA WITHDRAWAL

A small adjustment to the technique of simply ratifying the parties' recommendations solved these problems without sacrificing the technique's other virtues. Long after the endpoint of this study, the Massachusetts

Rules of Criminal Procedure formalized this adjustment by requiring each trial judge to advise a defendant who pleads guilty under a plea agreement that the judge "will not impose a sentence that exceeds the terms of the [prosecutor's] recommendation without first giving the defendant the right to withdraw his plea."[86]

Note how gracefully this rule would set even the most skittish defendant at ease without imposing any constraint on the trial judge. A judge who wants to encourage defendants to plead guilty need not slavishly bow to prosecutors' sentencing recommendations. She may follow a prosecutor's recommendation—or not, as she pleases. She need merely permit the defendant to withdraw his plea when she disappoints his expectations. The rule therefore erases the prideful concerns of judges who chafed at being the D.A.'s rubber stamp. Yet even as the rule gives judges complete discretion to impose any sentence authorized by law, it grants prosecutors full power to promise defendants an assured concession in exchange for a guilty plea. In a sense, then, and in violation of all the laws of physics, the rule expands the sum total of sentencing power in the criminal courtroom.

It is no wonder that this plea-withdrawal rule or rules like it should have proved widely popular. In 1975 Congress amended Rule 11 of the Federal Rules of Criminal Procedure to embrace the plea-withdrawal technique. The rule now provides that although the judge should not, of course, participate in any plea discussions, the judge must, if she entertains a plea agreement offered under the rule but rejects the parties' recommendation, give the defendant the opportunity to withdraw the plea.[87] Both the American Bar Association and the American Law Institute had recommended such a rule before Congress's action, and several states besides Massachusetts have taken their advice.[88] There can be little doubt that the plea-withdrawal rule has contributed to the extraordinary dominance of plea bargaining in modern American courtrooms, where guilty plea rates above ninety or even ninety-five percent are common.[89]

Tracing the Plea-Withdrawal Rule's Roots

A far harder question is whether this rule—or some version of it—played any part in pushing the guilty plea rate in Middlesex County toward the ninety-percent mark in the closing decades of the nineteenth century.

There are several reasons to think it did not. For one thing, the description of practice from the 1920s quoted earlier gave no hint of ready permission to withdraw one's plea whenever the judge exceeded the district attorney's sentencing recommendation. Even as late as 1976, just a few years before Massachusetts adopted the plea-withdrawal rule as part of its new rules of criminal procedure, the Supreme Judicial Court refused to "break new ground" by requiring a judge to permit plea withdrawal whenever he exceeded the prosecutor's recommendation.[90] More importantly, I have found very little Massachusetts-based evidence of such a rule at work during the time frame of this study. The Supreme Judicial Court repeatedly held in the nineteenth century that plea withdrawal was not a right, but could be permitted or not at the discretion of the court.[91]

But the absence of contemporary evidence of the rule in Massachusetts is perhaps not conclusive, as I have found very little evidence at all of the specific procedures surrounding guilty pleas. None of the Supreme Judicial Court's several opinions on plea withdrawal addressed the situation that concerns us here, in which the defendant sought to withdraw a guilty plea after the court imposed a harsher sentence than the prosecutor recommended.[92] It may be that trial courts routinely permitted withdrawal in such circumstances and that the high court therefore never had cause to review these cases. Moreover, there is good reason to think that trial court records omitted mention of plea withdrawals when they took place. A Lowell newspaper reported an 1835 plea withdrawal that never appeared in the court's official records.[93]

Outside Massachusetts, evidence that the plea-withdrawal rule was in place in the late nineteenth century is compelling, if not conclusive. In 1889 Murat W. Hopkins, an Indiana practitioner, published an article on plea withdrawal in the *Criminal Law Magazine*.[94] Hopkins stated the rule in explicit terms:

> If, by reason of any side agreement with the prosecuting officer, a defendant under a criminal charge enters a plea of guilty, a more severe sentence than that agreed upon should not be awarded; and if a sentence more severe than the one indicated be inflicted, the defendant should be allowed to withdraw his plea of guilty, and plead not guilty, if he desires.[95]

The assurance with which Hopkins announced this formula suggests it was not merely his opinion of what the rule should be, but rather his observation of what the rule was. That his statement of the rule echoed its modern form so exactly is at least some evidence that this was a well-recognized principle and not merely one man's fancy. Yet of the three cases from two states that he cited for support,[96] only a single 1888 opinion of the Indiana Supreme Court supplied a clear precedent for the rule.[97]

My research students and I have searched extensively (if not exhaustively) through the large number of plea-withdrawal cases of the late nineteenth and early twentieth centuries in search of other statements of Hopkins's rule.[98] Although many courts endorsed a liberal attitude toward plea withdrawal generally,[99] we discovered only three that considered the specific question at hand: whether a defendant who pled guilty on the strength of a prosecutor's promised sentencing recommendation had the right to withdraw his plea if the judge exceeded that recommendation. These jurisdictions—Kentucky, Illinois, and Georgia—hardly constitute an American consensus, but it is notable nonetheless that all three endorsed the plea-withdrawal rule more or less as Hopkins stated it.[100]

Despite the meager rewards of our search, I hope that something more than an Eastern bias lies behind my suspicion that an Indiana practitioner's interpretation of an Indiana court's opinion did not alone give rise to a rule that grew to have national influence. For now, though, until further evidence turns up, I must concede that the subtle brilliance of the plea-withdrawal rule and the ease with which it dispatched several of the difficulties inherent in judicial plea bargaining may have come into play only much later in plea bargaining's progress. The point is not critical to our story, for judges could have achieved much of the benefit of the rule merely by accepting as a matter of course the sentencing recommendations of prosecutors. By this simple means, they would have escaped soiling their own hands in the bargaining process and avoided overtly ceding sentencing power to prosecutors even as they offered defendants sufficient assurance against unpleasant surprise to encourage a great number to plead guilty. As we saw earlier, at least by the 1920s a practice of ready judicial acceptance of the prosecutor's negotiated sentences was solidly in place in Massachusetts. This mechanism perhaps helped judges of the late nineteenth century overcome their prideful objections to the practice of plea bargaining just as an avalanche of tort suits threatened to bury their courts.

6

Social and Political Theories of Plea Bargaining's Rise

As this story turns the corner into the twentieth century, the victory of plea bargaining appears largely complete. The desire to see cases plead out rather than go to trial, which had infected public prosecutors almost from their inception, now had spread to judges, whose power to dictate sentences reached much further. Plea bargaining therefore could break loose from the narrow bounds to which prosecutorial charge bargaining once had confined it. Meanwhile, the supposed reform of permitting defendants to testify at trial had left those defendants who had criminal histories with little hope of winning at trial and little choice other than to seek the best plea deal they could get. With all of the system's power-holders now sharing a common interest in plea bargaining, trials grew exceedingly rare. The rate of guilty pleas, which had approached ninety percent in 1900, showed no sign of falling off by 1910.[1] And as we know from the history books, the rest of the century only advanced the dominance of plea bargaining.[2]

In the next chapter, I investigate whether the dynamic of powers and interests that drove the rise of plea bargaining in Massachusetts can explain the course of plea bargaining's progress elsewhere. But before leaving Massachusetts, it is important to consolidate the lessons learned here. The task is especially pressing because two prominent studies, including one rooted in Massachusetts, reach conclusions about the origins of plea bargaining that differ from mine and are attractive in their own right.

Mary Vogel's recent article on the history of plea bargaining in Massachusetts and a somewhat older article by Mike McConville and Chester Mirsky tracing plea bargaining's rise in New York devote far more attention than I do to the role of broader social and political forces. Some hint of the differences in our approaches emerges from the differing importance we give to the role of caseload pressure. I argued in Chapter 2 that rising caseloads operated directly on prosecutors' incentives to plea bargain. Working part-time, early Massachusetts prosecutors found their prosperity depended on shrinking the time they devoted to their prosecutorial duties so they could turn quickly to their more lucrative civil practices. In that context, I presented Vogel's dissenting view on the importance of caseloads. When I take up the history of plea bargaining in New York in the next chapter, I look briefly at McConville and Mirsky's similar dismissal of the role of caseload pressure.

In rejecting the importance of caseload pressure as a motivation in plea bargaining's rise, both Vogel and McConville and Mirsky declare an intention to move beyond an analysis staked in the personal interests of courtroom actors and to embrace a more complex vision of the plea-bargaining dynamic. Often—perhaps usually—taking a broader focus improves the telling of history. I do not believe this is one of those times. The evidence overwhelmingly suggests that plea bargaining was the work of those who labored in the criminal courts and that the course of its rise was a function of their personal interests and systemic power. Though these authors, and particularly Vogel, add richness and color to the story of plea bargaining's rise, and though I could with some ingenuity reconcile my telling with theirs, I think that any gain in color would be a loss in accuracy.

Because Vogel's article is more recent and more far-reaching than McConville and Mirsky's, and because she set her study in Massachusetts, I devote most of this chapter to an examination of her work. It is fair to say that Vogel's study, embracing both her article and an earlier dissertation on the same topic, now stands as the leading social history of plea bargaining. In assessing whether a "social" history—one that looks beyond the courtroom to broader cultural and political forces—is the appropriate discipline for a study of plea bargaining, I will turn to McConville and Mirsky's article when it offers support for Vogel's approach or takes an interestingly different tack of its own.

VOGEL'S CULTURAL AND POLITICAL APPROACH

At the outset, Vogel and I chose two very different bodies of data as the sources for our empirical studies. She conducted her research at the Boston Police Court, which occupied the lowest tier of Boston's judicial system.[3] Unlike the courts of the middle tier, which I studied in Middlesex County, the police court was a nonjury forum that usually operated without a professional prosecutor.

This difference in personnel entirely changed the dynamics of bargaining in the two forums. In the police court, the only authority with the power to grant the defendant a concession in exchange for his guilty plea was the presiding magistrate. That same magistrate also decided the issues of guilt and sentencing should the defendant choose trial. In such a setting, the notion of a plea "bargain" surely meant something very different than in a jury court. Once a police court magistrate told the defendant what he believed the case to be worth, the defendant knew the magistrate could achieve that result equally well after trial as after plea. The independent judgment of a jury could pose no obstacle to the sentence the magistrate intended to impose. In contrast, defendants in the courts of the middle tier could reject a plea offer in the hope of winning an acquittal from a jury and so could engage the authorities in a true bargaining process.

Such concerns about the roles and powers of various courtroom actors, central to my analysis, draw little of Vogel's attention. She sets her work apart from those who focus on "the prosecutor, the police, trial complexity, and crowding in the courts,"[4] and looks instead to the "social structural and institutional context" of plea bargaining.[5] Having concluded from her data that plea bargaining in Boston emerged in the 1830s and 1840s, Vogel focuses on the culture and politics of those decades.

It was a time of riots and unrest, she writes, and Boston's Whig elite found itself striving to regain social order.[6] But it was also a time of broadened voting rights, "which made it likely that state response [to social unrest] would take a form attuned to sustaining the popular consent."[7] The political elite resolved this tension through a pattern of "episodic leniency."[8] By rewarding guilty pleas with sentencing concessions, Boston's magistrates (appointed largely by the Whig power-holders) could secure convictions while dispensing grace and thereby maintain order while winning the voters' consent.[9]

It is an elegant theory, and Vogel richly details the social conflicts and political maneuverings of the day. Such factors no doubt influenced in some ways, great or small, the course of plea bargaining's rise, and at a few junctures in this study I bring the role of social forces to bear. In Chapter 5, for example, I argued that an explosion of mechanized industry and transportation in the late nineteenth century and a resulting flood of personal injury lawsuits helped drive judges into plea bargaining's ranks.[10] But in my analysis, social forces always played an indirect role. They were important to the extent they helped shape the powers or interests of courtroom actors. Vogel's analysis, in contrast, simply forgoes questions about the source of bargaining power and pursues the matter of interests only abstractly. More importantly, the claim of episodic leniency that undergirds her theory stands on very shaky evidence.

EVIDENCE OF EPISODIC LENIENCY

During the 1830s, 1840s, and perhaps 1850s, Vogel claims, the magistrates of Boston's police court dispensed leniency in exchange for guilty pleas and did so noticeably enough to help secure public consent in their law-enforcement mission. Vogel acknowledges one troublesome shortcoming in her evidence. Of the five types of cases she analyzes—drunkenness, being a common drunkard, nightwalking, larceny, and assault and battery—drunkenness cases were by far the most likely to end in guilty pleas.[11] In 1830, when guilty pleas accounted for only 19.1 percent of all pleas in larceny cases and 10.6 percent of all pleas in assault-and-battery cases, they accounted for a full three-quarters of all pleas in drunkenness cases. And although guilty pleas in larceny and assault-and-battery cases advanced notably in 1840, 1850, and 1860, the highest rate observed in these cases never matched even the lowest rate observed in drunkenness cases.[12]

These facts pose difficulties for Vogel's theory of episodic leniency because, as she frankly allows, those convicted of drunkenness appear to have won no leniency in exchange for their guilty pleas. In fact, they seem to have suffered a penalty for pleading guilty, drawing heavier punishments than those convicted after trial.[13] Faced with this discordant evidence, Vogel simply excises drunkenness cases from her theory of episodic leniency. She says it is more important to focus on "crimes against property and the person"—that is, on larceny and assault and battery—because the authorities who promoted the policy of episodic leniency were most concerned with "offenses [that] threatened the security of the goods, buildings, and facilities crucial for growth."[14] But this excision depends on four implausible facts: first, that the authorities believed that *both* larceny and assault and battery threatened the security of goods and buildings more than did drunkenness and that drunkenness did so little or not at all; second, that the authorities did not regard drunkenness itself as a threat to economic growth; third, that episodic leniency resulted in more complete (as opposed to more popular) law enforcement than did the relative harshness shown to drunkenness defendants; and fourth, that the point of episodic leniency—to secure popular consent in law enforcement—was more effectively achieved by showing leniency to thieves and assailants than to accused drunks.

Vogel's theory of episodic leniency meets an even larger empirical obstacle when she attempts to demonstrate its central claim—that the leniency shown to those who pled guilty in larceny and assault-and-battery cases was substantial enough to help win popular consent in law enforcement. Vogel claims that plea bargaining emerged in these cases in the 1830s and 1840s and that "concessions were most strikingly evident in 1840 and 1860."[15] She seems to acknowledge that her argument must fail unless the pattern of leniency was striking enough for the public to notice.

Table 6.1 reprints Vogel's analysis of sentencing concessions in the relevant years. The table compares the fates of those who pled guilty and those who were found guilty after trial along three dimensions: the likelihood of imprisonment versus fine, the length of any confinement, and

6.1.

Outcomes in Selected Case Types: Boston Police Court, 1840–1860

	LARCENY		ASSAULT AND BATTERY	
	PLED GUILTY	LOST AT TRIAL	PLED GUILTY	LOST AT TRIAL
1840				
% Imprisoned	80	70	0	7
% Fined	20	30	100	93
Avg. Term of Imprisonment[a]	3.5	4.0	N/A	6.0
Avg. Fine	$3.67	$4.58	$3.36	$3.54
1850				
% Imprisoned	31	38	11	18
% Fined	69	63	89	82
Avg. Term of Imprisonment[a]	2.4	2.5	—	—
Avg. Fine	$6.25	$6.33	$4.71	$3.63
1860				
% Imprisoned	36	38	9	14
% Fined	64	62	91	86
Avg. Term of Imprisonment[a]	4.0	2.5	2.0	3.5
Avg. Fine	$4.67	$9.71	$6.20	$4.46

SOURCE: Vogel, "Social Origins," 184, 189.
[a]Measured in months.

the size of any fine.[16] As Vogel suggests, the numbers show a pattern of lower penalties for those who pled guilty in larceny and assault-and-battery cases. Across eighteen points of comparison (three years *times* two crimes *times* three sentencing variables), the results suggest leniency for guilty pleas in twelve instances and a premium in only four.

But the benefits of pleading guilty were very small. On average—across crimes and across years, weighing each cell in the diagram equally—a guilty plea reduced the defendant's chances of going to prison from thirty-one percent to twenty-eight percent; reduced the average term of imprisonment from 3.7 to 3.0 months; and reduced the average fine from $5.38 to $4.81. Even if we focus on the two years in which, Vogel says, "[c]oncessions were most strikingly evident"—1840 and 1860—the concessions seem small. In these two years, pleading guilty to larceny or assault and battery reduced the chances of going to prison from thirty-two to thirty-one percent; reduced the average term of imprisonment from 4.0 to 3.2 months; and reduced the average fine from $5.57 to $4.48.[17] Because serious offenders might have been more likely to choose trial than were less serious offenders (a possibility Vogel allows),[18] the small margin of leniency shown here may reflect the relative seriousness of offenses rather than a reward for pleading guilty. In any event, absent evidence of episodic leniency more perceptible to the public, Vogel's arguments about its significance in explaining plea bargaining's rise must stand without empirical support.

EVIDENCE OF PLEA BARGAINING'S PUBLIC POPULARITY

Here I pursue one branch of Vogel's analysis further because other scholars have echoed the point and because it has a certain intuitive appeal. Plea bargaining arose in part, Vogel argues, because the voting public liked it. Its familiarity and accessibility won it support: "The plea bargain, in its customary simplicity, was more knowable (or 'cognoscible' in Bentham's term) than the arcana of common law—and so drew citizens into a relationship with a comprehensible state by clarifying what the law proscribed, the menu of costs associated with any breach, and facilitating a grasp of the consequences of those actions."[19]

In their study of the rise of guilty pleas in New York, McConville and Mirsky likewise point to the political popularity of plea bargaining as a factor in explaining its growth. They write that plea bargaining "avoided the discontent that imprisonment for convictions of the full indictment would engender among the immigrant underclass, who, under the movement for universal suffrage, had become part of the newly formed electorate."[20]

Public Knowledge of Plea Bargaining

Such arguments about plea bargaining's popularity demand evidence that the public knew about plea bargaining. Though McConville and Mirsky do not undertake such proof, Vogel does, and she points specifically to three signs of public awareness. First is a phenomenon Vogel terms "mirroring":[21] She says that in larceny and assault-and-battery cases, defendants more readily pled guilty when authorities more readily granted concessions in exchange—that is, defendants "mirrored" concessions with guilty pleas. "This mirroring," Vogel writes, "demonstrates that not only was a 'bargaining' process in place by 1840 but also that institutionalization was underway whereby members of the public, aware of concessions being granted, varied the frequency with which they individually pled guilty."[22] But evidence of mirroring speaks only to *defendants'* knowledge of concessions granted for pleas, and defendants—sometimes aided by counsel's advice—surely knew more about plea bargaining than the public at large. It would be hard to imagine a system of plea bargaining in which defendants did not more readily plead guilty when greater concessions were offered. Vogel's argument reduces, therefore, to a claim that all plea bargaining must be publicly known.[23]

Next, Vogel points to a monograph of courtroom vignettes published in 1837 by the court reporter of the *Boston Morning Post*.[24] "While not making too much of it," Vogel notes that the reporter used the term "bargain" to describe the practice we know as plea bargaining, and she suggests that this usage reflects a public awareness of the practice.[25] I have read through this 250-page volume with some care and have come across only three uses of the term "bargain." Two of these concerned merchandise sales.[26] In the third, the reporter wrapped up his account of an assault-and-battery case with these words: "After the case was proved against Toupet beyond all hope of defence, he retracted his plea of not guilty, paid a fine of $5.00 and costs, and departed pretty well satisfied with his end of the bargain."[27] Not only does the reporter's use of the idiom, "his end of the bargain," fall far short of proof that the notion of a plea bargain was abroad in the community, but the timing of the defendant's plea—apparently after the government had put in its case at trial—removes this case far from the mainstream of plea bargains.

Finally, citing only the legislature's report on its 1845 investigation into Asahel Huntington's charge-bargaining practices, Vogel claims that "public knowledge" of the use of plea bargaining to advance public policy "was widespread and the practice met with public approval."[28] Vogel is surely right that the Huntington inquiry did not escape public notice. But the only hint in the legislative record that the *public* (as opposed to the legislature) knew about Huntington's charge-bargaining practices was this highly partisan and apparently unpublished claim made in 1844 by Representative Cyrus Washburn, who first lodged the legislative complaint against Asahel Huntington for plea bargaining:

> [T]here is now and has been for some time past a common & current report among a large portion of the People of this Commonwealth that Asahel Huntington . . . is and has been guilty of malpractice . . . by receiving of Defendants in cases of prosecutions of Commonwealth against violators of laws regulating the sale of spirituous liquors, and others, sums of money much less than that which the statute laws fix[] . . . and thereby discharging the said Defendants in his own responsibility without a trial.[29]

Washburn almost certainly overstated the public's "common and current" attention to Huntington's plea bargaining. Perhaps he spoke from his bias against Huntington, or perhaps he spoke as an Essex County lawyer in whose small circle Huntington's doings loomed large.[30] In any event, Washburn's claim does not square with news accounts of the Huntington affair, which seem to have avoided the topic of plea bargaining almost entirely.

The *Lowell Daily Courier*, one of the most important surviving Middlesex County newspapers,[31] devoted considerable attention to the Huntington story, but made only the merest mention of plea bargaining. "Wonders will never cease," began the first of at least nine separate news items, six of them substantial, that the *Courier* devoted to the Huntington affair.[32] "Who would have thought yesterday that the subject under discussion in the House to-day would have been upon a grave charge of official misconduct against the able and distinguished District Attorney." The author said nothing of the charges themselves, however, though he assured his readers that they would "if true . . . seriously affect [Huntington's] standing in the community."[33] Another item on the same page summarized the charges in such a way that the more sensational charge of corruption simply swallowed up any reference to plea bargaining: Washburn had charged Huntington "with mal-practice in relation to the law granting licenses for retailing spirituous liquors, receiving money from prosecutions, from various individuals, and not accounting for the same, or paying the same into the Treasury of the Commonwealth, thereby *defrauding* the Commonwealth."[34]

A few days later the *Courier* reprinted the *Salem Register*'s condemnation of Washburn's "grave accusations of official misconduct,"[35] yet again made no reference to plea bargaining. Months passed with only two tiny notices of the investigation.[36] Then the *Courier* reprinted another attack by the *Register* on the "miserable, skulking and groundless" charges against Huntington, sustained by testimony that "would not convict a dog."[37] Though the paper noted that Huntington had "submitted a few remarks in explanation of his course," it again said not a word about plea bargaining.[38]

Finally, in its third-to-last notice of the affair and almost a year after the first, the *Courier* for the first and last time mentioned what is for us the real object of concern. In an article devoted not to the legislature's inquiry but to a related grand jury proceeding, a single sentence appears near the bottom: "These complaints, it is well known, refer to the compromises made by Mr. Huntington with the liquor-sellers, by which they paid sums of money to the Commonwealth in order to be relieved from their indictments."[39]

Perhaps these charges were "well known," but the balance of the evidence suggests otherwise. Each of the other news items referred in hushed tones to scandalous allegations of graft, very much unlike this matter-of-fact mention of Huntington's self-acknowledged dealings with liquor merchants. Less than three weeks later, when the *Courier* printed its last account of the legislature's investigation, it once again dismissed the charges as lacking "any foundation in fact" and as a mere "malicious attempt to injure the character and usefulness of one of the worthiest and best men in the State" and once again made no reference to plea bargaining.[40]

If we back away for a moment from the Huntington affair and search more generally, we find almost no evidence of public awareness of plea bargaining. I have cast a very broad net—topically, chronologically, geographically—in search of public notices about plea bargaining and related practices. In an extensive newspaper search that skipped across the century and focused in particular on the 1830s and 1840s—a period that Vogel, Theodore Ferdinand, and I all agree to be critical—I found no prominent mention of plea bargaining before District Attorney Albert Nelson's 1847 announcement of his pleading terms.[41] There was, it is true, the occasional bit of courthouse news that said almost in passing that a slate of liquor defendants had "submitted, and paid their fines and costs."[42] But there was little to suggest that the public had a real awareness of plea bargaining.

Nor was the Nelson notice the first of many pointed references. On the contrary, it was one of astonishingly few that I found in print anywhere in the nineteenth century outside of court reporters and legislative documents.[43] Nor have I ever, in any nineteenth-century source, seen the term *plea bargaining.* Even when I have looked specifically for commentary about particularly notable events in our story, I have found nothing of note. For example, although the *Lowell Journal* reported extensively on Barney Goulding's killing of his wife in Lowell in 1848,[44] it apparently ignored altogether his guilty plea and sentencing. Yet Goulding's may have been the first plea-bargained murder case in Middlesex history.

In fact, the blinkered reporting of the Huntington episode highlights what may seem at first to be an odd incongruity in my evidence. Even while the public remained largely uninformed about plea bargaining in the courts, legislators not only knew about it, but acted on it—investigating Huntington's handling of liquor cases in 1844, barring prosecutorial nol prosses in liquor cases in 1852, and forbidding the filing of such cases in 1865. Perhaps one explanation is that many of the legislators—including Cyrus Washburn, who first complained against Huntington—were lawyers and therefore unusually aware of goings-on in court. Another explanation may be that newspaper editors thought the public would not much care about plea bargaining even if legislators did.

But the most likely explanation is that legislative attention to plea bargaining simply was incidental to its concern with liquor law enforcement, probably the most enduring political issue in nineteenth-century Massachusetts. After all, the temperance movement, unlike plea bargaining, prompted substantial news pieces—sometimes whole columns long—in almost every issue of almost every newspaper.[45] And even as the legislature took up the problem of plea bargaining in liquor cases three different times, it apparently took no notice of plea bargaining in murder cases, although almost half of all murder prosecutions in the 1860s ended in clear plea bargains. The public surely was concerned about liquor laws and their enforcement. It simply did not know as much about the mechanics of that enforcement as did its elected representatives.

Evidence the Public Liked Plea Bargaining

Difficult as it is to find evidence of public awareness of plea bargaining, it is even harder to find evidence that the public thought well of the practice. Yet Vogel's theory, like McConville and Mirsky's, depends on the public's approval of plea bargaining. I have found some evidence of *disapproval* of practices *related* to plea bargaining. In 1841 the *Courier* called it "a very miserable piece of business" when a Boston constable let a thief go in exchange for information about where he had hidden the goods.[46] Others apparently agreed, for the constable was indicted for breach of duty.[47] In 1866 a Boston newspaper took to task those crime victims who compromised with criminals for return of their property: "This is all wrong,—wrong in itself, and wrong because it operates as an encouragement to crime, and a discouragement to industry, and as a weakener of the rights of property."[48] These practices were not plea bargains, however, because the defendants never pled and the court never passed judgment.

In New York, where McConville and Mirsky base their claim of the electoral benefits of plea bargaining, the practice's press was bad. In 1865 the *New York Times* denounced plea bargaining by the local prosecutor's office, especially in crimes of violence, and suggested that plea bargaining was to blame for the city's high crime rate:

> It is a growing custom with the District-Attorney to accept a plea of guilty of a minor offense from a party indicted for a high crime. . . . We cease to be startled at the frightful record of bloody affrays or violent robberies which the daily papers present, when we see that criminals seldom receive the punishment due to their crimes, but are let loose to tell their comrades how easy it is to escape justice in New-York.[49]

In other scattered references to plea bargaining in this time frame, the *Times* repeatedly portrayed the practice as a bar to good law enforcement.[50] And by the 1880s, as Carolyn Ramsey has found, the New York public "associated plea-bargaining with undue lenience toward defendants."[51]

In defense of Vogel's and McConville and Mirsky's theories, one might argue that plea bargaining could have won votes even without broad public approval so long as individual defendants left court gratified by their bargains and prepared to vote or to influence others who would. I have come across occasional evidence that defendants reacted—or were thought to react—in this way, though the earliest I have seen is from New York and is dated 1869. Defendants whom the district attorney never prosecuted, the *New York Times* surmised, "naturally feel grateful for this forbearance, and depraved though they may be, appreciating the purity of [the district attorney's] motives, testify their gratitude by working for him at elections."[52] A similarly cynical Bostonian told a meeting of the Massachusetts Temperance Alliance in 1885 that "the district attorney is omnipotent and need not prosecute any liquor dealer . . . if the defendant can control a few votes." Yet the Boston speaker's next remarks—that "District Attorney Stevens is efficient against the friendless, unefficient among politicians" and that he "is, indeed, the tool of the criminal classes"—suggest that there were in fact few votes to be gained by plea bargaining.[53]

Moreover, this speaker specifically addressed the on-file method of case disposition. On-file plea bargaining, which involved no immediate penalty at all, was a far more gentle way to treat influential liquor dealers than the charge-bargaining technique practiced by Middlesex prosecutors in the first half of the nineteenth century. It is hard to believe that the liquor license defendants whom Huntington or Train snagged with one of their multicount indictment forms and who submitted to one or more charges to escape the full force of the district attorney's volley left court eager to stump for him on election day. Nor is it likely that the district attorney would have traded the goodwill of the defendant's law-abiding neighbors, who regarded their local speakeasy merchants as pests, to gain the uncertain and tainted support of the barkeeps he hauled into court.

A district attorney of Huntington's day who wished to curry favor with a potential liquor defendant had a better route—both milder and quieter—than to bring public charges and then bargain them away: He could contrive to avoid an indictment. In 1843, for example, Huntington found himself confronted with the demands of angry neighbors that he prosecute a local selectman who dealt liquor for his bread:

> Dear Sir,
>
> I wish to trouble you once more with complaints respecting the Licence Laws; we have now a hard case the chairman of our Board of Select men Capt. Moses Phipps, has a store in the south part of this town where ardent spirit is continually being sold without licence, & it is quite a source of annoyance to the neighbourhood & they have requested me to communicate with you upon the subject.
>
> This may well be termed spirit-ual wickedness in high places. Mr. Phipps is a man of property & influence, but his influence is not always for good, he was once indicted for selling without licence & it cost him something, but that did not make him obedient, & people think it time to try him once more.
>
> I have been furnished with a long list of witnesses, & you will do well perhaps to summon them all, some are the buyers & drinkers, & some are those who have seen it put up for them; I know not the tenor of their testimony but it is said that people buy by the glass & drink at the store, or by the quantity to carry away. . . .
>
> Please keep my name out of sight, & oblige:
>
> > Yours truly,
> >
> > John A. Fitch[54]

Huntington dutifully summoned before the grand jury a flock of witnesses, including most or all of those Fitch named, but the grand jury declined to indict.[55]

Today, the failure of a grand jury to return an indictment is often, perhaps usually, a sign that the prosecutor did not want an indictment. I have no evidence that a grand jury of the 1840s, like a grand jury today, "would indict a ham sandwich."[56] But as early as 1893 we can find in the pages of the *Harvard Law Review* the complaint that "the grand jury is, in practice, mere clay in the hands of the prosecuting officer."[57] It is fair to suppose that another half-century earlier, Huntington typically could secure an indictment when he wanted one. Failing to do so was surely a more politic way to do a selectman a favor than to hit him with a multi-count indictment form and publicly cut a deal.[58]

The theory that plea bargaining was politically popular suffers not only from a lack of evidence that plea bargaining garnered political support, but also from solid contrary evidence that those who most needed political support did what they could to kill plea bargaining in liquor cases. The office of district attorney became elective only in 1856.[59] Yet even as unelected district attorneys perfected multicount liquor-indictment forms as plea-bargaining tools, elected legislators contrived to frustrate their use. In 1852, as we have seen, the legislature effectively halted charge bargaining in liquor cases by banning nol prosses except with the approval of the court. There is little reason to think that the legislature acted without the specific intent to kill prosecutorial plea bargaining. Although I have not found reference to this part of the law in the surviving legislative records, we can gather something of the legislature's intent from its persistence in maintaining the nol pros ban in its 1855 and 1869 reenactments of the prohibition law.[60] These reenactments followed long after it was clear that the ban had snuffed out prosecutorial charge bargaining of the pre-1852 variety.

We find stronger proof of the legislature's distaste for prosecutorial plea bargaining in the steps it took to kill the one form of prosecutorial plea bargaining in liquor cases that survived the 1852 law. As I reported in Chapter 3, in 1865 a series of witnesses disclosed to a legislative committee that prosecutors were placing cases on file to get around the nol pros ban.[61] The legislature promptly passed the "Act to Prevent Evasions," which provided that no liquor case "shall be laid on file or disposed of except by trial" without the court's approval.[62] Thereafter, the legislature remained vigilant, reenacting its bar against filing liquor cases in 1869 and 1885 and effectively banning prosecutorial plea bargaining in such cases for the balance of the nineteenth century.[63]

The Role of Conviction Statistics

Although Vogel cannot, I believe, sustain her claim that plea bargaining in Massachusetts was politically popular, she does point to another political mechanism that might have moved Massachusetts prosecutors to plea bargain when they could. Vogel notes that in 1832 the legislature demanded that local prosecutors file regular reports on the outcomes of their cases. She rightly supposes that prosecutors had reason to exaggerate their record of success—and had greater reason to do so after their offices became elective in 1856.[64] Earlier I quoted a district attorney (and future governor) who boasted in 1844 that he had handled 523 cases in the previous year and that "[t]he number of *acquittals* by the verdicts of juries [was just] *four*."[65] But though this district attorney repeated his boast elsewhere,[66] he did not bother to distinguish those convictions he achieved after a plea from those (perhaps far fewer) he won after trial. No doubt this prosecutor and others like him valued the reticence of their reports to the state, which, except in the 1860s, never distinguished between these two very different sorts of victories.

These reports, therefore, are not evidence of plea bargaining's political popularity, but of the opposite; not evidence of the public's awareness of plea bargaining, but of the opposite; and not evidence of the popularity of extending leniency to some criminal defendants, but of the opposite. That prosecutors seem to have found political advantage in reporting high conviction rates and in obscuring how they won them suggests that the public preferred severity to leniency and full convictions to bargained deals. These reports cannot support Vogel's or McConville and Mirsky's claims of broader social, cultural, or political forces at work in the rise of plea bargaining. They are instead evidence that individual prosecutors found personal and political advantage in securing the easy victories plea bargaining afforded. For all these reports suggest, prosecutors believed that the more clandestinely they could secure those victories, the better.

In disputing the role that Vogel and McConville and Mirsky assign to broad social and political forces in shaping plea bargaining's rise, I do not mean to insist that such impulses played no role at all. Any major role is not obvious, however, and probably could not have taken exactly the shape these authors suggest. More importantly, even absent the social and political impulses that perhaps buffeted plea bargaining this way or that over time, plea bargaining probably would have progressed along more or less the same course. That is, the dynamic of powers and interests that I have traced out over the last several chapters is enough, I believe, standing alone, to explain the course of plea bargaining's progress. Any institution that so well served the interests of each of the system's powerholders was destined in time to rise up and overrun other, less congenial mechanisms of justice.

7

Explaining Plea Bargaining's Progress Elsewhere

Plea bargaining entered the twentieth century with all the staying power that comes from serving the interests of power. Its course throughout the century proved to be one of consolidation of power, as institutions that might have threatened the dominance of plea bargaining fell by the wayside and others that fed its preeminence took hold. In the next two chapters, I will trace the progress of plea bargaining in the twentieth century. Now it is important to apply more broadly the lessons of its rise in the nineteenth century. For this study of Middlesex County will be of little use unless we can be sure that the principles of power and interest that steered the course of plea bargaining's rise there operated in other times and places.

I do not mean that we should expect to find plea bargaining dominant throughout time or ascending along the same trajectory everywhere. The particular posture of institutional actors in Massachusetts—the statutes that constrained their powers and the caseloads they faced—had no exact twin anywhere else, and for every change to one of these features of our story, we can expect to find a corresponding change in the plot line. That is, if prosecutors lacked the good fortune of a rigid penalty scheme and an unregulated power to nol pros, then we would not expect to see charge bargaining of the sort that Massachusetts prosecutors devised in liquor and murder cases. And if judges lacked the incentive of caseload pressure, then we would not expect to find them setting aside their principled and prideful objections to bartering away defendants' rights and sharing sentencing authority with prosecutors.

In this brief foray into other times and places, then, I ask only two questions: Who stood to gain from plea bargaining, and did those actors have the power to make it happen? I hope to learn only whether the dynamic of powers and interests at work in Middlesex can help explain the absence of plea bargaining where it was lacking and its success where it thrived. There is a certain randomness to this survey, as it depends largely on empirical research of others, who may or may not have been concerned to detect plea bargaining and whose interests may not have raised the same questions that I have pursued. Moreover, there simply are very few in-depth empirical examinations of old court records, and most, like mine, focus on a fairly narrow swath of time and space—and not all on the same swath. The analysis that follows consequently must reach across both time and distance to seek out common elements in the dynamic of plea bargaining.

THE ABSENCE OF PLEA BARGAINING IN EARLIER TIMES

We may begin by asking why plea bargaining appeared only recently on the penal landscape. Of course, we cannot be sure that it did. My figures from Middlesex County show that guilty pleas were by no means uncommon in the late eighteenth century, the earliest period I studied. I argued in Chapter 2 that these early guilty pleas probably were not plea bargains in the sense that the defendant won some understood concession in exchange for his plea,[1] but rather gestures of remorse or hopelessness or unsecured bids for judicial mercy. Still, other observers might read the data differently. As I know of no substantial empirical study of pleading practice in American criminal courts before the nineteenth century, there is no way to conclude with assurance that plea bargaining had no American foothold before then.

The understanding that plea bargaining is a latter-day phenomenon emerges more from English than American studies and most particularly from the work of Malcolm Feeley and John Langbein. They are among the very few to have looked for evidence of plea bargaining in eighteenth-century English court records.[2] Neither Feeley nor Langbein found any sign of plea bargaining at London's Old Bailey court. They argue that the very unmodern brevity of eighteenth-century trials, a handful of which fit into the average court day, removed modern temptations to shortcut trial procedures with rough-and-ready plea bargains.[3] Feeley reports that the landscape began to change in the late nineteenth century, when the length of the average trial at the Old Bailey more than doubled just as large numbers of criminal cases began to end in guilty pleas.[4] In this respect, his evidence accords with my own findings in Massachusetts in the 1890s, when both the length of the average murder trial and the proportion of murder cases ending in plea bargains increased sharply.

Examining the English Evidence

I agree with Feeley and Langbein that there was little or no plea bargaining at the Old Bailey in the eighteenth century—my own review of that court's business in 1715 and 1774 confirms as much. I am less inclined to agree that brevity of trials was the cause. That is in part because other evidence, which I will discuss shortly, reveals clear traces of plea bargaining in this era and yet no sign of unusually long trials. More importantly, there is an explanation for the general absence of plea bargaining that is so powerful as to eliminate the need for any other. Except in state trials such as treason, no public prosecutor took part in eighteenth-century criminal cases. Parliament did not institute public prosecutors to manage ordinary felony cases until 1879.[5] In the eighteenth century, no matter how serious the case, crime victims or their survivors managed the prosecution. And not until the very end of the eighteenth century did any substantial proportion of crime victims hire private lawyers to manage the proceedings in court.[6]

My work in Middlesex makes it plain that public prosecutors were the most important actors in the early days of plea bargaining. They had, first of all, the incentives to bargain. They wanted to win, and their workload pressures and part-time status made them want to win quickly. And they had, in limited contexts, the power to bargain. Whatever their incentives, crime victims in eighteenth-century English courts simply lacked the plea-bargaining power of Massachusetts prosecutors. In particular, they lacked the nol pros. The only officer in the kingdom with the authority to enter a nol pros and terminate prosecution was the attorney general.[7] As the attorney general appeared only in the occasional case of treason or other offense against the state, there normally was no authority in the courtroom who could summarily end the prosecution or reduce the charges in exchange for the defendant's guilty plea.

Given the utter lack of prosecutorial bargaining power in most cases, the absence of plea bargaining perhaps should not surprise us. And yet the Massachusetts experience suggests that the will to bargain often led to the way. Crime victims in eighteenth-century England probably had the will to bargain, as they had at least three incentives to do so. The first was money. Victims had to front the often considerable cost of transporting witnesses and lodging them near the court. Even if the court later reimbursed these expenses, the short-term hardship to many victims must have been great. The second incentive was time. Even if individual trials flashed by, victims and their witnesses had to travel to the court and then wait hours and perhaps days for their cases to be called—and time cost money, both in lost income and in extra nights' lodging for witnesses. The third was risk of loss. More than one-third of prosecutions mounted at London's Old Bailey in the eighteenth century ended in acquittals.[8]

Whether for these reasons or others, crime victims did bargain in ways that their limited powers permitted. Even without the nol pros, they had one way to reward those defendants who chose to bargain. They could fail to show up for trial and thereby guarantee that the court would find the defendant not guilty.[9] That victims sometimes accepted cash from defendants in exchange for their nonappearance is clear.[10] Measuring the frequency of such bargains is difficult. Victims abandoned prosecution in about five percent of cases before the Old Bailey in 1715 and in about two percent of cases in 1774, but whether they did so in exchange for payment or for some other reason does not appear in the case reports. Moreover, any bargains that took place *before* charges were filed do not show up in the case reports at all. In any event, this was a clumsy sort of bargaining, with narrow application. Victims of serious crimes presumably wanted more justice than they could get in cash from often destitute defendants. Moreover, authorities condemned this way of resolving cases as against the public interest.[11] Indeed, settling—or "compounding"—felonies out of court was itself a crime.[12]

There was a more nuanced way for crime victims to use the power to abandon prosecution, but it was not possible in every case—and it required some sophistication to devise and carry off. The French jurist Charles Cottu wrote of the "incredible transaction[s]" he witnessed in English forgery cases in the early nineteenth century.[13] Cottu explained that lawyers for the victimized banks would seek two indictments against each alleged forger. One indictment charged the capital crime of forgery, and the other charged the noncapital offense of possessing false notes with the intent to utter. Cottu reported that defendants who pled guilty to the noncapital offense were sentenced by the court to be transported to an Australian penal colony. When the capital forgery charge then proceeded to trial, counsel for the bank would announce that he had no witness, and the jury would acquit the defendant as a matter of course.

The banks' lawyers showed the same kind of ingenuity in their role as private prosecutors that public prosecutors in Massachusetts showed in cobbling together plea-bargaining regimes with the unlikely tools at hand. Just as Massachusetts prosecutors overcame their limited power to dictate sentences, so the banks' lawyers made the best of the one sentencing tool they had—abandoning prosecution. But this practice was unlikely to spread much beyond forgery cases. Not all crimes lent themselves to multiple indictments, and not all crime victims could afford lawyers to think up clever plea-bargaining techniques. Cottu's account suggests that plea bargaining was rare in this era in England not because there was no incentive to bargain—for the banks' lawyers apparently thought there was—but because private prosecutors generally lacked the legal tools and know-how to devise a plea-bargaining regime.

The absence of public prosecutors in England readily explains the general lack of prosecutorial charge bargaining of the sort seen in Massachusetts. Their absence also goes some distance toward explaining the lack of judicial sentence bargaining. Nineteenth-century Massachusetts judges rarely, if ever, took part directly in negotiating plea bargains. Instead, it appears they participated in plea bargaining mainly by ratifying the sentencing recommendations of the parties—a technique that spared them the indignity of bartering in public. But in England, before the advent of regular public prosecutors in the late nineteenth century, judges had no such curtain behind which they could pull the levers of power. In London's Old Bailey, the court that Feeley and Langbein studied most closely, judges' actions were particularly exposed to scrutiny. That court's business was recorded in sometimes striking detail in the *Old Bailey Sessions Paper*, which enjoyed both a popular and an official readership.[14] Even judges who had the power and the incentive to plea bargain might have hesitated before so publicly trimming their workdays by trimming the rituals of justice.

In pointing to the absence of public prosecutors, therefore, I perhaps have said enough to explain the general absence of plea bargaining at the Old Bailey in the eighteenth century. Still, it is worth noting that the bench of the Old Bailey also appears to have lacked any strong incentive to plea bargain. Between 1715 and 1774, the court's caseload grew only from 495 to 697—a rate of well below one percent per year. Even if one considers the increasing length of trials—from an average of about one-fifth of a court day in 1715 to about one-third of a day in 1775—the increase in total case pressure over the course of three generations was rather mild.[15] Nor does it seem that English judges of the eighteenth century faced an explosion of civil cases like that encountered by Massachusetts judges of the late nineteenth century.[16] From all that appears, Old Bailey judges in this era had no particular motive to plea bargain.

The Manchester Evidence

If we now travel some 150 miles north of the Old Bailey, we can examine the business of a court that had a very different caseload and that operated in relative obscurity, far from the glare of the *Old Bailey Sessions Paper* or anything resembling it. The magistrates in and near Manchester presided at that town's court of quarter sessions, where various minor offenses were tried. Some years back, I studied the business of this court during the last quarter of the eighteenth century. Though my purpose at the time was to investigate changing modes of punishment, I stumbled upon unmistakable evidence of judicial plea bargaining.

This evidence emerges from the sentencing pattern in cases of petty larceny, which accounted for between seventy and eighty-three percent of all cases heard.[17] The magistrates had discretion to punish petty larceny with either seven-year terms of transportation or up to two years in the house of correction. In the years that I sampled between 1774 and 1797, they passed sentence on 516 petty larcenists. Of the 369 who had chosen trial and lost, the justices sentenced 170, or almost half, to transportation. But of the 147 who had pled guilty, the justices sentenced *not one* to transportation and instead incarcerated all but a few.[18] As the average house-of-correction term for petty larceny never much exceeded nine months,[19] and as the prospect of a dangerous ocean-crossing and seven years abroad terrified many defendants, the justices' concession in imposing prison terms rather than transportation must have been more than enough to induce many defendants to plead guilty.

I have read many accounts of the court's business published in the *Manchester Mercury*, one of the leading local papers. The *Mercury* reported in a summary way on the goings-on in court, but supplied none of the factual or procedural detail of the *Old Bailey Sessions Paper*.[20] Typically, it noted only the names of those called before the court, whether they were convicted or acquitted, and the sentence imposed. The magistrates therefore could feel secure that their bargaining practices, which emerge clearly on close examination of the court's records, perhaps escaped public notice and almost certainly escaped the attention of national authorities.

Unfortunately, the utter lack of public comment on the justices' bargaining practices means that scholars, too, lack information about the motive behind the method. Here again, the court's records shed light. At the same time that the practice of plea bargaining was advancing dramatically, the court's caseload was growing at a daunting pace, quadrupling in the course of a generation (see Table 7.1).

Although it seems very likely that Manchester's magistrates began plea bargaining in petty larceny cases to help relieve the pressure of mounting caseloads, I do not believe they acted solely for this reason. It is possible they had as well a principled basis for their bargaining. As a group, the magistrates believed ardently in prison reform and regarded prison as a means of rehabilitation.[21] They may have believed that those defendants who confessed their guilt were better subjects for a reformatory prison regimen than those who contested guilt at trial. Such a belief would help

7.1.

Guilty Pleas in Cases of Petty Larceny at the Manchester (Salford)
Court of Quarter Sessions

YEARS	NUMBER OF PERSONS CONVICTED	NUMBER OF GUILTY PLEAS	PERCENTAGE OF GUILTY PLEAS
1774–1775	42	3	7%
1781–1782	48	8	17%
1786–1787	109	25	23%
1791–1792	143	31	22%
1796–1797	174	80	46%

SOURCE: Fisher, "Birth of the Prison," 1276 table 10.

NOTE: The Quarter Sessions Order Books, which are the only comprehensive and convenient record of the business of the Manchester court, present convictions but not acquittals (Fisher, "Birth of the Prison," 1249 n.49). This chart reflects petty larceny convictions only. Total convictions (including those for petty larceny) increased from 55 in 1774–1775 to 199 in 1796–1797 (ibid., 1252 n.62 table 5).

account for the large jump in the proportion of guilty pleas that (with some delay) followed the opening in 1790 of the magistrates' new house of correction, designed and operated according to the most modern reforming principles.[22] The magistrates may have wanted to fill their innovative prison with the most promising subjects for reform. As in Middlesex, then, we find that the bench responded both to caseload pressure and to more principled concerns about the purposes of sentencing.

Despite such moments of recognition, this short tour through eighteenth-century England has taken us past scenes that look quite unlike nineteenth-century Massachusetts. But these differences do not undermine the lessons that emerged from Middlesex County. If plea bargaining was rare in England before the late nineteenth century, so too were the conditions that fueled plea bargaining's rise in Middlesex. In the Old Bailey, where plea bargaining was wanting, we find that the relevant actors lacked either the power or the incentive to bargain. But where plea bargaining does poke through the historical record—as it does in Cottu's account of forgery prosecutions in the early nineteenth century—we find behind the record a prosecutor with a motive to deal who contrived to find the power. And where we can find magistrates who had an incentive to bargain and the discretion to shape sentences—as we do in Manchester's busy court—we find them at work striking deals.

PLEA BARGAINING'S RISE ELSEWHERE IN AMERICA

Our task now is to examine whether these same principles of power and interest can help explain the course of plea bargaining's rise in U.S. jurisdictions outside Massachusetts. Here the inquiry must focus on two states, California and New York, because I have found no substantial empirical study of sentencing practices before the twentieth century in any other jurisdiction. Fortunately, California and New York provide a useful sampling—one state far removed from Massachusetts both geographically and in cultural and economic development, and one state very much the same. In California, plea bargaining progressed more slowly than in Massachusetts, while in New York it advanced faster. The information at hand is limited, so my conclusions cannot be certain. But all signs suggest that both California's late start and New York's precociousness trace to the different bundles of powers and interests held by each courtroom actor.

California

Lawrence Friedman and Robert Percival's study of Alameda County[23] supplies most of what we know about criminal practice in California in the late nineteenth and early twentieth centuries. Their critical findings emerge from a sampling of superior-court case files from between 1880 and 1910 (see Table 7.2).

Three aspects of these figures stand out. First, the proportion of guilty pleas of all sorts was growing steadily and modestly from twenty-two percent between 1880 and 1889, to twenty-five percent between 1890 and 1899, to thirty-six percent between 1900 and 1910. Second, all these figures remained considerably below corresponding figures in Middlesex County Superior Court, where the guilty plea rate for all cases was seventy-seven percent in 1880, eighty-seven percent in 1900, and probably about the same in 1910.[24] Third, there was a "remarkable" increase, as Friedman

7.2.

Initial Pleas in Cases in Which Defendants Entered Pleas:
Alameda County, California, 1880–1910

	INITIAL PLEA			
YEARS	% NOT GUILTY	% GUILTY AS CHARGED	% GUILTY OF LESSER OFFENSE OR FEWER COUNTS	NUMBER OF CASES
1880–1889	78	12	10	171
1890–1899	75	19	6	185
1900–1910	64	32	4	295

SOURCE: Friedman and Percival, *Roots of Justice*, p. 174, table 5.12.

and Percival call it,[25] in the proportion of defendants who pled guilty to the charged offense as opposed to some lesser crime. At the same time, the proportion who pled to a lesser offense started small and grew even smaller.

We may begin by asking why the rate of guilty pleas should have been so much lower in Alameda than in Middlesex. If we look first (as we have done before) at the power of prosecutors, we come immediately to one obvious explanation: In 1851 the California legislature abolished the nol pros[26] and thereby eliminated the district attorney's power to charge bargain in the fashion of Massachusetts prosecutors in liquor and murder cases. In place of the nol pros, the legislature substituted a procedure for dismissing indictments, but put the power to dismiss in the judge's hands. Friedman and Percival recount cases in which the district attorney and the defendant nevertheless agreed that if the defendant would plead guilty to one of several counts or to a lesser offense of the crime charged, the balance of the indictment would be dismissed. But in all such cases the parties still had to convince the judge to enter the dismissal. "It was very, very rare for a judge to refuse," they write, but apparently not unheard of. The authors tell of one case in which the court rebuffed a deal and another in which the court went along only with difficulty.[27]

Despite what Friedman and Percival see as the court's ready acquiescence in charge bargaining, the rarity of this bargaining technique sug-

7.3.

Criminal Caseload in Alameda and Middlesex Counties

	NUMBER OF CASES	
YEAR	ALAMEDA COUNTY	MIDDLESEX COUNTY
1880	117	486
1890	78	not measured
1900	75	602
1910	185	not measured

SOURCES: Friedman and Percival, *Roots of Justice*, 41 table 3.1; Middlesex Super. Ct. R. Books; Middlesex Super. Ct. Docket Books.

gests that prosecutors and defense lawyers did not like having to submit their carefully crafted agreements for court approval. After all, as Table 7.2 shows, the proportion of defendants who pled guilty to a lesser offense or to fewer counts than those charged stood at only ten percent at the outset of Friedman and Percival's study and promptly fell to six percent and then to just four percent—and this at a time when guilty pleas of all sorts were rising. Perhaps judges resisted participation in a process that so clearly implicated them in plea bargaining. The authors report one judge's demand that a defendant deny he pled guilty as part of a plea bargain. Only after the defendant complied—"Oh no, sir. No, I would have pleaded guilty anyway."—did the judge dismiss the balance of the indictment in strict compliance with the plea bargain.[28]

But even if California prosecutors had wielded a unilateral power to charge bargain, they perhaps lacked sufficient incentive to mount a vigorous plea-bargaining practice. It is true that prosecutors in California, like prosecutors everywhere, must have valued plea bargaining because it delivered certain victory in individual cases. But Alameda prosecutors apparently carried a far lighter workload than those in Middlesex and consequently may have felt less time pressure to plead. In the period of Friedman and Percival's study, the Middlesex County criminal caseload ranged between four and eight times the size of that in Alameda (see Table 7.3).[29]

Meanwhile, the legal staff of the Middlesex district attorney's office appears to have consisted of just the district attorney and one assistant prosecutor as late as 1898.[30] In Alameda, although the district attorney worked alone as late as the 1870s, there were three lawyers on staff by 1885, six by 1901, and nine by 1910.[31] Still, these prosecutors did not work full-time, and the district attorney and two of his assistants even joined together in a civil-law partnership in 1893.[32] As I argued earlier, part-time prosecuting inevitably generated financial incentives to dispose of criminal cases quickly, no matter how small the prosecutorial workload.[33]

But lacking the nol pros power, prosecutors who hoped to plea bargain had to win the cooperation of judges. In Massachusetts at the time of Friedman and Percival's study, judges were becoming full-fledged partners in the plea bargaining regime. If California judges were of the same mind, then we might expect to see a good deal more plea bargaining than we do. In fact, Alameda judges probably felt far less incentive to bargain than did Middlesex judges. In 1900, when the criminal caseload of Middlesex County was about eight times that of Alameda,[34] there were eighteen superior court judges in Massachusetts, who rode circuit among the state's fourteen counties.[35] That year they devoted a total of 325 judge-days to Middlesex County business—the equivalent of perhaps one and one-half full-time judges—and only forty-four days to the county's criminal calendar.[36] In contrast, four full-time superior court judges sat permanently in Alameda.[37] Friedman and Percival do not measure the judges' civil caseload, but Friedman reports elsewhere that it was quite small. Between 1880 and 1900, there were on average only seventeen personal injury suits filed each year in Alameda County Superior Court.[38] Two facts now seem clear: Alameda courts had something less than three times the judicial resources of Middlesex courts, and they had a caseload many times smaller. The pressure to plea bargain must have weighed far more heavily on the Massachusetts judges.

There is, moreover, good reason to think that California criminal defendants, like California prosecutors and judges, had milder incentives to plea bargain than did their counterparts in Massachusetts. We saw in Massachusetts that two factors—the rate of counsel representation and the right to testify at trial—influenced defendants' changing inclination to plea bargain in the nineteenth century. The distinction between California and Massachusetts defendants did not lie in the right to testify at trial—defendants in both states won that right at virtually the same moment.[39] To the extent that defendant-testimony laws discouraged some defendants from opting for trial, they probably had a similar impact in the two states.

But while Massachusetts provided free lawyers only for those defendants charged with capital crimes,[40] California did so for all indigent defendants facing felony trials.[41] Probably as a result, the proportion of defendants with counsel in Alameda Superior Court ranged between eighty-three and eighty-nine percent over the period Friedman and Percival studied,[42] while in Middlesex County in the same period the figure hovered below fifty percent.[43] We saw earlier that having a lawyer in Massachusetts greatly increased defendants' chances of winning at trial and considerably increased the odds that they would go to trial rather than plead guilty.[44] It may be true that appointed counsel in California, who received no fee for their services, were not the best, and it appears to be true that Alameda County defendants did not always fare better at trial than Middlesex County defendants despite their higher representation rate.[45] But we nonetheless may expect that defendants with lawyers more commonly *saw* their chances of victory at trial as justifying the risk. If so, then the higher representation rate in California may help explain Alameda's lower guilty plea rate.

With California prosecutors lacking the unilateral power to charge bargain and with all three courtroom actors lacking motives to bargain as strong as those in Massachusetts, it is perhaps natural that plea bargaining showed far less vigor in late nineteenth-century California than in late nineteenth-century Massachusetts. We should turn, then, to Friedman and Percival's "remarkable" finding that over the course of their study, the proportion of defendants who pled guilty to the charged offense increased from twelve to thirty-two percent.[46] I believe we can find an explanation in a procedural change that took place at the very outset of Friedman and Percival's study, supplying prosecutors with a charge-bargaining tool that stood in for the abolished nol pros.

In 1880 the California legislature established the "preliminary examination" as an alternative charging mechanism to the grand jury. Prosecutors quickly abandoned the grand-jury process.[47] Because over half of all defendants had counsel at their preliminary examination,[48] the examination gave prosecutor and defense lawyer a built-in opportunity to meet and review the evidence *before* the prosecutor brought charges. Knowing that a judge who had limited incentives to plea bargain would have to approve any deal that involved reducing or selectively eliminating charges, the lawyers now could strike a different sort of deal. In exchange for the prosecutor's promise to press only certain charges at the preliminary hearing, the defendant would promise to plead guilty to the face of the complaint. Researchers in later times have seen a good deal of this sort of bargaining at preliminary hearings in some (though not all) California courts and in courts elsewhere.[49]

Another aspect of the penal code added force to this charge-bargaining technique. In 1872 the California legislature enacted a harsh penalty scheme governing repeat offenders that sometimes imposed stiff mandatory-minimum terms.[50] For example, if a person once convicted of a crime punishable by state prison time was later convicted of an offense punishable by a term of more than five years, the law imposed a minimum ten-year sentence.[51] And if a person once convicted of petty larceny was later convicted of any crime punishable by state prison time, the law required the court to impose the maximum term for the new offense.[52] For many defendants caught in this law's grip, the prosecutor's promise at the preliminary hearing to forgo the prior offense allegation must have been more than enough to make a plea bargain seem worthwhile.[53]

Friedman and Percival's finding that after the 1880s a growing number of defendants pled guilty to the charged offense now seems almost predictable. The introduction of preliminary hearings in 1880 gave prosecutors and defense lawyers a new forum for plea bargaining. The deals this new forum facilitated—that the defendant would plead to the face of the complaint if the prosecutor brought only certain charges—appeared in court records as pleas to the crimes charged. As lawyers mastered and internalized the new charge-bargaining technique, such pleas inevitably became more common.

So here is just another example of lawyers' making do with what they had in contriving a plea-bargaining regime. Although the scenery in Alameda is again quite unlike that in Middlesex, the principles of power and interest that drove plea bargaining's development appear—at this quick and distant glance—much the same.

New York

For New York there is no equivalent of the full-length treatment of the operations of the local justice system that Friedman and Percival give to Alameda County. Instead we must work from the scattered bundles of evidence gathered in Raymond Moley's classic 1928 exposé of the once-hidden world of plea bargaining and in Mike McConville and Chester Mirsky's fuller but still brief study.[54] These works agree about two critical facts—the kind of plea bargaining that the authors observed in New York and the timing of its rise.

McConville and Mirsky, who focus exclusively on New York City courts, report that the most common form of plea bargaining in the mid-nineteenth century was charge bargaining. Of the guilty pleas they observed in an 1865 sample, seventy percent were to lesser offenses and only twenty-eight percent to the face of the indictment.[55] Moley reported that eighty-five percent of all guilty pleas in New York City in 1926 were to an offense other than that charged—though the proportion was considerably smaller in the rest of the state.[56] These are extraordinary rates of charge bargaining. In Alameda, Friedman and Percival found that only forty-five percent of all guilty pleas between 1880 and 1889 were to lesser offenses and that the figure dropped to twenty-four percent between 1890 and 1899 and to a mere eleven percent between 1900 and 1910.[57] My findings in Middlesex show that after the middle of the century, when charge bargaining in liquor cases was defunct, charge bargains never amounted to even nine percent of all guilty pleas in the courts of the middle tier.[58] Only in murder cases, in which the mandatory death penalty gave prosecutors the power to charge bargain effectively, did charge bargaining dominate, accounting for virtually all guilty pleas.[59]

The second fact that stands out about guilty pleas in New York is how early the upward trend began. McConville and Mirsky report a negligible guilty plea rate from 1800 until about 1830 and then a nearly steady rise to a high of seventy-five percent of all dispositions in 1890, the last year of their study.[60] Moley's figures commence only in 1839, but they reveal that the guilty plea rate already had begun to grow. His charts show the rate passing seventy-five percent in New York City by 1879 and in rural counties by the late 1890s.[61]

To explain both the type and timing of New York plea bargaining, we are wise to look first at prosecutors. In Middlesex County, charge bargaining was primarily a prosecutorial device. Only the rare noncompliance of a grand jury could limit the prosecutor's prerogative to seek certain charges. And only extraordinary legislative action—such as the 1852 Massachusetts ban on nol prosses in liquor cases and the 1851 California ban on all nol prosses—could limit the prosecutor's prerogative to drop or reduce charges. Although neither Moley nor McConville and Mirsky provide information that would help us assess how busy New York prosecutors were, it seems reasonable to assume they were quite busy and, like Middlesex prosecutors, felt strong incentives to reduce their workloads.[62] That charge bargains were more common in New York City than in the rest of the state and that the rise of guilty pleas was steeper in the City than in rural counties might suggest that Gotham prosecutors were busier than the rest.[63]

New York Prosecutors' Power. The difficult question is where New York prosecutors got the power to engage in such a far-ranging practice of charge bargaining. In Middlesex County, the power to charge bargain in liquor cases arose from the peculiar penalty scheme of the liquor license law. The law required judges to impose a fixed fine—or a fine within narrowly fixed bounds—for each conviction and thereby enabled prosecutors to dictate sentences by manipulating charges. In the first three-quarters of the century, before the mounting pressures of their civil caseloads convinced judges of the wisdom of plea bargaining, prosecutors' unilateral power to control sentencing was essential to the success of charge bargaining.

It appears that New York's unusual criminal code of 1829 conferred a similar but more broad-based power on prosecutors. Before 1829, New York law had a comparatively clumsy and undifferentiated schedule of criminal penalties. Persons convicted of treason or murder were to suffer death. Those convicted "of any manner of rape, or of . . . burglary; or of . . . robb[ery]," forgery, or setting fire to a house or barn were to "be punished with imprisonment for life."[64] And those convicted of any other felony above the grade of petty larceny faced imprisonment for "any term not more than fourteen years."[65] This pre-1829 code, with its roughly calibrated penalty scheme, allotted prosecutors little power to charge bargain. Because New York law apparently forbade partial nol prosses,[66] once the grand jury had charged the defendant with a crime such as rape, the prosecutor apparently had no power, short of nol prossing the charge outright, to alter the defendant's potential sentence.

True, the pre-1829 codes were not altogether bereft of the sort of rigid formulas that, in theory, could sustain a charge-bargaining practice. Most importantly, both the 1801 and 1813 codes called for life sentences for those convicted a second time of any felony above the grade of petty larceny.[67] These provisions perhaps gave prosecutors the power to threaten defendants with the mandatory life terms established for repeat offenders and then, in exchange for the defendant's plea, to strike off the prior-offense allegation. Any such charge-bargaining power, however, extended only to the fairly narrow range of cases to which these repeat-offender provisions applied.

Various features of the 1829 code invested prosecutors with far broader bargaining powers.[68] The new code, which took effect just as the rate of guilty pleas in New York started steadily upward,[69] divided several crimes into different "degrees" that carried corresponding punishments. For example, first-degree burglary called for a penalty of not less than ten years; second-degree burglary for not less than five or more than ten years; and third-degree burglary for not more than five years.[70] What is more, the code provided—and abundant case law confirmed—that prosecutors could use multicount indictments to charge several degrees of the same crime.[71] Although prosecutors apparently lacked power to enter partial nol prosses, they specifically retained power to enter a nol pros "to the whole of any one or more of several counts" within an indictment.[72] Taken together, the ability to seek multicount indictments and to nol pros individual counts within such indictments gave New York prosecutors, like prosecutors of liquor law violations in Massachusetts, the leverage to exact guilty pleas in exchange for selectively nol prossing separate counts of the indictment.

But in New York this power extended beyond a single class of cases. With regard to several offenses, the 1829 code assigned a minimum term of imprisonment to the higher degrees of the crime. This was true of first- and second-degree burglary; first-degree robbery; first- and second-degree forgery; first-, second-, and third-degree manslaughter; and first-, second-, and third-degree arson.[73] Such minimum terms bestowed peculiar power on the prosecutor to bind the judge's hands in sentencing and hence to persuade defendants to plead guilty. A defendant charged with first-degree burglary who faced a minimum ten-year term in state prison might have leapt at the prosecutor's offer to plead guilty to third-degree burglary with its guaranteed five-year maximum—and even might have settled for second-degree with its certain ten-year maximum.

This technique of bargaining among different degrees of the same crime, made possible by the 1829 code, became an enduring hallmark of prosecution practice in New York. One hundred forty years later a commission undertook the task of drafting a new penal code for the state. When asked whether the need to facilitate plea bargaining had prompted the commission to split a raft of crimes into multiple degrees in the usual fashion, the head of the commission replied: "Decidedly! We were very conscious of the negotiation process, and that's the reason for our extensive degree structure. . . . [I]t's very important that one can take the negotiating process right down the line through the degrees."[74]

The 1829 code gave rise to other charge-bargaining techniques as well. A defendant charged with second-degree burglary who faced a minimum five-year term could plead guilty instead to *attempted* second-degree burglary, with its *maximum* five-year term.[75] Although the code did not do so explicitly, it seemed to make attempt a lesser-included offense of many or most crimes.[76] In a broad range of cases, therefore, prosecutors had the power to substitute a charge of attempt for the original charge in exchange for the defendant's plea. They apparently did so often. McConville and Mirsky report that of the seventy-three guilty pleas to lesser offenses that they observed in an 1865 sample, thirty-four—or forty-seven percent—involved reducing the charged offense to a mere attempt.[77]

The code's harsh treatment of two broad categories of repeat offenders, whom it exposed to substantial minimum penalties,[78] may have supplied the means for one last charge-bargaining technique. These repeat-offender provisions precisely tracked—and therefore must have inspired—the 1872 repeat-offender laws in California that I discussed earlier.[79] As in California, these mandatory penalties put the prosecutor in a position to threaten the defendant with a long prison term that the judge had no power to avoid. In California, where the legislature had abolished the nol pros years before, prosecutors had no power to terminate prior offense allegations after charges were brought. New York prosecutors, by contrast, may have held the power to wipe out prior offense allegations in exchange for the defendant's guilty plea to the present charge.

The Massachusetts penal code simply denied prosecutors these various broad-based charge-bargaining options. Of all the commonly prosecuted crimes, only liquor law violations, murder, and a few other very serious offenses that called for mandatory life imprisonment or mandatory death carried minimum penalties. And not until 1974 did the Supreme Judicial Court deem attempt to be a lesser-included offense of the substantive charge.[80] I did not observe a single nineteenth-century case in which the defendant pled guilty to attempt as part of a charge bargain. Moreover, in Massachusetts there was no law that generally heightened the penalty for second offenders, and not until 1887 did the state enact severe minimum penalties for third offenders.[81] Before then, the only such law I have seen in use, outside the context of the liquor laws, imposed a rather mild minimum three-year term on those convicted a second time of theft.[82]

The Nol-pros Mystery. The power of New York prosecutors to enter nol prosses leads to the one real mystery surrounding the state's vigorous charge-bargaining practice. Even as the 1829 code created vast new realms for creative charge bargaining, the code stripped the state's district attorneys of the power "to enter a *nolle prosequi* upon any indictment, or in any other way to discontinue or abandon the same, without the leave of the court having jurisdiction to try the offence charged."[83] I have not been able to trace the legislature's motivations in adopting this provision. A single cryptic clue to the law's purpose emerges from an 1841 opinion of the state supreme court, then an intermediate appellate court. In *People v. McLeod*,[84] the court pointed out that the state's attorney general and its several district attorneys formerly shared the nol pros power. The 1829 code left the attorney general's power unimpaired even as it withdrew power from the district attorneys. Apparently, the court surmised, the legislature had found the nol pros power in too "many hands, and fear[ed] its abuse."[85] What sort of abuse the court did not say.

Nor can I explain with any certainty why the nol pros provision did not halt the apparent progress of charge bargaining in New York. After all, when the Massachusetts legislature imposed a similar restriction on prosecutors' use of nol prosses in liquor cases in 1852, prosecutorial charge bargaining in these cases came to an abrupt stop.[86] The most likely explanation for the New York law's failure to squelch charge bargaining is that the law did not by its terms forbid the practice. A charge bargain did not require the prosecutor "to enter a *nolle prosequi* upon [the] indictment," or "to discontinue or abandon the same," but merely to nol pros one *count* of the indictment—hence the usefulness of the multicount charging practice I noted earlier. The Massachusetts legislature had drafted its nol pros ban of 1852 more broadly, providing that in liquor cases, "a *nolle prosequi* shall not be entered by the prosecuting officer, except with the concurrence of the court."[87] Faced with the New York legislature's narrower ban, trial courts in that state may not have felt empowered to interfere when prosecutors terminated separate counts of an indictment. Given that the nol pros power traditionally had lain with prosecutors, courts may have preferred to wait for less ambiguous authority.

Alternatively, one could surmise that the nol pros provision failed to slow charge bargaining because New York judges, unlike those in Massachusetts, readily gave their consent to the necessary nol prosses. The course of later legislation in New York, however, suggests that judges remained unfriendly toward prosecutorial charge bargaining for some time to come. When David Dudley Field, David Graham, and Arphaxed Loomis reported a code of criminal procedure to the New York legislature in 1849,[88] they proposed to deprive all prosecutors, including the attorney general, of the nol pros power. The Graham Code, as it came to be known, flatly declared that "neither the attorney general, nor the di[s]trict attorney shall hereafter discontinue or abandon a prosecution" and instead bestowed on judges an exclusive power to dismiss criminal actions either "of [their] own motion, or upon the application of the district attorney."[89]

The authors at first gave no reason for proposing a wholesale shift of the power to terminate prosecutions. They claimed simply that several components of their code, including this one, "are sufficiently explained by the provisions themselves."[90] But in a revision of the proposed code submitted the following year, they suggested that the court's 1841 ruling in *McLeod* had prompted their action.[91] The court had held that the nol pros provision of the 1829 code, which by its terms gave trial courts the power to veto prosecutorial nol prosses, gave courts no power to *enter* a nol pros "unless by consent or on motion of the district attorney." The Graham Code's authors argued that the court thereby had made "the power of the district attorney, in this respect, . . . greater than that of the court."[92]

Far better, they wrote, that the nol pros power rest "where it should alone rest, in the hands of the court."[93] The authors never explained why, if they sought merely to remedy the inability of judges to end criminal prosecutions on their own motion, they proposed to take all such power from prosecutors. Nonetheless, we may infer two things from their proposal. First, they believed that the 1829 code had not sufficiently restricted prosecutors' nol pros power. And second, they did not believe judges had connived in whatever abuses prosecutors had wrought with that power—for if they had suspected judicial complicity, they surely would not have handed all power to judges.

This complete ban on prosecutorial nol prosses did not become law for many years. In the meantime, by whatever mechanism, prosecutors appear to have retained their nol pros power despite the 1829 restriction. In 1869 the *New York Times* printed a front-page discourse on the ills of the state's criminal justice system. While pointing out the dangerous concentration of power in the prosecutor, the anonymous but seemingly well-informed author claimed that the prosecutor "can without question enter a *nolle prosequi* in any case where an indictment has been found."[94] "He may go further and accept a plea from a prisoner guilty of an offence many degrees lower in grade than that charged in the indictment by the Grand Jury."[95] Where the prosecutor got these powers the author did not say. At about the same time, though, a somewhat jaded observer commented that a district attorney's "motion for leave to enter a *nolle prosequi* is granted by courts almost invariably, their assent being well nigh a matter of form."[96] It was by this time, or not long afterward, that Massachusetts judges had begun to soften their resistance to plea bargaining.

Between 1850 and 1880, as the Graham Code languished unenacted, the proportion of cases ending in guilty pleas reached and surpassed seventy-five percent.[97] Most of these pleas took the form of charge bargains.[98] In 1881 the legislature finally put in force the entire proposed code, including the nol pros ban.[99] Whether lawmakers gave any attention to the parts of the code that concern us now, which amounted to only two provisions in a code that contained hundreds, is not clear. What is both clear and unsurprising is that if the legislature had intended to end charge bargaining in New York by depriving prosecutors of the power to enter nol prosses, it failed in its mission. Moley's figures show that the rate of guilty pleas in New York City, where charge bargains were most common,[100] dipped barely perceptibly after enactment of the new code and then climbed to a new high.[101] That this result is unsurprising is a consequence of what Middlesex County's history has taught: By 1881, judges were confronting an onslaught of new civil litigation. No doubt New York judges, like their Massachusetts counterparts, abandoned whatever antipathy they once might have borne toward prosecutorial plea bargaining and lent it what aid they could. As Moley observed in 1928, New York judges dismissed cases about as often as prosecutors in other states entered nol prosses. "The practice [of nol prossing] exists," he wrote, "although the name is gone."[102]

In New York, then, as in California and England, the principles that emerged from our study of Middlesex County go far toward explaining the course of plea bargaining's rise. If plea bargaining in New York more often took the form of prosecutorial charge bargaining than did plea bargaining in California or Massachusetts, it is because New York law gave prosecutors more leverage to manipulate sentences by manipulating charges. And if plea bargaining got an earlier start in New York, it is in part because the legal framework to support broad-based prosecutorial charge bargaining was in place by 1829. And in part, it is because the frenzy of life in the Metropolis perhaps taxed prosecutorial resources earlier and more harshly than did the relative quietude of California or even Middlesex County.

8

The Power of Plea Bargaining

We have seen that both within and outside Massachusetts, we can explain a good deal of plea bargaining's progress by asking who held the power to bargain and who had the incentive. Now we can move ahead to explore the broader consequences of plea bargaining's amassed power. By "plea bargaining's power," I mean its derived power, for the power of plea bargaining is the power of the courtier—the influence it has gained by serving well the interests of those in high places. I begin, therefore, by sorting the several ways plea bargaining has served the interests of those who hold power in the criminal courtroom. I then seek to uncover how plea bargaining's amassed power has helped or hindered the progress of other institutions of criminal justice.

THE SOURCES OF PLEA BARGAINING'S POWER

How Plea Bargaining Serves Courtroom Actors

One of plea bargaining's great attractions for prosecutors and judges was its efficiency. When Middlesex prosecutors of the 1840s found themselves staggering under bloated caseloads, they multiplied charge bargains in liquor cases and deployed on-file plea bargains in a whole range of cases.

And when Massachusetts judges of the last quarter of the century faced paralyzing demands from their civil calendars, they threw their considerable power behind the cause of plea bargaining by engaging in sentence bargaining on an ever greater scale. The sheer efficiency of plea bargaining as a means of clearing cases to some extent has frozen it in place. When prosecutors and judges manage to keep pace with fast-growing workloads either with no increase in staffing or with increases that lag behind the growth in case numbers, any appeal they might make to the legislature for more personnel will fall short. And as staffing fails to keep pace with mounting loads, any hope of easing reliance on plea bargaining fades.

But the efficiency of plea bargaining is not the only benefit it extends to power-holders. It is obvious that prosecutors like plea bargaining because it secures victory in the case. What is less obvious is that plea bargaining confers almost the same advantage on judges. True, most judges have no personal or professional stake in the defendant's conviction. But a plea bargain means that the judge "wins" to the extent that the bargain guards against the reputational blow of a reversal. Without a trial, after all, the judge cannot commit trial error.[1]

It is not clear when trial judges first began to regard reversals with dread and therefore to view this aspect of plea bargaining as a virtue. Massachusetts district attorneys first had to report their win-loss statistics to the attorney general in the 1830s, and at least one district attorney made a point of bragging about his conviction rate as early as 1844.[2] What evidence I have of judicial concern for reversal rates arises later—and hence accords with other evidence that judges came around to the cause of plea bargaining only decades after prosecutors had put in place the equipment of charge bargaining in liquor and murder cases.

It is no mystery why judges of the first half of the nineteenth century did not concern themselves much with reversal rates—there simply were too few appeals. Theodore Ferdinand reports that between 1814 and 1822, defendants appealed in only three percent of municipal-court cases in Boston, a figure that declined through the first half of the century to just over one percent between 1844 and 1850.[3] By the end of the century, the pace of appeals was growing fast. According to one study, criminal appeals in Massachusetts increased from about 2,200 in the early 1890s to about 3,500 in 1900—with larger increases to come.[4] In California at about the same time, Friedman and Percival saw only slight growth in the overall frequency of appeals, which generally occurred in about two or three percent of all cases, but at times reached as high as six percent.[5] But when they measured appeals as a proportion of convictions after trial, rather than as a proportion of all cases, they found that appeals had more than doubled from 8.4 percent in the 1880s to 17.7 percent in the 1890s and had fallen off only slightly between 1900 and 1910.[6]

One can find occasional anecdotal evidence of trial judges' concern with the possibility of reversal on appeal. In 1879 the Michigan Supreme Court reviewed the actions of a trial judge who had coerced a plea bargain apparently to avoid the risk of appeal. As the high court related the case, after the judge had rejected the defendant's pretrial motion to dismiss and the jury had returned a guilty verdict, "[s]ome very extraordinary proceedings followed. The defendant was given by the judge to understand that he must submit to a severe sentence or else withdraw his plea of not guilty, enter a plea of guilty and immediately pay $400 *and estop himself from bringing error.*"[7]

The earliest evidence that I have found of a more generalized desire among judges to avoid the risk of reversal dates only to the 1920s. A Massachusetts district attorney wrote in 1926 of trial judges' "[f]ear of reversal," though he drew no connection between that fear and judges' attitudes toward plea bargaining.[8] It was left to Raymond Moley to make this connection in his 1928 indictment of the newly "discovered" practice of plea bargaining. The prosecutor "does not run the risk of losing" when the case ends in a plea bargain, he wrote, and "the judge escapes the danger of being reversed on some point of law."[9]

As the twentieth century wore on and expanding procedural protections generated more criminal appeals,[10] three sets of actors felt the growing allure of plea bargaining. For prosecutors, more appeals inevitably meant both more time-consuming prosecutions and more reversals on appeal. The usefulness of plea bargaining to them grew even larger than before.[11] As trial judges saw the greater potential for reversals and the reputational damage that they brought, personal interests bound them ever tighter to the cause of plea bargaining. And as appellate judges suffered under the weight of their growing dockets, they, too, began to know the efficient promise of plea bargaining. It is little wonder, perhaps, that the

U.S. Supreme Court's definitive affirmation of the legality of plea bargaining—rendered as though "any other course would be unthinkable"—came amid a period of overwhelming growth of criminal appeals in the federal courts.[12] Between 1960 and 1980, the number of appeals filed in federal courts of appeal almost quintupled—with criminal appeals rising faster than civil appeals—while the number of judges merely doubled.[13]

The pressure of criminal appeals on appellate judges, like the pressure of criminal trials on trial judges, is to some extent a function of the judges' civil workloads. In Chapter 5, I argued that the civil-litigation revolution of the late nineteenth century had confronted trial judges not only with more civil trials, but with a more complex brand of negligence cases that absorbed far more time than the old nonpayment disputes that had typified their civil docket.[14] Likewise, appeals in negligence cases, as Roscoe Pound saw in 1939, "require an exceptionally critical consideration of details of evidence in voluminous records."[15] The changing nature of the civil appellate caseload therefore has generated even greater incentives to limit the criminal appellate caseload.

How Plea Bargaining Serves the System

At least three influential participants in the criminal justice system—prosecutor, trial judge, and appellate judge—came to see plea bargaining as a means toward efficient management of overgrown workloads. At least two—prosecutor and trial judge—valued it as a means to guard their reputations from the scent of fecklessness or incompetence. And criminal defendants, lest we forget them, regarded bargaining as a way to avoid uncertainty and to elude the most severe allowable sentence. But beyond these advantages that plea bargaining brought to individual participants in the justice system, it conferred another on the system as a whole: To the extent a plea bargain delivers a verdict that onlookers acknowledge to be truthful,[16] it protects the jury and the system that sponsors it from the risk of issuing the wrong verdict—or to be precise, a verdict the public will perceive to be wrong. That is, despite all the criticism heaped upon plea bargaining by those who think it deprives defendants of their trial right or the public of its right to uncompromised punishment, when it comes to the apparent accuracy of outcomes, plea bargaining helps protect the system's legitimacy.[17]

In fact, plea bargaining may do an even better job of protecting the system from the perception of wrongful verdicts than at first appears. In their monumental study, *The American Jury*, Harry Kalven and Hans Zeisel concluded that plea bargaining tends to remove from the jury system those cases in which the defendant faces the clearest evidence of guilt:

> If all controversies of criminal law were placed on a continuum from the weakest to the strongest in terms of the prosecution's case, the guilty plea . . . would be likely to withdraw cases from the strong side of the continuum, leaving the weaker cases for jury trial.
>
> The upshot is that, out of the great universe of criminal controversies, those surviving to jury trial . . . are likely to be the more controversial cases where, in the nature of things, the chances of disagreement are increased.[18]

As we might expect, when defendants regard their odds of conviction to be all but certain, they are more likely to seek a deal to cut their losses. If they sense freedom within their grasp, they are more likely to insist on trial.[19] Judges perhaps magnify this tendency if, as Milton Heumann suggests, they exact a penalty against plainly guilty defendants convicted after trial when there was "no realistically contestable issue 'justifying' a . . . trial."[20]

The usefulness of this division of labor between plea bargaining and jury trial, in which the bargaining process handles the easier cases and the jury the harder ones, becomes clear when we reflect on the consequences of the jury's returning a "wrong" verdict in a "clear" case. The system's legitimacy suffers its greatest strain when the public feels sure that the jury has erred. The two clearest examples of this phenomenon in recent American history are the first Rodney King trial and the O. J. Simpson criminal trial. In the King case, videotape captured the actual crime. The country watched as a group of Los Angeles police officers beat a handcuffed King with their clubs. In the Simpson case, a tight web of circumstantial evidence, including DNA tests, bound the defendant to the crime. In each, the jury's acquittal prompted broad (though not universal) public indignation and demands for systemic reform.

The sheer celebrity of these prosecutions made plea bargaining politically impractical for the elected Los Angeles district attorney.[21] In more typical cases, defendants who face such overwhelming evidence of guilt bargain for the best deal they can get. The jury, therefore, rarely faces a clear case and rarely risks being clearly wrong. Instead, as Kalven and Zeisel said, the jury gets "the more controversial cases where, in the nature of things, the chances of disagreement are increased."[22] These are the cases that the jury cannot as easily get "wrong." Even if the jury convicts the innocent or acquits the guilty, the uncertainty of the evidence will help keep the public from seeing the error. Precisely because these cases are controversial, and precisely because they present a greater chance of disagreement, the jury's verdict can settle all controversy and resolve all disagreement. As Charles Nesson has written in a slightly different context, "such cases fall within a realm of ambiguity that allows the public to defer to any decision the jury reaches."[23]

Plea bargaining and jury trial, then, have joined in a task of erasing all apparent error from the criminal justice system. Little clear error can escape from the black box of the jury's deliberation room as long as only controversial cases enter. And plea bargaining by its very nature hides both factual and legal error: By admitting guilt, the defendant eliminates any formal doubt of guilt. By renouncing trial and all right to complain of pretrial error, the defendant normally bars any court from declaring error on appeal. We should not wonder at the staying power of plea bargaining. Not only does it ease the workloads and protect the reputations of the two most powerful courtroom actors, judge and prosecutor, it protects the reputation of the system as a whole.

THE CONSEQUENCES OF PLEA BARGAINING'S POWER

Plea bargaining has used its enormous power, gained by promoting the interests of power, to help or hinder those procedural institutions that help or hinder plea bargaining. Here I return to the image of plea bargaining as a courtier. Though plea bargaining has no power of its own, the judges and prosecutors who dictate what goes on in our criminal courtrooms do have power—and they have strong interests in seeing plea bargaining thrive. I do not suggest that they act in concert or even that they always know the consequences of their actions, but only that they try to make plea bargains happen. And in so doing, they raise up those procedural institutions that help plea bargaining and beat down those that threaten it.

I argued in Chapter 3 that the steady and vigorous growth of probation was one consequence of this derivative power of plea bargaining.
Probation stands as an especially clear case of the symbiosis that can
develop between plea bargaining and a friendly procedural innovation:
Because prosecutors who sought a new method of plea bargaining made
use of the same procedural device that later took the name probation,
plea bargaining actually helped invent probation.

In the case of the two procedural innovations that I take up now—
indeterminate sentencing and public defenders—the formative influence
of plea bargaining has been less direct.[24] One can assign various causes for
the failure of the indeterminate sentence, which arose with such great
promise at the close of the nineteenth century. But a good deal of the evidence surrounding its demise traces to plea bargaining's door, and the
supporters of plea bargaining indeed had a motive to wish its downfall.
That is, those judges and prosecutors who found benefits in plea bargaining had reason to shun the indeterminate sentence and to limit its
growth. There are likewise various ways to explain the introduction and
success of organizations for the defense of the poor. Still, the evidence
seems clear that public defenders emerged at least in part because they
promised to ease the course of plea bargains. We therefore must examine
the possibility that they have thrived in part because they fulfilled that
promise.

The Indeterminate Sentence

When examining the interplay between the indeterminate sentencing
movement and the plea-bargaining system, we need to separate the principles of the indeterminate sentence from its reality. Its principles, as I
argued in Chapter 5, perhaps aided plea bargaining. By suggesting that
punishment should look forward and not backward, advocates of the
indeterminate sentence relieved judges of the strict obligation to learn all
they could about the defendant's past crime before imposing sentence—an
obligation that they once had met by hearing evidence at trial. And by
claiming that judges had no particular skill at predicting an offender's
future conduct—and that therefore prison and parole authorities should
decide the exact date of release—these advocates absolved judges from the
obligation to get the defendant's sentence exactly right. If the rough-and-

tumble of the bargaining process produced a sentence that was other than ideal, prison and parole authorities could tailor it to fit more suitably.

The reality of the indeterminate sentence, however, if ever enacted according to the highest ideals of its advocates, would have shrunk plea bargaining to insignificance. The movement's purest adherents thought its indeterminacy should be complete. Once the judge sentenced an offender to serve time, prison and parole authorities should determine when he had "reformed" and should release him then, neither earlier nor later, no matter how long it took.[25] Even in such a system, some amount of plea bargaining might have persisted as defendants offered to plead guilty in exchange for a term of probation rather than a potentially endless sojourn in prison. But those defendants whose crimes demanded that they serve time would have had no incentive to plead, because both judges and prosecutors would have lacked the power to promise a shorter term.

It is probably significant, then, that no state ever enacted a true indeterminate sentence.[26] Those legislatures that did pass "indeterminate" sentencing laws imposed, at the very least, a firm maximum on the length of incarceration, so that even unreformed inmates eventually had to go free. The Massachusetts indeterminate sentencing law of 1886, the nation's second, was typical. It provided that inmates convicted of certain less serious crimes must go free within two years and all others within five years unless the sentencing judge specified a longer term.[27]

Evading Indeterminacy—Sentencing Options. Even such imperfect indeterminate sentencing provisions could have hobbled plea bargaining. After all, they took a great deal of the power to shape sentences from judges' hands. But another, more substantial departure from complete indeterminate sentencing left judges' power to promise shorter terms in exchange for guilty pleas largely intact: Those states that enacted indeterminate sentencing (of the imperfect sort just mentioned)[28] simply made it an additional sentencing *option*. Some states explicitly gave judges the choice to impose an indeterminate sentence or not, as they pleased. Others required sentences to certain institutions to be indeterminate, but imposed no such requirement on sentences to other institutions—and left the choice of institution up to the judge.

The 1886 Massachusetts law, for example, provided in seemingly mandatory terms that "[w]hen a convict is sentenced to the Massachusetts reformatory, the court or trial justice imposing the sentence shall not fix or limit the duration thereof."[29] But the law by no means required judges to send convicts to the reformatory instead of the state prison or county house of correction or any one of several other possible places of confinement. In 1890, in an editorial titled "Indefinite Commitments," the *Boston Evening Transcript* complained that "[s]ome change in the right direction was made by the legislature of four years ago, but the law has not accomplished what was hoped. It is said that the reform has not been carried out by the judges to the full extent which it was expected . . . ."[30] The paper was right to claim that judges did not often make use of the indeterminate sentence. The records of the Middlesex Superior Court show that in 1890 judges chose the reformatory for barely ten percent of convicts who served time—a figure that rose to twenty-two percent in 1896 before falling back to eighteen percent in 1900 and only twelve percent in 1910.[31] These numbers are perhaps especially low given that the state reformatory was conveniently nearby— in Concord, at the heart of Middlesex County.

Although rarely used, the Massachusetts reformatory perhaps proved useful to the plea-bargaining regime. In his 1906 commentary on the operations of the criminal justice system in Manhattan, Arthur Train recognized the complicated relationship between New York's reformatory at Elmira, on which the Concord reformatory was modeled,[32] and the plea-bargaining system. On the one hand, Train wrote, because "the Elmira sentence is indeterminate, the defendant has nothing to gain by pleading."[33] On the other, court officers who wanted to encourage guilty pleas sometimes told defendants of the "joys of Elmira."[34] Despite the uncertain length of a sentence to Elmira, therefore, some defendants perhaps preferred that option because they feared worse conditions elsewhere. Other defendants might have had geographical preferences—the reformatory at Elmira (or Concord) might have been closer to family and friends than the state prison at Auburn (or Charlestown).

In any event, as long as judges had no *obligation* to send convicts to Elmira or Concord, then by adding this option to the mix, the legislature simply added one more vector along which judge, prosecutor, and defendant could cut a deal. In fact, although Middlesex judges exercised the

Concord option only rarely, the great majority of defendants who received a reformatory sentence had pled guilty. Only thirteen percent of those who went to the reformatory in 1890 had gone to trial and lost—a figure that rose to thirty-one percent in 1896, but then shrank to eight percent in 1900 and a mere five percent in 1910. The corresponding figures for other institutions were almost always between two and five times as great.[35]

From Train's description of Elmira and this evidence of sentencing practices in Middlesex, we may conclude three things: First, because indeterminate sentences generally did not appeal to defendants, judges and prosecutors rarely found the reformatory option helpful in the plea-bargaining process. The great majority of convicts therefore served their time elsewhere. Second, when defendants did happen to prefer a sentence to the reformatory over one to another institution, judges were pleased to accommodate them in the interests of gaining a plea. And third, when defendants instead refused to plead guilty, insisted on their trial right, and lost, judges rarely sent them to the reformatory. That is, judges generally did not delegate the measure of punishment to the authorities who controlled release from the reformatory. The court could not be sure, after all, that those authorities would tax the defendant sufficiently for having burdened the court with a trial. Instead, judges usually punished defendants who lost after trial by imposing a more definite sentence to a specified term in another institution.

With the reformatory enjoying but small popularity among Massachusetts judges, the legislature tried to advance the ideal of the indeterminate sentence in other ways. In 1894 it instituted parole for state prisoners and in 1895 required judges to specify minimum and maximum terms to the state prison. The 1894 law made state prisoners eligible for release on parole at the discretion of a parole board after serving two-thirds of their term.[36] Advocates of the true indeterminate sentence dismissed parole regimes as poor imitations because they merely permitted a limited discount from an otherwise fixed sentence. Yet of all regimes that approached true indeterminacy, parole surely was the most significant. By 1900 twenty states had adopted some form of parole, while only eleven had put in place a more nearly indeterminate sentence along the lines of the Concord–Elmira model.[37]

With the 1895 law, the Massachusetts legislature tried to advance the simple parole system one step closer to true indeterminacy. The law provided that "the court imposing the sentence [to state prison] shall not fix the term of imprisonment, but shall establish a maximum and minimum term for which said convict may be held in said prison."[38] It then provided that the convict would be eligible for parole after serving the minimum term.[39] Again, the law by no means achieved true indeterminacy: Not only did the judge dictate both a floor and a ceiling for every sentence, but the maximum terms defined by statute still capped the judge's maximum.[40] Laws following this form spread across the nation, taking hold in twenty-three states by 1925.[41]

Even the limited indeterminacy introduced by these two laws might have slowed plea bargaining's progress by shrinking judges' power to promise defendants a particular sentence. As it was, however, the laws lost much in the translation from theory to practice and soon proved to be no more an obstacle to plea bargaining than was the Concord reformatory. As with the reformatory, Middlesex judges simply made little use of these new indeterminate sentences. In 1890, before the laws took effect, the state prison was the destination for nineteen percent of incarcerated convicts. That figure promptly fell to ten percent in 1896 and eight percent in 1900 before recovering somewhat to eleven percent by 1910.[42] In their reluctance to impose minimum and maximum terms to the state prison, Massachusetts judges followed New York judges, who reportedly spurned a similar sentencing option enacted in that state in 1889.[43]

When Middlesex judges did impose state prison sentences under the new parole regime, they very rarely did so in connection with plea bargains. In 1890, before enactment of the new laws, fifty-six percent of state prison sentences followed guilty pleas. In 1896, with the laws in place, only fourteen percent did so. These figures go some distance toward explaining the odd retreat in the overall rate of guilty pleas that I found in 1896.[44] Yet by 1900, the rate of guilty pleas not only had recovered, but had advanced a good ways. Eighty-one percent of state prison sentences that year followed guilty pleas. Something must have changed.

Evading Indeterminacy—Predictable Release Dates. The change appears in the statute book. In 1898, three years after the legislature had required judges to specify minimum and maximum terms to the state prison, it amended the parole law to provide that state prison inmates "shall be entitled to release from said prison upon the expiration of the minimum term" if they have observed all prison rules and were not punished for prison misconduct.[45] For any state prison inmate who behaved behind bars, the judge's sentence now dictated the exact date of release. Notwithstanding the claimed indeterminacy of sentences to the Massachusetts state prison, parties engaged in plea negotiations therefore could predict the date of release with near certainty. My search has uncovered no evidence of the legislature's motives in changing the law, but the results of the change were both predictable and immediate. With virtually all the indeterminacy boiled out of the state prison sentencing scheme, plea bargaining returned and advanced apace.

Evidence from many other states reveals a similar aversion to any parole scheme that approached true indeterminacy. Like Massachusetts, New Hampshire required automatic release at the end of the minimum term for prisoners who had not misbehaved behind bars.[46] Pennsylvania's parole statute did not directly require release at the end of the minimum term, but by commanding the relevant authorities to explain any decision *not* to release "in writing . . . in detail," the law probably achieved the same result.[47] In other states, even absent such statutory directives, decisions of parole boards became very easy to predict. In New Jersey a 1917 report complained of the threat such predictability posed to the theory of the indeterminate sentence:

> In actual practice parole is granted as a matter of course at the expiration of the minimum term, except in those cases in which the applicant has had his minimum term extended as a penalty for misconduct in prison. . . .
>   Thus, in all the state institutions[] is the aim of the indeterminate sentence defeated by the policy of the paroling authority.[48]

Next door in New York, evidence of highly predictable parole release dates spans the first quarter of the century. As early as 1906 Arthur Train had reported that a convict sent to Elmira to serve a supposedly indeterminate sentence "will be released in fourteen months if his conduct appears to warrant it"[49] A decade later the state's prison association claimed that more than ninety percent of New York parolees had won parole either immediately upon completing their minimum terms or within one month afterward.[50] And by the 1920s the New York Board of Parole found itself dogged by well-publicized and often-repeated complaints about its seemingly automatic release policy. In 1923, for example, the *New York Times* declared that "the paroling of prisoners in this State now has become largely automatic, . . . and that is quite contrary to the theory of the indeterminate sentence."[51]

Parole officials sought refuge in the authority of New York's indeterminate sentencing law, which they claimed mandated the board's practices. At an inquiry into the state's parole system in 1926, board chairman George W. Benham contended (as paraphrased by the *Times*) that "it was obligatory on the board to parole men who had served their minimum sentence and were in 'good standing.'" He added that "if the courts imposed a minimum sentence, the rule must be that [prisoners] could go on parole when that minimum was served." Another board member maintained that a prisoner "had the *right* of parole after he had served his minimum sentence, provided he had not broken prison rules."[52] And in an extract of its annual report issued after the hearing, the board said it based its release policy on the indeterminate law itself.[53] As the *Times* observed later, if that is how the system works, then "the indeterminate sentence has become a determinate sentence, fixed at the minimum."[54]

But New York's indeterminate sentence law required no such thing. Rather it provided that if "there is reasonable probability that [the] applicant will live and remain at liberty without violating the law, then [the] board may authorize" his release.[55] The law said nothing to imply a right of release after completion of the minimum term. Even on a finding of "reasonable probability" that the prisoner would live by the law if released, the board apparently retained the discretion *not* to grant release. The use of the word "may" in the statutory language would suggest as much. In 1927, probably in response to the board's misinterpretation of its governing law, the New York Crime Commission recommended pointedly that "the determination of what prisoners shall be released on parole and at what time, after the serving of the minimum sentence, shall be entirely in the discretion of the Board of Parole and not a matter of right as interpreted in the past."[56]

Although New York parole authorities may have been unique in tailoring their operations to a nonexistent parole law, their practice of releasing the great majority of inmates at the end of the minimum term appears to have been as much the rule as the exception. In 1937 the *Harvard Law Review* observed that "[t]he correctional benefits which should result from imprisonment under an indeterminate sentence have often been lost by the mechanical application of parole."[57] And looking back from later in the century, Charles Newman concluded that "release at the earliest possible date was [in these early years] a right rather than a privilege."[58] For our purposes, the significance of such predictability is clear: "Indeterminate" sentences can have posed no great obstacle to plea bargaining if negotiating parties could say with confidence when such sentences would end.[59] In fact, in an odd way, a parole system that embraced automatic release dates might have been the best of worlds for plea bargaining. Such a scheme permitted the parties to agree on a sentence that sounded long enough to satisfy the public's desire for harsh punishment, but in reality was short enough to entice the defendant to plead.[60] As Albert Alschuler noted some years back, "Defendants care about when they will 'hit the streets,' and the State's Attorney cares about a sentence that looks severe."[61]

Still, it is not clear why parole boards should so quickly have abandoned the principles of parole and adopted a practice of nearly automatic release dates. Sheer overwork must have played a part. In the early 1920s, after a far-ranging study of the operations of the Massachusetts parole board, Professor Sam B. Warner of the Oregon Law School concluded it was "impossible" for the two full-time members and one part-time member of the state's parole board "to make a careful personal investigation into the merits of each prisoner's claim to parole."[62] In a similar report of the Illinois parole system, Dean Albert J. Harno of the University of Illinois Law School noted that between 1917 and 1927, four persons reviewed every parole case in the state. "It soon became apparent," he wrote, "that [they] were unable to hear enough cases to unburden the prisons of their congestion, even through the parole of such prisoners who were good parole prospects. . . . [T]hose who were paroled were little short of having been 'guessed out' of prison."[63]

Circumstances in New York were similar or worse. One review committee found that during a twelve-month period in 1917 and 1918, the state's parole board met forty times to consider 1,411 parole applications—or about thirty-five applications per day.[64] As the board's sittings normally ran at most five hours, the average case must have consumed less than ten minutes of public hearing time.[65] The general secretary of the state's prison association claimed matters were worse than that. "The cases are handled very rapidly," the *Times* quoted him as saying, "perhaps less than five minutes to a case."[66] Defending the board, one of its members admitted "[i]t may be true . . . that cases are disposed of in a few minutes," but argued that the more challenging cases sometimes occupied the board for a full hour. Moreover, both prison and parole officials gave cases "long consideration" in advance of public hearings.[67] Nonetheless, one suspects that the board often could not make an intelligent individualized judgment about each prisoner's fitness for parole.

In these circumstances, conscientious parole officials might have felt the only fair alternative was to adopt a rigid policy of releasing prisoners at their earliest eligibility date. Perhaps, too, prison overcrowding simply demanded release at the earliest date. Harno apparently thought it the duty of the Illinois Parole Board "to unburden the prisons of their congestion." New York prisons were also overcrowded. The *Times* reported early in 1927 that "[p]ublic demand for longer prison terms and fewer paroles has created a serious penal problem in the State of New York, which has all of its prisons filled to capacity at present with the largest criminal population in its history."[68] But whether the pressure to release inmates on their earliest eligibility date grew from prison overcrowding or from parole boards' own inability to draw considered distinctions among cases, we see at work the same impulse toward efficiency that helped power the plea-bargaining system.

Evading Indeterminacy—Narrow Penalty Ranges. Judges did not depend entirely on early release dates and the cooperation of parole boards to maintain the determinacy of supposedly indeterminate sentences. In Massachusetts, after the 1898 law change ensured release at the end of the minimum term of those prisoners who did not misbehave in prison, judges attempted to keep control of the release dates of even those inmates who broke prison rules and had to serve out their maximum terms. In 1900 the average state prison sentence in Middlesex County called for a minimum term of 4.0 years and a maximum term of 5.2 years. The judges therefore rejected the advice of Warren Spalding, an advocate of the indeterminate sentence and former secretary to the state board of prison commissioners. Spalding had written in 1895 that to accomplish the goals of the indeterminate sentence, judges should leave a margin of at least three years between the minimum and maximum terms of short state prison sentences and a margin of at least five years in longer sentences.[69]

By compressing the gap between minimums and maximums, judges deprived the parole board of almost all discretion to set release dates. In 1910 Middlesex judges approached closer to Spalding's target and imposed an average state prison sentence of 5.8 to 8.2 years. Still, commentators in Massachusetts and elsewhere continued to press demands that judges not squeeze all the indeterminacy out of minimum–maximum sentencing schemes.[70] As the *Harvard Law Review* wrote in 1937, "[T]he history of indeterminate sentence legislation is not without attempts by judges to defeat the purpose of these acts by fixing the minimum term at slightly less than the maximum."[71] Several states specifically legislated against this judicial avoidance tactic.[72]

Evading Indeterminacy—Parole Officials' Cooperation. Of course, it is possible that judges resisted the indeterminacy of the new sentencing schemes merely because they resented the legislature's invasion of their sentencing power and not because they wished to facilitate plea bargaining.[73] The feeling of New York judges that they, "with their years of experience, are better able to determine the proper disposition to be made of any case than the Parole Commission" probably reflected the attitude of most judges.[74] To that extent, plea bargaining was the lucky beneficiary of judges' prideful resistance to indeterminate sentencing. It is also possible that the nation's parole boards regularly released inmates at their earliest eligibility date only because it was efficient to do so and not because such predictable practices aided plea bargaining. It is possible, in other words, that the link between plea bargaining and the downfall of the indeterminate sentence was causal only in the sense that both served the interests of judges and both served the interests of efficiency. Other evidence, however, suggests a more direct and purposive connection between plea bargaining and the receding ideal of the indeterminate sentence.

We begin to see a glimmer of such a link in Professor Warner's 1920s report on the Massachusetts parole board.[75] Warner focused on parole from the Massachusetts reformatory.[76] As we have seen, the reformatory scheme came rather close to true indeterminate sentencing.[77] Judges imposed no minimum or maximum term except for sentences of more than five years, and the controlling statute simply set a ceiling on term length. Warner found that in the exercise of its very broad discretion to set the date of release, the parole board gave a clear if modest preference to those convicts who had pled guilty rather than go to trial. Although about eighty percent of those granted parole had pled guilty, only sixty-seven percent of those *not* granted parole had done so.[78] Warner did not provide the statistic that would have been most useful for my purposes: the proportion of those who pled guilty, versus those who lost at trial, who won parole. But the numbers he did present suggest that one reward for pleading guilty may have been a readier release on parole.

A far stronger causal link between plea bargaining and early release on parole emerges from Dean Harno's 1928 report on the Illinois parole system.[79] Harno and fellow members of a review committee "found that occasionally serious problems arise between the [Parole] Board and the state's attorney and even the trial judge over representations made to a prisoner when his plea of guilty is secured."[80] Harno condemned the practice of making "a promise to the [defendant] or [giving] an intimation to him that if he pleads guilty he will be released, or is likely to be released, after a specified period of confinement."[81] He quoted one prosecutor who frankly wrote the superintendent of the state's reformatory in reference to three young inmates: "Prior to sentence Judge . . . and I agreed that on a plea of guilty we would recommend parole on the minimum time, providing, of course, that the boys, or any one or more of them, had conducted themselves in a manner to warrant parole."[82]

Other letters to the parole board followed—from the judge, defense counsel, police chief, and (again) the prosecutor—all relating or suggesting the same deal.[83] One defense lawyer noted that the judge and prosecutor "advised me they had never known of any case wherein the Parole Board had disregarded a joint recommendation from the State's Attorney and the Presiding Judge."[84] He added that "the State of Illinois will do these boys a great injustice if they do not admit them to parole now."[85]

Another lawyer on the case wrote that "the State should in good faith try to carry out that to which the State's Attorney and the Trial Judge pledged them in so far as they had the power to pledge them."[86] Although Harno's study did not extend beyond Illinois, and although I have found no clear evidence of "parole bargaining" in Massachusetts or other states, I suspect nonetheless that the practice was widespread. After all, by the time of Harno's report, guilty plea rates in the vast majority of American cities exceeded seventy percent, and almost every state had a parole law.[87]

Evading Indeterminacy—Latter-Day Tactics. There is one last piece of evidence—this one of a more modern vintage—suggesting that the indeterminate sentence's demise may have proceeded directly from judges' and prosecutors' determination to persevere in plea bargaining. Around the turn of the twentieth century, at least six states, including California, adopted parole laws that approached close enough to a true indeterminate sentencing scheme to raise a genuine challenge to the vitality of plea bargaining. In a certain range of cases, these statutes deprived the judge of all power to measure the term of confinement to state prison.[88] Instead, when a judge sent a convict to state prison, the parole board unilaterally set the date of release, constrained only by the minimum and maximum terms imposed by law.

Such a regime raised obvious obstacles to any plea-bargaining scheme. Not only did it leave judges powerless to promise a particular release date to defendants who pled guilty, it also disabled them from imposing a certain and harsher penalty on defendants who risked trial and lost. That is, even if judges or prosecutors could have persuaded parole authorities to release convicts who pled guilty at their earliest eligibility dates—an action that might have suited the boards' interests in relieving prison overcrowding or in developing a uniform rule for the treatment of most prisoners—persuading those same boards to penalize convicts who did *not* plead guilty by keeping them *beyond* their first release dates might have proved far more difficult. In contrast, under a typical parole system, judges could readily punish recalcitrant defendants who burdened the court with a trial. They simply imposed harsh terms that, even when reduced by the amount the parole law permitted, still penalized defendants for their imposition on the court.

Despite these obstacles, California judges, prosecutors, and defense lawyers adapted their plea-bargaining tactics to this unfriendly sentencing regime—and they did so in ways that frustrated the goals of the indeterminate sentence. Lynn Mather's study of the operations of the Los Angeles County courts in the early 1970s shows that by that time, only six percent of accused felons ultimately convicted of a crime ever went to state prison. Instead, the vast majority of convicts originally charged with felonies secured a mere misdemeanor conviction and either received probation or served time in a lesser institution or both.[89] The most important vector along which plea bargaining took place was the distinction between a state prison term and no state prison term. Mather reports that when the charged offense called for mandatory state prison time, plea bargaining often took the form of prosecutorial charge bargaining, for without a prosecutor's motion, the judge could not reduce the charge to one that permitted a lesser penalty.[90] But when the judge had the discretion to choose between imposing and not imposing state prison time, plea bargaining tended to take place directly between the judge and defense counsel in a process known as "chamberizing": The judge and lawyers would meet in the judge's chambers, where the judge could spell out or hint at the sentence she would impose should the defendant plead guilty.[91]

Albert Alschuler reports another means of evading the power of California parole authorities to dictate the length of sentence. In the 1960s, when Alschuler observed court business in San Francisco, defendants often pled guilty and were then sentenced to an indeterminate term in state prison. Instead of putting that sentence into effect, however, the judge would suspend it and impose probation during the term of suspension. Then, as a condition of probation, the judge would impose a fixed term in the county jail.[92] By judicial sleight of hand, a seemingly illegal jail term took the place of a seemingly mandatory state prison term—all in accord with the law. Thanks to such ingenious devices, by the time California officially abandoned its experiment with the indeterminate sentence in 1976, there was very little indeterminacy left.[93]

This brief sketch of the indeterminate sentence's slide from prominence suggests that several different causal strands may have tied plea bargaining's continued rise to the indeterminate sentence's demise. Judges, prosecutors, and defense lawyers, first of all, may have evaded the indeterminacy imposed by the new laws by bargaining for definite sentences at certain institutions rather than indefinite sentences at others. Second, some state legislatures acted to require or encourage release on parole at the earliest opportunity and thus restored the predictability that plea bargaining needed to thrive. Third, some judges may have erased the indeterminacy from minimum and maximum sentences by setting the minimum term very close to the maximum. Fourth, parole officials may have rewarded those convicts who pled guilty with earlier release dates. Fifth, some judges and prosecutors appealed to parole authorities to live up to negotiated deals that involved release on parole by a certain date. Finally, a single cause—overcrowding in the criminal justice system—may have promoted both the efficiency of plea bargaining and the nearly automatic decisions of some parole boards to release convicts on their earliest eligibility date, a practice that in turn facilitated plea bargaining by making release dates more predictable.

This multiplicity of mechanisms makes it highly unlikely that the historical correlation between plea bargaining's rise and the indeterminate sentence's fall was simple coincidence. By various devices, the forces that impelled plea bargaining's progress also compelled that the indeterminate sentence make way.

Public Defenders

Moving from the indeterminate sentence to public defenders, we change focus from an institution that threatened plea bargaining and was defeated by it to an institution that promoted plea bargaining and was fostered by it. At the moment of their founding, public defenders' offices and other organizations for the defense of the poor owed a direct debt to plea bargaining. The advocates who promoted these institutions in the early decades of the twentieth century staked their case in part on the claim that public defenders would be good for plea bargaining and therefore good for the justice system. Whether these advocates indeed believed or hoped that public defenders would encourage more guilty pleas is not so clear—it is clear only that they perceived a strategic advantage in claiming that this result would follow. They therefore borrowed from plea bargaining's prestige in the echelons of legal power to promote the cause of their pet reform. That the institutions they created have helped plea bargaining consolidate its position may not have been the reformers' intent, but it was the nearly inevitable result of their actions.

The Founders' Promise. Not all early advocates claimed that public defenders would facilitate guilty pleas,[94] but one of the most prominent did so frankly. In 1915 Mayer Goldman saw his proposals for a public defender fail before the New York legislature.[95] In a defense of his bills published two years later,[96] Goldman seemed at first to promise that under a public defender system, there would be *fewer* guilty pleas. He complained that the lawyers who were assigned to represent indigent defendants under the system that then prevailed in New York persuaded even their innocent clients to plead guilty,[97] and he claimed the public defender system would "minimize[]" guilty pleas.[98]

In several passages in his short book, however, Goldman made it clear that he wished to minimize guilty pleas only by *innocents* and that his proposed public defender would strive to secure guilty pleas from the guilty:

> His function would not be to defeat justice—but to promote it. He should co-operate with the district attorney, whenever not inconsistent with his duty to his client, and wherever possible, in order to bring about an ideal administration of the law. His duty should be to protect the innocent—not to acquit the guilty. He should see that the guilty is fairly punished—not over-punished.[99]

"The law would not require nor expect a public defender to endeavor to acquit a guilty person," Goldman continued later, "any more than that the prosecutor is expected to convict an innocent person."[100] Goldman quoted a New York judge who predicted that "[i]f the public defender's office were well and honestly conducted, I think . . . that a large number of perjured defenses would be eliminated and honest defenses or pleas of guilty substituted which would not only be conducive to good public morals but would save much time and labor in the courts and would reduce the calendar."[101]

Perhaps taking their cue from Goldman's advocacy, the nation's fledgling public defenders declared it to be their goal to win guilty pleas from guilty clients. In a 1918 report, the Los Angeles public defender took unabashed pride in his office's pursuit of efficient and truthful outcomes:

We have not felt that it was our duty to oppose the district attorney, but rather to cooperate with him in setting all the facts before the courts. . . . Our office has tried to keep uppermost the idea that justice should be done and even in criminal cases attorneys should not try to get the defendants "off" regardless of the merits. We have not asked for unnecessary delays and have not resorted to technicalities. . . . *In cases where there is no question of the guilt of the accused, it is the established rule of the office that no trials should be held but that pleas of guilty be entered, thereby saving the county the expense and delay of trials.*[102]

In even more emphatic language, the Los Angeles defender reported in 1922 that "[i]f the defendant admits his guilt we do not go to trial. We require, if we represent him, that he enter a plea of guilty even though that plea will send him to State Prison."[103]

In New York the Voluntary Defenders' Committee announced in its 1917 prospectus that "[w]hen a voluntary defender finds that he has a guilty man on his hands he will not set out to acquit him."[104] Rather, "[t]he first essential step towards improvement is a confession of guilt."[105] A few years later the committee added that "counsel's duty does not require that the state be compelled to prove the guilt of a defendant confessedly guilty."[106] In Omaha the newly established public defender likewise emphasized his attitude of cooperation with the district attorney: "The examination by the county attorney and public defender in all alleged crimes, results in many judgments by the court satisfactory to both the state and the accused, thus saving Douglas County considerable sums that would otherwise be expended in useless trials."[107]

The Omaha defender's claim of cost efficiency, echoed by both the Los Angeles and New York defenders,[108] raises suspicions that such declarations were more public relations gestures than expressions of honestly held views. After all, defenders' offices relied on public or donated funds to provide a service often seen as subversive of effective law enforcement. And just as claims of cost efficiency went far to win public acceptance, so perhaps did eager denials of ambitions to gain freedom for the guilty. It is not easy at this distance to disentangle the beliefs of early public defenders and their sponsors from their rhetoric. Michael McConville and Chester Mirsky, whose work led me through many of the materials I have cited here, emerged from their investigation convinced that the rhetoric was genuine. After reviewing the many studies and commentaries that accompanied the rise of New York's Voluntary Defenders' Committee, they concluded that "[t]he primary goals of the indigent defense system have been and remain to make the criminal law a more effective means for securing social control at minimal expense to the state and to the private bar. The method minimizes adversarial advocacy, and therefore the cost of criminal defense, by compelling guilty pleas and by other non-trial dispositions."[109]

I am less sure. In the heated atmosphere of the early days of the public defender movement, as state legislatures and private bar associations balked at the expense of the new advocates and fretted about their potential to empower the guilty poor,[110] disavowals of zealous advocacy made too much strategic sense to be taken at face value. It is worth noting that one of the more temperate and establishment-bound of the early backers of the public defender system, Reginald Heber Smith of the Boston law firm Hale and Dorr,[111] made it plain he believed even confessedly guilty clients should have a trial and a defense if they wanted one.[112] And although Smith reported with no apparent disapproval the success of public defenders in persuading their guilty clients to plead guilty,[113] he did not hail the promise of increased guilty pleas as a reason to embrace the new institutions. Clara Foltz, an earlier and more radical advocate of the public defender, avoided even the pretense of promising that a good defender would encourage guilty pleas. Instead she lamented that defendants without counsel and those represented by inadequate assigned counsel had little choice but to plead guilty,[114] and she insisted that "one-half of those arrested and charged with crime are actually innocent, and in the eyes of the law all of them are so."[115]

But Foltz's words, written in 1897, moved no legislature to establish a public defender. By the second decade of the next century, when Goldman wrote his defense and the first cautious legislatures dared take up the experiment,[116] supporters had grown savvier. They now promised cost efficiency and ready plea bargaining. It is perhaps a bit of a paradox that this new advocacy frankly recognized the importance of plea bargaining, which the exposés of the *next* decade pretended to reveal to the world. Apparently, while the world was waiting for a series of law professors to discover the prevalence of plea bargaining,[117] those lawyers and other officials who worked in the courts already understood how useful it could be to claim that the public defender would spread plea bargaining even further.

Fulfilling the Promise of Cooperation. Having come into being on a promise, however strategically and insincerely made, that they would facilitate plea bargaining, public defenders apparently proceeded to do just that. Figures comparing the work of early public defenders with that of other criminal lawyers are rare, but they do exist for Los Angeles from 1913 to 1914. The public defender reported that his office resolved seventy percent of its cases by guilty plea—as opposed to sixty-two percent for private counsel assigned to represent indigent defendants and a mere forty-nine percent for paid lawyers.[118] A few years later, both the Los Angeles public defender and the New York Voluntary Defenders' Committee claimed they had persuaded every client who confessed guilt to counsel to do so in court.[119] And a 1923 report of the New York committee proudly told how staff lawyers confronted clients with evidence of their guilt to persuade them to plead guilty: "The notable feature of our work is the large number of persons who plead guilty . . . . These pleas are not always the immediate and open confession of guilt which the figures might imply. We have often been compelled to make extensive investigations into facts, which when revealed to our clients, have resulted in their admissions of guilt."[120]

That these offices in fact promoted plea bargaining is not surprising given their promises to do so. Whether public or charitable, institutional defenders had to report on their operations and constantly justify their continued funding. Regular boasts that high guilty plea rates were yielding the promised cost savings constituted a centerpiece of their survival strategy. The New York Voluntary Defenders' Committee made such claims almost annually.[121] Decades later, long after the public defender had become an established American institution, the same strategy was at work. In 1969 the San Jose public defender reported to a national defenders' conference that by driving down the rate of felony trials from eleven percent to six percent, his office had won the approval of the court's presiding judge. The judge had praised the program as having "'materially assisted the court in the administration of justice . . . at considerable savings to the taxpayers of Santa Clara County.'"[122]

Broader institutional pressures no doubt also played a role in generating high guilty plea rates. Because public defenders did all of their lawyering within a single county before a limited set of judges and against a fixed group of prosecutors, they were apt to be more concerned than more mobile lawyers with earning and keeping the goodwill of those judges and prosecutors. Their reasons were not necessarily selfish. If judges became disaffected with the public defenders and refused to appoint them to represent indigent defendants, then clients would suffer too.

Good relations with the district attorney could also be good for the clientele. The Los Angeles defender explained the benefits in 1922:

> The most cordial relations exist between the office of the District Attorney and that of the Public Defender. This makes it possible to discuss cases frankly and candidly with the purpose of arriving at the truth, so that justice may be done. By reason of this open discussion many cases are dismissed before trial, because after all the evidence available on both sides has been considered the District Attorney sometimes realizes the weakness of his case and moves its dismissal on the ground that the evidence is not sufficient.[123]

In the same vein, an early official of the New York Voluntary Defenders' Committee wrote in 1928 that when a defender's client was innocent, the lawyer would lay the evidence of innocence before the district attorney, who would "recommend to the Court the immediate dismissal of the charge."[124] Given this perceived value of accommodation, public defenders bragged in a decidedly nonadversarial way about how their high guilty plea rates won praise and cooperation from their courtroom counterparts.[125]

Beyond securing the support of their financial sponsors and the approval of prosecutors and judges, defenders had a more selfish interest in seeing their clients plead guilty: They were overworked. As McConville and Mirsky write, "The first forty years of the existence of the Defenders' Committee were marked by moderate increases in staff size and a great expansion of its caseload."[126] Unlike private lawyers who earn more when they work more and can adjust their workloads to their needs, public defenders have only limited power to moderate their labors.[127] They are, in fact, in nearly the same position as prosecutors and judges, whose ranks only the legislature can expand. And the legislature, which shares none of their workload, faces instead the constant pressure to cut costs. The imperative of efficiency that moved both prosecutors and judges to embrace plea bargaining therefore now works to ensure that a large proportion of the defense bar shares in the same cause.

PRINCIPLES OF PROCEDURAL CHANGE

The Impact of Plea Bargaining

If plea bargaining's symbiotic relationships with probation and public defenders and its unhappy encounter with the indeterminate sentence had been three disconnected stories, then we would have a trilogy of evolutionary tales but no theory of evolution. I believe, though, that a fairly simple evolutionary thread runs through these stories. To find it, we should not focus on the ways these three institutions helped or hurt plea bargaining. Those mechanisms were as different as the institutions themselves. Hence probation aided plea bargaining both by offering a new penalty for which minor offenders could bargain and by supplying an officer who told the court about the crime and criminal, making it possible to pass a well-informed sentence without trial. Public defenders helped plea bargaining by funneling many defendants into an advocacy institution so chronically overburdened that it had little recourse but to join prosecutors and judges in a regular practice of plea bargaining. And the indeterminate sentence endangered plea bargaining by threatening to deprive judges and prosecutors of the power to promise fixed concessions that could tempt defendants to plead guilty.

The theme that unites these three stories is not their impact on plea bargaining, but rather plea bargaining's impact on them. In each case, two fairly simple causal mechanisms ensured that those institutions that helped plea bargaining would thrive and any that hurt it would wither. The first was the sheer exercise of power by judges and prosecutors, who stood united in a common preference for bargains over trials. The second was the pressure of business and the consequent imperative of efficiency, which impelled judges and prosecutors toward their common preference for pleas and operated directly on other actors in the system to move them to assist in plea bargaining's rise.

In the case of probation, we saw the first mechanism most clearly at work. I argued in Chapters 2 and 3 that during the second quarter of the nineteenth century, when the practice of on-file plea bargaining took root, part-time prosecutors felt enormous pressure to lighten their loads. Judges felt this pressure less keenly, and they had other objections to plea bargaining as well, so prosecutors had to seek out plea-bargaining methods that required no participation by the judge. The on-file technique served this purpose by empowering prosecutors to promise a fixed concession (that no sentence would be imposed unless the defendant again broke the law) without any endorsement by the court. More versatile than prosecutorial charge bargaining, which relied on the fortuity of a rigid penalty scheme, on-file plea bargaining became more popular as the century wore on.

Eventually it won the favor of judges, who gradually took it over. By the last quarter of the century, when the civil caseload revolution demanded that judges sharply limit their criminal workloads, the on-file technique had become arguably the most important weapon in plea bargaining's arsenal. In 1900 on-file plea bargains accounted for forty-one percent of all case adjudications. The number of defendants who insisted on trial and still secured the favor of a filing approached zero. As this same technique—putting cases on file and staying sentence unless the defendant again misbehaved—eventually took the name probation, it is fair to say that prosecutors and judges fashioned probation as an instrument of plea bargaining.

In the case of the public defender, both evolutionary mechanisms took part in ensuring that this new friend of plea bargaining would find fortune. The early twentieth-century advocates of the public defender thought it wise to claim that defenders would encourage guilty pleas. That claim was sure to please the judges and prosecutors who sponsored plea bargaining, and their good opinion no doubt influenced the legislatures and private legal foundations that established the first public defenders. Once in place, the new defenders found that staying in the judge's favor was essential to survival because the judge dictated who would represent an indigent defendant. Staying in the prosecutor's favor was important because the prosecutor's cooperation could ensure the quick and certain release of innocent clients. The wages of such favor, of course, were taking part in plea bargaining and not contesting the guilt of the guilty.

Though the ethics of such devil's deals might have troubled some defenders, sheer overwork perhaps eased their consciences. Here the second evolutionary mechanism—the imperative of efficiency—came into play. Unable to represent more than a fraction of their clients at trial, public defenders must have felt justified in allocating scarce trials to those who seemed innocent and in negotiating the best possible deals for the rest.

The case of the indeterminate sentence likewise revealed both evolutionary mechanisms at work. The first mechanism, in which judges and prosecutors protected plea bargaining's viability by directly discouraging the indeterminate sentence, operated most prominently. Many judges spurned broad use of their new indeterminate sentencing options. In Middlesex County and elsewhere, they rarely imposed indeterminate sentences to the state reformatory, made less use of the state prison when sentences to that institution became less determinate, and contrived to defeat the purpose of minimum–maximum sentencing laws by squeezing out the gap between minimum and maximum terms. At least occasionally, judges or prosecutors compromised the parole process by promising parole release on a certain date as part of a deal and then asking parole authorities to go along.

We see the second evolutionary mechanism at work in the decisions of parole boards to avoid thousands of individualized decisions by adopting automatic or nearly automatic release dates. Automatic release eased the boards' workloads and, at the same time, helped relieve prison overcrowding. As a happy side effect, they restored enough certainty to the length of confinement to permit plea bargaining to carry on.

The Hallmark of Plea Bargaining's Dominance

In the end, though, the best evidence that plea bargaining has held evolutionary sway over its sibling criminal-justice institutions may not be our ability to spell out evolutionary principles that link the success of those institutions to the interests of plea bargaining. Rather, the most convincing proof may be our inability to name a single important procedural innovation of the last 150 years that threatened to choke off plea bargaining and yet flourished. I have considered already all but two of the most prominent innovations in this period. The two that remain are the due-process revolution of the Warren Court, accomplished in the third quarter of the twentieth century, and the advent of sentencing guideline systems in the fourth quarter. The latter is the topic of the next chapter. The former I take up now.

The Warren Court's sweeping guarantees of a variety of rights to the criminal accused, both time-consuming in themselves and time-consuming to enforce, surely threatened the systemic efficiency that plea bargaining served so well. These newly announced rights did nothing, however, to threaten plea bargaining itself. Precisely because they added so much time to the processes of trial and appeal,[128] these rights supplied both advocates and judges with greater incentives to achieve compromise. Efficiency aside, the due-process revolution deepened the concerns trial judges and prosecutors had for the apparent legitimacy of their acts. Facing a trial minefield littered with exploding error, they were even readier to bargain than before.[129]

Fortunately, the same new rights that created these incentives to plea bargain also created the opportunity to do so. Every new right supplied a new vector along which a bargain could be struck. By sacrificing the chance of freedom promised by a sloppy search warrant, a defendant could win an extra concession on a plea.[130] Fortunately, too, the Supreme Court considered few of its newly guaranteed rights to be nonwaivable. The court declared without embarrassment that the defendant could bargain away virtually all of them in exchange for the prosecutor's promise to demand something less than her due.[131]

In only one, largely insignificant way has the due-process revolution crimped plea bargaining's progress. I argued in Chapter 4 that the defendant-testimony laws of the latter half of the nineteenth century, which gave defendants the right to testify in their own defense, moved many of the most accomplished criminals to plead guilty. Because juries would regard the silence of a defendant who had the right to speak as a sign of guilt, and because prosecutors could impeach those defendants who did speak with evidence of their past convictions, defendants who carried the burden of a criminal record found themselves trapped in a procedural catch-22.

The situation was worst in those states that permitted prosecutors to comment to juries on the defendant's silence and thereby stir up their natural suspicions.[132] But in 1965, the Supreme Court ruled that such comment violated a defendant's right against self-incrimination.[133] Moreover, the law of evidence has evolved to make judges somewhat slower to admit evidence of past crimes to impeach criminal defendants who take the stand in their defense.[134] No doubt these developments operate against plea bargaining's interests by making trials more viable for defendants who otherwise might have felt compelled to strike a deal.

And yet these changes have had no far-reaching impact. Defendant-testimony laws appear to have played a smaller role in plea bargaining's progress than, for example, the civil caseload revolution of the same period or the rise of probation. Moreover, prosecutorial comment on silence probably added little to the power of defendant-testimony laws to discourage trials. As Arthur Train wrote in 1906 in a state that barred such comment,[135] "The writer has heard more than one talesman say, in discussing a verdict, 'Of course we couldn't take it against him, but we *knew* he was guilty because he was afraid to testify.'"[136] Or as Judge Seth Ames wrote in 1867 in another such state, the defendant's silence "will, and inevitably must, create a presumption against him, even if every page of the statute-book contained a provision that it should not."[137] Such sentiments surely continue to discourage trials among defendants with bad records except when they are able to persuade the court to keep out evidence of their records. That is, if a ruling that bars comment on the defendant's silence constitutes the only procedural advance of the last century and a half that challenges plea bargaining's onward march, then plea bargaining has faced remarkably feeble resistance.

9

The Balance of Power to Plea Bargain

Here the reader might object that at least one twentieth-century procedural innovation, the nonjury trial, has arisen in the path of plea bargaining. Until now, I have used "trial" as a shorthand for "jury trial" because a jury sat in judgment at virtually every trial held in the intermediate and upper-tier courts of Middlesex County during the nineteenth century.[1] It is true that on the lowest tier of the Massachusetts judiciary, a lone magistrate rendered verdicts in the most petty criminal trials.[2] It is also true that other states provided more broadly for nonjury trials in misdemeanor cases.[3] But not until the early twentieth century did more than a few states give defendants facing felony charges the option to waive a jury trial and put themselves instead on the judgment of the court.[4]

There are two reasons to expect that giving defendants a broad right to choose nonjury trials might have stalled the plea-bargaining juggernaut. The most obvious is that nonjury trials appear to eliminate or at least moderate the main incentives to plea bargain. Because they are relatively quick,[5] they make the efficiency advantages of plea bargaining less weighty. Because experienced and savvy judges are less likely to reject powerful evidence of guilt than are a dozen randomly chosen laypersons, prosecutors can be less fearful of capricious acquittals and more willing to go to trial. And because it is more difficult to generate reversible error before a judicial fact-finder, judges can be less fearful of reversals and the resulting damage to their reputations.

The second reason to expect that nonjury trials might have slowed plea bargaining's rise looks not to the balance of incentives between trial and plea, but to the balance of power between judge and prosecutor. Raymond Moley, probably the earliest theorist of the dynamics of plea bargaining, predicted in 1928 that nonjury trials would reallocate courtroom power in a way that might cause "an immediate decline in the proportion of pleas of guilty."[6] "It would seem," he wrote, "that the way to restrict the discretion of the prosecutor is to give wide powers to the judge." Nonjury trials would undermine prosecutors' power to plea bargain in a way that no "direct attack upon the practice of prosecutors" could—by investing judges with a competing power to resolve cases efficiently.[7]

History has proved false all such theories of the impact of nonjury trials. Within a decade of Moley's prediction, most states permitted nonjury felony trials,[8] and by 1960 every state did so.[9] But plea bargaining marched on and now accounts for a higher proportion of criminal dispositions than it did when virtually every felony had to be tried by jury.[10] Informed by this hindsight, we can see now that there never was good reason to think that a broader right to nonjury trial would hold back plea bargaining's progress.

Consider first how the incentives of costs and risks play themselves out in the typical plea negotiation. Assume the defendant regards his chances of acquittal at trial to be, say, thirty percent.[11] In exchange for his guilty plea, he normally will demand a deduction of about thirty percent from the sentence he would have faced had he gone to trial and lost. Those defendants who value certainty for its own sake will demand a smaller deduction. Those who regard immediate prison time (following a quick plea) as more painful than future time (following an extended trial) will demand a larger deduction.

Meanwhile the prosecutor, who is spared a thirty-percent risk of loss, normally will be willing to grant a thirty-percent reduction in sentence *plus* a concession that reflects the saved expense and effort of trial.

Because the prosecutor is willing to give more than the defendant demands, the parties almost always find common ground. And because the judge is spared both the time of trial and the risk of reversal, she almost never stands between the parties and their deal. Trials therefore take place only when the parties calculate the likely post-trial sentence or the odds of acquittal differently or something else interferes with their freedom to bargain.

There is no reason the option of a nonjury trial should alter this dynamic greatly. Because the Constitution guarantees defendants a jury trial in all but petty cases, a nonjury trial happens only when the defendant elects it. Yet no defendant would do so who plans ultimately to plead guilty. Because nonjury trials confront prosecutors with both smaller costs and smaller risks, prosecutors presumably will offer a smaller discount from the post-trial sentence in exchange for the defendant's plea. So only those defendants who are bent upon trial would choose trial before a judge. Because juries are typically more likely than judges to find reasonable doubt where the evidence is strong, only a select few defendants spy advantage in electing trial before a judge. A defendant charged with child abuse, for example, especially if the prosecution's evidence is weak, might decide that a judge would weigh emotional facts more dispassionately than a jury. But such defendants are the exception.

If the availability of nonjury trials has influenced the rate of plea bargaining, therefore, it is not because nonjury trials have altered the parties' incentives to deal. Rather, it is because a small amount of plea-bargaining power now has shifted from prosecutor to judge. Moley anticipated such a power shift. But because he misperceived the existing dynamic of bargaining power, he got the significance of the shift exactly backward. His belief that prosecutors alone drove the plea-bargaining process prompted him to conclude that judges would restrict plea bargaining if only they could. In fact, increasing judicial power by easing access to nonjury trials merely has made plea bargains that much more likely.

As our long immersion in the records of Middlesex County made plain, prosecutors never could do much plea bargaining on their own. Absent judges' cooperation, Massachusetts prosecutors of the first three-quarters of the nineteenth century maintained, at best, an underground resistance of plea bargaining. They built a narrow charge-bargaining practice upon the rigid penalty structures of the liquor and murder laws. And from their procedural power to withhold a motion for sentence, they fashioned a quiet scheme of on-file plea bargaining. Only after judges came over to the side of plea bargaining in the last quarter of the nineteenth century did plea bargaining achieve the dominance that Moley discovered in his studies of the 1920s. Nothing but the full-fledged participation of judges could explain how the guilty plea rate in Middlesex County reached eighty-seven percent by the end of the century. As the vast majority of these cases arose under statutes that assigned broad sentencing discretion to the judge, most plea bargains depended on the judge's confederacy in the cause.

In fact, judges may have grown to be even greater advocates of plea bargaining—or at least of certain plea bargains—than prosecutors. Consider the relative interests that judge and prosecutor bring to the bargaining process. In the average case, a bargain saves time for both the judge and the prosecutor, but also hands victory to the prosecutor. So we are accustomed to think of the prosecutor as having the greater interest in striking a deal. In many cases, however, the judge maintains an efficiency-based interest in a plea bargain, as well as an interest in avoiding the risk of reversal, but the prosecutor stands opposed.

Most prosecutors, after all, must face reelection before a constituency that may regard plea bargaining as the prosecutor's capitulation to expediency. Even if the public stands indifferent to plea bargaining in general, it is likely to demand the full measure of punishment in those cases that prompt great fear or outrage.[12] In contrast, even those judges who must face the electorate rarely take responsibility for plea bargains, which the public usually blames on prosecutors. And on the higher plane of principle, prosecutors trained as advocates might see the defendant's crime as more vile and might peg the odds of conviction higher than would the judge and therefore might consider the case to be "worth" more on a plea. As a consequence, the judge might be more willing than the prosecutor to offer the defendant a concession great enough to induce a plea.

Normally, such disagreements between judge and prosecutor pose no obstacle to a successful plea bargain. The judge, after all, controls the sentence and therefore simply offers the defendant a larger concession than the prosecutor thinks right. But where the statutory penalty scheme imposes a harsh minimum sentence for a particular offense, the prosecutor's refusal to reduce the charge can thwart the judge's desire to deal. Now we see how the nonjury trial can shift the balance of power decisively toward the judge. When the judge believes that a plea bargain on the defendant's terms is appropriate, but the prosecutor withholds the nol pros that could make the deal possible, the judge has a trump card. The judge can advise the defendant to elect a nonjury trial on the understanding, spoken or otherwise, that the judge will fashion her own nol pros simply by finding the defendant not guilty of that part of the prosecutor's charge that stands in the way of the lower sentence the judge wants to impose.[13]

The prosecutor now confronts a dilemma: He may persist in his refusal to deal and embark upon a time-consuming nonjury trial with a predetermined result. Or he may succumb to the terms of the bargain and secure the sentence that the judge perceives as fair without the trial.[14] Overpowered by the judge, the resource-wise prosecutor submits—and deals. Now we see the magnitude of Moley's error. For judges have deployed the new power given them by nonjury trials not to rein in plea bargaining, but to spur it on in the face of occasional prosecutorial opposition.

In a world in which plea bargaining dominates the mechanisms of criminal justice, the option of nonjury trials may achieve the best possible balance of the power to deal. The defendant who wishes to regulate her risks by striking a bargain can hold out for the best terms that either judge or prosecutor will offer. The defendant's deal-making need not be subject to the whims of either officer because the agreement of one normally is enough for the deal to proceed. The judge, as I have said, can strike a bargain even without the prosecutor's compliance. If, on the other hand, the judge rejects a deal arranged between defendant and prosecutor, the prosecutor often can limit the judge's sentencing options by selectively nol prossing charges or parts of charges to guarantee the defendant a concession in exchange for her plea. In the end, it is rare that either judge or prosecutor can scuttle a deal by insisting on a harsher sentence than the other thinks right.

But two conditions, coming together, can destroy this balance of power. The first is that the prosecutor be granted the power to veto a nonjury trial and insist instead on trial by jury. In our federal system and in many states, the prosecutor indeed holds this power.[15] With it, he can exact the full measure of punishment prescribed by those statutes that impose a minimum punishment below which the judge may not dip. The second condition is that there be many such statutes. In our federal system and in those states that have adopted rigid sentencing guidelines, the entire criminal code now approaches this form. Guidelines systems assign a narrow range of sentencing options to virtually every criminal violation and allot judges only limited power to impose a sentence below that range. They thereby invest prosecutors with the power, moderated only by the risk of loss at trial, to dictate many sentences simply by choosing one set of charges over another.

The New Order

Until the United States Sentencing Guidelines took effect in November 1987, federal criminal statutes commonly gave judges unreviewable discretion to choose any sentence of days or decades, constrained only by widely separated minimum and maximum penalties.[16] By impressing a rigid and finely graduated penalty scheme onto the entire criminal code, the Guidelines wiped out much of this old discretion. The watchword of the guideline-writing process was *uniformity*, and Congress aimed to ensure that offenders with similar histories who committed similar acts would be treated alike.[17]

As both mechanism and metaphor of the new rigidity, the U.S. Sentencing Commission conceived a 258-celled "sentencing table" (see Figure 9.1).[18] Across the top, the table assigns each defendant a criminal history score of between one and six, mounting with the gravity of his past convictions. Down the side, it carves the forms of criminal conduct into forty-three levels of increasing magnitude. For each offender and every offense, the sentencing judge must plot the box that lies at the intersection of these scores. Each of the 258 boxes prescribes a permissible

SENTENCING TABLE
(in months of imprisonment)

	Offense Level	Criminal History Category (Criminal History Points)					
		I (0 or 1)	II (2 or 3)	III (4, 5, 6)	IV (7, 8, 9)	V (10, 11, 12)	VI (13 or more)
	1	0-6	0-6	0-6	0-6	0-6	0-6
	2	0-6	0-6	0-6	0-6	0-6	1-7
	3	0-6	0-6	0-6	0-6	2-8	3-9
	4	0-6	0-6	0-6	2-8	4-10	6-12
Zone A	5	0-6	0-6	1-7	4-10	6-12	9-15
	6	0-6	1-7	2-8	6-12	9-15	12-18
	7	0-6	2-8	4-10	8-14	12-18	15-21
	8	0-6	4-10	6-12	10-16	15-21	18-24
Zone B	9	4-10	6-12	8-14	12-18	18-24	21-27
	10	6-12	8-14	10-16	15-21	21-27	24-30
Zone C	11	8-14	10-16	12-18	18-24	24-30	27-33
	12	10-16	12-18	15-21	21-27	27-33	30-37
	13	12-18	15-21	18-24	24-30	30-37	33-41
	14	15-21	18-24	21-27	27-33	33-41	37-46
	15	18-24	21-27	24-30	30-37	37-46	41-51
	16	21-27	24-30	27-33	33-41	41-51	46-57
	17	24-30	27-33	30-37	37-46	46-57	51-63
	18	27-33	30-37	33-41	41-51	51-63	57-71
	19	30-37	33-41	37-46	46-57	57-71	63-78
	20	33-41	37-46	41-51	51-63	63-78	70-87
	21	37-46	41-51	46-57	57-71	70-87	77-96
	22	41-51	46-57	51-63	63-78	77-96	84-105
	23	46-57	51-63	57-71	70-87	84-105	92-115
	24	51-63	57-71	63-78	77-96	92-115	100-125
	25	57-71	63-78	70-87	84-105	100-125	110-137
	26	63-78	70-87	78-97	92-115	110-137	120-150
Zone D	27	70-87	78-97	87-108	100-125	120-150	130-162
	28	78-97	87-108	97-121	110-137	130-162	140-175
	29	87-108	97-121	108-135	121-151	140-175	151-188
	30	97-121	108-135	121-151	135-168	151-188	168-210
	31	108-135	121-151	135-168	151-188	168-210	188-235
	32	121-151	135-168	151-188	168-210	188-235	210-262
	33	135-168	151-188	168-210	188-235	210-262	235-293
	34	151-188	168-210	188-235	210-262	235-293	262-327
	35	168-210	188-235	210-262	235-293	262-327	292-365
	36	188-235	210-262	235-293	262-327	292-365	324-405
	37	210-262	235-293	262-327	292-365	324-405	360-life
	38	235-293	262-327	292-365	324-405	360-life	360-life
	39	262-327	292-365	324-405	360-life	360-life	360-life
	40	292-365	324-405	360-life	360-life	360-life	360-life
	41	324-405	360-life	360-life	360-life	360-life	360-life
	42	360-life	360-life	360-life	360-life	360-life	360-life
	43	life	life	life	life	life	life

Figure 9.1. Sentencing table. Source: U.S. Sentencing Commission, *Guidelines* (1999), ch. 5, pt. A, at 310.

sentencing range in which the upper term rarely exceeds the lower term by more than twenty-five percent.[19] Absent unusual circumstances, the sentencing judge must choose a penalty that falls within the range.

Even as the Guidelines first took form, observers worried that such a system of narrowly confined sentencing options could work a massive transfer of sentencing discretion from judges to prosecutors. As in the old Massachusetts liquor cases, narrowly fixed penalty provisions would mean the prosecutor could constrain the judge's sentencing options by manipulating the slate of charges. If the prosecutor refused to drop or alter the charges, the judge would have only limited power to avoid the sentence commanded by law.[20] The likely consequence was that in any plea negotiation, the prosecutor's power to promise the defendant a particular sentence in exchange for his plea would be greater than before—while the judge's power to make a similar promise would be less.

As the Sentencing Commission set about the task of guideline-writing, it specifically noted the risk of increased prosecutorial discretion and took five steps to keep prosecutors' sentencing and bargaining power in check.[21] Two of these—establishing "guideline education programs" and funding research into the Guidelines' operation—warrant little notice.[22] Though both have proved more substantial than skeptics might have predicted,[23] they probably have had little impact on courtroom practice. A third, to encourage the Department of Justice to enforce the terms of the Guidelines on rank-and-file prosecutors,[24] probably had some bite. Still, enforcing the Guidelines can have had little effect beyond what the Guidelines themselves require. So we must look at the last two of the Commission's steps if we hope to find meaningful limits on prosecutors' power to dictate sentences. Each of these measures, by assigning specific countervailing powers to sentencing judges, appeared aimed at preserving the careful balance of bargaining power that the Guidelines threatened to unsettle.

The most far-reaching step sought to ensure that when assigning an offense level of between one and forty-three, the sentencing judge would consider more than the offense charged. All parties saw that to permit the stated charges to dictate the severity of the offense simply would commit all sentencing authority to prosecutors. Instead, the Guidelines require the judge to consider certain broadly defined "Relevant Conduct" of the defendant, whether embraced by the charges against him or not.[25] On a finding by a mere preponderance of the evidence that such conduct took place, the judge normally must choose a sentence that reflects the full gravity of that conduct, capped only by the maximum statutory penalty for the crime charged.[26] Federal probation officers, meanwhile, were assigned the duty to act as the court's "independent investigator" and to inform the judge of the defendant's relevant conduct, even when the prosecutor and defense counsel would prefer to keep it hidden.[27] As the Commission explained, its aim was to scuttle prosecutorial charge bargains of the old-fashioned kind—"to limit the degree to which the prosecutor's choice of charge will ultimately dictate the guideline sentence."[28]

The Commission's second means of balancing sentencing authority between judge and prosecutor was more direct. In a series of policy pronouncements, the Guidelines simply call upon judges to reject plea bargains proposed by the prosecutor and defense lawyer whenever those bargains threaten to "undermine the sentencing guidelines."[29] Although there is a good deal of controversy about whether judges *must* scuttle such deals,[30] few doubt judges have the power to do so if they choose.

In making these two measures the mechanism for constraining prosecutors' sentencing discretion, the Commission seems to have repeated Raymond Moley's mistake of a half-century before. Moley had predicted that permitting nonjury trials would empower judges to slow the advance of prosecutorial plea bargaining. But judges long since had joined forces with prosecutors in promoting plea bargaining and had little interest in undermining the practice. On the contrary, nonjury trials enabled judges in some circumstances to push the bounds of plea bargaining past where prosecutors wanted to take them—by offering defendants better terms than the prosecutor's best offer.

In empowering judges to keep prosecutorial bargaining from "undermin[ing]" the Sentencing Guidelines, the Commission betrayed its ignorance of this history. The Commission gave judges meaningful discretion to impose sentences *harsher* than those offered by the government in the course of a plea negotiation. There simply is no reason to suppose, however, that a modern American trial judge should want to frustrate a prosecutorial deal in the average case by demanding harsher terms than the prosecutor thinks right. Least of all would a judge do so when the only alternative is a full-fledged jury trial. Yet a jury trial is the only plausible consequence of unsettling a prosecutor's deal, for few defendants would elect a nonjury trial once the judge has announced her preference for a harsh result. It is particularly ironic that the Commission should have expected judges to guard against *undermining* the Guidelines, when so many judges have complained so loudly about the steep penalties locked in place by the Guidelines and by certain mandatory sentencing laws that took effect at about the same time.[31]

A good deal of evidence suggests that many judges have gone far to avoid the oversight role Congress assigned them. Many pointedly look the other way when prosecutors and defense lawyers conspire to hide relevant conduct that otherwise would compel a stiffer sentence.[32] It is true that probation officers, as agents of the court, have a duty to make independent investigations of offenders' conduct and to report their findings to the court. It is also true that many probation officers discharge this task in earnest—though many others do not.[33] But even when a probation officer presents the court with evidence of conduct warranting a tougher sentence than the lawyers have proposed, the judge often ignores such findings in favor of the facts as presented by the parties.[34]

Judges' Limited Powers of Leniency

Had the Commission genuinely hoped to establish a balance of bargaining power between prosecutor and judge, it would have empowered sentencing judges to undermine the Guidelines *further* than prosecutors chose. That is, it would have enabled them to offer plea bargains on *easier* terms. Defendants then would have had a second bargaining partner, one with interests less antagonistic to their own.

But doomed to repeat Moley's mistake, the Commission sought to control prosecutorial charge bargaining by investing judges with powers badly suited to the task. Neither of the most significant steps the Commission took to limit prosecutors' power bears any promise of yielding a more favorable deal for the average defendant than that offered by the prosecutor. The Guidelines' requirement that sentencing judges consider an offender's relevant conduct merely empowers judges to impose harsher terms than the prosecutor sees fit. And provisions authorizing judges to reject prosecutorial plea bargains simply allow judges to demand jury trials instead—a result most judges would rather avoid. Defendants therefore normally will find that the best deal they can get is the one the prosecutor offers.

Still, judges do not lack all power to impose a lower sentence than that sought by the prosecutor. A resourceful judge can find such power tucked in at least three of the Guidelines' procedural crannies.[35] All of these sources of power, though, prove on closer inspection to be shallower than they first appear.

Granting Discounts for Acceptance of Responsibility. In the introduction to the original Guidelines, the Commission noted that "inasmuch as those who currently plead guilty often receive lesser sentences, the guidelines also permit the court to impose lesser sentences on those defendants who accept responsibility" for their misconduct.[36] At first, the Commission limited this reward to a two-step reduction in offense level, yielding a discount from the offender's sentence of somewhere between twenty and thirty-five percent.[37] In 1992 it created an option for a three-step reduction.[38]

In practice, however, this grant of discretion invests judges with little power to undercut prosecutors' desired sentences. The Department of Justice explicitly authorizes federal prosecutors to agree to reductions for acceptance of responsibility in the course of plea bargaining.[39] Plea bargains so routinely involve these discounts that they have become part of the background noise of plea negotiations under the Guidelines. In the rare case in which prosecutors object to such discounts, they perhaps can frustrate them simply by bringing more or higher charges in the first place—especially if those charges carry mandatory sentencing provisions. Conversely, prosecutors who feel more generous than the judge usually can outdo the judge's bounty simply by pruning back these same charges. So it will be an unusual case in which a judge can use a discount for acceptance of responsibility to offer the defendant a more lenient sentence than that favored by the prosecution.

Rejecting Relevant Conduct. A resourceful judge also can reduce an offender's sentence by finding that certain "relevant conduct" did *not* take place. That is, a prosecutor may bring a slate of charges in the confidence that a judge's findings of relevant conduct will result in imposition of a stiff sentence. By finding that no such conduct took place, the judge can disappoint the prosecutor's expectation of a long sentence. Yet this judicial power, too, is less potent than it seems. To prevail on the question of relevant conduct, the prosecutor need merely prove such conduct by a preponderance of the evidence.[40] And the relevant conduct in question— such as the weight of drugs sold or the quantity of money stolen or the fact of a victim's injuries—often is among the most readily proved parts of the government's case.[41]

In these circumstances, the average judge may lack the moxie to declare the behavior not proved.[42] Even if the judge dared, prosecutors often have ways of circumventing such rulings. Instead of tacking alleged relevant conduct onto an underlying charge, a prosecutor could bring separate or higher charges that reflect the totality of the offender's conduct. A defendant who pleads guilty to such charges—or who is found guilty of them by a jury—normally must be sentenced based on the totality of the conduct charged. The judge will have no capacity to reduce the sentence merely by finding that certain (charged) conduct did not take place. The prosecutor's hand will be especially strong if the crimes charged carry mandatory-minimum sentencing provisions that the judge has no power to undermine.[43]

Departing Beneath the Guideline Range. Finally, a resourceful judge can find meaningful power to undercut a prosecutor's proposed sentence in the limited authority Congress granted judges to "depart" from the penalty ranges dictated by the sentencing table. The law permits such departures if "there exists an aggravating or mitigating circumstance of a kind, or to a degree, not adequately taken into consideration by the Sentencing Commission in formulating the Guidelines."[44] Yet even as the law allots judges this discretion to depart, the guidelines snatch much of it back by specifically discouraging several of the most attractive grounds for departure. The offender's youth, mental soundness, employment history, and family responsibilities are all deemed "not ordinarily relevant" in granting departures.[45] In 1991 the Commission reported that 86.6 percent of district judges surveyed said there were circumstances in which they would like to depart, but felt constrained from doing so by the guidelines.[46] Despite such complaints, the Commission lengthened the list of disapproved grounds for departure by adding the offender's military or public service, his charitable work, and his lack of guidance as a youth.[47]

Those judges willing to depart on some other basis face a second disincentive to leniency. Congress gave prosecutors the right to appeal downward departures from the guideline range.[48] We have seen already how judges fear the flame of reversal on appeal. When the question is whether to grant a downward departure, judges' fears of reversal have proved particularly well-founded. On the one hand, federal prosecutors challenge judges' decisions to depart relatively rarely—in an average of just two dozen cases each year—suggesting that prosecutors perhaps overlook more modest judicial departures. On the other hand, when prosecutors do appeal, they normally prevail. Between 1996 and 2001, the government lost only twenty-nine percent of its appeals on departure issues.[49]

Set against the very real risk of reversal that judges face when they dare depart from the Guidelines is the almost complete security from such risk they enjoy when they don't. As long as the judge makes no legal error in applying the Guidelines and as long as she understands she has the power to depart, neither prosecutor nor defendant may appeal her decision not to do so.[50] As Kate Stith and José Cabranes have written, the "slightest comprehension of human nature" would suggest the inevitable consequence of this incentive structure—that judges rarely will risk offense by departing.[51]

The numbers generally bear out Stith and Cabranes's prediction. Judges virtually never depart above the guideline range, thereby evading almost any risk of a defense appeal. Upward departures have not occurred in even one percent of all cases since 1995.[52] Though less wary of prosecutors' appeals, judges do not risk them often. At first, however, the numbers appear deceptively large. Downward departures took place in a record 35.4 percent of all cases in 2001.[53] But prosecutors specifically requested the great majority of these departures as part of either a plea agreement or a cooperation arrangement with the defendant.[54] It is a fact worth emphasizing that the single largest category of downward departures is that for "substantial assistance," granted defendants in exchange for information against others. Yet both the Guidelines and case law, following a statutory lead, make clear that absent exceptional circumstances, a judge may depart downward for substantial assistance only after the prosecutor has "authorized" the court to do so.[55] If our concern for the moment is to identify those downward departures that reflect a judge's bid to undercut the prosecutor's desired sentence (and therefore those that risk a prosecution appeal), then we must exclude from the list departures granted pursuant to plea agreements and those based on substantial assistance.

We also should exclude the large number of departures granted because the defendant consented to be deported. It is likely that prosecutors either specifically requested or failed to object to many or most such departures—after all, the defendant's prompt exit from the country serves some of the goals of punishment while sparing scarce prison space.[56] Once we subtract deportation departures from the list, we are left with a small bundle of downward departures arguably granted against prosecutors' wishes—the only downward departures that pose any real risk of appeal. While growing more common in recent years, such departures never have occurred in more than 12.8 percent of all cases nationwide.[57] Historically they have been far rarer, averaging only 7.3 percent of all cases since the Guidelines took effect.[58] Even these numbers probably exaggerate judges' willingness to grant downward departures in the face of government opposition. One suspects that many downward departures besides those specifically labeled as having been granted "[p]ursuant to plea agreement" arose out of a deal in which the prosecutor promised, in exchange for the defendant's plea, not to challenge downward departures requested by the defendant.[59]

In short, most judges probably share the sentiments of one who said "the best departures" are those "that aren't appealed."[60] I do not, however, want to exaggerate judges' unwillingness to risk reversal. Some surely are readier than others to antagonize prosecutors by giving shorter sentences than the government bargained for. In the District of Connecticut, for example, where the federal bench has shown little fondness for the Guidelines, judges apparently have deployed probation officers to assist them in undermining prosecutors' desired sentences. Judges have asked that probation officers report on offenders' personal characteristics, even though the Guidelines largely deem such characteristics "not ordinarily relevant" to the decision whether to depart.[61] While the average federal judge departed downward for reasons other than substantial assistance in 18.3 percent of all cases in 2001, Connecticut's judges did so in 33.8 percent of all cases.[62]

Unfortunately, it is impossible to know how common such maverick judges are. Although the Commission publishes data showing how often judges in different districts grant downward departures, its district-by-district figures do not break down the specific grounds for such departures beyond separating those for substantial assistance from all others. We cannot know, therefore, what proportion of these downward departures genuinely antagonize prosecutors and risk reversal. For example, it is likely that the four judicial districts with the nation's highest rates of "other downward departures"—Arizona, the Southern District of California, New Mexico, and the Eastern District of Washington (which has a large population of Mexican migrant farmworkers)—also have many cases in which defendants face deportation and receive downward departures on that basis, perhaps unopposed by the government.[63] And a great many marijuana traffickers in the first three of these districts receive downward departures by agreement with the prosecutor under the government's "fast track" program, established along the Mexican border, which rewards low-level drug dealers and immigration defendants who plead guilty promptly or waive deportation proceedings.[64]

Elsewhere in the country, a high rate of "other downward departures" in a particular district likewise may be evidence not of maverick judges willing to risk reversal by undercutting prosecutors' deals, but of maverick prosecutors bent on cutting those deals and willing to agree to downward departures to get them. Moreover, not all maverick judges truly are mavericks in the sense that they flout the risk of reversal when they authorize departures over the prosecutor's objection. The controlling case law in some circuits—including the Second Circuit, which embraces Connecticut—extends trial judges a substantial measure of freedom to depart downward from the guideline range.[65]

Evidence of Imbalanced Bargaining Power

Despite such variations across districts and regions, two central facts remain. Under the Guidelines, judges have far less power to undersell prosecutors' sentencing offers than they had in pre-Guidelines days. And prosecutors necessarily have greater power to dictate sentences in the course of plea negotiations.[66] If early commentators perhaps exaggerated the magnitude of this power shift,[67] so have recent revisionists reached too far in minimizing it. Indeed, two such revisionists, Frank Bowman and Michael Heise, having set out to disprove such a power shift, instead produced convincing evidence of its occurrence.

In a detailed 2001 study, Bowman and Heise sought to debunk the old "articles of faith" that the Guidelines and new mandatory-minimum sentencing laws "conferred immense discretionary authority on federal prosecutors" and "handcuffed judges, depriving them of the power to ameliorate harsh sentences."[68] Bowman and Heise's argument faced criticism on its own terms,[69] but whatever its inherent merits, the authors themselves proved to be its undoing. In an intensive district-by-district follow-up study published early in 2002, they found that between 1992 and 1999, average drug sentences fell in just over half the nation's federal judicial districts. They wisely concluded that rising plea-bargaining rates were a prominent force behind falling drug sentences. But they admitted their surprise at another "odd" and "puzzling" finding—that although falling drug sentences correlated strongly and consistently with rising prosecutorial workload (measured as cases per prosecutor), drug sentences showed no statistically significant correlation with judicial workload.[70]

These results would not have puzzled Middlesex prosecutors of the late nineteenth century. They knew, as Bowman and Heise surmised, that rising workloads prompted judges as well as prosecutors to cut deals where they could. Yet they also knew that no official, judge or prosecutor, could plea bargain without the power to *reduce* the defendant's sentence below the sentence he would face after trial and conviction. And both the Guidelines and the mandatory sentencing provisions that apply to many of the nation's drug laws confer that power on prosecutors while largely denying it to judges.

In one stroke, then, Bowman and Heise helped confirm three critical features of the dynamic of plea bargaining. First of all, plea bargaining responds to caseload pressure. As the authors concluded with evident reluctance, "maybe it's the workload, stupid."[71] Second, plea bargaining depends on the prosecutor's (or judge's) power to assure the defendant a lower sentence than he would face after trial. And third, the federal

Sentencing Guidelines, by stripping judges almost entirely of the power of leniency, have made plea bargaining the prosecutor's prerogative. As Bowman and Heise acknowledged, again reluctantly, "it may be that prosecutors are better able to manipulate sentencing outcomes to relieve caseload pressure than are judges."[72]

The Consequences of Imbalanced Bargaining Power

Bowman and Heise's findings merely confirm what a commonsense evaluation of the Guidelines, informed by the lessons of history, suggests. The question is not whether prosecutors hold more bargaining power today than in pre-Guidelines days—they surely do. The question is only what impact we might expect this power shift to have on the course of plea bargaining.

Severity of Sentences. We should expect, most directly, that defendants will face longer sentences after guilty pleas. This conclusion at first seems paradoxical, for Bowman and Heise found that prosecutorial plea bargaining produces lower sentences. Their data, however, showed merely that plea bargaining, even when conducted by prosecutors, yields lower sentences than trials. At the same time, plea bargaining *with prosecutors alone* yields higher sentences than plea bargaining with *both* prosecutors and judges in a system that allots each the power of leniency.

In non-Guidelines systems, defendants often can sound out both judge and prosecutor and take the best deal offered by either. But in today's federal courts, the only actor fully empowered to undermine the prosecutor's desired sentence is the jury. Unless the judge risks reversal by departing downward from the guideline range, the prosecutor's bottom line normally will be the best deal the defendant can get. The Guidelines therefore have left most defendants with a single bargaining partner, and he is the partner least likely to look at things the defendant's way.

It is probably impossible, however, to confirm that our new imbalance of bargaining power has resulted in longer sentences after pleas. There is no question that the typical federal sentence today is far longer than in pre-Guidelines days.[73] But the dominant causes of this increase are very likely the mandatory-minimum sentencing provisions that took effect in the late 1980s and the Guidelines themselves, which locked in place greater penalties and would have prompted considerably longer sentences even absent the new bargaining dynamic.[74] The difficulty of disentangling these causal strands makes it unlikely one could ever succeed in isolating the impact of the new imbalance of bargaining power. We nonetheless can be confident, I believe, that a substantial part of the overall increase in sentence length seen in the past dozen or so years traces to this source.

Frequency of Pleas. Though we can feel sure that prosecutors' increased bargaining strength has lengthened post-plea sentences, the new imbalance of bargaining power is unlikely, standing alone, to have made plea bargains more common. It is true that in Massachusetts during the first three-quarters of the nineteenth century, prosecutors' power to dictate penalties by manipulating charges in liquor and murder cases helps explain why plea bargaining emerged first in those contexts. But times have changed. In the early nineteenth century, judges did not share the prosecutorial urge to plea bargain. By the time the Guidelines took effect in the late 1980s, however, judges so rarely opposed plea agreements struck between defendants and prosecutors that plea bargaining took place with enormous regularity even when the governing statutes gave judges a nearly free hand in sentencing. In fact we might have expected that by depriving judges of much of their former power to undercut prosecutors' desired sentences, the Guidelines would have *reduced* the likelihood of guilty pleas. After all, judges now have far less freedom to sweeten the deal to entice recalcitrant defendants to plead in those rare cases in which prosecutor and defendant are unable to come to terms.

And yet since the creation of the Sentencing Guidelines, plea bargaining in American federal courts has advanced with striking speed. The Guidelines officially took effect in November 1987, but they did not begin to dictate the vast majority of federal sentences until after the Supreme Court declared them constitutional in 1989.[75] In that year eighty-four percent of adjudicated federal cases ended in guilty pleas (see Table 9.1). By 1991 the guilty plea rate had begun its relentless climb, reaching ninety-four percent by century's end. During the last decade of the twentieth century, therefore, the rate of federal criminal trials fell from sixteen percent of adjudicated cases to only six percent,[76] a drop of more than three-fifths.[77]

9.1.

Plea Bargaining in Federal District Courts:
Cases Ending in Pleas of Guilty or No Contest
as a Proportion of All Adjudicated Cases

YEAR	PERCENTAGE OF CASES
1984	84
1985	85
1986	84
1987	85
1988	84
1989	84
1990	84
1991	85
1992	86
1993	88
1994	89
1995	90
1996	91
1997	92
1998	92
1999	94
2000	94
2001	94

SOURCE: Bureau of Justice Statistics, *Sourcebook of Criminal Justice Statistics Online—2001*, table 5.21 (2001) (available at http://www.albany.edu/sourcebook/1995/pdf/t521.pdf).

Whether the Guidelines gave rise to plea bargaining's stunning end-of-century triumph is perhaps open to some question. Although the current guilty plea rate of ninety-four percent appears to be unprecedented, the rate had reached as high as ninety percent in both 1949 and 1951 before declining to a postwar low of seventy-seven percent in 1980. Even before the Guidelines came into being, the rate had begun to climb. Meanwhile, the federal caseload, which reached a ten-year low of 36,560 disposed cases in 1980, more than doubled to a record 75,650 cases by 2001.[78] It is surely possible that the increase in guilty pleas owed as much to this rising caseload—or to some other factor not imagined—as to the Guidelines.

Post-Trial Sentencing Discretion. Still, there are at least two reasons to think the Guidelines supplied much of the force behind plea bargaining's latest advance. One has to do with the new allocation of bargaining power I described over the last several pages. But here the proper focus is not on which party—judge or prosecutor—has the power to offer the best deal on a guilty plea. Because modern judges are almost as anxious as prosecutors to see cases end in plea bargains, the allocation of this power should have relatively little impact on the bargaining rate. The same is not true, however, of the power to control the sentence imposed *after trial.* Here a shift in discretion from judge to prosecutor is likely to cause a substantial increase in the rate of pleas.

It takes just a moment to see why. Begin with the proposition that prosecutors and defendants will settle successfully on a deal whenever the sentence a defendant faces after trial (discounted by the possibility of acquittal and adjusted for other factors) exceeds the sentence the prosecutor offers on a plea. In such a world, the rate of plea bargaining will rise together with the prosecutor's power to widen the gap between these two numbers. The true genius of the plea-bargaining strategy devised by Massachusetts prosecutors in the early nineteenth century was that it exploited prosecutors' power to do exactly that. Plea bargaining took hold in the old liquor and murder cases because rigid penalty schemes gave prosecutors the power *both* to guarantee a sentencing concession should the defendant plead guilty *and* to guarantee a harsher sentence should the defendant stand trial and lose—and to do both without the judge's help. The Guidelines, like the Massachusetts liquor laws, enable prosecutors to maximize the defendant's sentencing exposure by filing charges that reflect the whole range of his behavior. Then, by striking off those charges in the course of a plea bargain, prosecutors normally can assure the defendant a better fate.

In pre-Guidelines days, prosecutors generally lacked power to threaten defendants who rejected an offered deal with a particular post-trial sentence. Most penal statutes gave judges complete discretion to choose any sentence between probation and a long term of years. The prosecutor's choice of charges therefore rarely dictated the judge's sentence. Prosecutors' incapacity on this score would not have slowed plea bargaining's progress had judges been willing to state before trial how they would view the case upon conviction. In that event the prosecutor's promise to recommend a certain (lower) sentence on a plea (a recommendation judges almost always followed)[79] could have created a great enough gap between the post-trial and post-plea sentences to persuade all but a hardy few defendants to plead guilty.

I have seen no evidence, however, that judges typically made such pretrial predictions of post-trial sentences. Many judges no doubt would have thought this practice both untrue to the principles of sentencing, which traditionally looked to facts revealed at trial, and unfaithful to the dignity of their offices. Moreover, both the Federal Rules of Criminal Procedure and federal case law disapproved of any such direct participation by judges in the bargaining process.[80] And even if a judge had risked reproof by predicting the sentence she would impose after trial, the defendant knew the judge could change her mind and impose an entirely different sentence on judgment day. For that matter, even if the judge adhered to her earlier prediction, a judge's sentence in pre-Guidelines days gave the defendant only a rough sense of his actual release date. Parole authorities, and not the judge, determined when the defendant would walk free.[81]

Before the Guidelines, then, defendants generally could not predict with confidence the costs of wagering trial and losing. In the face of this uncertainty, we may expect that many defendants measured those costs too low and unreasonably passed up the benefits of a plea. After all, those persons who face criminal charges already have proved themselves unreasonably confident of their capacity to beat the system.

The Guidelines altogether reshaped this dynamic. At the outset of this section, I examined how the Guidelines have choked off much of the old judicial discretion to offer a lower sentence after a guilty plea than that offered by the prosecution. For all the same reasons, judges have little discretion today to award a lower sentence after trial and conviction than that demanded by the prosecutor's slate of charges. Just as most judges are reluctant, for example, to depart beneath the guideline range after a plea, so they are reluctant to do so after trial. The prosecution's charges, taken together with the defendant's relevant conduct, therefore normally dictate the lower bounds of the defendant's post-trial sentence. What is more, the same 1984 act that created the Sentencing Commission also abolished parole.[82] The result is that the sentence a judge awards under the Guidelines, itself closely constrained by the prosecutor's charging decisions, almost directly determines the time the offender will serve.[83]

Together, the relatively precise way in which the Guidelines allocate punishment and the abolition of parole mean that in counseling her client on the consequences of risking trial and losing, a defense lawyer now can state those risks with a great deal more precision than before. In the Commission's words, the Guidelines have altered the nature of plea bargaining by "creat[ing] a clear, definite expectation in respect to the sentence that a court will impose if a trial takes place."[84] Defendants inclined to think wishfully about winning a sentencing concession even after losing at trial now have less luxury to do so. Even if the Guidelines have not actually increased the difference between post-plea and post-trial sentences (a very difficult thing to measure),[85] they have made that difference loom larger in the eyes of those who face charges. The natural consequence should be that more of them will be willing to plead guilty.

The impact of this new predictability on the rate of plea bargaining will grow with the gap that separates sentences offered on a plea from those threatened after trial. It should also grow with the rigidity of post-trial sentences. This is where the mandatory-minimum sentencing provisions enacted in the late 1980s come into play.[86] For as stingy as the Guidelines are in granting judges the power to undermine a prosecutor's desired sentence, these laws are even stingier. Although prosecutors have multiple mechanisms to spare defendants the fate of a mandatory-minimum sentence—refraining from charging, dropping the charges once brought, or moving to depart in exchange for the defendant's substantial assistance—judges have no general discretion to sentence beneath the minimum.[87] Deprived of even a distant hope that the sentencing judge will show mercy, a defendant facing prosecution under one of these statutes should give full measure to the gap between the mandatory-minimum term and the deal offered by the prosecution.

Not only are these mandatory sentencing laws rigid, they are harsher than what went before. Together with the Guidelines themselves, they have produced far longer sentences than in pre-Guidelines days.[88] In the process, they perhaps have made it easier for prosecutors to widen the gap between the sentence they offer on a plea and the one they demand should the defendant risk trial and lose. There is, after all, a sentence below which prosecutors will not go even to attract a plea bargain. Unreasonably low sentences may both offend their sense of justice and risk public outrage. The newly inflated sentences called for under the Guidelines and under mandatory sentencing laws allow prosecutors to offer sentences that might seem low to defendants—because they are so much lower than what could befall them after trial—even while appearing appropriately harsh to the public, which may compare them with the shorter sentences awarded in pre-Guidelines days or in state court.[89] As a result, prosecutors perhaps can offer bigger sentencing discounts—and induce more pleas—without risking their tough-on-crime images.

Both more inexorable and more severe than what went before, these new sentencing mechanisms perhaps have proved potent instruments of plea bargaining. Rising plea rates arguably merely confirm what a comparison of the new order with the old Massachusetts liquor laws might have predicted: that by investing prosecutors with greater post-plea and post-trial sentencing discretion, Congress ensured that more cases would end in guilty pleas.

The Guidelines' Hidden Bargaining Tools

The second reason to think the Guidelines helped drive plea bargaining's late-century advance is that their Byzantine pathways conceal a variety of vectors along which parties may deal. We have seen throughout this history that those systemic actors with an interest in bargaining will seek out whatever bargaining mechanisms the system affords, limited only by their ingenuity in discovering them. By the late twentieth century, all of the system's major players—judge, prosecutor, and (often) defense counsel—shared an interest in plea bargaining. Hence all participated in the hunt.

Judges, for example, have wielded their power to award discounts for acceptance of responsibility in a way that generally encourages bargaining. In 1998, 89.5 percent of defendants who pled guilty in federal court received a discount for acceptance of responsibility, while only 7.1 percent of those convicted after jury trials were so lucky.[90] Though one might wonder why judges would grant *any* defendant convicted after trial a discount for acceptance of responsibility,[91] it remains true that the average defendant, in choosing trial, must abandon all realistic hope of this reward.

In fact, the Commission has encouraged judges in this direction. As originally issued in 1987, the commentary that accompanied the guideline section on acceptance of responsibility advised that "[a] defendant may manifest sincere contrition and take steps toward reparation and rehabilitation even if he exercises his constitutional right to a trial."[92] Three years later, the Commission amended the commentary and advised that "[t]his adjustment is not intended to apply to a defendant who puts the government to its burden of proof at trial by denying the essential factual elements of guilt, is convicted, and only then admits guilt and expresses remorse." The Commission deemed it the "rare" case in which the defendant "clearly demonstrate[s] an acceptance of responsibility for his criminal conduct even though he exercises his constitutional right to a trial."[93]

Defense lawyers, meanwhile, readily join with prosecutors to find ways to reduce the sentences of defendants who plead guilty under the Guidelines. In defense lawyers' hands, the many and varied complexities of the sentencing regime "are like little prizes hidden in the Guidelines" — just so many tools for creative bargaining.[94] Hence the Guidelines have spawned *fact bargaining,* in which prosecutor and defense lawyer contrive to hide the defendant's unflattering relevant conduct from the court.[95] They do so despite the Commission's injunction that, when the lawyers submit a statement of facts pertinent to sentencing, they "must fully and accurately disclose all factors relevant to the determination of sentence."[96]

Likewise, the Guidelines have given rise to *range bargaining,* in which defense lawyer and prosecutor agree to recommend that the judge impose a sentence at the lower end of the guideline range. And they have prompted *guideline-factor bargaining*: If the judge has the power to grant a two- or three-level discount for acceptance of responsibility, then the prosecutor may agree to recommend this discount in exchange for the defendant's plea. If the judge has the power to adjust a defendant's sentence based on the role he played in the crime, then the parties may agree that he was the gang's dupe and not its leader.[97] And most importantly, the lawyers take part in *substantial-assistance bargaining.*[98] A great many defendants readily plead guilty in exchange for the prosecutor's promise to authorize the court to depart downward for substantial assistance.

All along there remains charge bargaining, which our long journey suggests may be the original form of bargaining. Thanks to the Guidelines' rigid sentencing structure, charge bargaining does not merely survive but thrives. And the practice of *pre*-charge bargaining has fared especially well.[99] In pre-charge bargaining, the defendant agrees to plead guilty to the prosecutor's original slate of charges as long as the prosecutor agrees to bring only certain charges in the first place. This device relieves prosecutors of the need to drop existing charges—as occurs in regular, *post*-charge bargaining—and therefore avoids awkward explanations to superiors and the public about why prosecutors are abandoning charges they once thought worth bringing. And unlike regular charge bargaining, this mechanism does not advertise to the judge that the deal proposed by the parties involves ignoring certain "relevant conduct" on the defendant's part.[100] Just as Friedman and Percival found a century ago in Alameda County, when the law acts to limit prosecutors' power to drop charges at will, prosecutors and defense counsel respond by doing their bargaining before charges are brought.[101]

A LAST LOOK BACK

The rise of the federal Sentencing Guidelines rightly claims this place at the end of our story. As the force that shapes the sentences of some 60,000 federal convicts each year, the Guidelines stand as the country's most influential source of sentencing law. They have prompted us, moreover, to look again at the dynamic of powers and interests that fueled the growth of plea bargaining in nineteenth-century Massachusetts. Like the liquor and murder statutes that played so large a role early in our story, the Guidelines have erected the kind of rigid penalty scheme that can support a broad and effective charge-bargaining regime. Even as they foretell plea bargaining's future, therefore, the Guidelines replay much of plea bargaining's past.

At the opening of the twentieth century, eighty-seven percent of adjudicated cases in Middlesex Superior Court ended in guilty pleas. As the century approached its close, the rate of guilty pleas in American federal courts trailed somewhat short of that number. Now, in the few years since the federal Sentencing Guidelines took force, we have left that figure far behind. It appears that by converting almost the entire criminal code to the form of the old Massachusetts liquor laws, the Guidelines have set off a plea-bargaining frenzy.

With this odd juxtaposition of the old Massachusetts liquor laws and our very modern Sentencing Guidelines, we now can see how far we have come. Something more than 150 years ago, plea bargaining in Massachusetts claimed but a tiny beachhead. Supported only by the desire of prosecutors to manage their crushing workloads and to gain an occasional effortless conviction, plea bargaining extended no further than the sentencing power of prosecutors. In liquor and murder cases, the legislature's perhaps imprudently designed penalty schemes gave prosecutors the sliver of power they needed to support a meager charge-bargaining practice. By the middle of the nineteenth century, plea bar-gaining had stolen to a larger outpost, the on-file form of plea bargaining, left exposed to prosecutors by the procedural fluke that judges could not pass sentence until the prosecutor so moved. There the progress of plea bargaining might have stalled, for the sentencing power of prosecutors reached little further.

Then, in the last quarter of the nineteenth century, judges found themselves confronted by an onslaught of new, and newly complex, civil suits brought on by the ravages of industrial machinery. They saw no choice but to make terms with the new order in the criminal courts. They embraced plea bargaining and turned their considerable sentencing power to its purpose. Sustained now by the two most powerful courtroom patrons, plea bargaining swiftly became the dominant force in criminal procedure. It pushed aside the indeterminate sentence, and it supported those institutions, such as probation and the public defender, that aided its cause. Finally, plea bargaining grew so entrenched in the halls of power that today, though its patrons may divide its spoils in different ways, it can grow no more. For plea bargaining has won.

Appendix A
A Note on the Cases

Many of my arguments and conclusions rest on an analysis of a large body of nineteenth-century Massachusetts court cases, drawn mainly from Middlesex County. In various footnotes throughout the book, I have described the records themselves and the protocols I followed in classifying and counting them. For those who would like to pursue similar research or to analyze my findings more critically, I have tried to gather together the most important points about the database and my method of analyzing it in this appendix.

THE RECORDS AND WHERE TO FIND THEM

I have relied most heavily on records of the middle-tier courts: the Court of General Sessions of the Peace through 1803; the Court of Common Pleas from 1804 through the first two sessions of 1859; and the Superior Court from late 1859 on.[1] For a few years during the 1840s, I examined the records of the Essex County Court of Common Pleas, held by the Archives Division of the Supreme Judicial Court. Otherwise, my research of middle-tier courts focused exclusively on Middlesex County. The Massachusetts Archives in Boston houses all records of the middle-tier courts of Middlesex for 1859 and earlier. Records for 1860 and later are stored off site by the Archives Division of the Supreme Judicial Court. The record books for most years between 1771 and 1808 and between 1823 and 1839 may be purchased on microfilm from the Genealogical Society of Utah in Salt Lake City.

The records of the court's work take three forms. First are the record books themselves, probably compiled at the end of each session of court, which lay out all case dispositions in beautiful script (until the advent of clerk-typists sometime in the late 1880s) and in an organized way. Cases not disposed of—for example, those continued until the next session of court—are not mentioned. Typically, the record-book entry for each case transcribes the indictment or other charging document and lays out various facts documenting the case's progress through the court. These include the defendant's plea, any nol pros entered by the prosecutor, the names of jurors, the jury's verdict, and the judge's sentence. The record book typically does not say who testified at trial, whether the defendant had counsel, or what facts were proved. Beginning in the late 1840s, record books usually include long lists of cases that are identified only by the defendants' names and are noted, simply, as having been placed on file or nol prossed.

In the earlier years of this study, the clerk's docket books largely repeat information contained in the record books. Beginning in 1844, however, the docket books fill in several missing details. They tell us which cases the court continued from one session to the next, whether defendants had counsel, what charges were involved in the "filed" and "nol prossed" cases listed in the record books, and whether the defendants in these cases pled guilty. They also tally the days consumed by each session of court. Unfortunately, the docket books are far more difficult to read than the record books—entries are both messier and more abbreviated. Moreover, not until the last third of the century did the clerk note each case's docket number in the record books. For earlier years, the task of cross-referencing cases listed in both books is arduous.

The files for each case are the richest source of information, but also the least convenient. They include the original indictment, witness subpoenas, tables of costs, occasional moving papers submitted by one of the lawyers, and (very occasionally) other notes or letters to or from the lawyers. All these are neatly folded together, bundled with ribbons, hardened with time, and boxed away.

I have read the record-book entry for every case relied on in this study. For many, I have read the docket-book entry. For several dozen or perhaps more, I have examined the file papers. For most of the years studied, I have read every case handled by the court that year. As the century wore on and the court's caseload grew, I sometimes read only those cases decided at one or two of the three annual sessions. To extrapolate these partial studies into totals that represent the whole year's work, I have assumed that the caseload of each session of court was proportional to the days consumed by that session. In 1870, for example, I studied only the February session of court. In that session, a single judge sat for thirty-three days and disposed of 183 cases. As the June and October sessions of court consumed forty-eight judge-days between them, I have calculated the year's total workload as 449 cases:

$$((33 + 48) , 33) \cdot 183 = 449.$$

In all, I examined 4,142 middle-tier cases in Middlesex. This figure does *not* include cases identified in the record books merely as having been nol prossed or placed on file unless I also examined the docket-book entry for those cases. Therefore, the number of cases I examined tends to be larger for those years for which I also studied the docket books (see Table A.1).

In calculating the court's caseload after 1844, I have included only those years for which I have read the docket books. To maintain consistency across years, I counted only *disposed* cases—that is, those cases that traditionally had been listed in the record books—and omitted any case (such as those continued from one session of court to the next) listed in the docket books but not mentioned in the record books. I believe these protocols guard against the possibility that the caseload boom of the late 1840s, depicted in Figure 2.1, was simply an artifact of the appearance in 1844 of more elaborate docket books.

My study of the records of the Supreme Judicial Court was more limited (see Table A.2). For the early part of the century, before the legislature transferred jurisdiction over all but capital cases to the Court of Common Pleas,[2] I examined the entire business of the high court in sev-

A.1.

Case Database: Middlesex County Superior Court
and Its Predecessor Courts

YEAR	NUMBER OF CASES EXAMINED	COURT SESSIONS	DOCKET BOOKS EXAMINED?
1789	15	All	N/A
1790	8	All	N/A
1799	17	All	N/A
1800	21	All	N/A
1805	21	All	N/A
1806	26	All	N/A
1809	14	All	N/A
1810	20	All	N/A
1814	25	All	N/A
1815	45	All	N/A
1819	24	All	N/A
1820	38	All	N/A
1824	48	All	N/A
1829	41	All	N/A
1834	95	All	N/A
1839	42	All	N/A
1843	101	All	N/A
1844	123	All	Yes
1849	443	All	Yes
1853	482	All	Yes
1859	415	All	Yes
1864	225	Feb. & Oct.	Yes
1870	183	Feb.	Yes
1874	153	Feb.	No
1880	140	Oct.	Yes
1885	105	June	No
1890	232	Feb.	In Part
1896	144	Oct.	No
1900	602	All	Yes
1910	294	All	No
TOTAL	4142		

SOURCES: Middlesex Ct. Gen. Sess. Peace R. Books; Middlesex Ct. C.P. R. & Docket Books; Middlesex Super. Ct. R. & Docket Books.

A.2.

Case Database: Supreme Judicial Court (Sitting in Middlesex County)

YEAR	NUMBER OF CASES EXAMINED	COURT SESSIONS
1799	12	All
1809	24	All
1819	30	All
1824	36	All
1829	20	All
1834	7	All
1839	1	All
1843	0	All
1849	4	All
TOTAL	134	

SOURCES: Sup. Jud. Ct. R. Books (Middlesex sittings).

eral different years. For these early years, the Supreme Judicial Court's docket books added little or no useful information to the record-book entries, and I rarely examined either the docket books or the file papers. All relevant Supreme Judicial Court records are housed at the Massachusetts Archives in Boston.

My study of the disposition of capital cases extended to the Supreme Judicial Court's business for the entire state, not merely Middlesex County. I drew most of my data from the attorney general's annual reports, which usually stated in greater or lesser detail (depending on the year) the procedural course of every capital case heard by the court. The attorney general submitted his reports to the legislature, which published them, and they are widely available in both hardbound and microfilm formats. They did not, however, appear before 1832. For earlier years, I have relied on my survey of the Middlesex sittings of the court as well as on a thorough study of the Suffolk County (that is, Boston) sittings between 1820 and 1832.[3] For those later years in which the attorney general either did not exist or produced no useful report (1840–1848 and 1853), I have examined the court's record books for its sittings in Suffolk,

Middlesex, Bristol, Hampden, Norfolk, and Worcester counties.[4] This strategy omitted any capital case arising in one of the state's other eight counties. Still, I am confident I have captured the great majority of the state's capital cases in these years.

COUNTING CASES AND STATISTICAL PROTOCOLS

Although some of my research assistants (and in particular Dan Levin) helped me code cases onto a spreadsheet for analysis and others (Josh Greenberg and Craig Estes) helped with the technical task of counting cases, I read every case myself, determined how to classify it, and reviewed the coding for consistency. All of the middle-tier cases from Middlesex are on a single document that is available to others for analysis.

I made several decisions about how to count cases. I believe that all of them are defensible, but few are self-evidently the only right approach. First, I chose not to count as part of any year's court business those cases that were adjudicated in an earlier year, whether by trial or by plea, unless they were re-adjudicated in the year under study. That is, if a case tried in 1858 happened to be disposed of in 1859—perhaps because sentencing was delayed—the clerk typically would record the entire proceedings in the 1859 record book. In my analysis of the business of 1859, I have omitted such cases.

Second, when performing any count designed to assess the workload of prosecutors or judges (as when calculating caseload for Figure 2.1), I counted each case as one case even if it involved several defendants. When assessing decisions made by judges, juries, or litigants, however, I followed a different course. Consider, for example, Figure 4.1, which represents defendants' tendency to plead guilty rather than go to trial. If a particular case had, say, four codefendants, and if all four went to trial (or all four pled guilty), then I counted the case as one case. But if three of four defendants pled guilty while one went to trial, I counted the case as two separate cases: one that ended in a guilty plea and one that went to trial. Although others might count such a case as *four* cases (three that ended in a plea and one in a trial), I believe my method is more likely to represent the reality behind courtroom decision making. With surprising frequency, codefendants acted (and were treated by the jury) as a unit, a tendency perhaps magnified by the frequent appearance of only one defense lawyer in a case involving multiple codefendants. As my goal generally was to examine *decisions* and not outcomes per se, I believe the number of different decisions—rather than the number of actors controlled by those decisions—was the better proxy.

Third, when drawing cross-century comparisons, I often have excluded both liquor cases and cases placed on file. For reasons I have discussed at length in the text, these case types were different from the rest, particularly because the prosecutor possessed far more control over sentencing than he did in other cases. Because both liquor cases and filed cases were either rare or absent early in the century, I thought that including them would too greatly distort any analysis that spanned the century.[5] For similar reasons, I have excluded them from most analyses designed to gauge judicial decision making. As the century wore on, however, prosecutors lost their peculiar powers in liquor cases and (to a lesser extent) in filed cases,[6] so for late-century studies of judicial decision making, I sometimes have included them.[7] In all cases, I have tried to specify which course I took.

Fourth, the distinction between liquor and nonliquor cases was itself tricky. Because the significance of this distinction was the rigid penalty scheme that gave prosecutors the unilateral power to charge bargain, as I described in Chapter 1,[8] I have limited "liquor cases" to those cases that arose under the liquor-license laws or under the liquor-prohibition laws. These laws traditionally—and fairly consistently—maintained mandatory penalty schemes.[9] I therefore counted drunkenness and common-drunkard cases as "nonliquor cases" because the penalty schemes governing those crimes granted the judge considerable discretion and frustrated prosecutorial charge bargaining of the sort seen under the license laws.[10] After some deliberation, I decided that the odd category of "liquor nuisance" cases, first created by the legislature in 1855 and retained throughout the balance of the century,[11] fits comfortably under neither "liquor cases" nor "nonliquor cases." Because the nature of the offense is essentially unauthorized liquor-selling—the same activity punished by the license and prohibition laws—it seems strained to call these nonliquor cases. But because the penalty scheme did not closely resemble the license and prohibition laws' rigid formulas,[12] it would be wrong to

A.3.

Pleas of No Contest as a Proportion of All Pleas of Either Guilty or No
Contest: Middlesex Superior Court and Its Predecessor Courts

YEAR	TOTAL PLEAS	% NO CONTEST PLEAS
1789–1790	16	13
1799–1800	21	57
1805–1806	23	57
1809–1810	14	57
1814–1815	19	47
1819–1820	28	57
1824	27	52
1829	21	48
1834	19	16
1839	16	0
1843–1844	82	26
1849	129	9
1853	72	29
1859	107	14
1864	77	5
1870	59	3
1874	57	0
1880	73	7
1885	69	3
1890	101	6
1896	66	5
1900	471	6
1910	224	3

SOURCES: Middlesex Ct. Gen. Sess. Peace R. Books; Middlesex Ct. C.P. R. & Docket Books;
Middlesex Super. Ct. R. & Docket Books.

classify nuisance cases as liquor cases. I therefore have excluded liquor
nuisance cases from both categories, although they are included in tallies
of "total" cases, and they appear as well (for reasons explained there) in
Table 5.1 and occasionally in other tallies.[13]

Fifth, throughout the text, I have tried to distinguish between pleas of
guilty and pleas of no contest. At times, however, if the context was clear
or the distinction unimportant, I have used "guilty pleas" as a shorthand
to represent both. The legal distinction between these pleas was almost

insignificant,[14] but because a plea of no contest was easier for some defendants to swallow, this option often smoothed negotiations toward a plea. Although the earliest clear plea bargains I observed in liquor cases (those in the 1820s and earlier) always involved pleas of no contest, for later years I saw relatively few no contest pleas (see Table A.3).

Finally, I have made many other, more minor decisions about how to count cases. The most important of these is that, unless specified otherwise, I counted as a "conviction" any case in which the jury convicted the defendant of any part of the crime charged. I have kept a record of the other decisions I have made and am happy to share them—as well as any of my other data—with future researchers.

Ferdinand's Category of "Vice or
Regulatory Offenses"

This appendix refers back to Note 42 of Chapter 2, where I deferred an analysis showing the affinity between what Theodore Ferdinand calls "vice or regulatory" offenses and what I call liquor law violations.

Ferdinand tells us that "[r]egulatory offenses include liquor law violations, offenses against religion (blue law violations), and city ordinance violations."[1] "Offenses against religion," he then adds, "consisted basically of violations of blue laws prohibiting taverns from serving alcoholic beverages on Sunday."[2] Section 5 of the 1832 liquor license law punished Sunday liquor sales by a mandatory ten-dollar fine for each offense.[3] By assigning a fixed fine to each offense, this provision gave the prosecutor the same power to engage in multiple charging and charge bargaining that I described in Chapter 1 with regard to the rest of the liquor license law.[4] Asahel Huntington often charged multiple counts of Sunday sales just as he charged multiple counts under other provisions of the license law; one of Huntington's preprinted multicount forms contained four Sunday sale counts.[5]

Although Ferdinand does not tell us which city ordinances the category of "city ordinance violations" comprehends, he does say that "in the late 1830s and early 1840s, arrests for city ordinance violations, liquor law violations, and offenses against religion began to climb sharply . . . , suggesting that all three were part of the temperance campaign against liquor abuses. When city ordinance violations took a sharp jump in 1848, the other two declined; and when liquor law violations spurted in 1850, city ordinance violations fell back."[6] From this, we can conclude that the substance of the ordinance in question, like that of "offenses against religion," concerned liquor sales. Without more, we cannot be sure of the ordinance's penalty scheme, and we cannot know whether it was suited to prosecutorial charge bargaining. It is fair to guess that this city ordinance was punishable by a fine only, though whether it attached a fixed fine to each offense I cannot say.

"Vice offenses," Ferdinand tells us, "include gambling and prostitution."[7] He does not itemize the offenses that fall under "gambling," and there are several possibilities. First are the "gaming" offenses addressed by section 11 of the 1832 liquor license law. The law punished those who permitted "dice, cards, bowls, billiards, quoits," or other games on their premises with a ten-dollar fine for each offense and punished those who took part with a ten-dollar fine.[8] Like the rest of the liquor license law, this provision gave the prosecutor the power to manipulate the sentence by manipulating charges. A different gaming provision also provided for a fixed ten-dollar fine.[9] Other statutes bearing on offenses that could be labeled gambling, however, supplied no fixed penalty.[10] Without a finer breakdown of Ferdinand's "gambling" category, it is hard to know whether his findings support or challenge my arguments.

The second of Ferdinand's vice offenses, prostitution, clearly does not fall within my charge-bargaining paradigm. Ferdinand does not specify the statute governing the offense in question, but there seem to be only two possibilities: Being a "common night walker[]" made one liable to confinement for up to six months,[11] and "keep[ing] a house of ill fame" carried a penalty of up to two years or three hundred dollars.[12] These wide-open penalty schemes did not permit the kind of charge bargaining I have discussed, and yet Ferdinand reports some facts suggesting a high incidence of plea bargaining in these cases.[13] On the other hand, Ferdinand reports that the overall rate of guilty pleas in prostitution cases was slightly less than that for the average common law crime, including property offenses and felonies against the person.[14]

As prostitution apparently was not prosecuted in the middle-tier courts of Middlesex County, I cannot apply my own data to the task of explaining Ferdinand's findings. Of course, a guilty plea by a friendless prostitute might have been as much the product of hopelessness as of negotiation—something I suggested earlier with regard to drunkenness prosecutions.[15] And a judge's compassion for an accused prostitute who showed remorse by pleading guilty also need not have been the result of bargaining. Moreover, I cannot tell whether Ferdinand's findings in prostitution cases represent on-file plea bargaining of the sort I discussed in Chapter 3. Ferdinand does distinguish cases left on file from those ending in guilty pleas,[16] but he does not tell us how he counts those cases that were placed on file after a guilty plea—the mark of an on-file plea bargain.[17] On-file plea bargaining was, as I argue in Chapter 3, simply probation by another name, and John Augustus, Boston's probation pioneer, devoted much of his labor in the latter part of the 1840s to prostitution defendants.[18] As Ferdinand reports a near-tripling in the percentage of prostitution cases left on file in the 1840s,[19] there is a real possibility that he is seeing on-file plea bargaining and simply failed to distinguish it from other forms. So again, without more detail, it is impossible to say whether Ferdinand's findings support or challenge my own.

Notes

1. J. S. Cockburn discovered what is perhaps the earliest clear evidence of plea bargaining anywhere. He found that between 1587 and 1590 as many as half of the defendants who came before the assize courts of the English Home Circuit pled guilty (Cockburn, "Trial by the Book?," 73). These defendants seem to have earned two kinds of rewards for their pleas, both of which Cockburn attributes to judicial action. First, judges apparently altered indictments to reduce the charges. Second, judges granted benefit of clergy—a mechanism for avoiding execution—more readily to those defendants who pled guilty.

2. Although one of the first studies of the patterns of plea bargaining recognized the probable impact of the rush of cases brought on by national prohibition in the 1920s (see American Law Institute, *Business of the Federal Courts*, 31–32, 57), the first study I am aware of which hints that state liquor laws of the nineteenth century may have played a role in plea bargaining's rise is by Albert Alschuler: "Plea Bargaining and Its History" (see p. 6).

3. Though the ranking of the counties was unstable, Middlesex was the largest during every census from 1840 to 1870. See *A Compendium of the Ninth Census*, 56.

4. Roger Lane has detailed the unwillingness of Boston police to enforce the state's liquor-prohibition laws in the third quarter of the nineteenth century (see Lane, *Policing the City*, 87).

5. See Act of April 5, 1859, ch. 196, §§ 1–3, 1859 Mass. Acts 339, 339–40, which established the superior courts; Act of March 9, 1804, ch. 89, §§ 3–4, 1804 Mass. Acts 490, 491, which enlarged the jurisdiction of the courts of common pleas and transferred the criminal jurisdiction of the Court of General Sessions of the Peace to the Court of Common Pleas. Catherine Menand's suggestion that there were several shifts in criminal jurisdiction between 1803 and 1827 results, I think, from a misreading of the relevant statutes (see Menand, *Research Guide*, 50). In any case, my examination of the records of the Court of Common Pleas and the Court of General Sessions of the Peace for Middlesex County revealed no shift in criminal jurisdiction after 1804.

6. See Act of July 3, 1782, ch. 15, 1782 Mass. Acts 157, 157, which established courts of general sessions of the peace.

7. See § 10, 1859 Mass. Acts at 342, which established the dates and locations of roving civil and criminal courts in Middlesex County; Act of February 14, 1821, ch. 79, § 2, 8 Mass. Laws 545, 546, which established a Court of Common Pleas for the

Commonwealth of Massachusetts. Before 1821, the Court of Common Pleas consisted of separate judges for each county or for small groups of counties, rather than a corps of judges who rode circuit (see Davis, *History of the Judiciary*, 201–4). At various times, Boston (that is, Suffolk County) had criminal tribunals distinct from this statewide system (ibid., 205–6).

8. In the early years treated in this study, individual justices of the peace presided alone over trials of the more petty criminal offenses. Their judgments could be appealed to a jury trial before the courts of the middle tier (see Menand, *Research Guide*, 60). In time, a system of police courts and finally district courts would succeed to the jurisdiction of the individual justices, but these courts continued to sit without a jury and without even the regular attendance of a public prosecutor (ibid., 61–67).

9. Ibid., 37–38.

10. See Act of June 6, 1891, ch. 379, § 1, 1891 Mass. Acts 966, 966, which transferred jurisdiction of capital trials to the superior courts; Act of October 17, 1859, ch. 282, § 1, 1859 Mass. Acts 632, 632, which returned jurisdiction of capital trials to the Supreme Judicial Court; §§ 1, 21, 1859 Mass. Acts at 339, 344, which established the superior courts and briefly transferred jurisdiction of capital trials from the Supreme Judicial Court to the superior courts; Act of March 14, 1832, ch. 130, 12 Mass. Laws 396, which enlarged the jurisdiction of the Court of Common Pleas in criminal cases, regulated the appointment and duties of prosecuting officers, and transferred the Supreme Judicial Court's criminal trial jurisdiction, except in capital cases, to the Court of Common Pleas. In his book, *Prison and Plantation* (p. 93), Michael Stephen Hindus notes that by 1852, murder was the only offense that remained capital in Massachusetts. One other capital crime apparently existed—the voluntary and wrongful release of a capital prisoner by an official. The Supreme Judicial Court noted in 1866 that this crime apparently had never been committed (see *Green v. Commonwealth*, 94 Mass. [12 Allen] 155, 168 [1866]).

11. As I explain later, I do not always rely directly on the Supreme Judicial Court's own records, but often refer instead to the state attorney general's annual summaries of his business before that court. The Supreme Judicial Court's records did prove important in filling gaps when the attorney general's reports were missing or ambiguous.

12. My data set includes 4,142 cases heard in the middle-tier courts of Middlesex County between 1789 and 1910, as well as several hundred cases from the Supreme Judicial Court and the courts of Essex County. The data set is described in more detail in Appendix A.

13. See, e.g., American Law Institute, *Business of the Federal Courts*, 12–14, 51–54, 56–58, 97; Morse and Beattie, *Criminal Justice in Oregon*, 136–50; Fuller, *Criminal Justice in Virginia*, 148–55; Illinois Association for Criminal Justice, *Illinois Crime Survey*, 470–74; Crime Commission of New York State, "Report," 47–54, 83–90, 116–30; Missouri Association for Criminal Justice, *Missouri Crime Survey*, 148–51, 314–18; Pound and Frankfurter, *Criminal Justice in Cleveland*, 149 and n.1, 181,

322; Georgia Department of Public Welfare, "Crime and the Georgia Courts," 190–92, 215; "Report of the Minnesota Crime Commission," 15–17, 31.

14. Justin Miller, "Compromise."

15. Moley, "Vanishing Jury." Moley edited the final report of the subcommission on statistics of the New York Crime Commission, and there is a good deal of overlap between that 1928 report and his article of the same year (see Crime Commission of New York State, "Report," 39, 47–54).

16. Miller, "Compromise," 1–2.

17. See Moley, "Vanishing Jury," 97.

18. Ibid., 126.

19. Miller identified himself as the former district attorney of Kings County (Miller, "Compromise," 1 n.*).

20. Ibid., 2–10.

21. Ibid., 16–19.

22. Ibid., 20. Miller mentions as well a fourth cause for increasing compromises: "the unwillingness of people to admit criminal liability." I have excluded this reason from the text because it seems paradoxical in the context of those forms of compromise involving guilty pleas.

23. Mike McConville and Chester Mirsky suggest that certain reports on which Moley relied were incomplete. See McConville and Mirsky, "Rise of Guilty Pleas," 470 n.17.

24. See Moley, "Vanishing Jury," 123–24.

25. Ibid., 103–04.

26. Ibid., 127. Moley thought that giving judges the power to hear cases without a jury (on the defendant's consent) would empower judges to counter prosecutors' attempts to plea bargain.

27. National Commission on Law Observance and Enforcement, Report on the Enforcement of the Prohibition Laws of the United States 56 (1931).

28. Heumann, "Note." Heumann later republished much of this study in his 1977 book on plea bargaining: see Heumann, *Plea Bargaining*, 24–33.

29. See Heumann, "Note," 520–21.

30. Langbein, "Torture," 9; Alschuler, in his article "Plea Bargaining and Its History" (p. 41), writes that "[f]or all the praise lavished upon the American jury trial, this fact-finding mechanism has become so cumbersome and expensive that our society refuses to provide it."

31. See Langbein, "Torture," 12–19.

32. Ibid., 10. It is, however, possible that Langbein exaggerated the brevity of the old trials. He writes (p. 10) that "[i]n the Old Bailey in the 1730s we know that the court routinely processed between twelve and twenty jury trials for felony in a single day." But Malcolm Feeley and Charles Lester report that the average judge at the Old Bailey in 1735 conducted something fewer than five trials per day (see Feeley and Lester, "Legal Complexity," 352).

33. See Alschuler, "Plea Bargaining History," 41.

34. Many less prominent and less developed theories surfaced during the second wave. In a quick summary of the possibilities, Albert Alschuler lists several forces that "may have ... played their parts" in plea bargaining's rise: "Urbanization, increased crime rates, expansion of the substantive criminal law, and the professionalization and increasing bureaucratization of the police, prosecution, and defense functions" (Alschuler, "Plea Bargaining History," 42). To this list, John Langbein adds "changes in the social composition of victim and offender groups; ... and the intellectual influence of the marketplace model in an age when laissez faire was not an epithet" (Langbein, "Understanding," 265 n.7).

35. Friedman and Percival, *Roots of Justice*, 194.

36. Mike McConville and Chester Mirsky report that their study of prosecutions in New York in the first two-thirds of the nineteenth century reflects no increased sophistication in policing practices even as the rate of guilty pleas grew markedly (see McConville and Mirsky, "Rise of Guilty Pleas," 461–63, 466).

37. See Friedman and Percival, *Roots of Justice,* 174 tbl. 5.12, 179. They note that a growing proportion of defendants pled guilty to the face of the indictment, while a shrinking proportion pled guilty to lesser or fewer offenses than those originally charged. I discuss this finding more fully in Chapter 7 at Notes 25 and 46–54 and accompanying text.

38. Ferdinand, *Boston's Courts*; Vogel, *Courts of Trade*; Vogel, "Social Origins"; McConville and Mirsky, "Rise of Guilty Pleas."

39. See Chapter 5, Note 8.

NOTES TO CHAPTER I

1. Dana (1767–1835) was appointed by Massachusetts Governor James Sullivan. For the date of his appointment, I rely on Davis, *Bench and Bar*, vol. 2, 33. It is true that Davis refers here to the *Essex* County attorney. Other sources make it clear, however, that Dana was the Middlesex County attorney. See, e.g., Massachusetts House of Representatives, *Report*, 1.

The legislature had created the office of county attorney in 1807, probably to relieve the attorney general and solicitor general of the burden of managing public prosecutions statewide. See Act of June 20, 1807, ch. 18, § 1, 1807 Mass. Acts 172, 172, which delineated the offices and duties of the attorney general, solicitor general, and county attorneys. Dana had held the role of prosecutor provisionally since 1804. In that year, the Court of Common Pleas appointed him to prosecute cases for the Commonwealth "until further notice of this Court" (Middlesex Ct. C.P. R. Book 338 [September 1804]).

Dana was the son of Rev. Samuel Dana of Groton. He was a lawyer in Groton before his appointment as county attorney. Later he sat as a judge on the Circuit Court of Common Pleas, served as president of the Massachusetts Senate, and held a brief tenure as Congressman. See Dana, *Memoir*, 5–7, 10–13; Davis, *Bench and Bar*, vol. 2, 33.

2. Massachusetts House of Representatives, *Report*, 10. The legislative investigating committee alleged that Dana wrote his letter of complaint after the judges refused him a continuance (ibid., 7).

3. See Massachusetts House of Representatives, *Report*, 5–7.

4. Section 2, 1807 Mass. Acts at 171.

5. The legislature's investigating committee charged that when Dana helped crime victims seek reimbursement from the court for the costs of bringing charges, he listed his own five-dollar fee for providing this assistance as one such cost. Then, in his official role, he certified this table of costs to the court, which reimbursed the victim, who then paid Dana's fee. Massachusetts House of Representatives, *Report*, 2–3.

6. Section 2, 1807 Mass. Acts at 171.

7. Massachusetts House of Representatives, *Report*, 3.

8. Dana, "Mr. Dana's Answer," 10–11.

9. Ibid., 8–9.

10. Ibid., 2–3.

11. Ibid., 7.

12. Ibid., 11.

13. Dana addressed his offending letter to the "Justices of the Court of Common Pleas for the County of Middlesex, at December Term, 1808." Massachusetts House of Representatives, *Report*, 8. Court records show that the same judges who sat in December 1808 (James Prescott, James Winthrop, and Ephraim Wood) were also sitting in September 1809, when the Court of Common Pleas appointed Asahel Stearns to be Middlesex County attorney. Stearns's appointment permits the strong inference that Dana was out (see Middlesex Ct. C.P. R. Book 289, 723 [September 1809]; Middlesex Ct. C.P. R. Book 339 [December 1808]). That Stearns appeared again in the following session of court strengthens the inference (see Middlesex Ct. C.P. R. Book 513 [December 1809]).

In his rather exhaustive history of the Massachusetts courts, William Davis reported that Dana was reappointed as county attorney on September 3, 1811; that he was succeeded by one Timothy Fuller on November 20 of the same year; and that Stearns did not take office until August 20, 1813 (see Davis, *Bench and Bar*, vol. 2, 33). The confusion seems traceable to acts of the legislature. On June 20, 1809, the legislature repealed that part of the 1807 Act creating the office of county attorney that provided for the means of appointment: see Act of June 20, 1809, ch. 32, 1809 Mass. Acts 37, 37. In so doing, the legislature presumably transferred power to appoint county attorneys from the governor to the court. It then reversed course in 1811 and restored the 1807 Act, returning the appointment power to the governor: see Act of June 18, 1811, ch. 10, § 1, 1811 Mass. Acts 279, 279.

14. See Act of June 21, 1811, ch. 33, § 2, 1811 Mass. Acts 424, 424–25, which

established circuit courts of common pleas; Davis, *History of the Judiciary*, 202–4. The court's records show that at the first three sittings of 1811, Judges Prescott, Winthrop, and Wood still presided. At the December sitting, Dana presided as chief together with Judges William Wetmore and Stephen Minot. See Middlesex Ct. C.P. R. Book 249 (December 1811); Middlesex Ct. C.P. R. Book 1 (September 1811); Middlesex Ct. C.P. R. Book 1 (June 1811); Middlesex Ct. C.P. R. Book 1 (March 1811).

15. See Massachusetts House of Representatives, *Report*, 3, 6–8.

16. See Act of February 28, 1787, ch. 68, 1786 Mass. Acts 206, 206; *Commonwealth v. Josiah Stevens*, Middlesex Ct. C.P. R. Book 803 (December 1808).

17. Two earlier cases had come before the Court of Common Pleas. In September 1804 William Collins Hookway was tried before a jury and convicted and fined as a liquor dealer (*Commonwealth v. William Collins Hookway*, Middlesex Ct. C.P. R. Book 333 [September 1804]). At about the same time—but apparently shortly afterward—the court appointed Dana to prosecute cases for the Commonwealth (ibid., 338). In 1805 Dana handled the case of Amos Brown, charged with keeping an unlicensed tavern. Dana nol prossed the complaint after Brown paid the costs of prosecution (*Commonwealth v. Amos Brown*, Middlesex Ct. C.P. R. Book 191 [March 1805]). This exchange in some ways resembled a plea bargain, but it lacked a critical feature, as Brown never pled either guilty or no contest.

I studied the work of the court that preceded the Court of Common Pleas—the Court of General Sessions of the Peace—during 1789–1790 and 1799–1800. That court heard three liquor cases in those four years. The first, *Commonwealth v. William Barker*, took an interesting form that I discuss in Chapter 3, Note 21. The second and third each concerned the same defendant, Samuel Brown. Each case charged a single count of unlicensed sale, and in each, Brown pled no contest and was fined and assessed costs. There is no indication in these two cases of any sort of concession granted to the defendant in exchange for his plea. See *Commonwealth v. Samuel Brown*, Middlesex Ct. Gen. Sess. Peace R. Book 532 (September 1800); *Commonwealth v. Samuel Brown*, Middlesex Ct. Gen. Sess. Peace R. Book 532 (September 1800).

18. *Stevens*, Middlesex Ct. C.P. R. Book at 804.

19. Ibid. The odd amount of the fine—$6.67—can be traced to the statute, which set the penalty for an unlicensed sale at "a sum not exceeding *six pounds*, nor less than *forty shillings* [i.e., two pounds]" (1786 Mass. Acts at 207). In 1820 the records of the Court of Common Pleas noted that "the sum of five pounds [is] equal to sixteen dollars sixty six cents and six mills" (*Commonwealth v. Grosvenor Tarbell*, Middlesex Ct. C.P. R. Book 273 [September 1820]). At this conversion rate, two pounds would equal $6.67.

20. *Commonwealth v. Nathan Corey*, Middlesex Ct. C.P. R. Book 380 (March 1809).

21. Ibid. It appears that the court by then had abandoned the cumbersome fine

of $6.67 (see 1786 Mass. Acts at 207; this chapter, n.19), and had chosen to round up the figure to seven dollars.

22. See Act of March 9, 1804, ch. 154, §§ 3–4, 1803 Mass. Acts 788, 789, which enlarged the jurisdiction of the court of common pleas.

23. Or sixteen cases out of twenty-two. By *adjudicated cases*, I mean those in which the defendant went to trial or pled guilty or no contest.

24. Or twenty-one cases out of thirty-two.

25. Or seven cases out of twelve.

26. The third case followed the form but lacked the substance of the *Stevens* and *Corey* bargains. In 1790 George Peters faced several indictments for theft, including one that charged that he had stolen a pair of spectacles and a pair of scissors. To this indictment, he said that he was "guilty of taking the spectacles but not guilty of taking the scissors" (*Commonwealth v. George Peters*, Middlesex Ct. Gen. Sess. Peace R. Book 7 [September 1790]). A lawyer who acted temporarily for the government announced that he would "no further prosecute as to the scissors." But unlike Stevens and Corey, Peters won little benefit from the government's "concession." The charge remained unchanged because subtraction of the scissors did not alter the grade of the theft. It altered only the measure of the restitution, set in the usual way at three times the value of the goods stolen, and now reduced by three times the value of the scissors.

27. The statute did not define the offense of being a "common seller" as charged in count one, and I have not found elsewhere a definition that governed at this time. In an 1852 law that established liquor prohibition in Massachusetts, the legislature provided that "three several sales . . . shall be sufficient to constitute" the offense of being a common seller (Act of May 22, 1852, ch. 322, § 12, 1852 Mass. Acts 48, 50). Perhaps there is earlier case law, unknown to me, establishing such a definition. In that case, Dana's indictments might be redundant, but not designedly excessive.

28. Even in these very early years, the Court of General Sessions of the Peace and the Court of Common Pleas readily accepted pleas of guilty. In 1789–1790 there were fourteen guilty pleas while there were only two pleas of no contest. In 1799–1800 there were nine guilty pleas and twelve pleas of no contest. Until the 1830s, however, all of the clear plea bargains I saw in liquor cases involved pleas of no contest. Except in sparing defendants automatic liability in related civil cases, a plea of no contest had the same legal effect as a guilty plea:

> It is only where the party is sued in a civil action for doing the thing for which he was indicted, . . . that the distinction between these pleas is material. The plea of *nolo contendere* pleaded with a protestation that the party was not guilty, would clearly not conclude the party in his defence against the civil action.
>
> But so far as the Commonwealth is concerned, the judgment of conviction follows as well the one plea, as the other. And it is not necessary that the *court* should adjudge that the party was guilty, for that follows by necessary legal inference from the implied confession. But the court thereupon proceeds to pass

the sentence of the law affixed to the crime. (*Commonwealth v. Horton*, 26 Mass. [9 Pick.] 206, 208 [1829])

29. See *Commonwealth v. Andrews*, 2 Mass. (1 Tyng) 408, 414 (1807): "The Court never [enters a nolle prosequi], but at the instance of the counsel for the government."

30. See Act of February 28, 1787, ch. 68, 1786 Mass. Acts 206, 207.

31. On the exchange rate, see this Chapter, Note 19.

32. For being a common victualler, innholder, taverner, or seller, the penalty was twenty pounds (1786 Mass. Acts at 207). For permitting a patron to drink to excess, for serving hard alcohol to minors or servants, or for serving to those identified by town selectmen as neglecting their families, the penalty was twenty shillings, or one pound (ibid., 210). For serving to persons identified by the selectmen as common drunkards, the penalty was thirty shillings, or one and a half pounds (ibid., 214).

33. Ibid., 210.

34. *Mass. Rev. Stat.* ch. 141, § 8 (Dutton & Wentworth 1836): "All costs, arising in criminal prosecutions, . . . shall be taxed by the attorney general, or by the district or county attorney, and the allowance thereof shall be certified by the clerk, under the direction of the court."

35. See ibid. ch. 125, § 15, which discussed unarmed robbery; ibid. ch. 126, § 11, which stated the penalties for shop breaking and entering; ibid. ch. 126, § 17, which set out the penalties for petty and grand larceny; ibid. ch. 127, § 4, which discussed forgery. These penalties prevailed after 1836. Before then, there were more crimes that carried mandatory penalties. Robbery, for example, carried mandatory life in prison (see Act of March 16, 1805, ch. 143, § 7, 1804 Mass. Acts 240, 243). Prosecutors still could not take advantage of this rigidity, however, because it was not yet clearly established that prosecutors had the power to enter *partial* nol prosses. In liquor cases, prosecutors could bring multiple charges and then nol pros whole counts of the complaint to reduce the defendant's sentence. As most robberies involved but a single allegation, the only way a prosecutor could contrive to lower the defendant's sentence was by reducing a greater charge to a lesser one by entering a nol pros as to part of the charge. It became clear only in 1838 that prosecutors had this power. See this chapter, Notes 101–9 and accompanying text.

36. See *Commonwealth v. Tuck*, 37 Mass. (20 Pick.) 356, 366 (1838): "If the attorney general may enter a *nolle prosequi* as to the whole of an indictment, or of a count, so he may do it as to any distinct and substantive part of it." The power to enter a partial nol pros was uncertain before this 1838 decision. See this chapter, Notes 101–9 and accompanying text.

37. Not all of the sixteen nonliquor defendants whose cases ended in clear plea bargains benefited from pleading guilty in terms of a lower maximum potential penalty. I have already discussed the 1790 case of George Peters (this chapter, Note 26). Other defendants, like Peters, were willing to plead, but only if the prosecutor first struck specific allegations as to which the defendant apparently maintained his inno-

cence. Although these partial nol prosses lessened somewhat the seriousness of each case, there was no change in the formal designation of the defendant's crimes. See, e.g., *Commonwealth v. Emerson Elwell*, Middlesex Ct. C.P. R. Book 216 (June 1843), which reported a breaking-and-entering case alleging the theft of thirty dozen saws, as to two dozen of which the prosecutor entered a nol pros; *Commonwealth v. Benaiah S. Conner*, Middlesex Ct. C.P. R. Book 2 (February 1843), which reported a petty larceny case in which a partial nol pros extended to some of the allegedly stolen goods; *Commonwealth v. Timothy Peterson*, Middlesex Ct. C.P. R. Book 218 (November 1839), which reported a similar case.

38. These are my findings for the relevant years:

Clear Plea Bargains in Liquor and Nonliquor Cases:
Middlesex Court of Common Pleas and Its Predecessor Court

YEAR	NUMBER OF ADJUDICATED DEFENDANTS		NUMBER OF CLEAR PLEA BARGAINS	
	NONLIQUOR	LIQUOR	NONLIQUOR	LIQUOR
1789–1790[a]	21	1	1	0
1799–1800[a]	30	2	0	0
1805–1806[a]	39	0	0	0
1809–1810[a]	27	1	0	1
1814–1815[a]	36	0	2	0
1819–1820[a]	41	5	1	1
1824	27	12	1	3
1829	18	9	0	0
1834	58	7	0	4
1839	35	1	1	0
1843–1844[a]	135	42	8	4
1849	167	56	2	20
TOTAL	634	136	16	33

SOURCES: Middlesex Ct. Gen. Sess. Peace R. Books; Middlesex Ct. Gen. Sess. Docket Books; Middlesex Ct. C.P. R. Books; Middlesex Ct. C.P. Docket Books.
[a] Two-year totals.

By *liquor cases*, I mean cases brought under the liquor license law, which I have described above, Notes 16, 30–33, and accompanying text. By *nonliquor cases*, I mean those in which the charge does not concern the sale or distribution of alcohol. In Appendix A, I trace out the line between liquor and nonliquor cases more exactly.

As I noted previously in note 23, *adjudicated* cases are those in which the defendant went to trial or pled guilty or no contest. Beginning in 1849, a great many cases at each term of court were placed "on file." As I explain in Chapter 3, filed cases present a different aspect of the prosecutorial pleading power and must be considered separately. I therefore have been careful to note whether my figures for 1849 or any later year include filed cases. My figures for 1849, listed in the table in this note, do not.

39. Though perhaps not continuously. See this Chapter, Note 13.

40. It is often difficult to tell from the face of the record book whether a liquor case involved multiple counts. The clerk often noted only that the defendant was charged with a violation of "the License-law." See, e.g., *Commonwealth v. John Wilson*, Middlesex Ct. C.P. R. Book 79 (June 1853). The shorthand of the notation leaves one unable to conclude that only a single count was brought. For the nine cases just noted in the text, I have examined the indictments themselves, which are retained as part of the file papers and stored at the Massachusetts Archives, to confirm that there was just a single count. See *Commonwealth v. John Wade & Bowen Bucknam*, Middlesex Ct. C.P. R. Book 405 (June 1824); *Commonwealth v. William Rogers*, Middlesex Ct. C.P. R. Book 404 (June 1824); *Commonwealth v. Thomas Jameson*, Middlesex Ct. C.P. R. Book 403 (June 1824); *Commonwealth v. John Howe*, Middlesex Ct. C.P. R. Book 402 (June 1824); *Commonwealth v. Ebenezer Davis*, Middlesex Ct. C.P. R. Book 401 (June 1824); *Commonwealth v. John Fowle*, Middlesex Ct. C.P. R. Book 401 (June 1824); *Commonwealth v. Andrew Cochran*, Middlesex Ct. C.P. R. Book 400 (June 1824); *Commonwealth v. Jacob Butters*, Middlesex Ct. C.P. R. Book 399 (June 1824); and *Commonwealth v. Isaac Brooks*, Middlesex Ct. C.P. R. Book 201 (March 1824).

41. "Implicit plea bargaining takes place when a defendant pleads guilty without an explicit promise or deal, but knowing (or assuming) that better deals go to those who 'cooperate' and spare the public the bother and expense of a trial" (Friedman, "Courts over Time," 38). Raymond Moley recognized the phenomenon a good many years ago, noting that the defendant may plead in exchange for an "expressed or implied assurance" of a concession (Moley, "Vanishing Jury," 103).

42. The conviction took place in *Commonwealth v. Josiah Howard*, Middlesex Ct. C.P. R. Book 241 (March 1820). Stearns's other liquor trial ended in an acquittal. See *Commonwealth v. John Houch*, Middlesex Ct. C.P. R. Book 685 (December 1829). Although in some jurisdictions, costs could be assessed even after an acquittal, that was not the case in Massachusetts during the period of my study. In a 1799 case resulting in a not-guilty verdict, the records make clear that costs were to be paid by the county (see *Commonwealth v. John Johnson*, Middlesex Ct. Gen. Sess. Peace R. Book 432 [March 1799]).

43. See *Commonwealth v. Jacob Carter*, Middlesex Ct. C.P. R. Book 244 (March 1820).

44. *Commonwealth v. William Fletcher & Archibald McIntire*, Middlesex Ct. C.P. R. Book 174 (March 1814).

45. In two cases, the costs were unspecified, and in one they were set at $9.97.

46. The records bear this theory out. In all of the cases just noted, defendants who paid the same costs came from either the same or contiguous towns. I have exam-

ined Stearns's accounting of costs in the file papers for several of these cases and have noted nothing that seems contrived or fudged.

47. Throughout the period of my study, it was quite unusual for the record books to disclose the presence of counsel. The court's docket books regularly recorded counsel beginning only in 1844. I argue in Chapter 4 (Notes 12–16 and accompanying text) that the rate of representation before that time was probably a good deal less than fifty percent.

48. In the eight years of his tenure that I studied—1809 (second half), 1810, 1814, 1815, 1819, 1820, 1824, and 1829—Stearns asked for costs in only four of the forty-eight cases in which defendants served time. For examples of the anomalous cases, see *Commonwealth v. Nathaniel Gilson*, Middlesex Ct. C.P. R. Book 515 (December 1809), a theft case in which the defendant was sentenced to two months in jail and was assessed costs of $29.66, and *Commonwealth v. Timothy Cole*, Middlesex Ct. C.P. R. Book 370 (June 1814), a theft case in which the defendant was sentenced to twenty days in jail and a fine of $20.00 and was assessed costs of $39.98. It was certainly true, however, that for *nonpayment* of costs, defendants often found themselves locked up. In fact, the typical sentence commanded that the defendant be committed until costs were paid.

49. The license law of 1832 made second offenders liable to a term of up to 90 days (Act of March 24, 1832, ch. 166, § 15, 1832 Mass. Acts 473, 481–82). An act of 1855 made prison time mandatory even for a first offense (see Chapter 3, Note 1, and accompanying text).

50. *Commonwealth v. Samuel Elliot*, Middlesex Ct. C.P. R. Book 327 (September 1834), indictment form on file with the Massachusetts Archives.

51. *Commonwealth v. Amos Adams*, Middlesex Ct. C.P. R. Book 477 (December 1834), indictment form on file with the Massachusetts Archives.

52. See, e.g., *Commonwealth v. Patrick Maurice*, Middlesex Ct. C.P. R. Book 336 (September 1834), indictment form on file with the Massachusetts Archives. Maurice pled guilty to one count of making a single sale, and Huntington nol prossed the other two counts (ibid).

53. *Commonwealth v. Henry Sprague and Albert H. Sprague*, Middlesex Ct. C.P. R. Book 423 (October 1843), indictment form on file with the Massachusetts Archives.

54. *Mass. Rev. Stat.* ch. 47, §§ 1–4 (Dutton & Wentworth 1836). Like the 1787 license law (see this chapter, Notes 16, 30–33 and accompanying text), the 1836 code called for mandatory penalties throughout the liquor-licensing provisions. It imposed a five-dollar fine for selling to minors or servants, a ten-dollar fine for selling on Sundays, and a twenty-dollar fine for selling to persons cut off by town selectmen (*Mass. Rev. Stat.* ch. 47, §§ 11, 13, 15–16). Only in the case of second offenders, whom the court had the discretion to sentence to up to ninety days in the common jail, did the act create any flexibility in sentencing (ibid, sec. 29). But second-offender prosecutions were exceedingly rare.

55. *Commonwealth v. Daniel McCrillis*, Middlesex Ct. C.P. R. Book 521 (June 1849).

56. See, e.g., *Commonwealth v. Daniel L. Richardson*, Middlesex Ct. C.P. R. Book 611 (October 1849), which reports a case in which the defendant pled to two twenty-dollar counts and was fined forty dollars and assessed court costs of thirty-five dollars.

57. *Commonwealth v. Tuck*, 37 Mass. (20 Pick.) 356, 365–66 (1838).

58. *Case of Asahel Huntington: Report*, H. Doc. No. 4, at 3–5 (Mass. 1845). Robert Hampel seems to be the first modern scholar to cite the Huntington case (Hampel, *Temperance and Prohibition*, 214 n.11).

59. H. Doc. No. 4, at 7.

60. *Order for Committee of Asahel Huntington*, H. Doc. No. 1499, at 2 (Mass. 1844), on file with the Massachusetts Archives.

61. H. Doc. No. 4, at 7.

62. The committee's report lists sixteen witnesses to the allegations of plea bargaining (ibid., 5). I have been able to identify only three. Two were defendants in liquor cases heard in the March 1842 session of the Essex Court of Common Pleas (*Commonwealth v. Joshua Peckham*, Essex Ct. C.P. R. Book 124 [March 1842]; *Commonwealth v. John N. Martin*, Essex Ct. C.P. R. Book 124 [March 1842]). One of these and one other appeared as liquor defendants in the September term of the same court (*Commonwealth v. Joseph Perley*, Essex Ct. C.P. R. Book 105 [September 1842]; *Commonwealth v. John N. Martin*, Essex Ct. C.P. R. Book 105 [September 1842]). In the March term, Huntington had seven liquor cases, and although he consistently charged multiple counts, he was forced to trial in five of them (the two just cited being the exceptions). In the September term, when Huntington had eighteen liquor cases, his tactics were more successful. He charged all but two liquor defendants with multiple counts, secured pleas of no contest in all but five cases, entered nol prosses on payment of costs in four, and nol prossed the last case outright.

63. H. Doc. No. 4, at 8–10.

64. Ibid., 6–7.

65. Ibid., 7–8.

66. Ibid., 7.

67. See Act of March 24, 1843, ch. 99, 1843 Mass. Acts 60.

68. H. Doc. No. 4, at 7.

69. Ibid., 8.

70. Ibid., 9.

71. Ibid., 8.

72. It appears that Albert H. Nelson took office as district attorney in December 1845. The *Lowell Courier* noted his appointment on December 10, 1845 ("Albert H. Nelson, Esq.," *Lowell Daily Courier*, December 10, 1845, 2). A correspondent to the *Lowell Journal* is the source of the supposition that Huntington "felt constrained to resign on account of the inadequacy of the salary" (*Lowell Journal*, October 8,

1847, 1). I discuss the district attorneys' disgruntlement with their workloads and salaries in Chapter 2 (Notes 14–28 and accompanying text).

73. "License Cases," *Lowell Journal*, April 2, 1847, 2. Lowell is one of the prominent cities of Middlesex County. Newburyport is in Essex County and, although not large, was the site of one of the four annual sittings of the Court of Common Pleas in that county. The two counties together formed the Northern District, of which Nelson was district attorney. Tami Swiger, one of my research assistants, spotted this notice of Nelson's practice.

74. Nelson made his last appearance in the Court of Common Pleas Record Books in the October 1847 session; Train made his first in February 1848 (Middlesex Ct. C.P. R. Book [February 1848], on file with the Massachusetts Archives; Middlesex Ct. C.P. R. Book [October 1847], on file with the Massachusetts Archives).

75. The one exception is *Commonwealth v. Charles McDermot*, Middlesex Ct. C.P. R. Book 448 (February 1849). McDermot was charged with six liquor counts on a preprinted form. As far as the records indicate, he offered a general guilty plea, but was sentenced on only two counts and fined twenty dollars on each. The records do not specify that Train nol prossed the remaining counts. I might have hesitated to call this case a clear plea bargain, but the court's docket book specifically noted that the case was disposed of "*without costs*" (ibid.). This was a rare concession. Viewing it together with the other circumstances, I felt justified in including this case with the others.

Another seven of Train's 1849 liquor cases look very much like clear plea bargains—but not enough for me to count them as such. Most took the form of *Commonwealth v. Jonathan M. Marston*, Middlesex Ct. C.P. R. Book 437 (February 1849). Marston was charged with one count of being a common seller (carrying a hundred-dollar fine) and two counts of making single sales (each carrying a twenty-dollar fine). He pled guilty, but the record does not say whether he pled to all counts. He was fined one hundred dollars and assessed an unspecified amount of court costs. We may infer that Marston was convicted only of the common-seller count, but there is no sign of what happened to the other counts. Because the defendant paid a fine on the most expensive count, and because the record makes no explicit statement that the district attorney nol prossed the other counts, I have decided not to consider Marston's case or the others like it to be clear plea bargains. I have also excluded on-file plea bargains from the twenty cases noted in the text. These are the topic of Chapter 3.

76. See Act of March 24, 1843, ch. 99, 1843 Mass. Acts 60.

77. See Act of May 1, 1849, ch. 186, 1849 Mass. Acts 117.

78. See *Commonwealth v. William Goldsmith*, Sup. Jud. Ct. R. Book 456 (Middlesex, April 1845).

79. See *Commonwealth v. George Hunnewell*, Sup. Jud. Ct. R. Book 102 (Middlesex, October 1847).

80. See *Commonwealth v. Alexander Roy*, Sup. Jud. Ct. R. Book 103 (Middlesex, October 1847).

81. See *Commonwealth v. Barney Goulding*, Sup. Jud. Ct. R. Book 226 (Middlesex, October 1848); *Lowell Journal*, March 24, 1848, p. 4.

82. *Goulding*, Sup. Jud. Ct. R. Book at 228.

83. Ibid.

84. Ibid.

85. *Commonwealth v. Battis*, 1 Mass. (1 Will.) 94, 94–95 (1804). I have come across four other pleas to capital charges in the nineteenth century. See *Commonwealth v. Edwin Ray Snow*, listed in *Report of the Attorney General for the Year Ending January 17, 1900*, Pub. Doc. No. 12, at xii (Mass. 1900); *Commonwealth v. Daniel Gleason*, listed in *Report of the Attorney General for the Year Ending December 31, 1872*, Pub. Doc. No. 12, at 5–6 (Mass. 1873); *Green v. Commonwealth*, 94 Mass. (12 Allen) 155, 157 (Mass. 1866); *Commonwealth v. Edward W. Green*, listed in *Report of the Attorney General for the Year Ending December 31, 1864*, Pub. Doc. No. 14, at 12 (Mass. 1865); *Commonwealth v. John Roach*, Sup. Jud. Ct. R. Book 682 (Worcester, September 1845).

In the *Gleason* and *Snow* cases, the governor commuted the defendants' death sentences to life in prison. The attorney general's report of the *Gleason* case gave no reason for the commutation, but in *Snow*, the attorney general said he had recommended a commutation because the defendant was only seventeen at the time of the murder in question. See *Snow*, Pub. Doc. No. 12, at xii. Although it is possible that Snow pled guilty in exchange for the attorney general's promise to recommend commutation, this purpose seems unlikely, because the parties could have accomplished the same result—life in prison—with a second-degree murder deal, and because the prosecutor presumably could not guarantee the governor's action.

In the first half of the nineteenth century, about twenty percent of state prison inmates in Massachusetts were released by governors' pardons (see Kuntz, *Criminal Sentencing*, 124–25). Because I have not seen evidence that defendants pled guilty in anticipation of such forgiveness, I have not included the pardoning power in this study.

86. It is quite possible that other plea bargains escaped my notice. The attorney general began to produce comprehensive accounts of his business before the Supreme Judicial Court in 1832. My examination of his reports disclosed no plea bargaining in capital cases between 1832 and 1840. For the years 1820 to 1832, I examined the Supreme Judicial Court's own records of its criminal business in Suffolk County, which generated far more capital cases than any other county. I also studied the records of the court's criminal business in Middlesex County during 1799, 1809, 1819, 1824, and 1829. In none of these records did I find any evidence of plea bargaining in capital cases—but the state contained many other criminal jurisdictions, and I left many other years unexamined.

87. See *Commonwealth v. Susan Boston*, Sup. Jud. Ct. R. Book 152 (Bristol, April 1841). Boston, charged with murdering a man with a knife, pled guilty to manslaughter. Austin nol prossed so much of the complaint as charged murder, and the court sentenced Boston to three years in the house of correction.

88. See *Commonwealth v. Michael Larry*, Sup. Jud. Ct. R. Book 363 (Suffolk, November 1841).

89. It appears that the only other capital crime after midcentury was an official's voluntary and wrongful release of a capital prisoner—an offense that the Supreme Judicial Court noted in 1866 had never, to the court's knowledge, been committed. See *Green*, 94 Mass. (12 Allen) at 168.

90. See *Commonwealth v. John Cunningham*, Sup. Jud. Ct. R. Book 46 (Bristol, November 1845).

91. Although the office of attorney general was not abolished until 1843, the A.G.'s annual reports for 1840–1842 contained no account of the cases he prosecuted before the high court. The attorney general did not resume this practice until 1849, when the office was reinstated. For each of the intervening years, I examined the Supreme Judicial Court's own records of its sittings in the counties of Suffolk, Middlesex, Bristol, Hampden, Norfolk, and Worcester. Although this survey excluded eight other counties, most of those eight generated little criminal business.

92. Clifford served as attorney general from 1849 until 1853, when he left the post to become governor, and then again from 1854 until 1858. See Davis, *Bench and Bar*, vol. 1, 290; Davis, *History of the Judiciary*, 286.

93. I have found no reported case and no commentary, judicial or otherwise, bearing on these prosecutorial charge bargains in murder cases. It is the nature of prosecutorial charge bargains that they require no judicial cooperation and that indeed judges have little power to interfere. Still, the absence of negative comment by the Supreme Judicial Court, which presided over pleas in murder cases, casts doubt on the general claim that "appellate courts accepted [plea bargaining] only after almost a century of severe disapproval" (Alschuler, "Plea Bargaining History," 19 n.106).

94. In 1844 the figure fell just shy of ten percent. The single charge bargain in 1790 (see above, note 26), amounted to 11 percent of that year's nine adjudicated nonliquor cases. As I noted earlier, it is not altogether clear that this case should be considered a charge bargain at all.

95. I am not including filed cases, the topic of Chapter 3, in this calculation.

96. See, e.g., Alschuler, "Plea Bargaining History," 5–16, 19–24.

97. See this chapter, Notes 15–21 and accompanying text.

98. At least two scholars have reported earlier Massachusetts cases that at first appear to have involved capital charge bargains. I do not believe, however, that any of the five cases they cite actually charged a capital offense, and in four of the cases, I am certain that there was no charge bargain.

Adam Hirsch points to a series of "burglary" cases that came before the Supreme Judicial Court in 1784 and 1785, in which, he writes, "defendants pleaded innocent, and subsequently entered amended guilty pleas" (Hirsch, *Rise of the Penitentiary*, 164 n.77). These four cases, however, all involved breaking and entering a shop or warehouse rather than a home. See *Commonwealth v. Nero Fanueil*, Sup. Jud. Ct. R. Book 75 (February 1785), charging a shop break; *Commonwealth v. James*

Daken, Sup. Jud. Ct. R. Book 67 (February 1785), warehouse break; *Commonwealth v. Elijah Austin Smith*, Sup. Jud. Ct. R. Book 263 (September 1784), shop break; and *Commonwealth v. Thomas Joyce*, Sup. Jud. Ct. R. Book 231 (August 1784), shop break. I believe that the use of the word *burglariously* in the charging language in each of these cases indicated not that these cases involved "burglary," but only that they involved nighttime break-ins.

In any event, as the burglary statutes Hirsch cites make clear, capital burglary was restricted to *home* invasions. See Act of April 26, 1770, ch. 16, §§ 2–3, 5 Mass. Prov. Acts 43, 43–44, which expanded the circumstances in which the invasion of a "dwelling-house" shall be deemed a capital offense; Act of May 25, 1715, 1 Geo. 2, at 253 (Mass.), which defined capital burglary as a nighttime break into an inhabited "Dwelling House." In each of the cited cases except *Daken*, at least one codefendant retracted an initial not-guilty plea, pled guilty *to the crime charged*, and was sentenced accordingly—that is, noncapitally. (Daken and his codefendant initially pled guilty.) Retracting an earlier not-guilty plea in this way was quite common—at least in the nineteenth century—but such a plea did not manifest a charge bargain (involving a reduction in the charged offense) and perhaps represented no understood bargain at all.

David Flaherty reports an apparent charge bargain from 1749 in which the acting attorney general nol prossed so much of the indictment as charged "burglary" (David H. Flaherty, "Criminal Practice," 191, 220 n.9; see also Alschuler, "Plea Bargaining History," 17–18, in which he elaborates on Flaherty's finding). But again, the case in question involved breaking into a ship, not a home (see *Commonwealth v. John Patterson*, Super. Ct. Adjudicature R. Book 224 [1747–1750]). Although it was not capital, the case does appear to have involved a charge bargain. The acting attorney general nol prossed the "Burglary therein charged, [and the defendants] pleaded guilty of the stealing therein charged" (ibid). Flaherty reports that "this episode is the only concrete evidence found on plea bargaining" in his research into criminal practice in colonial Massachusetts (Flaherty, "Criminal Practice," 220).

99. *Commonwealth v. Barney Goulding*, Sup. Jud. Ct. R. Book 228 (Middlesex, October 1848).

100. *Commonwealth v. Michael Larry*, Sup. Jud. Ct. R. Book 363 (Suffolk, November 1841).

101. See *Commonwealth v. Tuck*, 37 Mass. (20 Pick.) 356, 356–57, 359 (1838).

102. Ibid., 366.

103. Ibid.

104. *Commonwealth v. M'Monagle*, 1 Mass. (1 Will.) 517 (1805); *Commonwealth v. Lewis*, 1 Mass. (1 Will.) 517 (1805). Only a year later, the court's chief justice wrote that courts should make no recommendations whatever on the use of nol prosses. See *Commonwealth v. Wheeler*, 2 Mass. (1 Tyng) 172, 174 (1806) (Parsons, C. J.): "Certainly, the court are not legally competent to give any advice on this

subject. The power of entering a *nolle prosequi* is to be exercised at the discretion of the attorney who prosecutes for the government, and for its exercise he alone is responsible."

105. *Commonwealth v. Briggs*, 24 Mass. (7 Pick.) 177, 179 (1828).

106. Ibid., 179–80. The prosecutor had sought, after trial, to nol pros so much of the indictment as charged that the defendant was a repeat offender. The court feared that the defendant had been prejudiced by the jury's knowledge of his former conviction.

107. It is not a foregone conclusion that the court should have approved partial nol prosses. They apparently were disallowed in New York. See *People v. Porter*, 4 Park. 524, 526 (N.Y. Oyer & Terminer 1860), which reports the opinion of a single judge of a court of oyer and terminer that, "[a]s I have before said, a *nolle prosequi* may be to the whole indictment, or to the whole of any one or more of several counts, but cannot be to a part of any one count."

108. See Washburn, *Manual*, 205 n.4.

109. See *Commonwealth v. Wakelin*, 230 Mass. 567, 572 (1918), citing the 1838 case and none earlier; *Commonwealth v. Uhrig*, 167 Mass. 420, 423 (1897), citing only the 1838 case; *Commonwealth v. Wallace*, 108 Mass. 12, 13 (1871), citing both the 1838 case and the 1828 case; *Commonwealth v. Jennings*, 105 Mass. 586, 588 (1870), citing both the 1838 case and one of the 1805 cases.

110. See Act of March 27, 1858, ch. 154, 1858 Mass. Acts 126. The new law defined first-degree murder as murder committed with premeditation, with extreme atrocity or cruelty, or while committing or attempting to commit a life felony. Second-degree murder was all other murder (ibid., §§ 1–2).

111. Ibid., §§ 4–5.

112. See *Commonwealth v. Edward Owens*, listed in *Report of the Attorney General for the Year Ending December 31, 1863*, Pub. Doc. No. 17, at 7 (Mass. 1864); *Commonwealth v. Thomas Coyne*, listed in Pub. Doc. No. 17, at 7.

113. In the 1860s, guilty pleas to second-degree murder accounted for thirty-two percent of all plea bargains in murder cases, while pleas to manslaughter still made up sixty-eight percent. In the 1870s, 1880s, and 1890s, pleas to second-degree murder accounted for a steady sixty-one percent of all murder deals and manslaughter pleas for the balance of thirty-nine percent. These figures are gathered from the attorney general's reports of the relevant years studied.

NOTES TO CHAPTER 2

1. This figure represents all cases disposed of by the Court of Common Pleas in 1849, including those that were listed in merely summary fashion in the record books. I discuss this class of cases in Chapter 3.

2. See Ferdinand, *Boston's Courts*, 138, fig. 5.1, which shows the rising case-

load in Boston's municipal court, the counterpart to the Court of Common Pleas, beginning in the mid-1830s. The municipal court's caseload turned more steeply upward in the 1840s. In 1844 the Suffolk County district attorney reported 750 cases for the previous year (see S. Doc. No. 68, at 6 [Mass. 1844], petition of Samuel D. Parker). He reported 1,672 cases for 1848 (see H. Doc. No. 63, at 4 [Mass. 1849]).

3. See U.S. Census Office, *Twelfth Census of the United States*, vol.1, part 1, 24, table 4. In 1844 the Suffolk County district attorney complained to the legislature that the county's "criminal business . . . has kept equal pace with the increased population of the city" (S. Doc. No. 68, at 6, petition of Samuel D. Parker). The population of Boston more than doubled between 1820 and 1845 to about 99,000 (see Handlin, 239, table xiv). Population growth alone, however, cannot account for the increased caseload. Michael Stephen Hindus reports that the *rate* of criminal prosecutions in Massachusetts grew from 169 per 100,000 in 1831–1840 to 277 per 100,000 in 1841–1850 (Hindus, *Prison and Plantation*, 77).

4. We are more likely to see such an impact in Boston, where the legislature authorized the creation of a police force in 1838 (see Act of April 17, 1838, ch. 123, 1838 Mass. Acts 421), than in the rest of the state, where the legislature did not grant similar authority until 1851 (see Act of May 15, 1851, ch. 162, 1851 Mass. Acts 657).

5. Theodore Ferdinand (*Boston's Courts*, 14) reports that "[t]he Commonwealth made a concerted effort to limit the sale of spirits in the late 1830s and 1840s through licensing, and liquor violations grew by leaps and bounds." Robert Hampel (*Temperance*, 152) adds that "[i]n each one of the seven years from 1845 to 1851, [liquor] license cases made up between 30 percent and 40 percent of the business of the [Massachusetts] courts." It is possible that part of the increase in liquor cases was due to a shift of cases from the lower police courts. Ferdinand saw such a shift in his study of Boston's courts (*Boston's Courts*, 84 table 3.9).

6. The 1832 jurisdictional shift slashed the criminal workload of the Supreme Judicial Court sitting in Middlesex County to nearly nothing:

Middlesex County Criminal Caseload: Court of Common
Pleas and Supreme Judicial Court

	NUMBER OF CASES	
	---	---
YEAR	COURT OF COMMON PLEAS	SUPREME JUDICIAL COURT
1799	17	12
1809	14	24
1819	24	30
1824	48	36
1829	41	20
1834	95	7

(table continued on next page)

NUMBER OF CASES

YEAR	COURT OF COMMON PLEAS	SUPREME JUDICIAL COURT
1839	42	1
1843	101	0
1849	443	4

SOURCES: Middlesex Ct. C.P. R. Books; Middlesex Ct. Gen. Sess. Peace R. Books; Sup. Jud. Ct. R. Books (Middlesex sittings), on file with the Massachusetts Archives.

7. The caseload was as follows:

Appeals from Lower Tribunals:
Middlesex Court of Common Pleas and Its Predecessor Court

YEAR	NUMBER OF CASES	NUMBER OF APPEALS	APPEALS AS % OF TOTAL
1789–1790[a]	23	0	0
1799–1800[a]	38	2	5
1805–1806[a]	47	3	6
1809–1810[a]	34	1	3
1814–1815[a]	70	5	7
1819–1820[a]	62	2	3
1824	48	2	4
1829	41	3	7
1834	95	1	1
1839	42	1	2
1843–1844[a]	224	12	5
1849	443	134	30

SOURCES: Middlesex Ct. C.P. R. Books; Middlesex Ct. Gen. Sess. Peace R. Books; Sup. Jud. Ct. R. Books (Middlesex sittings), on file with the Massachusetts Archives.
[a] Two-year totals.

8. I argue in Chapter 4 (Notes 13–16 and accompanying text) that the proportion of defendants who had lawyers probably increased in the early part of the century. It is clear that defendants with lawyers accounted for the great majority of cases appealed to the Court of Common Pleas from lower tribunals—seventy-three percent of them in 1849, although only sixty percent of all defendants had lawyers in that year. See Table 4.1; Middlesex Ct. C.P. R. Book (1849); Middlesex Ct. C.P. Docket Book (1849). A former Massachusetts assistant district attorney wrote in the early 1920s that "[i]n a large majority of appeal cases, defendants have counsel" (quoted in Grinnell, "Legislative Problems," 7, 9).

9. See Act of February 16, 1848, ch. 16, 1848 Mass. Acts 605; Act of March

14, 1832, ch. 130, § 9, 1832 Mass. Acts 396, 404–6. The Essex County caseload was smaller than that of Middlesex, but not by much. In 1842, for example, 126 criminal cases were addressed in the Middlesex Court of Common Pleas and 102 cases in Essex (Middlesex Ct. C.P. R. Book [1842], on file with the Massachusetts Archives; Essex Ct. C.P. R. Book [1842], on file with the Essex County Superior Court).

    10. See Act of May 1, 1849, Ch. 186, 1849 Mass. Acts 117; Act of March 24, 1843, Ch. 99, 1843 Mass. Acts 60. Suffolk County District Attorney Samuel D. Parker complained to the legislature in 1844 that "[t]he office of Attorney General has been abolished;—capital trials in [my] county have been added to [my] department, as well as the task of arguing all questions of law in the Supreme Judicial Court, in which the Commonwealth is a party, formerly the exclusive duty of the Attorney General" (S. Doc. No. 68, at 6 [Mass. 1844], petition of Samuel D. Parker). The district attorney for the Southern District, J. H. Clifford, echoed Parker, noting that by eliminating the attorney general's office, the legislature had "largely increased" the labors of the district attorneys (ibid., 7, 8).

    11. *Lowell Courier*, July 15, 1845, 2. This item was reprinted from the *Salem Register*.

    12. I have seen no reference to an assistant prosecutor anywhere in Massachusetts before 1852, when one was appointed by the Boston Municipal Court (see Ferdinand, *Boston's Courts*, 191). In 1875 the legislature provided for a part-time assistant district attorney for the Northern District (Middlesex) and others (see Act of February 11, 1875, ch. 12, 1875 Mass. Acts 602, 602). An 1873 law permitted appointment of a clerk to assist district attorneys (see Act of May 12, 1873, ch. 278, 1873 Mass. Acts 707, 707).

    13. See Middlesex Ct. C.P. R. Book 147–50 (October 1845). Nelson, Huntington's successor, fared little better. At the end of the next year, he nol prossed 229 cases, and as he prepared to leave office at the end of 1847, he nol prossed another 182. See Middlesex Ct. C.P. R. Book 323 (February 1848), which notes the first appearance of Nelson's successor, Charles Russell Train; Middlesex Ct. C.P. R. Book 299–300 (October 1847); Middlesex Ct. C.P. R. Book 223–29 (October 1846).

    14. See Massachusetts House of Representatives, *Report*, 4.

    15. See Davis, *History of the Judiciary*, 219–20. In his response to legislative charges of malfeasance in 1809, Dana mentioned that he had been "engaged at the Legislature" during the June 1808 sitting of the Court of Common Pleas. Dana, "Mr. Dana's Answer," 5.

    16. Stearns was county attorney of Middlesex between about 1809 and 1832 (see Chapter 1, Note 13, and accompanying text; Table 1.1, p. 28). He served in Congress from 1815 to 1817 and as principal professor at Harvard Law School from 1817 to 1829 (see Davis, *Bench and Bar*, vol. 1, 561). Isaac Parker, chief justice of the Supreme Judicial Court, served as the Royall Professor of Law at Harvard, but "[f]or the twelve years of his incumbency, Judge Parker had no closer direct connection with the Law School than was afforded by the attendance of the students at his lectures and

a vague understanding that he was occasionally to visit the school and examine the men. The working member of the faculty was Asahel Stearns" (Grinnell, "Courts and Lawyers," 263).

In 1826 Stearns reported on the burdens of his professorship to the college president:

A large portion of the Professor's time is employed in selecting and preparing suitable questions and cases for argument at the moot court, and in assisting the students to put them into this form of judicious action, examining their declarations, pleas, replications, demurrers, bills of exceptions, motions, etc., and directing them in the course of their investigations and researches. But of the amount of time thus employed, and of that also which is devoted to answering the numerous questions, and solving the doubts which occur to the students, (and which they are encouraged and desired to suggest with freedom when they occur), it is impossible to make any correct estimate. (Warren, *History of Harvard Law School*, vol. 1, 357 [quoting Stearns])

17. John H. Clifford, who was district attorney of the Southern District during the 1840s, was said to have maintained "the leading civil practice on the circuit" (Clifford Papers, Box 1845–1851, January–October 1850 folder). This claim appears in a handwritten biography or autobiography of Clifford kept among his papers.

It is likely that most American prosecutors supplemented their incomes with civil practices. Friedman and Percival (*Roots of Justice*, 50–51) report that Alameda County prosecutors of the late nineteenth century had civil practices on the side.

18. This letter of Daniel Wells, district attorney for the Western District, was reprinted in S. Doc. No. 68, at 10, 12 (Mass. 1844). Wells suggested that he "could afford to do the duties of the office for a less compensation, if the business of the court admitted of the establishment of separate criminal terms" (ibid., 12). Whether for this reason or others, the various counties moved toward separate criminal and civil sessions, a step Middlesex County took in 1839. See Middlesex Ct. C.P. R. Book (1839), on file with the Massachusetts Archives, which records June 1839 as the first Middlesex sitting of the Court of Common Pleas that held separate civil and criminal sessions. In other counties, the change came later. See H. Doc. No. 63, at 15 (Mass. 1849), which reports the complaint of the district attorney for the Eastern District about the "urgent necessity for the separation of the criminal from the civil business of the Court of Common Pleas . . . as in some of the other large districts of the Commonwealth."

19. Similar pressures came to bear on prosecutors in New York. See Gould et al., "Report on Common Jails," 149 (1866): "[W]here the district attorney has private practice in the court, for which he is paid, it is natural that he should attend to that in preference to the criminal business for which he is not paid otherwise than by salary."

20. See Alschuler, "Prosecutor's Role," 59 n.31.

21. See Act of March 7, 1843, ch. 9, 1843 Mass. Acts 6, 6. This act reduced the salaries of most of the state's district attorneys from one thousand to seven hundred dollars a year. The salary of the Suffolk County district attorney, whose position was

nearer to full-time, was cut from eighteen hundred to fifteen hundred dollars. Associate justices of the Court of Common Pleas earned eighteen hundred dollars per year during most of the first half of the century (see Act of February 14, 1821, ch. 79, § 10, 1821 Mass. Acts 545, 551), though the legislature also reduced their salaries in 1843 to seventeen hundred dollars (see § 1, 1843 Mass. Acts at 6). "[I]ndustrious laboring men" earned three hundred dollars per year in the 1830s (see "Moderate Drinking a Losing Business," *Lowell Courier*, November 29, 1836, 1).

22. See S. Doc. No. 68, at 7, 9 (Mass. 1844), memorial of J. H. Clifford. By contrast, the Suffolk County district attorney was well paid at two dollars a case (ibid., 6, petition of Samuel D. Parker).

23. Ibid., 10, 11, letter of Daniel Wells.

24. See H. Doc. No. 63, at 4, 5 (Mass. 1849), which abstracts from the report of Samuel D. Parker, the county attorney for Suffolk County. Theodore Ferdinand reports that Parker's caseload grew from 228 cases in 1830 to 1,532 in 1850 (see Ferdinand, *Boston's Courts*, 67).

25. "Letters from the Editor.—No. 6," *Lowell Courier*, January 14, 1845, 2.

26. "Massachusetts Legislature," *Lowell Courier*, January 21, 1845, 2.

27. See Act of February 10, 1845, ch. 36, 1845 Mass. Acts 412, 412, which set the salary of the district attorney for the Northern District of the Commonwealth; Act of January 29, 1845, ch. 14, 1845 Mass. Acts 401, 401, which set the salary of the district attorney for the Southern District. But in restoring the district attorneys' salaries to one thousand dollars, the legislature failed to squelch prosecutorial discontent or editorial criticism. In 1847, as Albert Nelson prepared to leave office (apparently because of his low salary), another local paper called the legislature "niggardly" ("Mr. Attorney Nelson," *Lowell Journal*, October 1, 1847, 2).

28. See Act of May 1, 1849, ch. 186, 1849 Mass. Acts 117, 117.

29. Vogel, *Courts of Trade*, 163; see also Heumann, "Note on Plea Bargaining," 516–17. Heumann surveyed studies holding that caseload pressure played a large role in bringing about the rise of plea bargaining.

30. Vogel, *Courts of Trade*, 163.

31. Vogel conducted her research for the years before 1866 in the Boston Police Court (see Vogel, "Social Origins," 176). The records of the police court apparently did not reveal clear plea bargains, in which the exchange of plea for concession was apparent on the face of the records. Vogel therefore engages in an elaborate examination of the pattern of concessions across cases over time (see ibid., 180–95). But as this procedure permitted her to draw no firm conclusion about whether any particular case was a plea bargain or a simple guilty plea, her comparison of caseload and plea bargaining had to rely on guilty plea rates (ibid., 219).

32. See ibid., 220; Vogel, *Courts of Trade*, 163–64.

33. Vogel, "Social Origins," 219; see also Vogel, *Courts of Trade*, 163.

34. See Vogel, "Social Origins," 176; Vogel, *Courts of Trade*, 59.

35. The graph is titled "Guilty plea rates and caseload pressure." Vogel, "Social Origins," 220.

36. Vogel, "Social Origins," 220.

37. Ibid., 176; Vogel, *Courts of Trade*, 59.

38. Ferdinand also studied the Boston Police Court, a nonjury forum from which prosecutors generally were absent (see Ferdinand, *Boston's Courts*, 82). As I explain in more detail in Chapter 6, I do not think that the work of the police court can shed much light on the operations of a jury forum in which prosecutors conducted business for the state. With regard to the police court, Ferdinand sometimes endorses and sometimes dismisses a link between caseload pressure and plea bargaining's rise. At one point (*Boston's Courts*, 65), he writes that "[t]he Police Court initiated plea bargaining for the same reason that it was developed in the Municipal Court: to ease the burdens of prosecution." At another (*Boston's Courts*, 93), Ferdinand says that "there was no prosecutor in the Police Court, and little if any relationship between caseload and plea bargaining."

39. Ibid., 138.

40. Ibid., 81. Ferdinand reports that between 1832–1840 and 1842–1850, the proportion of municipal court cases ending in pleas of either guilty or no contest grew by more than half—from 19.3 percent to 31.8 percent (ibid., 100, table 4.1). Ferdinand prefers to consider those cases in which the defendant offered an *initial* plea of guilty or no contest separately from those in which the defendant initially pled not guilty and later changed her plea to guilty or no contest (ibid., 100–101).

If we focus on only the latter cases, then the 1840s look like a true revolution in plea bargaining: Changed pleas surpassed seventeen percent of all cases after the 1840s, although they never amounted to three percent before that decade. The starkness of the increase suggests that something significant took place, and Ferdinand may well be right that a retracted plea is a sign that prosecutor and defendant conferred after the initial plea and reached a deal (ibid., 74–77, 100–101). The large increase in the number of changed pleas, however, also may have resulted from a change in record-keeping practices—that is, from a decision to record both pleas when only the final plea generally had been recorded before. As Lynn Mather notes ("Comments," 284–85), an initial plea of guilty could result from an explicit charge bargain made before charges were finalized.

41. Ferdinand, *Boston's Courts*, 93.

42. Ibid., 81. Of the two categories, regulatory crimes (which included liquor-law violations) showed the most striking increase in guilty plea rates during the 1840s and the highest overall incidence of guilty pleas—55.2 percent between 1842 and 1850. The guilty plea rate in vice offenses never surpassed thirty-five percent (ibid., 59, table 2.3). See also Appendix B, in which I analyze Ferdinand's category of "vice or regulatory" offenses.

43. Ferdinand, *Boston's Courts*, 93.

44. See Act of May 16, 1856, ch. 173, § 1, 1856 Mass. Acts 98, 98–99, which concerned the election of district attorneys and other county officers; Act of March 14, 1832, ch. 130, § 8, 1832 Mass. Acts 396, 403–04; Vogel, "Social Origins," 218–19; Vogel, *Courts of Trade*, 136.

45. Letter of J. H. Clifford, January 20, 1843 [sic], reprinted in S. Doc. No. 68, at 7, 9 (Mass. 1844). Clifford became attorney general in 1849 and governor in 1853. See Davis, *Bench and Bar*, vol. 1, 290.

46. In Clifford's papers, there is a handwritten biography or autobiography presumably prepared for a run for office. On page six, the biography states that "while there were from three to four hundred cases yearly, there were just seventeen verdicts of not guilty rendered in the district in criminal cases, during the entire decade over which his incumbency of the office extended" (Clifford Papers, January–October 1850 folder). The biography attributes Clifford's success to his firm course of "abandoning a prosecution, when he became satisfied that the jury ought to entertain reasonable doubts of the guilt of the accused."

47. The Massachusetts attorney general began making annual reports to the legislature in 1832. Except when the office itself was suspended for six years in the 1840s, these reports appeared throughout the nineteenth century. Until 1870 they included abstracts of the business of the various district attorneys. From 1832 through 1859, these abstracts made no distinction between convictions after trial and convictions after plea. A single category, "Convictions," presumably included both phenomena. See, e.g., S. Doc. No. 20, pt. 2, at 19–35 (Mass. 1842), annual report of the attorney general.

Between 1860 and 1869, however, the abstracts of the district attorneys' business took on far greater detail and, in particular, noted the number of guilty and no contest pleas in each of the various categories of crime. See, e.g., Pub. Doc. No. 23, app. at 22–26 (Mass. 1860), annual report of the attorney general for the year ending December 31, 1860. In 1870 this experiment with full disclosure stopped as suddenly as it had begun. Throughout the rest of the century, the reports of the attorneys general excluded altogether the abstracts of the district attorneys' business. See, e.g., Pub. Doc. No. 12 (Mass. 1871), annual report of the attorney general for the year ending December 31, 1870.

I have not found the reason for the great candor of the 1860s. Four different men served as attorney general in that decade, and neither the beginning nor the end of the decade coincided with a change of office holders (see Morse, "Historical Outline," 111–12).

48. Moley, "Vanishing Jury," 103; see also Pound, *Criminal Justice in America*, 184: "[P]rosecutors publish statements showing 'convictions' running to thousands each year. But more than ninety per cent of these 'convictions' are upon pleas of guilty, made on 'bargain days,' in the assured expectation of nominal punishment, as the cheapest way out, and amounting in effect to license to violate the law."

49. See *Commonwealth v. Henry Howard*, Middlesex Ct. C.P. R. Book 193 (October 1853).

50. See Davis, *Bench and Bar*, vol. 1, 389; Davis, *History of the Judiciary*, 289.

51. Two-thirds of the way through the 1859 court year, the Superior Court supplanted the Court of Common Pleas. But for its new name and new roster of judges, the new court looked very much like the old, and record-keeping practices continued virtually unchanged. See Act of April 5, 1859, ch. 196, 1859 Mass. Acts 339, 339, which established the superior courts; Middlesex Ct. C.P. R. Book (1859), on file with the Massachusetts Archives; Hindus, *Prison and Plantation*, 17.

52. In my study of selected years' records of the first half of the century, I did not come across any breaking-and-entering or larceny-from-a-building case that charged separate counts for nighttime and daytime. In unsystematic browsing through other years, I came upon only one such case—in 1846 (*Commonwealth v. Francis Smith*, Middlesex Ct. C.P. Docket Book No. 274 [October 1846]).

53. Only one of the four deals ended the way one might expect—with the defendant's pleading guilty to the daytime count and the prosecutor's nol prossing the nighttime count: see *Commonwealth v. Harry Peterson*, Middlesex Ct. C.P. R. Book 94 (February 1859). The other three took the opposite form: see *Commonwealth v. William C. Riley*, Middlesex Ct. C.P. R. Book 209 (June 1859}; *Commonwealth v. John Petite*, Middlesex Ct. C.P. R. Book 113 (February 1859); *Commonwealth v. Joseph Merrett*, Middlesex Ct. C.P. R. Book 88 (February 1859).

54. See *Mass. Gen. Stat.* ch. 161, §§ 11–12, 14 (William White 1860). The penalties were stiffer if the offender was armed or assaulted someone present in the building (ibid. §§ 10, 13), but there was no such allegation in any of these cases. The crime of larceny from a building carried a five-year maximum, apparently without regard to whether it was committed by day or by night (ibid. § 15).

55. Defendants in two of the thirty-nine cases were found not guilty at trial, and those in two others were found guilty of or pled guilty to larceny only. See *Commonwealth v. James Smith*, Middlesex Ct. C.P. R. Book 201 (June 1859), which reported a not-guilty finding after trial; *Commonwealth v. Michael Manyer*, Middlesex Ct. C.P. R. Book 193 (June 1859), which reported that the defendant was found guilty after trial, but that the prosecutor then nol prossed the part of the indictment that alleged that the theft was from a building; *Commonwealth v. George W. Giles*, Middlesex Ct. C.P. R. Book 105 (February 1859), which reported a not-guilty finding after trial; *Commonwealth v. Thomas Murray*, Middlesex Ct. C.P. R. Book 92 (February 1859), which reported that the defendant pled guilty to larceny only and that the prosecutor nol prossed the balance of the indictment. The number of defendants found guilty was actually greater than thirty-five, because several cases had more than one defendant.

The two cases in which sentences exceeded five years do not include two cases involving the same defendant, both of which ended in five-year consecutive sentences: see *Commonwealth v. Angus Mannon*, Middlesex Ct. C.P. R. Book 86 (February 1859); and *Commonwealth v. Angus Mannon*, Middlesex Ct. C.P. R. Book 84 (February 1859).

56. It appears that those defendants who entered into a charge bargain with Morse received more lenient sentences than those who went to trial and lost, but not more lenient than those who simply pled guilty to the entire indictment. Not all these cases are comparable in terms of seriousness, but we can isolate for comparison the eight that charge breaking and entering a residence, since three of the four charge-bargained cases fall in this group. The defendants in the charge-bargained cases received an average sentence of thirty-six months: see Middlesex Ct. C.P. R. Books (February, June 1859); and Middlesex Super. Ct. R. Book (October 1859). In two cases, which involved the same defendant, the defendant went to trial, was convicted each time, and received two sixty-month sentences, to be served consecutively. In each of the other cases, the defendant pled guilty without any form of charge bargain and received an average sentence of twenty-three months: see Middlesex Ct. C.P. R. Books (February, June 1859); and Middlesex Super. Ct. R. Book (October 1859).

57. Of the thirty-nine cases, fifteen went to trial. Two ended in not-guilty verdicts. The jury returned a split verdict—guilty on one count and not guilty on the other—in eight cases. In three of the remaining five cases, the jury returned a general guilty verdict, and Morse then nol prossed one count of the indictment. In the two cases in which the general verdict apparently stood, there is no sign that the defendant was sentenced on both counts: see Middlesex Ct. C.P. R. Books (February, June 1859); Middlesex Super. Ct. R. Book (October 1859).

58. Although Morse did not abandon charge bargaining in breaking-and-entering cases, the tactic never caught on, and he may have lost enthusiasm for it. In 1864 he charged separate daytime and nighttime counts in nine of thirteen indictments for either breaking and entering or larceny from a building. In 1870 he did so in only seven of fifteen such indictments. None of the 1864 cases and only one of the 1870 cases ended in a charge bargain involving a nol pros of one of the two counts: see Middlesex Super. Ct. R. Books (February, October 1864; February 1870).

59. Act of May 22, 1852, ch. 322, § 13, 1852 Mass. Acts 257, 257.

60. See Chapter 1, Notes 74–75, and accompanying text.

61. The sample size here is small, however. The records in 1853 disclose only seven cases in which the clerk made it clear both that Train sought an indictment under the new prohibition law and how many counts he charged. The rest of the adjudicated liquor cases came to the Court of Common Pleas not via grand jury indictment, but as appeals from lower tribunals. It does not appear that the district attorney dictated the charging practices in such cases, and they only rarely involved multiple counts either before or after the law change of 1852. Unfortunately the clerk often recorded only that a case charged violations of the liquor license law or of the prohibitory law, without enumerating counts: see Middlesex Ct. C.P. R. Book (1853), on file with the Massachusetts Archives.

62. In 1855 the legislature broadened the state's criminal nuisance law to embrace the act of keeping a liquor tenement: see Act of May 19, 1855, ch. 405, 1855 Mass. Acts 803, 803. Thereafter, "liquor nuisance" cases became quite common.

Because the penalty scheme of the nuisance law was very different from those of the old license law and of the new prohibition law, it would be wrong to lump the liquor nuisance cases with the rest. Whenever I refer simply to *liquor* cases, therefore, I mean either liquor license cases or prohibition cases, depending on the governing statute at the time—but not liquor nuisance cases. Liquor nuisance cases must languish in limbo, as neither liquor nor nonliquor cases. See Appendix A.

63. Because the prohibition law, as reenacted in 1855, called for mandatory imprisonment, these defendants all served time. See Act of April 20, 1855, ch. 215, §§ 15, 17, 24, 1855 Mass. Acts 623, 630, 631, 635; *Commonwealth v. James Campbell*, Middlesex Ct. C.P. R. Book 144 (June 1859), which notes a sentence of twenty days and a fine for a single sale of liquor; *Commonwealth v. John Healey*, Middlesex Ct. C.P. R. Book 22 (February 1859), which likewise notes the same sentence; *Commonwealth v. John Healey*, Middlesex Ct. C.P. R. Book 24 (February 1859), which notes the same sentence.

64. See Act of June 19, 1869, ch. 415, § 60, 1869 Mass. Acts 706, 723, which states that "the prosecuting officer . . . shall not enter a *nolle prosequi* [in any case arising under this act] except with the concurrence of the court"; Act of April 20, 1855, ch. 215, § 35, 1855 Mass. Acts 623, 641, which states that "a *nolle prosequi* shall not be entered by the prosecuting officer [in any case arising under this act], excepting with the concurrence of the court." The 1855 reenactment followed a decision by the Supreme Judicial Court in 1854 declaring unconstitutional certain search-and-seizure provisions of the 1852 prohibition law: see *Fisher v. McGirr*, 67 Mass. (1 Gray) 1, 21 (1854).

65. The anomalous cases are *Commonwealth v. Richard Barrett*, Middlesex Super. Ct. R. Book 85 (February 1874); *Commonwealth v. Edward Riordan*, Middlesex Super. Ct. Docket Book No. 510 (February 1864); *Commonwealth v. Nicholas Mullen*, Middlesex Super. Ct. Docket Book No. 488 (February 1864); and *Commonwealth v. Catherine Conley*, Middlesex Super. Ct. Docket Book No. 461 (February 1864). In *Barrett*, the record does not specify that the prosecutor in fact entered a nol pros. I have included this case in the list, however, because it is clear that Barrett pled to one count among several, that he was fined only on that count, and that the one count carried only a small fine. The case had all of the other earmarks of a liquor charge bargain.

66. Act of May 22, 1852, ch. 322, §§ 7, 12, 1852 Mass. Acts 257, 257. Unlike the old law, though, the new law provided mandatory prison terms on third offenses and required the posting of one-thousand-dollar or two-thousand-dollar bonds as surety against future violations.

67. See *Commonwealth v. Joseph Jeffrey Jr.*, Middlesex Ct. C.P. R. Book 375 (December 1824), in which Asahel Stearns nol prossed one of two counts of damaging a highway after the defendant pled no contest to the other; *Commonwealth v. Simeon Gigger*, Middlesex Ct. C.P. R. Book 34 (December 1820), in which the defendant, who was charged with breaking and entering a dwelling house and committing

assault and battery, pled guilty to assault and battery only and was sentenced on that basis; *Commonwealth v. Simeon Ford*, Middlesex Ct. C.P. R. Book 450 (June 1815), in which the prosecutor nol prossed one of two counts of traveling on a Sunday after the defendant pled guilty to the other; *Commonwealth v. George Peters*, Middlesex Ct. Gen. Sess. Peace R. Book 7 (September 1790), which is discussed in Chapter 1, Note 26. In a fifth case, there was a clear concession but not precisely a charge bargain. See *Commonwealth v. Jonathan Curtis*, Middlesex Ct. C.P. R. Book 371 (June 1814), in which Asahel Stearns nol prossed an assault-and-battery charge upon payment of costs after the defendant pled no contest.

68. I am excluding liquor cases from this portion of the study because in those cases, prosecutors held the balance of sentencing power. In later years, breaking-and-entering and assault-and-battery cases were common enough to allow analysis (see Chapter 5, Table 5.1). In the years I studied between 1789 and 1829, however, there were only a handful of breaking-and-entering convictions, and although assault-and-battery cases were more plentiful, far too few (only six) ended in convictions after trial to permit comparison with convictions by plea.

69. See, e.g., *Commonwealth v. Daniel Nix*, Middlesex Ct. Gen. Sess. Peace R. Book 458 (September 1789), in which the sentence provided for various alternatives, including whipping, restitution, sale into servitude, and incarceration at hard labor.

70. See Act of February 14, 1821, ch. 79, § 10, 8 Mass. Laws 545, 551. This act established the "Court of Common Pleas for the Commonwealth," one variant in the institution's evolution (see Prologue, Note 7).

71. See Act of March 14, 1832, ch. 130, § 10, 12 Mass. Laws 396, 406.

72. See Act of March 7, 1843, ch. 9, § 1, 1843 Mass. Acts 6, 6.

73. Letter from B[enjamin] R. Curtis to John H. Clifford (April 28, 1849), Clifford Papers, Box 1845–1851, 1848–1849 Folder.

74. A bill proposed in 1811 would have made it a "high misdemeanor" for any Court of Common Pleas judge to appear as an attorney before a state or federal court or to take part in any civil case. See *Act To Prohibit the Justices of the Court of Common Pleas from Practising as Attornies or Counsellors*, on file with the Harvard Law School Library. This bill does not seem to have become law and in any event would have fallen under a general repeal provision of the 1821 legislation: see Act of February 14, 1821, ch. 79, § 12, 8 Mass. Laws 545, 551.

75. The only evidence I have seen of a judge's doing legal work on the side appears in the diaries of Charles Thompson (1827–1894), a lawyer based in Salem who was appointed to the superior court in 1885. Thompson's diaries note that in May 1886 he "went to Probate Court on Probate of will of Fitz E. Riggs" (Thompson, Diaries, vol. 13 [May 8, 1886]). Thompson had handled the Riggs will before his appointment to the bench. See ibid., February 24, 1885, which makes reference to the will of Fitz E. Riggs; ibid., vol. 11, October 14, 1885, which notes his nomination to

the Superior Court. There is no reason to believe that Thompson took on new business after his appointment, but neither did he immediately wrap up his old business.

Samuel Dana served in the Massachusetts Senate from 1811 to 1813 and in Congress from 1814 to 1815 even while he sat on the Court of Common Pleas (Davis, *History of the Judiciary*, 202–04, 219–20). Perhaps for this reason, the legislature provided that its 1821 salaries were "in full for [the judges'] services" and that if any judge should accept a legislative seat or federal position, "his office of the Justice of the Court of Common Pleas shall thereby be vacated" (§ 10, 8 Mass. Laws at 551). But as the legislature repealed this restriction four months later (Act of June 16, 1821, ch. 23, § 4, 8 Mass. Laws 595, 595), it is possible that other judges took multiple posts in later years.

76. See § 1, 1843 Mass. Acts at 6; Alan J. Dimond, *Superior Court*, 78 (1960).

77. Davis, *History of the Judiciary*, 244.

78. Dimond, *Superior Court*, 75–76.

79. Act of April 6, 1859, ch. 216, § 1, 1859 Mass. Acts 371, 371.

80. Davis, *History of the Judiciary*, 244; see also "Court of Common Pleas," *Lowell Journal*, September 10, 1847, 1: "Something ought to be done to enable our courts to d[i]spatch business, so that parties going to law, may do so with a reasonable prospect of settling their disputes in their lifetime."

81. See Act of May 6, 1872, ch. 352, § 1, 1872 Mass. Acts 320, 320.

82. In 1875 the legislature provided for a part-time assistant district attorney for the Northern District (Middlesex) and others (see Act of February 11, 1875, ch. 12, § 1, 1875 Mass. Acts 602, 602). A law of 1873 permitted appointment of a clerk to assist the district attorneys (Act of May 12, 1873, ch. 278, § 1, 1873 Mass. Acts 707, 707). The first indication I have seen of a possibly full-time assistant prosecutor in Middlesex is in an 1881 county payroll showing $1,000, disbursed for an assistant district attorney, raised to $1,500 the following year (Middlesex County, *Statement of Receipts . . . 1881*, 5; Middlesex County, *Statement of Receipts . . . 1882*, 5).

83. See Chapter 2, Note 13 and accompanying text.

84. See *Mass. Gen. Stat.* ch. 160, § 18 (William White 1860).

85. This was also true elsewhere. See Train, *Prisoner at the Bar*, 178, which notes that sentences in New York as of 1906 "cannot be considered or reversed on appeal."

86. *People v. Brown*, 54 Mich. 15, 20 (1884). After the defendant pled guilty but before sentencing, the judge told others who approached him on the defendant's behalf "that I would examine into the previous history of the respondent and consider any mitigating circumstances that there might be in his case, and that I was not prepared to announce in advance what his sentence would be" (ibid., 21). Of course, as the quoted statement comes from the judge's own account of events supplied to the state's supreme court on the defendant's appeal following his guilty plea, it perhaps says more about the appropriate response to a defense lawyer's inquiry than about the actual response.

87. An 1837 issue of the *Lowell Courier* reported that at the Court of Common Pleas, a defendant "pleads guilty, and on examination of witnesses is sentenced to common gaol 2 mos" ("Court of Common Pleas," *Lowell Courier*, September 14, 1837, 2). The same report includes several other cases in which defendants pled guilty and were sentenced without any mention of further proceedings. I cannot say whether the first case was exceptional or—what seems just as likely—the reporter simply neglected to mention a similar hearing in other cases. The court's records never mention sentencing hearings, though they surely were common.

Superior Court Judge Charles Devens wrote in an 1867 trial notebook that a defendant "plead Guilty of assault & Battery—as to sentence Mr W.E Jewett states that it was an accidental struggle" (Devens, Notebooks, Norfolk, April 1, 1867). Although it seems likely that Jewett was the defendant's lawyer and not a witness, this entry nevertheless makes it clear that there was a sentencing hearing at which the judge was paying attention, suggesting no previous agreement on sentence.

On March 9, 1886, a New Bedford lawyer recorded the following charge bargain in his diary: "In Taunton A.M. . . . engaged in the trial of John Connerlly for larceny &c. The case was nol pros & Connelly [sic] plead guilty to receiving stolen goods &c." (Barney, Diaries, vol. 3, 26). The next day the lawyer wrote that he had returned to Taunton "about Connlly [sic] sentence" (ibid.). He noted at least one other time that he had addressed the court on the question of sentence after his client had pled guilty (ibid., vol. 1, September 22, 1859, 82). See also Thompson, Diaries, vol. 11; May 13, 1885, 77: "At Newburyport—Case of Geo W Colburn[.] He plead guilty. Spoke as to sentence & matter postponed."

An Illinois statute of 1845 provided that "[i]n all cases where the courts possess any discretion as to the extent of the punishment, it shall be the duty of the court to examine witnesses as to the aggravation and mitigation of the offence" (Act of March 3, 1845, ch. 300, § 183, 1845 Ill. Rev. Stat. 185, 185). Friedman and Percival report that according to a California statute (Act of April 20, 1850, ch. 119, § 480, 1850 Cal. Stat. 310, 310), "[a]fter conviction, the judge was supposed to wait at least two days before fixing sentence . . . . But over one-third of the defendants waived their rights and were sentenced the day they were convicted" (Friedman and Percival, *Roots of Justice*, 201). A 1904 Iowa case reported that a trial judge heard witnesses to determine an appropriate sentence after the defendant had pled guilty (*Iowa v. Hortman*, 122 Ia. 104, 104, 108 [1904]).

Arthur Train reported in his 1906 book that a particular defendant pled guilty, after which "his pedigree [was] taken and a day set for his sentence" (Train, *Prisoner at the Bar*, 152–53). At sentencing hearings, "[a]ffidavits, letters, newspaper clippings and memoranda are submitted tending to show that [the defendant] is of either good or bad character, [and] has had a reputable or a disreputable past" (ibid., 193).

88. *State v. Conway*, 20 R.I. 270, 273 (1897).

89. Ex–Chief Justice Emery, "The Nolle Prosequi in Criminal Cases," 6 *Me. L. Rev.* 199, 202 (1913).

90. Ibid., 202–3.

91. Ferdinand reports that his "data collection team" coded over 36,000 cases from the Boston Police Court between 1826 and 1850 and 9,200 cases from the Boston Municipal Court, the analogue to the Court of Common Pleas elsewhere in the state (Ferdinand, *Boston's Courts*, 215).

92. Ibid., 50, table 2.2. Ferdinand concludes that "[t]here is little evidence that common law crimes or private disputes were regularly plea bargained in either [the Police or the Municipal] court during the antebellum period" (ibid., 92; see also pp. 74–81).

93. Ibid., 59, table 2.3, which shows a leap in the rate of guilty pleas in "regulatory offenses" from 24.2 percent of all cases in 1814–1840 to 55.2 percent in 1842–1850). See also Appendix B, which describes regulatory offenses as defined by Ferdinand.

94. Ferdinand, *Boston's Courts*, 77, 79, table 3.6.

95. Ibid., 77. Ferdinand does not say what became of the other counts.

96. Ibid., 13, 15, 66, 95, 186.

97. Ferdinand gives a broader label than "liquor cases" to those violations in which he finds a high rate of plea bargaining in the Boston Municipal Court for the first half-century. He calls them "vice or regulatory" cases (Ferdinand, *Boston's Courts*, 81). Regulatory offenses consisted entirely or almost entirely of liquor-selling crimes, and vice offenses included some that were punishable under the liquor license law. Demonstrating the affinity between what Ferdinand refers to as vice or regulatory offenses and what I call liquor law violations requires some close statutory analysis, which I undertake in Appendix B.

98. Ferdinand, *Boston's Courts*, 93: "The complainant in such cases was inevitably someone who would understand and accept a reduced punishment." Ferdinand adds that "[s]ince few victims followed the prosecution of these cases or took note of their resolution, regulatory and vice cases offered a wide latitude for experimentation" (ibid., 60).

99. See Chapter 6, Note 54, and accompanying text, which reprints a long excerpt from a townsman's letter to Asahel Huntington. See also *Commonwealth v. Asa B. Cobleigh*, Middlesex Ct. C.P. File Papers, No. 130 (February 1850), which contains a letter to Charles Russell Train from a citizen who complained of the defendant's gambling activities and who listed witnesses to the defendant's gambling and liquor selling. In Appendix B, I address the connection between the liquor law and gambling offenses.

100. Ferdinand, *Boston's Courts*, 93.

101. Robert Hampel reports that in Taunton, Massachusetts, between 1834 and 1845, "[t]he great majority of the complainants [in liquor prosecutions] . . . were volunteers" of various temperance organizations (Hampel, *Temperance*, 148). He adds, with regard to the state as a whole, that "[t]he task of prosecuting sellers and drunkards did not fall on the local police." Boston was surely a very different place

from Taunton, and Hampel does not appear to have studied Boston in any depth, but his findings counsel caution in reaching conclusions about Boston.

102. Ibid., 93.

103. Only twenty-six percent of burglary defendants pled guilty over the course of Ferdinand's study (Ferdinand, *Boston's Courts*, 50, table 2.2).

104. Ibid., 94.

105. Ferdinand notes almost in passing that "defense attorneys were not common" in the Boston Municipal Court in the period of his study (ibid., 99). He writes that "[d]efendants were permitted lawyers, . . . but most often they were unrepresented" (ibid., 185). Still, it is possible that the particular documents he examined would not have disclosed the presence of counsel in most cases. Ferdinand's appendix on his method, although not quite clear on the point, suggests that he looked only at the "record books" for the municipal court (see ibid., 211, 213, 215). In my work in the Middlesex Court of Common Pleas (a close analogue of the Boston Municipal Court) I found that the record books rarely noted defense counsel. Beginning in 1844, however, the court's "docket books" regularly recorded counsel in criminal cases. As I report in Chapter 4 (Table 4.1), over half of all defendants in the Middlesex Court of Common Pleas had counsel at the century's midpoint.

NOTES TO CHAPTER 3

1. See Act of April 20, 1855, ch. 215, § 15, 1855 Mass. Acts 623, 630, which called for a ten-dollar fine and a twenty- to thirty-day term for illegal sale, with mounting mandatory penalties for subsequent offenses; ibid. § 17, 1855 Mass. Acts at 631, which imposed a fifty-dollar fine and a three- to six-month term for being a common seller, with mounting mandatory penalties for subsequent offenses; ibid. § 24, 1855 Mass. Acts at 635, which imposed a ten-dollar fine and twenty-day term for keeping liquor with the intent to sell.

2. See Act of April 5, 1859, ch. 196, §§ 1–3, 1859 Mass. Acts 339, 339–40, which established superior courts.

3. Three of the tried cases did not appear in the record book, but only in the docket book.

4. See, e.g., Middlesex Ct. C.P. R. Book 18 (February 1859).

5. I draw this conclusion from the high quality of the volumes themselves and the obvious care taken in their preparation. It is not clear exactly when the record books were written in relation to each term of court, but it is clear from both their neatness and their mode of organization that they were not produced in court as the business was ongoing. I think it is most likely that the clerk prepared the record book after each term of court.

6. The abbreviation "L.L." was a throwback to the days before 1852, when the state had a "license law" as opposed to full-scale alcohol prohibition, but now it signified simply "liquor law." Even in the docket books, the clerk maintained a distinc-

tion between violations of the prohibition law and violations of the liquor nuisance statute. My discussion here is limited to the former, as the nuisance act carried neither the nol pros ban nor (at this time) mandatory prison (see Chapter 2, Note 62).

7. *Commonwealth v. Bridgit Durgin*, Middlesex Ct. C.P. Docket Book No. 817 (February 1859).

8. *Commonwealth v. Eldridge H. Spinney*, Middlesex Ct. C.P. Docket Book No. 112 (February 1859).

9. Middlesex Ct. C.P. Docket Book No. 789 (February 1859).

10. *Commonwealth v. James Quinlan & John Callahan*, Middlesex Ct. C.P. Docket Book No. 664 (February 1859).

11. See F. W. Grinnell, "Probation," 601–04, 610–12.

12. See *Commonwealth v. Jerusha Chase* (Boston Mun. Ct. 1831), in Woodman, *Reports of Criminal Cases,* 267.

13. Grinnell, "Probation," 604, quoting from the court record.

14. See *Jerusha Chase*, in Woodman, *Reports of Criminal Cases,* 267; Grinnell, "Probation," 604.

15. It appears that the record book for the June 1849 session of the Middlesex Court of Common Pleas was the first to list cases placed on file. See Middlesex Ct. C.P. R. Book 461 (June 1849).

16. For example, in *Commonwealth v. Joseph Reed* (Middlesex Ct. C.P. Docket Book No. 78 [October 1844]), the defendant pled no contest to a liquor charge in February 1843. His case was then continued until October 1844, when the district attorney entered a nol pros. See also *Commonwealth v. Elias Messenger*, Middlesex Ct. C.P. Docket Book No. 108 (October 1843), which followed a similar chronology.

17. Nelson made this announcement before a court session in Essex County, also part of his district, and not in Middlesex, but there is no reason to think that his practice that year would have varied greatly between the two counties. I have examined the records of the Essex Court of Common Pleas for the June 1847 session—the next session after Nelson's announcement. The court's record book, unsurprisingly, makes no mention of cases handled in the way just described, and the court's docket book appears to be missing. The file papers for individual cases, however, have survived. I found ten liquor cases in which the defendant pled guilty or (in two cases) no contest and then pledged or posted two hundred dollars as security for his appearance in the future. No fines are noted.

18. "License Cases," *Lowell Journal*, April 2, 1847, 2; Chapter 1, Note 73, and accompanying text.

19. See, e.g., *Commonwealth v. David Chandler*, Essex Ct. C.P. File Papers No. 279 (June 1847), on file with the Essex County Superior Court. Chandler, having pled guilty to a liquor indictment, pledged or posted two hundred dollars to appear in the future and to keep the peace.

20. *Commonwealth v. C. Robinson*, Essex Ct. C.P. File Papers No. 394 (December 1847), on file with the Essex County Superior Court.

21. I found what might be a surprisingly early example of this mechanism at work in the earliest liquor case that my research turned up. In 1790, William Barker came before the Court of General Sessions of the Peace charged with a single unlicensed sale. He pled guilty and then, on his motion, the court suspended judgment until the next term of court (*Commonwealth v. William Barker*, Middlesex Ct. Gen. Sess. Peace R. Book 4 [September 1790]). At the next term, the court again deferred passing sentence (*Commonwealth v. William Barker*, Middlesex Ct. Gen. Sess. Peace R. Book 16 [November 1790]). Finally, at the *next* term, the prosecutor who appeared on the case (probably appointed temporarily by the court), "by advice of the Court," nol prossed the case (*Commonwealth v. William Barker*, Middlesex Ct. Gen. Sess. Peace R. Book 26 [March 1791]). Although it surely seems possible that this chain of events manifested the same process that I have described at work in 1847, I would be reluctant to claim too much of an isolated example—and I did not see this procedure repeated until the 1840s.

22. As the Supreme Judicial Court wrote decades later, ordering cases on file "dispenses with the necessity of entering formal continuances upon the dockets" (*Commonwealth v. Dowdican's Bail*, 115 Mass. 133, 136 [1874]).

23. For example, in *Commonwealth v. David Wheeler*, Middlesex Ct. C.P. Docket Book No. 921 (October 1847), the defendant pled guilty to a liquor charge and entered into a recognizance; the case was then "[p]laced on file." In *Commonwealth v. Bernhard Moosback*, Middlesex Ct. C.P. Docket Book No. 862 (October 1847), a larceny case, the clerk noted similar facts and added that the defendant was "used as witness."

24. In two cases, the clerk did not name the charge.

25. Ferdinand's figures from Boston also show a greatly expanding use of the on-file mechanism in the 1840s. Unfortunately, he does not distinguish between cases that also involved a guilty finding and those in which the defendant defaulted, a witness left town, or the case for some other reason was abandoned. See Ferdinand, *Boston's Courts*, 60.

26. Ibid., 69.

27. See Act of April 26, 1878, ch. 198, 1878 Mass. Acts 146, 146.

28. In 1916, in the course of ruling that federal trial courts had no power to suspend the imposition of sentence in the absence of federal probation legislation, the U.S. Supreme Court canvassed state practice and found Massachusetts to be in the minority of states that recognized a nonstatutory practice of staying sentences indefinitely (see *Ex parte* United States, 242 U.S. 27, 47 & n.1, 48 & n.1, 50–52 [1916]).

29. Grinnell, "Probation," 604.

30. See *Commonwealth v. Jerusha Chase* (Boston Mun. Ct. 1831), in Woodman, *Reports of Criminal Cases*, 268; Davis, vol. 1, *Bench and Bar*, 223. It is clear from these sources that Austin served at the relevant times as county attorney and that he handled at least the later proceedings in *Chase*. It is possible that he did not personally conduct every stage of the prosecution.

31. See Chapter 1, Notes 87–89, and accompanying text.

32. Middlesex Ct. C.P. R. Book (February 1859).

33. Middlesex Ct. C.P. R. Book 55 (June 1853).

34. See, e.g., Middlesex Super. Ct. R. Book 145–46 (June 1870); Middlesex Super. Ct. R. Book 1 (February 1870); Middlesex Super. Ct. R. Book 133 (October 1864); Middlesex Super. Ct. R. Book 2 (February 1864).

35. See, e.g., *Commonwealth v. Jeremiah Dempsey*, Middlesex Super. Ct. Docket Book No. 52 (October 1864).

36. See, e.g., Middlesex Super. Ct. R. Book 1–2 (February 1877).

37. For example, in *Commonwealth v. Patrick Brady*, Middlesex Ct. C.P. Docket Book No. 957 (February 1859), the clerk noted that the case was "ordered on file by Court." In fact, there is confusion even within the 1859 Record Book. Although the district attorney is credited with having placed the long list of cases on file, there are five other cases (none of them liquor cases) to be found elsewhere in the record book, all of which the court placed on file. See, e.g., *Commonwealth v. Edward Dyer & Thomas E. Berry*, Middlesex Ct. C.P. R. Book 181 (June 1859): "The Court ordered that the defendants go on probation, and that the indictment be placed on file against them."

38. Ferdinand, *Boston's Courts*, 71–72. Ferdinand writes nonetheless that the growing practice of putting cases on file "represented a clear expansion of [the prosecutor's] powers" (ibid., 69). Elsewhere, he analyzes the various judges of the municipal court partly in terms of their willingness to place cases on file (ibid., 128–33).

39. *Commonwealth v. Dowdican's Bail*, 115 Mass. 133, 136 (1874).

40. Act of May 12, 1865, ch. 223, § 1, 1865 Mass. Acts 617, 617.

41. See this chapter, Notes 43–45 and accompanying text.

42. See Act of June 19, 1869, ch. 415, § 60, 1869 Mass. Acts 706, 723–24, which provided that "[n]o case in court for the violation of . . . this act . . . shall be laid on file or disposed of except by trial," except with the concurrence of the court.

43. I infer that the hearings led to the "Act to Prevent Evasions" from the coincidence of two legislative documents. The minority report of the committee that conducted the hearings, which complained of the practice of putting liquor cases on file, was issued on the same day that the bill to prevent evasions was reported by a separate committee. Compare S. Doc. No. 201, at 1, 6 (Mass. 1865) (the minority committee report), with S. Doc. No. 205, at 1, 1–3 (Mass. 1865) (which reports the bill).

44. S. Doc. No. 200, at 22 (Mass. 1865), statement of George P. Sanger. Sanger was speaking of prosecutions under the liquor nuisance act, not the prohibition act, but because the "Act to Prevent Evasions" applied to both acts, the distinction is unimportant here.

45. S. Doc. No. 201, at 6, minority committee report. The minority opposed the recommendation of the committee that the state revert from a prohibition law to a license law. See S. Doc. No. 200, at 44–45.

46. See *Commonwealth v. Joseph Alexander*, Middlesex Super. Ct. Docket Book No. 874 (February 1870).

47. I am counting both license law and liquor nuisance cases, as the 1865 Act and its successors barred prosecutors from putting either kind of case on file without the court's leave.

48. The clerk's papers for *Commonwealth v. Dowdican's Bail*, 115 Mass. 133 (1874), contain the judge's "certificate" that the act requires before a liquor case may be placed on file. The preprinted form reads, "In this case, No. [blank] of 18[blank], against [blank] I certify that I am satisfied the cause relied on in the annexed affidavit exists, and that the interests of public justice require the allowance of the motion to lay the case on file" (Judge's certificate (June 5, 1867), *Dowdican's Bail* (No. 2024), on file with the Supreme Judicial Court Archives, Boston). The underlying affidavit to which the form refers appears to have been lost, but it is described in the case notes to the Supreme Judicial Court's opinion as having claimed that the indictments in question were duplicative of another (*Dowdican's Bail*, 115 Mass. at 134).

49. *Commonwealth v. Jerusha Chase* (Boston Mun. Ct. 1831), in Woodman, *Reports of Criminal Cases*, 268.

50. Ibid.

51. Ibid., 267.

52. Ibid., 269.

53. Ibid.

54. "License Cases," *Lowell Journal*, April 2, 1847, 2; Chapter 1, Note 73, and accompanying text.

55. I think it is fair to assume that Nelson's promise not to "press for the fines" amounted to a promise not to move for sentence—or at least not to do so immediately. The only other possibility is that Nelson intended to nol pros each case on payment of costs after a guilty plea. But part of the deal he proposed was that the defendant would "enter into recognizance to observe the law" in the future (ibid). I have not seen this condition attached to a nol pros, whereas it was, as we will see, often part of an on-file plea arrangement. I think it is more likely that Nelson was promising that the case would be continued, following a guilty or no contest plea, without disposition in a manner analogous to the on-file mechanism. Court records show that Nelson often employed this procedure in 1847.

56. S. Doc. No. 200, at 5 (Mass. 1865).

57. *Commonwealth v. Tuck*, 37 Mass. (20 Pick.) 356, 366 (1838).

58. Brief for the Commonwealth at 2, *Commonwealth v. Dowdican's Bail*, 115 Mass. 133 (1874) (No. 2024), on file with the Social Law Library, Boston.

59. *Dowdican's Bail*, 115 Mass. at 136 (emphasis added).

60. Harris, *Report of District Attorney*, 116. Two pages later, Harris wrote, "We [the district attorneys] can 'continue for sentence,' 'place on file,' or allow the men to go on their own recognizance" (ibid., 118).

61. 265 Mass. 436 (1929).

62. Act of June 4, 1895, ch. 469, § 1, 1895 Mass. Acts 532, 532.

63. *Kossowan*, 265 Mass. at 438.

64. Ibid.

65. *Commonwealth v. Carver*, 224 Mass. 42, 44 (1916).

66. Ibid.

67. Harris, *Report of District Attorney*, 116.

68. *Carver*, 224 Mass. at 44.

69. Frank A. Goodwin, "Community vs. Criminal," 16. The author continued: "There are hundreds of cases where the machinery of the State, at great expense, has been used to convict a man and then for months and even years the record reads 'still pending for sentence.'"

70. See this chapter, Notes 54 and 56, and accompanying text.

71. See *Commonwealth v. Jerusha Chase* (Boston Mun. Ct. 1831), in Woodman, *Reports of Criminal Cases*, 267.

72. Grinnell, "Probation," 604, which quotes the original record.

73. "License Cases," *Lowell Journal*, April 2, 1847, at 2; see also Chapter 1, Note 73, and accompanying text, which quotes the press account of Nelson's announcement in full.

74. See this chapter, Notes 23–25 and accompanying text.

75. Grinnell, "Probation," 604, which quotes the original record.

76. See *Commonwealth v. Jerusha Chase* (Boston Mun. Ct. 1831), in Woodman, *Reports of Criminal Cases*, 267. Chase's situation was similar to that of the modern probationer, whose probation can be revoked on a probable cause showing of a further crime even if a jury has refused to convict by the standard of beyond a reasonable doubt.

77. Ibid., 268.

78. Ibid.

79. Ibid.

80. Ibid., 269.

81. In a concluding footnote to Thacher's opinion, the reporter noted that the Supreme Judicial Court had pronounced the judgment correct in an opinion by Chief Justice Lemuel Shaw and "that the principles of the above decision have often been recognized in our courts" (ibid., 270 n.1). The high court's opinion is apparently missing (see Grinnell, "Probation," 603).

82. *Commonwealth v. Dowdican's Bail*, 115 Mass. 133, 136 (1874).

83. Ibid.

84. The time lapse in *Dowdican's Bail* itself, which the court implicitly approved by upholding judgment against the defendant's sureties, was six years (ibid., 133–34).

85. Grinnell, "Probation," 593. In this sentence and the next, Grinnell was quoting from a brief he cowrote with R. W. Hale. Grinnell implies that the brief was largely his work, and as that seems likely, given the context, I am attributing these quotes to him.

86. Ibid., 593.

87. Ibid., 593 and footnote * on that page.

88. Grinnell supplied no date for *Macey*, but he did say that the judge's name was Bell (see ibid., 593 n*), and the only Bell to sit on the superior court bench (as of 1900) was appointed in 1898 (Davis, *History of the Judiciary*, 254–55, 267, 417).

89. See this chapter, Notes 127, 135–37, and accompanying text.

90. *Commonwealth v. Jerusha Chase* (Boston Mun. Ct. 1831), in Woodman, *Reports of Criminal Cases*, 268–69.

91. S. Doc. No. 200, at 28–29 (Mass. 1865), statement of William A. Smith.

92. S. Doc. No. 200, at 22 (Mass. 1865), statement of George P. Sanger.

93. I am including data only from those years for which I studied both the record and the docket books of the court: 1853, 1859, 1864 (February and October only), 1870 (February only), 1880 (October only), and 1890 (incomplete count of docket entries).

94. See *Commonwealth v. Maloney*, 145 Mass. 205, 210 (1887).

95. Ibid., reporter's statement of the case.

96. Ibid., 210 (emphasis added), citing *Commonwealth v. Dowdican's Bail*, 115 Mass. 133 (1874).

97. *Commonwealth v. Jerusha Chase* (Boston Mun. Ct. 1831), in Woodman, *Reports of Criminal Cases*, 268.

98. Ibid.

99. S. Doc. No. 200, at 22 (Mass. 1865), statement of George P. Sanger. The context was the Senate's 1865 hearings on enforcement of the liquor law. The assistant clerk of courts for Worcester testified, "It is always made a condition to promise to go out of the business, before placing a case on file, and there is always a conviction by plea of guilty, or by a verdict" (ibid., 28–29, statement of William A. Smith).

100. Brief for the Commonwealth at 2, *Commonwealth v. Dowdican's Bail*, 115 Mass. 133 (1874) (No. 2024), on file with the Social Law Library, Boston.

101. Ibid.

102. Grinnell, "Probation," 604, which quotes from the municipal-court record).

103. See this chapter, Notes 13–14 and accompanying text.

104. See Augustus, *Report of the Labors*, 4–5, 7. Charles Newman (*Sourcebook on Probation*, 14) wrote that "[i]t was in America that the combination [of factors that constitute probation] was first set in motion, by the judges of the Boston Municipal Court in cooperation with John Augustus." And, according to N. S. Timasheff (*One Hundred Years*, vol. 1, 7), "[i]n this country, the idea of probation as a distinct method of treating offenders is quite correctly ascribed to John Augustus."

105. See Augustus, *Report of the Labors*, 4–5, 34; see also ibid., 37, which refers to his role as "surety." As Timasheff (*One Hundred Years*, vol. 1, 17) wrote, "the unofficial and benevolent persons who helped the judge in the application of pro-

bation, and who were to oversee the behavior of the probationer, [were] commonly sureties."

Augustus was typically obscure about the procedural posture of the cases he described in his chronicle. I have found only one explicit reference to placing cases "on file" in his work, and although the context is somewhat ambiguous, I think the most natural reading suggests that most of his cases were placed on file. Toward the end of his chronicle, Augustus described a case involving a seven-year-old boy charged with rape—a case unusual in itself but also more serious than most of those in which Augustus took part (see Augustus, *Report of the Labors*, 95–96). Augustus wrote that the court granted his request to place the case on file before trial. He then added, "This is the only case where I became bail [i.e., surety] when the indictment was laid on file on a plea of not guilty, except perhaps, when parties have died" (ibid., 95). I read this sentence to mean that most of the rest of Augustus's cases were placed on file *after* a guilty plea or verdict. Elsewhere, Augustus refers to a court that "continued [a group of his cases] from term to term for several months, as a season of probation" (ibid., 34). A continuance "from term to term" was often used by courts as a near synonym for the on-file mechanism, differing only in that it required a regular reexamination into the case's status. See this chapter, Notes 21–22 and accompanying text.

One of the few clear descriptions of the procedural status of defendants Augustus helped comes from an account he reprinted from the *Christian World* of 1848:

Twelve boys, all of about nine or ten years of age, were brought into the Boston Municipal Court one afternoon last week, to receive sentences for various criminal offences. They had been convicted, or had pleaded guilty, and their sentences had been standing postponed; some for nearly a year; others for less periods,—meanwhile they had been under bail. Most of them had been bailed by John Augustus .... [The judge] delayed sentence further .... (Augustus, *Report of the Labors*, 58)

Note that the boys had already been convicted and awaited only sentencing. This postponement of sentence was the critical feature of the on-file mechanism.

Note also that this reporter omitted any mention of the prosecutor's role and left the impression that the judge could freely delay sentencing. Another news account reprinted by Augustus gave a fuller sense of the prosecutor's role, but remained at least ambiguous about whether the judge had the power to postpone sentence in the face of a prosecutor's motion for sentence. The reporter quoted the district attorney as acceding to Augustus's request for a further continuance of sentence in a petty-larceny case: "We do not wish to punish, except for a purpose of warning others. I will not urge a sentence now" (ibid., 20; this quotes an undated report from the *Morning Post*). The reporter concluded, "His Honor listened attentively to the remarks of the worthy philanthropist, and granted the request" (ibid).

Of course, in a petty-larceny prosecution, in which the allowable sentence range was zero to one year or zero to three hundred dollars (*Mass. Rev. Stat.* ch. 126, § 17 [Dutton & Wentworth 1836]), the question whether the prosecutor could demand sentence at a particular time may have been academic, because the judge could pass a sentence of nothing at all. In any event, the power the prosecutor most needed to do on-file plea bargaining, as I discussed earlier in this chapter, was the power to *block* sentencing by withholding a motion for sentence. The power to demand sentencing was important but unessential and, as we have seen, was at least uncertain at the time of *Dowdican's Bail* in 1874. See this chapter, Notes 82–84 and accompanying text.

106. Augustus, *Report of the Labors*, 34.

107. Ibid., 35.

108. Ibid.

109. Ibid., 103. Augustus (ibid., 37) wrote that "[a]lmost all the cases in which I stood as surety were settled without being brought to trial; and pleas of guilt being put in, a door was opened for the mercy of the court."

110. See Act of April 26, 1878, ch. 198, 1878 Mass. Acts 146, 146, which provided for the appointment of a probation officer for Boston. Grinnell ("Probation," 612) wrote that the act "is reputed to be the first act by any legislative body using the word 'probation'" in the relevant sense.

111. § 1, 1878 Mass. Acts at 147.

112. Grinnell, "Probation," 614. Likewise, Timasheff (*One Hundred Years*, vol. 1, 17) wrote that "[i]t is obvious that this statute introduced nothing essentially new into the common-law practice."

I have relied a good deal on Grinnell's study. Most importantly, he pointed out the strong connection between the practices described in *Chase* and probation as it later developed. I disagree with his analysis, however, in two ways. First, I think he gave somewhat too much importance to a law adopted in the Massachusetts 1836 code that gave lower tribunals authority to release a defendant charged with certain minor crimes "upon his entering into a recognizance, . . . with sufficient sureties, for his good behavior for a term not less than six months, nor more than two years" (*Mass. Rev. Stat.* ch. 143, § 9 [Dutton & Wentworth 1836]; see also Grinnell, "Probation," 609–10, which quotes the statute and places it in a chronology of probation's development). As N. S. Timasheff argued, this law "merely gave statutory sanction to the common-law practice of *replacing* punishment by recognizance for good behavior" (Timasheff, *One Hundred Years*, vol. 1, 16 n.2). The statute did not embrace the peculiar procedural posture shared by the on-file mechanism and modern probation: The defendant is released after conviction but before sentence, so that the penalty for bad behavior is not merely forfeiting bonds, but being sentenced on the original indictment.

Second, I believe Grinnell attempted to minimize the degree of prosecutorial control over the on-file mechanism, especially in the early years. Although he acknowledged that Thacher's opinion in *Chase* made it clear that "the practice of suspending sentence was in fact by the consent of both parties to a case, because the government could move for sentence at any time and the defendant also," Grinnell argued that this fact "does not necessarily lead to the conclusion that the power of the Court rests upon the consent of the parties" (Grinnell, "Probation," 631). But as I argued earlier (see this chapter, Notes 77–80 and accompanying text), other language in Thacher's opinion suggests he thought the government's forbearance from moving for sentence was essential.

113. *Maloney*, 145 Mass. at 211.

114. See *Mass. Pub. Stats.* ch. 212, §§ 74–81 (Rand, Avery, & Co. 1882).

115. See Act of June 19, 1885, ch. 359, 1885 Mass. Acts 817.

116. *Commonwealth v. McGovern*, 183 Mass. 238, 239 (1903).

117. Grinnell, "Probation," 604. As Robert Harris (*Report of District Attorney*, 120) wrote, "[t]he probation officer . . . becomes [the defendant's] surety for his appearance in court when wanted."

118. *McGovern*, 183 Mass. at 239. Although I am not sure, I believe that the court's reference to an "oral agreement made between [McGovern] and the Commonwealth" (ibid.) refers to an agreement with the probation officer, acting perhaps as a "fiduciary" of the court (ibid.) rather than with the district attorney. Elsewhere in the same paragraph, the court refers to both probation officer and prosecutor by title, so its ambiguous reference to an agreement with "the Commonwealth" seems odd. But as the court repeats the same ambiguous formula five times in its short opinion (see ibid., 239–40), the word choice cannot have been unintended. Unfortunately, none of the court's repetitions of the phrase clarified its meaning.

119. See, e.g., *Commonwealth v. Charles McCannon*, Middlesex Ct. C.P. Docket Book No. 656 (February 1859), on file with the Massachusetts Archives. I noted seven cases in the docket books of 1859 and two in the record books that explicitly equated putting a case on file and on probation in this manner.

120. See, e.g., *Commonwealth v. George B. Avery*, Middlesex Super. Ct. R. Book 316 (1903); *Commonwealth v. George B. Avery*, Middlesex Super. Ct. Docket Book No. 30 (1903); *Commonwealth v. Thomas H. McNabb*, Middlesex Super. Ct. R. Book 316 (1903); *Commonwealth v. Thomas H. McNabb*, Middlesex Super. Ct. Docket Book No. 61 (1903).

121. See Middlesex Super. Ct. R. Book 509, 513 (1910), unpublished document, on file with the Massachusetts Trial Court.

122. Ibid., 513.

123. See this chapter, Notes 32–36, 83–90 and accompanying text.

124. Act of April 26, 1878, ch. 198, § 1, 1878 Mass. Acts 146, 147.

125. Act of March 22, 1880, ch. 129, § 4, 1880 Mass. Acts 87, 87. In addition to providing for the appointment of probation officers, this act created the first parole-like regime in Massachusetts, a development I discuss in Chapter 5 (ibid. §§ 6–10, 1880 Mass. Acts at 88–89).

126. Act of May 28, 1891, ch. 356, § 3, 1891 Mass. Acts 920, 920.

127. Act of June 8, 1898, ch. 511, § 1, 1898 Mass. Acts 474, 474–75.

128. See this chapter, Notes 49–72 and accompanying text.

129. See this chapter, Notes 60–71 and accompanying text.

130. § 1, 1878 Mass. Acts at 147.

131. See Act of March 22, 1880, ch. 129, 1880 Mass. Acts 87.

132. See Act of May 28, 1891, ch. 356, 1891 Mass. Acts 920.

133. *Marks v. Wentworth*, 199 Mass. 44, 46 (1908).

134. See Harris, *Report of District Attorney*, 116, 118.

135. § 1, 1898 Mass. Acts at 475.

136. Harris, *Report of District Attorney*, 119.

137. Ibid., 122, 119.

138. See this chapter, text preceding Note 94.

139. See Act of February 23, 1903, ch. 34, 1903 Cal. Stat. 34, 34, which said that "the court shall have power, in its discretion, to place the defendant upon probation." Friedman and Percival (*Roots of Justice*, 227) quote from a 1910 sentencing hearing in which it was clear that the judge both held and wielded the decision-making power.

140. See Friedman and Percival, *Roots of Justice*, 225. They report that between 1900 and 1902, just before the probation law passed, 32.2 percent of accused felons pled guilty, while 49.4 percent did so between 1903 and 1910 (ibid., 227).

141. Ibid., 227, which quotes from the 1910 sentencing hearing.

142. Ibid., 226.

143. Friedman and Percival write, "[c]learly, a guilty plea opened the doors to probation. Word of this must have gotten around to defendants and defense. The message—'plead guilty'—rang through loud and clear" (ibid., 181).

NOTES TO CHAPTER 4

1. *Green v. Commonwealth*, 94 Mass. (12 Allen) 155, 176 (1866). *Green* was at least the second time the Supreme Judicial Court addressed guilty pleas in capital cases. In the first, *Commonwealth v. Battis*, 1 Mass. (1 Will.) 94 (1804), the defendant already had been executed at the time of the court's opinion, and the court did not review the legality of the proceedings. Since the defendant had pled guilty before the high court, however, and since three justices of that court must have passed the death sentence (see Menand, *Research Guide*, 37), there is no reason to think that the court disapproved of the proceedings. The *Battis* trial court did take great care to give the defendant a chance to reconsider his self-destructive plea, and in *Green* the court wrote that "[i]t is the well settled practice in all courts . . . to receive and record with great reluctance and caution a confession of guilt in a capital case" (*Green*, 94 Mass. [12 Allen] at 175–76). But as I noted in the text, the court denied itself the power to refuse such a plea. Lending support to this reading, Barry Fisher ("Judicial Suicide," 183–91) recently argued that in the nineteenth century and before, the law generally did not bar defendants from pleading guilty to capital crimes.

2. "Adjudicated cases" are those in which the defendant went to trial or pled guilty or no contest. I have excluded from Figure 4.1 both liquor cases and cases placed on file to avoid the distorting impact of the large shifts in prosecutorial plea-bargaining

power that I described in Chapters 1 and 3. Moreover, for comparisons that span the century, it is important to keep the mix of case types relatively stable. "Filed" cases so called did not appear until the 1840s, and liquor cases were quite rare in the first decades of the nineteenth century, so including them could badly distort some findings.

3. See, e.g., Alschuler, "Plea Bargaining History," 5–16, 19–24. Mary Vogel (*Courts of Trade*, 52) writes that "the courts, at the beginning of the [nineteenth] century were reluctant to accept a guilty plea under any circumstances." Michael Millender (*American Criminal Trial*, 187) agrees: "Even in the North, courts . . . at the beginning of the nineteenth century . . . only reluctantly accepted guilty pleas." Examining an earlier period, John Langbein ("Short History of Plea Bargaining," 264) concludes that before the mid-eighteenth century not only was there "no particular pressure to . . . encourage the accused to waive his right to jury trial," but "the sources reveal an opposite pressure."

4. *Green*, 94 Mass. (12 Allen) at 158. Others have adopted the court's allusion to suicide. A correspondent to the *New York Times* ("Guilty Pleas of Murder," *New York Times*, August 5, 1924, 16, letter of Charles Maitland Beattie) wrote in 1924 that pleading guilty in a capital case "would really be a way by which a man could commit judicial suicide." More recently, Albert Alschuler ("Plea Bargaining History," 11) suggests that "[w]hen a guilty plea is an act of suicide, it is understandable that the acceptance of it should evoke squeamish feelings."

5. Ibid., 176. In the latter half of the eighteenth century, Blackstone explained the judicial suspicion toward guilty pleas specifically in the capital context: "Upon a simple and plain confession, the court hath nothing to do but to award judgment: but it is usually very backward in receiving and recording such confession, out of tenderness to the life of the subject; and will generally advise the prisoner to retract it" (Blackstone, *Commentaries*, vol. 4, *329). Likewise, in the mid-seventeenth century, Sir Matthew Hale suggested that judges encouraged capital defendants in particular to go to trial rather than plead guilty: "[B]ut it is usual for the court, especially if [the crime] be out of clergy [i.e., capital], to advise the party to plead and put himself upon his trial" (Hale, *History of the Pleas of the Crown*, vol. 2, 225).

6. Washburn, *Manual*, vi, 132; see also Davis, *History of the Judiciary*, 247–48, which provides biographical information about Washburn. After this quotation, Washburn cited *Commonwealth v. Battis*, 1 Mass. (1 Will.) 94 (1804), which involved a guilty plea in a murder case. Washburn's reliance on *Battis* suggests that *Battis* should not be interpreted as evidence that Massachusetts judges were suspicious of *all* guilty pleas.

7. See Chapter 1, Note 85.

8. *Craig v. State*, 49 Ohio St. 415, 416 (1892).

9. See Chapter 2, text preceding Note 1.

10. See Chapter 1, Notes 35–38, and accompanying text.

11. Prosecutors did have the power to set costs, and as I noted earlier, costs typically were higher after trial than after a plea (see Chapter 1, Notes 34, 41–44,

and accompanying text). It is very hard to say how effectively prosecutors could have wielded the cost-setting power as a plea-bargaining tool in the general run of cases. The court never ordered costs against defendants who were found not guilty after trial and very rarely did so against defendants sentenced to serve time. Defendants who went to trial therefore had a good chance of escaping costs altogether. And a defendant was unlikely to plead guilty simply to win the prosecutor's promise of freedom from costs when the prosecutor had no power to promise freedom from incarceration. The prosecutor's power to set costs therefore probably worked best as a plea-bargaining tool in cases that were likely to be punished by a fine—among them, liquor cases.

12. See Chapter 2, Notes 70–90 and accompanying text.

13. Mary Vogel's research in these early years focused on the Boston Police Court, where defense counsel probably were rare. Her work says little about counsel. And Ferdinand (*Boston's Courts*, 81) reports that the records of the Boston Municipal Court do not systematically record counsel, though as I noted earlier, it seems possible that he did not use the court's docket books as a source (see Chapter 2, Note 105).

14. See Feeley and Lester, "Legal Complexity," 355. Their study provides only tentative support because its setting is an ocean away and because the authors report an anomalously high rate of representation in 1795—about 40 percent—that interrupts very low rates that prevailed throughout the eighteenth century and in 1815. The authors suggest no explanation for their discordant figures in 1795.

15. See Chapter 2, Note 6, and accompanying text.

16. Although Massachusetts law provided for free counsel in capital cases, it made no provision for indigents accused of lesser crimes, and as late as 1952, appointed counsel were confined to cases of first-degree murder (see Callagy, "Legal Aid," 611). New York apparently provided free counsel to all indigent defendants at least by 1810, so almost all defendants had lawyers (see McConville and Mirsky, "Rise of Guilty Pleas," 454–55).

17. These are my findings for the years before the 1832 jurisdiction shift:

Disposition by Plea of Guilty or No Contest in the Supreme Judicial Court
(Sitting in Middlesex County)

YEAR	NUMBER OF ADJUDICATED CASES	NUMBER OF PLEAS	PERCENTAGE OF PLEAS
1799	11	6	55%
1809	22	2	9%
1819	27	8	30%
1824	32	12	38%
1829	20	2	10%

SOURCE: Sup. Jud. Ct. R. books (Middlesex sittings).

After the jurisdiction shift, there were too few cases left in the Supreme Judicial Court to allow for meaningful analysis. See Chapter 2, Note 6, and accompanying text.

18. Some uncertain corroboration for my finding that cases with lawyers were more likely to go to trial comes from McConville and Mirsky's work in New York. They report near-universal representation by counsel at the beginning of the century (presumably because New York apparently provided free counsel to all indigent defendants at least by 1910) and a rate of trials that fell just below eighty percent (see McConville and Mirsky, "Rise of Guilty Pleas," 454–55, 466). In 1897 Clara Foltz argued that many unrepresented defendants "are recorded as pleading guilty and railroaded into jail because too dazed to understand their rights and legal position" (Foltz, "Public Defenders," 393).

19. Friedman and Percival (*Roots of Justice*, 174) note that "[m]ost defendants who pled guilty at arraignment had waived counsel. They cite a survey of inmates at Folsom Prison taken in the late 1880s in which 33.9 percent of those who pled guilty said that they did so because they "had neither money nor friends" (State Board of Prison Directors of the State of California, *Eighth Annual Report* 88 [Sacramento, J.D. Young 1887], cited in Friedman and Percival, *Roots of Justice*, 180 n.77). It is hard to imagine the relevance of the lack of money and friends except that, without either, one cannot hire a lawyer. As California defendants were entitled to free counsel in felony trials after 1872 (see *Cal. Penal Code* § 987 [Sumner Whitney & Co. 1881]), it is a puzzle why a defendant would plead guilty for want of counsel. Appointed counsel got no fees, so defendants may have been correct in believing that they got what they paid for. Friedman and Percival do present some evidence that appointed counsel were less zealous in their work than paid counsel (see Friedman and Percival, *Roots of Justice*, 172, 201–2).

20. Clara Foltz ("Public Defenders," 397) wrote that the defendant "know[s] that to go into court without counsel would be equivalent to an invitation to convict which a jury would readily accept."

21. John Langbein ("Understanding," 269 n.12) notes that "[w]here assigned counsel was not readily available, an indigent accused in nineteenth-century America may have had a considerable incentive to plead guilty rather than try to defend himself at trial . . . against a lawyer–public prosecutor."

22. S. Doc. No. 68, at 7 (Mass. 1844), petition of Samuel D. Parker.

23. My findings are as follows:

Proportion of Liquor and Nonliquor Defendants with Counsel:
Middlesex Court of Common Pleas and Superior Court

YEAR	LIQUOR LICENSE DEFENDANTS	NONLIQUOR DEFENDANTS
1844	62%	40%
1849	68%	58%

(table continued on next page)

YEAR	LIQUOR LICENSE DEFENDANTS	NONLIQUOR DEFENDANTS
1853	72%	31%
1859	59%	48%
1864	64%	52%
1870	59%	53%
1880	57%	36%
1900	81%	44%

SOURCES: Middlesex Ct. C.P. R. Books; Middlesex Ct. C.P. Docket Books; Middlesex Super. Ct. R. Books; Middlesex Super. Ct. Docket Books.

24. See Act of May 22, 1852, ch. 322, § 13, 1852 Mass. Acts 257, 257.

25. See Chapter 1, Notes 98–109, and accompanying text.

26. I found only five such pleas to capital charges throughout the century: see Chapter 1, Note 85.

27. See Lane, *Policing the City*, 60.

28. See Act of May 26, 1866, ch. 260, 1866 Mass. Acts 245, 245. The first two states to pass such acts were Maine and California. See Act of April 2, 1866, ch. 644, § 1, 1866 Cal. Stat. 865, 865; Act of March 25, 1864, ch. 280, § 1, 1864 Me. Laws 214, 214.

29. See Davis, *History of the Judiciary*, 194–95.

30. 1866 Mass. Acts at 245.

31. [Ames], "Testimony," 444. David Gold (*Nineteenth-Century Law*, 188 n.22) identifies Ames as the author of the quoted work.

32. [Ames], "Testimony," 445.

33. Ibid., 445. William Maury ("Validity of Statutes," 762–63) argues in the same vein that even those defendant-testimony laws that bar a negative inference from silence "force [the defendant] to take the stand to protect himself from the inference of guilt which is almost sure to be drawn against him if he fail to do so." A century after Ames wrote, Harry Kalven and Hans Zeisel referred to "the common-sense inference of the defendant's guilt, if he chooses not to talk" (Kalven and Zeisel, *American Jury*, 145).

34. [Ames], "Testimony," 447.

35. Ibid., 444. Kalven and Zeisel reported on the basis of their 1950s sample that eighty-two percent of defendants took the stand at trial (Kalven and Zeisel, *American Jury*, 33 n.1, 144).

36. [Ames], "Testimony," 447.

37. See Act of May 22, 1852, ch. 312, § 60, 1852 Mass. Acts 235, 235, which stated that "the conviction of any crime may be shown to affect the credibility of any person testifying"; Wigmore, *Treatise*, vol. 3, § 980(1)(a), p. 538.

38. The rule permitting impeachment by evidence of past conviction was more than a century old. Wigmore (*Treatise*, vol. 3, § 980, p. 539) cites seventeenth-century

examples of its application. But because those convicted of any infamous crime were altogether disqualified from testifying, the impeachment rule probably did not come up often. A Massachusetts act of 1852 (§ 60, 1852 Mass. Acts, at 235) abolished the rule disqualifying felons and at the same time provided that all witnesses could be impeached with evidence of past crimes.

39. See *Gorham*, 99 Mass. at 420.

40. Ibid., 421, which cites *Commonwealth v. Bonner*, 97 Mass. 587 (1867).

41. "The New Law," *New York Times*, September 13, 1869, 2; see also Act of May 7, 1869, ch. 678, § 1, 1869 N.Y. Laws 1597, 1597.

42. For example, Federal Rule of Evidence 609(a)(1) permits a litigant to impeach witnesses *other* than criminal defendants with evidence of their past crimes as long as the probative value of the evidence is not substantially outweighed by the risk of unfair prejudice. But the rule admits such evidence against criminal defendants only if its probative value outweighs the risk of unfair prejudice. The stricter weighing test supplies criminal defendants with an extra measure of protection against this sort of impeachment.

In Massachusetts the governing statute does not itself distinguish between impeachment of defendants and other witnesses (see *Mass. Gen. Laws Ann.* ch. 233, § 21 [Law. Co-op. 1986]). But the Supreme Judicial Court has recognized that "[t]he admission of evidence of prior convictions presents the risk that the fact finder's attention may be diverted from the question of the defendant's guilt to the question of the defendant's bad character" and therefore has required trial judges to balance the impeachment value of the evidence against the "danger of unfair prejudice" before admitting evidence of past crimes against criminal defendants (*Commonwealth v. Fano*, 400 Mass. 296, 303 [1987]).

43. *Bonner*, 97 Mass. at 588.

44. Ibid.

45. Ibid., 589.

46. In *Commonwealth v. Sullivan*, 150 Mass. 315, 317 (1889), the court wrote simply, "[t]he defendant having testified, the record of her conviction of a crime was admissible to affect her credibility." The court since has recognized that a criminal defendant faces a particular danger of unfair prejudice "if a prior conviction is substantially similar to the crime being tried" (*Fano*, 400 Mass. at 303).

47. See *National Cyclopedia*, vol. 14, 427.

48. Train, *Prisoner at the Bar*, 164.

49. Ibid., 161. Train cited the experience of one of his colleagues: "Out of three hundred defendants tried by the writer's associate, Mr. C. C. Nott, twenty-three failed to take the stand in cases submitted to the jury. Of these twenty-one were convicted, one was acquitted, and as to one the jury disagreed" (ibid., 163).

50. Ibid., 164.

51. Ibid., 148.

52. Ibid., 161.

53. Ibid., 148.

54. Ibid.

55. Ibid., 169.

56. See *Ferguson v. Georgia*, 365 U.S. 570, 577 & n.6 (1961).

57. See this chapter, Note 28.

58. Proceedings upon Sentence at 5–6, *People v. Schroeder*, No. 4025 (Alameda Super. Ct. 1910), quoted in Friedman and Percival, *Roots of Justice*, 181.

59. See Proceedings upon Sentence, *People v. Sullivan*, No. 4837 (Alameda Super. Ct. 1910), which quotes a judge who justified a heavy sentence to the defendant by noting that "[y]ou were not only willing to commit the offense, you were willing to go upon the witness stand and state that which was not true" (cited in Friedman and Percival, *Roots of Justice*, 214). Heumann ("Note," 526 n.18) notes the same principle at work in modern-day Connecticut.

60. "The New Law," *New York Times*, September 13, 1869, 2.

61. See George Fisher, "Jury's Rise," 656–98.

62. Augustus, *Report of the Labors*, 19.

63. See Savage, *Annual Report*, 1–2, 8. Under the heading "First Offences," Savage wrote that "very few are probated who have once been in prison." He urged courts to give "mature consideration" to their apparent belief "that there is little hope for a second comer" (ibid.). According to the *Boston Evening Transcript* ("Probation," Jaunuary 15, 1880, 1), which cited Savage's first annual report, as many as ninety-five percent of his cases were first offenses.

In 1889 Savage wrote that "a large majority of the cases recommended are for first and minor offences" (Savage, *Probation Work*, 16). That same year, the probation officer for the South Boston district reported that during his seven-year tenure, 1,129 of 1,598 disposed probation cases involved first offenders (ibid., 22). (For the claim that Savage was Boston's first regular probation officer, see Savage, *Police Records*, xiii.)

A generation later a Chicago lawyer wrote, "It is assumed that a probation system is one which results in the establishment of the principle that a first offender . . . shall be relieved of punishment" (Kocourek, "Unconsidered Element," 9, 10). Lynn Mather reports that in Los Angeles in the 1970s, when the offense was minor, the "lack of prior record indicated the likelihood that probation would be granted" (Mather, *Plea Bargaining or Trial?*, 32).

64. When New York acted to permit suspended sentences (an elaboration of the probation procedure) in 1893, it limited the practice to persons not previously convicted of a felony. See Act of April 4, 1893, ch. 279, § 1, 1893 N.Y. Laws 559, 559. According to a 1905 rule, abandoned in 1918, convicted felons could never be granted probation. See Act of May 6, 1918, ch. 457, § 1, 1918 N.Y. Laws 1339, 1339–40; Act of May 29, 1905, ch. 655, § 1, 1905 N.Y. Laws 1664, 1664; see also Timasheff, *One Hundred Years*, vol. 1, 19, 54. Maryland's 1894 probation act limited the practice to first offenders found guilty of noncapital offenses: see Act of April 6, 1894, ch. 402, § 1, 1894 Md. Stat. 583, 583–84. In 1926 the Massachusetts legisla-

ture declared that "no person convicted of a felony by a district court shall be placed on probation by said court . . . if it shall appear that he has been previously convicted of any felony" (Act of April 23, 1926, ch. 271, § 1, 1926 Mass. Acts 267, 267).

NOTES TO CHAPTER 5

1. See Chapter 4, Notes 18–21, and accompanying text.

2. Act of May 22, 1852, ch. 322, § 13, 1852 Mass. Acts 257, 264 (emphasis added).

3. See Chapter 2, Notes 59–65, and accompanying text.

4. Act of May 12, 1865, ch. 223, § 1, 1865 Mass. Acts 617, 617, which concerns evasions of provisions of the general statutes regarding liquor cases; see also Chapter 3, Notes 39–40, 45–48, and accompanying text.

5. Moreover, only one of these twenty-seven cases looked like an old liquor charge bargain in that the prosecutor's manipulation of the charges dictated the sentence. That was a murder case, in which the prosecutor reduced a charge of first-degree murder, which called for mandatory death, to second-degree murder, which called for mandatory life imprisonment, in exchange for the defendant's plea (*Commonwealth v. William H. Kelley*, Middlesex Super. Ct. R. Book 368, No. 26 [1900]). The legislature had transferred jurisdiction to try murder cases from the Supreme Judicial Court to the superior court in 1891 (Act of June 6, 1891, ch. 379, § 1, 1891 Mass. Acts 966, 966; see also Davis, *History of the Judiciary*, 254).

In almost all the other cases, the judge's sentence was well below the maximum of the reduced charge, and so the defendant arguably won only the collateral rewards that might have come with a lesser crime of conviction. For some defendants, these rewards might have been substantial, but the very small total number of charge bargains suggests that for most defendants, they held little allure.

6. See Chapter 4, Table 4.1, p. 97.

7. If anything, those defendants unfortunate enough to come to court without lawyers had reason to be more hopeful than in years past. In 1900, of thirty-four defendants with counsel who went to trial, twenty won acquittals or hung juries—a success rate of fifty-nine percent. Fifteen of the thirty-nine unrepresented defendants (thirty-eight percent) who risked trial also won acquittals or hung juries. Having counsel was still a benefit, but going to trial alone proved less hopeless than it had in the first half of the century. See Chapter 4, Table 4.3, p. 99. I cannot explain why unrepresented defendants fared better at trial in later years.

8. Figure 4.1 understates the proportion of defendants who pled guilty at century's end because I excluded liquor prosecutions and filed cases from that diagram. I did so to avoid the distorting impact of the prosecutors' power to bargain in those cases, especially in earlier decades, as well as the distorting impact of changes in the liquor laws and in the rates of liquor prosecutions. By the last third of the century, of

course, prosecutors had lost their power to charge bargain in liquor cases, and by the last two decades of the century, judges perhaps had assumed more of the power to place cases on file (see Chapter 3, Notes 81–90, and accompanying text). When I return the excluded cases to the pool, the proportion of adjudicated cases settled by plea in 1900 rises to eighty-seven percent.

9. See Chapter 3, Notes 81–90, and accompanying text.

10. In 1880, for example, on-file plea bargains made up thirty-four percent of all pleas. By 1900, that figure had climbed to forty-eight percent. See Middlesex Super. Ct. R. Books (1880, 1900); Middlesex Super. Ct. Docket Books (1880, 1900).

11. Thompson, *Diaries*, vol. 11, October 14, 1885.

12. Ibid., vol. 13, October 22, 1885. Because Thompson kept separate diaries in his two offices, different volumes sometimes cover the same dates.

13. Ibid., vol. 13, October 26, 1885.

14. Ibid., vol. 13, November 9, 1885.

15. After writing in an entry dated November 9 that he "[w]ent to Greenfield [and] held Court for a fortnight," Thompson made no further note of his itinerary until this entry—"Monday December 1885 Went to Greenfield"—which he followed with this vague comment: "Held Court . . . Wednesday Night Dec. 9." Thompson then became more specific, noting that he "went to Boston and held court till Thursday night 24, 1885." He spent the Christmas week at home (ibid., vol. 13, undated entries).

16. Volume 13 of Thompson's diaries contains the chronicle of his busy schedule. In an undated entry following January 5, 1886, he noted that he sat court in Boston and Barnstable, then in Boston again; on May 13, 1886, he recorded a sitting in Worcester; on June 30, 1886, he wrote that he sat court in East Cambridge; on December 24, 1886, he noted sittings in Bristol, Lowell, East Cambridge, Boston, Plymouth, Dukes County, and Nantucket; on October 4, 1887, he noted sittings in Springfield and Boston, then in Springfield again, and then in Boston; finally, on November 12, 1887, he wrote that he sat in Pittsfield. His three remarks about how busy he was all appear in undated entries in volume 13, following his entry of January 5, 1886.

17. Ibid., vol. 13, October 4, 1887: "Rode with horse [from Springfield] to Beverly."

18. In the 1830s and 1840s the *Lowell Courier* remarked several times on unfinished business left by the Court of Common Pleas. In 1836, for example, it noted "the present crowded and overflowing state of the dockets of the C.C.P." The next year it reported that "[n]o civil action has been tried [at the present sitting of the Court of Common Pleas], and none will be. The number of new entries is 436, of old about 900." And in 1841, after the court had adjourned its June sitting, the *Courier* reported that "[m]uch business remained undisposed of, but Chief Justice Williams . . . being obliged to hold the Term in Boston . . . and the other members of the Court having engagements in other parts of the Commonwealth," the court was forced to adjourn.

See "To Our Friend of the Concord Gazette We Send Greeting," February 20, 1836, 2; "Court of Common Pleas," September 14, 1837, 2; "Criminal Cases Disposed of at the Late Session of C.C.P.," July 8, 1841, 2.

19. See Chapter 2, Notes 14–28, 81–83, and accompanying text.

20. Langbein, "Torture," 11.

21. The attorney general never recorded trial time with any precision. Most often, he noted the trial as a span—for example, "December 1–9" for an 1868 murder case. See *Commonwealth v. Samuel M. Andrews*, listed in *Report of the Attorney General for the Year Ending December 31, 1868*, Pub. Doc. No. 16, at 17 (Mass. 1869). In such cases, I have assumed that the trial consumed both the beginning and ending day and every day in between. As I expect—but do not know—that courts were closed on Sundays, and as I have not determined which dates were Sundays, I have simply excluded one day in seven whenever the time span noted exceeded six days. Hence I have assumed that the *Andrews* case, quoted above, consumed eight days.

22. I have limited myself to murder trials, rather than considering all capital trials, because murder cases may have taken more or less time to try than cases involving other capital offenses—and because, after mid-century, murder was virtually the only capital offense.

23. See Act of June 6, 1891, ch. 379, § 1, 1891 Mass. Acts 966, 966.

24. S. Doc. No. 68, at 7 (Mass. 1844), petition of Samuel D. Parker.

25. See Chapter 4, Table 4.1, p. 97.

26. As the table makes clear, I have measured the number of "judge-days"— that is, if two or more judges were presiding in separate courtrooms for a span of days, I have multiplied the number of judges by the number of days.

27. In this respect, the table slightly understates the efficiency of the later years. Because of the district attorney's workload, he nol prossed or simply placed on file (without a plea) a higher proportion of cases in the middle of the century than toward the end, when he became a full-time official and took on assistants. The bench therefore had to deal with a greater proportion of the total cases coming into the court as the last half of the century wore on.

28. Friedman and Percival report an average length of trial in Alameda County of 1.5 days in 1880–1889 (Friedman and Percival, *Roots of Justice*, 185). Trials in Middlesex were a good deal shorter. In 1890 the Middlesex Superior Court heard 1.7 trials per judge-day—suggesting a trial length of about three-fifths of a day, minus enough time to make room for cases not resolved by trial. Except in murder cases (see Table 5.3, p. 119), I did not see a substantial increase in trial length at century's end. Friedman and Percival, in contrast, report an average trial length of 2.6 days in 1890–1899 (ibid.).

Probably the most important reason for the immoderate—or at least unmodern—quickness of these nineteenth-century trials was that the same two juries sat throughout each session of the court with only slightly shifting memberships to suit the needs of each trial. The prosecutor had no right to make peremptory challenges in Massachusetts until 1862, further shortening the time taken in jury selection (see Act of March 22, 1862, ch. 84, § 1, 1862 Mass. Acts 64, 64). The practice of keeping the same jury from case to case helps to explain the very fast trial rates that John Langbein observed in late-seventeenth- and eighteenth-century London and that Friedman and Percival saw in Leon County, Florida, in the 1890s. Langbein ("Understanding," 262) notes an average trial rate at the Old Bailey of between twelve and twenty felony cases a day well into the eighteenth century. Friedman and Percival (*Roots of Justice*, 194 and n.97) report that Leon County trials "took, on the average, half an hour at most."

29. I am not able to draw a perfect comparison between case dispositions in 1900 and those in 1910 because I could find only the record books and not the docket books for 1910. Without the docket books, it is impossible to know how many of the filed cases, which appear simply as long lists of names in the record books, involved guilty pleas. But the record books for the two years suggest a remarkably similar pattern of case disposition. In 1900 the record book discloses 313 adjudicated nonfiled cases, of which 240—or 77 percent—were resolved by plea. In 1910 the record book lists 288 adjudicated nonfiled cases, of which 222—or 77 percent—were resolved by plea.

30. But Langbein's thesis might very well help to explain the continued advance of plea bargaining in the twentieth century. Langbein reports ("Torture," 9 and n.11) plea-bargaining rates in some American jurisdictions of up to ninety-nine percent. And Alschuler ("Plea Bargaining History," 38) cites studies showing that the length of the average felony trial grew from 3.5 days in 1964 to 7.2 days in 1968 in Los Angeles, and from 1.9 days in 1950 to 2.8 days in 1965 in the District of Columbia.

31. For studies adhering to the accepted wisdom, see those cited by Heumann, "Note," 516–17, and McConville and Mirsky, "Rise of Guilty Pleas," 474 n.125. Both Heumann and McConville and Mirsky seek to debunk the importance of case-load pressure. McConville and Mirsky argue that New York City courts "absorb[ed]" and "accommodated" a fivefold increase in criminal caseload between 1839 and 1865 "without requiring the court to adopt alternative methods of case disposition" (McConville and Mirsky, ibid., 463–64).

Heumann's is the most sustained attack on the theory that caseload pressure prompted the rise of plea bargaining, but as I noted in the Prologue, his analysis is not entirely convincing. He compares trial rates in low-volume and high-volume superior courts in Connecticut and finds that "trial rates between them varied minimally, and indeed often the low volume courts tried proportionately fewer cases" (Heumann, "Note," 521–22). Heumann admits that this mode of analysis is "rough" because, without knowing the number of prosecutors and judges in each court, "we cannot be sure that volume reflects pressure" (ibid., 520–21). Moreover, Heumann does not say whether the judges of the Connecticut Superior Court rode circuit over the period of his study or were otherwise shifted from one court to another when the first court's business was done. If so, we would expect to find little variation in judicial caseload pressure between those courts with many cases and those with few, and hence not much variation in the rates of trials.

32. For example, Friedman and Percival (*Roots of Justice*, 42–43, 48) don't mention the civil caseload when arguing that the Alameda "Superior Court's workload was not . . . oppressive," although a majority of the court's judges devoted themselves to the civil caseload. Albert Alschuler ("Plea Bargaining History," 34) addresses the caseload problem only in terms of case pressure on the U.S. attorney's office and does not consider civil case pressure on judges. And Milton Heumann ("Note," 523 n.10) acknowledges that his data would not permit analysis of the impact of civil caseload.

33. Because the court did not begin to hold separate criminal and civil sessions until partway through 1839, I began recording the time devoted to each session in 1840. Although the court of common pleas underwent a substantial reorganization in 1821 (see Act of February 14, 1821, ch. 79, § 1, 8 Mass. Laws 545, 545–46), the fundamental operations of the court did not change again throughout the nineteenth century. At least since 1821, each judge of the court of common pleas and the superior court could preside alone over sessions of the court (ibid). Although the record and docket books are not absolutely clear on this point, I believe that judges always or almost always sat alone.

In 1891, when the legislature transferred trial jurisdiction in capital cases to the superior court from the Supreme Judicial Court, it required three judges to preside at such trials (Act of June 6, 1891, ch. 379, § 2, 1891 Mass. Acts 966, 966), but then reduced the figure to two in 1894 (Act of April 5, 1894, ch. 204, 1894 Mass. Acts 186, 186). There were, however, no murder trials in Middlesex County in 1896 or 1900, the two years that I studied after these law changes, so I did not need to figure either change into my calculations. Occasionally, two or more judges presided in different courtrooms at the same time, each of them sitting alone. When calculating the number of judge-days for Figure 5.1—as well as for Table 5.4—I multiplied the number of judges sitting by the number of days.

34. To figure the judges' total annual workload, we would have to repeat this analysis in each of the state's other thirteen counties. If the business of Middlesex County was proportional to its population, then it accounted for about eighteen percent of Massachusetts court work in this era (see *Compendium of the Ninth Census*, 56; *Compendium of the Tenth Census*, vol. 1, 34). It is likely, however, that Middlesex actually accounted for a smaller proportion of total workload because Boston (Suffolk County) apparently accounted for more than its share of both criminal and civil business (see Note 36, this chapter).

35. For these figures, I divided the number of cases brought before the judges for resolution (257 in 1859, 546 in 1900) by the number of judge-days in criminal sessions (78 in 1859, 44 in 1900). These case counts exclude from the total caseload those disposed of by complete nol prosses, by being placed on file without a guilty plea, or because the defendant defaulted. I presume such cases absorbed little of the judges' time.

36. Alan Dimond (*Superior Court*, 93, 96) cites legislative reports showing a

doubling of civil cases entered on the superior court docket statewide between 1880 and 1900 and noting continued increases afterward. Likewise, Michael Stephen Hindus and his coauthors (*Files*, 193) report an increase in the civil caseload of Suffolk County from 24,785 cases in 1860–1869 to 52,293 cases in 1890–1899 to 115,784 cases in 1920–1929. Because both the civil and criminal caseloads of Suffolk County seem to have been several times greater than those of Middlesex, which apparently was its closest rival, what happened in Suffolk probably influenced judges' behavior more than events elsewhere. Two of the smaller counties actually saw their civil caseloads shrink in this time frame. Berkshire County's civil caseload fell from 4,374 to 2,202 between 1860–1869 and 1890–1899, and Hampshire County's fell from 1,453 to 1,400 after rising as high as 3,179 in 1870–1879 (ibid., 190, 192).

Although I have seen no study that measures the time consumed by civil caseloads in jurisdictions outside Massachusetts, several studies have measured the number of cases filed. The results generally do not show so steep an increase in civil filings as in Massachusetts, and some even show declines. Randolph Bergstrom (*Courting Danger*, 16), relying on a sampling, reports a decline in civil filings in the New York City Supreme Court from about 5,110 in 1870 to 4,740 in 1890 and then a rise to 6,150 in 1910. Marc Galanter ("Reading the Landscape of Disputes," 40) cites a study showing that the rate of civil filings in Menard County, Illinois, measured in terms of cases per thousand people, fell from 16.4 in 1870 to 5.5 in 1890. Galanter often reports the *rate* of civil cases filed because he examines our society's litigiousness. For my purposes, however, the important question is the burden on courts, which might be something very different. For example, Galanter cites a study of St. Louis that shows a sharply falling rate of civil litigation at a time when the number of civil cases filed was rising healthily (ibid., 39).

37. See Friedman, *History of American Law*, 339; Hurst, *Growth of American Law*, 149–50. The phrase, "transformations of American law," of course must be credited to Morton Horwitz.

38. Hindus and his coauthors (*Files*, 139) write that "[t]he rise of tort actions came about in large measure because of technological changes in the means of transportation." They echo Roscoe Pound's 1940 observation (*Organization of Courts*, 200) that "[t]he transition to a mechanical era [after the Civil War] led to the rise of the law of torts as one of the great subjects of the law." Hence the appearance of such texts as *The Law of Railroad Accidents in Massachusetts* in 1897 and *The Law of Passenger and Freight Elevators* in 1896 (Silverman, *Law and Urban Growth*, 167 n.7, 187 n.14). Robert Silverman notes that the number of tort cases filed in Boston's courts against street railways rose from 15 in 1880 to about 1,400 in 1900 and that negligence cases against gas utilities rose from "a handful" in 1880 to about 400 in the same period (ibid., 191 n.47, 109).

The Massachusetts legislature created wrongful death actions for families of railroad workers in 1881 (Act of April 12, 1881, ch. 199, § 1, 1881 Mass. Acts 521, 521); permitted employees or their survivors to sue for work-related injuries due to railroad negligence in 1883 (Act of June 16, 1883, ch. 243, § 1, 1883 Mass. Acts 532, 532); and extended wrongful death actions to all survivors of work-related accidents in 1887 (Act of May 14, 1887, ch. 270, § 2, 1887 Mass. Acts 899, 900).

Not all of the increase in the Superior Court's business arose directly out of technological change. The number of negligence actions involving a fall or a falling object filed in Boston's courts rose from about fifty in 1880 to more than six hundred in 1900 (see Silverman, *Law and Urban Growth*, 112). Moreover, the legislature shifted large chunks of judicial business from the Supreme Judicial Court to the superior court. In 1880 it removed all jurisdiction over torts from the Supreme Judicial Court (Act of February 20, 1880, ch. 28, 1880 Mass. Acts 31, 31); in 1883 it gave the superior court equity jurisdiction concurrent with that of the Supreme Judicial Court (Act of May 13, 1883, ch. 223, § 1, 1883 Mass. Acts 510, 510); and in 1887 it gave the superior court exclusive jurisdiction over divorces and custody actions (Act of May 31, 1887, ch. 332, 1887 Mass. Acts, 954, 954). The legislature also tried to relieve the superior court of its civil case burden by shunting some of its jurisdiction to the lower courts (see Act of May 11, 1877, ch. 211, § 3, 1877 Mass. Acts 595, 596).

39. See Silverman, *Law and Urban Growth*, 113.

40. Hindus and his coauthors (*Files*, 138, 140) report that from 1875 to 1905, the proportion of tort cases in the civil docket of Suffolk and Hampshire counties rose from 7.1 percent to 37.4 percent, with continuing increases thereafter, while the proportion of contract cases fell from 80.6 percent to 50.5 percent during the same period. Bergstrom (*Courting Danger*, 16–17) notes that tort cases in New York City consistently made up a proportion of "contested cases" roughly four times larger than their proportion of all cases between 1870 and 1910.

41. Hindus and his colleagues (*Files*, 139) write that "[t]ort actions were generally more subjective than the often clear-cut promissory note and simple debt cases that had dominated the docket in earlier decades." Silverman (*Law and Urban Growth*, 135–36) adds that plaintiffs were more likely to claim jury trials in personal injury litigation, expecting "to win sympathy from their peers." And Moorfield Storey (*Reform*, 51–52), estimated that personal injury suits took up at least three-quarters of the time allotted by Boston courts to jury trials.

42. Silverman (*Law and Urban Growth*, 115–16, 118) reports that at the turn of the century, the Boston Elevated Railway was the defendant in nearly thirty percent of all personal injury suits in Boston and that a few law firms handled most of the defense work. He cites the minutes of the Boston Bar Association, which expressed concern in 1897 that contingency fees prompted the poor, in league with their lawyers, to bring unmeritorious negligence suits. Hindus and his coauthors (*Files*, 139) point out the importance of contingency fees in this era.

43. In *Roots of Justice* (p. 56), Friedman and Percival note that the American population grew by 97 percent between 1870 and 1900, while the population of lawyers grew by 186 percent. Closer to the study, Silverman (*Law and Urban Growth*, 30) reports that the membership of the Boston bar "nearly doubled" between 1880

and 1900, while over the same period the population of Suffolk County increased a mere fifty-eight percent (U.S. Census Office, *Twelfth Census of the United States*, vol. 1, 24, table 4).

44. See *Mass. Rev. Laws* ch. 173, § 112, at 1569 (Wright and Potter 1902); *Shanahan v. Boston & N.S. Ry.*, 193 Mass. 412, 414 (1907). I would like to thank Bob Gordon for pointing out to me the importance of remittitur in this context.

45. The legislature approved the concept of additur only in 1945 (Act of July 10, 1945, ch. 578, § 1, 1945 Mass. Acts 590, 590). The word *additur* appears to have been used for the first time in a Massachusetts appellate case report in 1959 (see *Murach v. Massachusetts Bonding & Ins. Co.*, 339 Mass. 184, 185 [1959]). More than a century before, the state's high court had recognized the concept of enhancing damages in a contract action, where "the damages are capable of estimation," but suggested that judges should do so only very rarely in "actions for personal wrongs" (*Taunton Mfg. Co. v. Smith*, 26 Mass. [9 Pick.] 11, 12 [1829]). In her article, "New Trial for Verdict Against Law" (pp. 505, 554), Renée Lettow notes that in the United States in the early nineteenth century, "remittitur was more widely accepted than additur."

46. See Hindus et al., *Files*, 148.

47. In both Suffolk and Hampshire Counties, it took twice as long to resolve the average civil case in 1895 as in 1865, and given the huge increase in the number of cases, there is no way the settlement rate could keep up with the increasing pressure on the docket (see ibid., 150; and this chapter, Notes 38–39, 46, and accompanying text). In 1890 the governor complained to the legislature that despite a recent addition of two judges to the superior court bench, "the present volume of business is so great that it is difficult to obtain a trial of an action until a long time after its commencement" (Dimond, *Superior Court*, 93, quoting the governor). In 1903 a different governor made a very similar statement (ibid., 98). In 1909 the legislature was forced to create a commission "To Investigate the Causes of Delay in the Administration of Justice in Civil Actions" (H. Doc. No. 1050, at 3–4 [Mass. 1910]). Studies from other jurisdictions suggest that a good deal of the growth in civil settlements took place only in the twentieth century (see Alschuler, "Foreword," 2–5).

48. I say "arguably" impartial because the earliest probation statute, that of 1878, provided that the probation officer "shall be under the general control of the chief of police" of Boston (Act of April 26, 1878, ch. 198, § 1, 1878 Mass. Stat. 146, 147). Both the 1878 act and 1880 probation acts envisioned that probation officers might be appointed from the police force (see Act of March 22, 1880, ch. 129, § 1, 1880 Mass. Stat. 87, 87; § 1, 1878 Mass. Stat. at 146). In fact, Boston's first public probation officer, Edward H. Savage, was the city's retiring police chief (see Savage, *Police Records*, xiii). The legislature gave the courts, rather than municipal authorities, the power to appoint probation officers by acts of 1891 and 1898, so that the probation officer perhaps became "in every way an officer of the Court" (Act of May 28, 1891, ch. 356, § 1, 1891 Mass. Stat. 920, 920; Act of June 8, 1898, ch. 511, § 1, 1898 Mass. Acts 474, 474–75; Grinnell, "Probation," 612–14).

49. § 1, 1878 Mass. Stat. at 146–47.

50. §§ 3, 11, 1880 Mass. Stat. at 87, 89.

51. Savage, *Annual Report*, 7–8.

52. Savage, *Probation Work*, 15.

53. Ibid., 14. At least one observer from the late 1890s confirmed that Savage and his colleagues did as he claimed: Probation officers "visit the home or place of employment. They search the court records to see if it be the first offense. If circumstances warrant, they may recommend to the judge, who is largely guided by their report, that the person be either discharged at once or be put upon probation" (Allen, *Prison Reform*, 5).

54. See §§ 3–4, 1880 Mass. Stat. at 87; § 1, 1878 Mass. Stat. at 147. By requiring probation officers to investigate "persons charged with or convicted of crimes" (the 1878 act) and "every person arrested for crime" (the 1880 act), the acts make it clear that the duty to investigate arises before conviction, but this language says nothing about the stage at which the probation officer should "recommend" probation to the court.

55. § 11, 1880 Mass. Stat. at 89 (emphasis added).

56. Commonwealth of Mass., *Probation Manual* 17 (1916).

57. Ibid.

58. Ruggles-Brise, *Some Observations*, 20, 21–22 (emphasis added). On Ruggles-Brise, see Leon Radzinowicz and Roger Hood, *History of English Criminal Law*, vol. 5, 596–99.

59. See Edward Lindsey, "Historical Sketch," 18–20. The Cincinnati meeting, known as the National Congress on Penitentiary and Reformatory Discipline, helped put indeterminate sentencing on the political agenda, but it was not the first American encounter with the concept. As early as 1839, George Combs, a Scottish philosopher, articulated a proposal for a true indeterminate sentence (see Newman, *Sourcebook*, 34–35). And a half-century before Combs, Philadelphia's Benjamin Rush had advocated a system in which there would be fixed penalties for crimes, but prisoners would not be told what these penalties were (Rush, *Enquiry*, 11). I thank Al Alschuler for pointing me to this aspect of Rush's work.

60. See Chapter 8, Notes 26–27, and accompanying text.

61. See Spalding, "Indeterminate Sentence," 7, 13; Lewis, "Indeterminate Sentence," 20–21.

62. Spalding, "Indeterminate Sentence," 14; see also Conlon's Case, 148 Mass. 168, 169 (1889), which identifies Spalding as the Secretary of the Board of Commissioners of Prisons. As early as the 1840s, S. J. May wrote that "[o]ne of the greatest improvements in the administration of our penal code would be to withhold from the judges all discretion as to the time for which convicts shall be confined" (quoted in Wilcox, *Parole*, 9). By the end of the century, complaints about the "absurd[ity]" of judicial sentencing were common. Frederick Allen (*Prison Reform*, 9–10) wrote in 1898 that "[t]he prevalent system . . . is absurd. A convict is usually sentenced for a fixed period—supposedly determined by his crime. Apart from the difficulty of dis-

criminating as to a man's guilt [is] the personal equation of the disposition and mood of different judges." The next year Charlton Lewis ("Indeterminate Sentence," 17–18) added that "[o]ur penal codes . . . leave it to the trial judge to fix the duration of imprisonment within [broad] limits according to his view of the criminal's deserts. This system has often been exposed as absurd in principle and as grossly wrong and injurious in practice."

63. In 1899 an Ohio judge and advocate of indeterminate sentences expressed in mild terms the objections of other judges to the drift of the indeterminate sentence movement: "Some learned judges and statesmen hesitate to apply the principles of an indefinite sentence . . . , holding that the trial judge can better fix a correct limit of just punishment . . . than can the officer who keeps the prisoner. These thinkers seem to be held by the principle that the confinement and punishment of the criminal must equal the character of the offense, and that no one but a commissioned judge should limit the time" (Follett, "Indeterminate Sentence," 22).

In 1891 the Michigan Supreme Court declared unconstitutional a state law that had given judges the option to impose indeterminate prison terms (see *People v. Cummings*, 88 Mich. 249, 263 [1891]). Although judges retained the right to impose definite sentences instead, the court condemned the statute because it appeared to transfer to a parole board "judicial power in determining the term of imprisonment" (ibid., 251). The court wrote that the trial judge is "the one person best calculated, from his knowledge of all the incidents and circumstances of the commission of the crime and of the character of the prisoner, to exercise a discretion in fixing the term of imprisonment" (ibid., 253). Dissenting in *Miller v. State* (149 Ind. 607, 628 [1898]), one judge argued that "the right to assess the punishment, and thereby fix the term of imprisonment provided, within the limits of the statute [is] a judicial function, of which the court . . . cannot be deprived by the legislature." Newman (*Sourcebook*, 35) notes that "[t]he main opposition to the enactment of indeterminate sentence laws came from the judges who were unwilling to relinquish their traditional privilege of fixing the time prisoners must serve."

64. See Act of March 24, 1858, ch. 77, 1858 Mass. Acts 58, 58, which addresses jails and houses of correction; Act of May 30, 1857, ch. 284, § 1, 1857 Mass. Acts 72, 72, which deals with state prisons. Although New York and Tennessee instituted good-behavior reductions in 1817 and 1836, respectively, Ohio's 1856 law seems to have sparked the concept's adoption nationwide (see Act of April 15, 1817, ch. 269, §§ 5, 19, 1817 N.Y. Laws 310, 312, 316; Act of April 8, 1856, § 17, 1856 Ohio Laws 126, 133–34; Act of February 20, 1836, ch. 63, § 4, 1835–1836 Tenn. Pub. Acts 171, 171; see also Wines, *Monograph on Sentences*, 15 n.*.

65. See Act of March 22, 1880, ch. 129, § 6, 1880 Mass. Acts 87, 88.

66. See Act of May 21, 1884, ch. 255, 1884 Mass. Acts 220; and ibid., §§ 3, 12–14, 33, 1884 Mass. Acts at 221, 223, 227. The Governor and Governor's Council had to approve the release of any convict sentenced to state prison.

67. See Act of June 24, 1886, ch. 323, § 1, 1886 Mass. Acts 296. The act

required that sentences to the Massachusetts reformatory "not fix or limit the duration" of confinement, unless they exceeded five years. But judges had the choice of other institutions, and reformatory sentences proved to be much more the exception than the rule (see Chapter 8, Notes 30–31, and accompanying text). Even reformatory sentences of less than five years were not strictly indeterminate, for the act capped confinement of such sentences at either two or five years, depending on the crime.

68. See Act of June 5, 1895, ch. 504, §§ 1–2, 1895 Mass. Acts 624, 629, which required judges to impose minimum and maximum terms to the state prison and provided for release on parole at any time after the expiration of the minimum term; Act of May 26, 1894, ch. 440, § 1, 1894 Mass. Acts 492, 492, which provided for release on parole from the state prison at the expiration of two-thirds of the judge's sentence.

69. Ruggles-Brise, *Some Observations*, 17.

70. Ibid.

71. The four others received forty-eight months, sixty months, sixty-three months, and seventy-two months. See *Commonwealth v. Maurice C. McCarthy*, Middlesex Super. Ct. R. Book 146 (February 1890), which reports a sentence of forty-eight months after trial and conviction in a breaking-and-entering case; *Commonwealth v. Arthur N. Neil*, Middlesex Super. Ct. R. Book 101 (February 1890), which reports a sentence of sixty months; *Commonwealth v. John Heffernan*, Middlesex Super. Ct. R. Book 101 (February 1890), which reports a sentence of sixty-three months; *Commonwealth v. Cornelius Sheehan*, Middlesex Super. Ct. R. Book 101 (February 1890), which reports a sentence of seventy-two months.

72. Similarly, all four defendants who pled guilty to assault and battery in the October 1880 term of the Middlesex Superior Court received fines instead of prison sentences, while all three convicted of that crime after trial went to prison. The cases that resulted in fines were *Commonwealth v. Michael Hennessy*, Middlesex Super. Ct. R. Book 243 (October 1880); *Commonwealth v. Frederick Measures*, Middlesex Super. Ct. R. Book 244 (October 1880); *Commonwealth v. Jeremiah Ahern*, Middlesex Super. Ct. R. Book 245 (October 1880); and *Commonwealth v. William L. Orcutt*, Middlesex Super. Ct. R. Book 255 (October 1880). The cases that resulted in prison terms were *Commonwealth v. Christopher Flynn*, Middlesex Super. Ct. R. Book 205 (October 1880); *Commonwealth v. Daniel Driscoll*, Middlesex Super. Ct. R. Book 227 (October 1880); and *Commonwealth v. Patrick Ford*, Middlesex Super. Ct. R. Book 228 (October 1880).

73. As I did earlier (see this Chapter, Table 5.1, p.115), I am excluding home breaks to avoid the distortion of that more serious offense.

74. Mather and others have reported the practice (see Mather, *Plea Bargaining or Trial?*, 31–32, 58). In my years as a Middlesex County prosecutor, I regularly witnessed judicial plea bargaining.

75. *State v. Stephens*, 71 Mo. 535, 536 (1880).

76. *People v. Brown*, 54 Mich. 15, 21, 29 (1884).

77. Ibid., 20.

78. See White, *John A. Peters*, 35–36. I thank David Gold for this reference.

79. In Middlesex County in the late 1980s and early 1990s, when I served as a prosecutor, judges in the district (lower) courts often stated the terms of their plea offers openly and on the record. Superior court judges were more discreet and usually proposed terms in chambers with only counsel present. Mather reports that Los Angeles judges avoided on-the-record barters and that lawyers adopted the verb "chamberize" for the process of cutting deals with the judge behind closed doors. See Mather, *Plea Bargaining or Trial?*, 31.

80. Grinnell, "Legislative Problems," 8, which quotes from a report of the Massachusetts Judicature Commission of 1923, which in turn quoted from a letter by the former prosecutor.

Although I have no evidence that Massachusetts judges did (or did not) habitually follow the parties' sentencing recommendations in the late nineteenth century, I can report evidence that lawyers *made* specific sentencing recommendations to the court in this time frame. An 1879 report in the *Boston Globe* ("Charles P. Stickney," *Boston Daily Globe*, March 5, 1879, 1) recounted a sentencing proceeding in superior court in which the defense lawyer appealed for a sentence in the house of correction rather than in state prison, and the prosecutor requested "the full sentence of the law—namely, five years in the state prison."

81. Albert Alschuler reported that in the late 1960s Houston judges generally did not participate directly in plea bargaining and instead adhered rigorously to prosecutors' sentencing recommendations (Alschuler, "Trial Judge's Role," 1060–65).

82. Grinnell, "Legislative Problems," 8.

83. *Commonwealth v. Raffaele Scorpio* (Bristol Super. Ct.), listed in *Report of the Attorney General for Year Ending January 17, 1893*, Pub. Doc. No. 12, at vi (Mass. 1893).

84. See, e.g., *Commonwealth v. William McGrath*, listed in *Report of the Attorney General for Year Ending December 31, 1868*, Pub. Doc. No. 16, at 4 (Mass. 1869), where the attorney general stated, "I accepted a plea of guilty of murder in the 2d degree."

85. Grinnell, "Legislative Problems," 8.

86. Mass. R. Crim. P. 12(c)(2).

87. Fed. R. Crim. P. 11(e)(1)(c), 11(e)(4)(slated to be recodified as of December 1, 2002, as Rules 11(c)(1) and 11 (c)(5)(B).

88. See *Model Code of Pre-Arraignment Procedure* § 350.6 (1975); *Standards Relating to Pleas of Guilty* § 2.1 (1968).

89. See Heumann, "Note," 515 n.1; Langbein, "Torture," 9 n.11; Ch.9, p.223.

90. See *Commonwealth v. Taylor*, 370 Mass. 141, 146 (1976). Most, but not all, state courts that considered this issue in the 1960s and 1970s reached a similar result. See Alschuler, "Trial Judge's Role," 1072 n.45.

91. See *Commonwealth v. Ingersoll*, 145 Mass. 381, 382 (1888); *Commonwealth v. Mahoney*, 115 Mass. 151, 152 (1874); *Commonwealth v. Winton*, 108

Mass. 485, 485–86 (1871); *Commonwealth v. Hagarman*, 93 Mass. (10 Allen) 401, 402 (1865).

92. All four of the cases cited in the previous note addressed a different fact scenario: The defendant pled guilty or no contest in a lower court and then, on appeal for a trial de novo in superior court, sought to withdraw that plea and plead not guilty. Such defendants often wished merely to get the best deal that either court would give them on a guilty plea, but of course they needed to withdraw their earlier guilty pleas in order to have any leverage in the higher court. Judges often resisted such forum-shopping by refusing to allow plea withdrawal. The judges' refusal in this context says little about their willingness to permit plea withdrawal when doing so would facilitate standard (single-court) plea bargaining.

93. On September 26, 1835, the *Lowell Courier*'s summary of the business of the court of common pleas included this small account: "*Martin Murtoy*, Lowell— Assault with a shoe knife and an attempt to kill and murder; Plea, Guilty; sentence— 3 days solitary and 5 years in State Prison. Afternoon, retracted his plea of guilty, pleaded not guilty, and stood for trial" (*Lowell Courier*, September 26, 1835, 2). Both the record book and the docket book of the court of common pleas omit any mention of the *Murtoy* case in their reports of the court's September 1835 session. Murtoy did appear, however, in the records of the court's December session, at which a jury found him guilty of simple assault and battery but not guilty of acting with intent to kill, and the court sentenced him to a mere year in the house of correction (see *Commonwealth v. Martin Murtoy*, Middlesex Ct. C.P. R. Book 525–26 [December 1835]).

For our purposes, the most significant aspect of the record is the clerk's summary of the case's procedural history, which notes only that Murtoy had appeared at the previous session of the court and pled not guilty and says nothing of his earlier guilty plea and sentencing: "This Indictment was found at the Court of Common Pleas holden [in] . . . September last, when and where the said Martin Murtoy was set to the bar, and had this Indictment read to him, he said that thereof he was not guilty, and thence said Indictment was continued to this time" (ibid., 525). The clerk's silence about Murtoy's earlier plea and plea withdrawal leaves us to suspect that, for all the records of the Middlesex courts disclose, defendants perhaps commonly have offered guilty pleas only to withdraw them when dissatisfied with their sentence.

I have found occasional—but only occasional—cases in which the clerk did record the defendant's withdrawal of a guilty plea. See, for example, *Commonwealth v. Henry O'Hapgood*, Middlesex Ct. C.P. R. Book 309 (October 1847); and *Commonwealth v. Hosmer Lew*, Middlesex Ct. C.P. R. Book 43 (June 1844).

94. See Hopkins, "Withdrawal"; see also *New York Times*, December 17, 1955, 23, which identified Hopkins as an Indiana lawyer and gave his first name.

95. Hopkins, "Withdrawal," 480; see also *Corpus Juris Criminal Law (Plea of Guilty)*, vol. 16, § 730 (1918), which noted that if the defendant pleads guilty under the belief, induced by the prosecutor, "that sentence less severe than the maximum allowed would be given, defendant should be allowed to withdraw the plea."

96. See Hopkins, "Withdrawal," 480, which cites *Myers v. State*, 18 N.E. 42 (Ind. 1888); *State v. Kring*, 71 Mo. 551 (1880); *State v. Stephens*, 71 Mo. 535 (1880). Hopkins's statement of the rule follows immediately upon and within the same paragraph as his discussion of *Sanders v. State* (85 Ind. 318 [1882]), but that case seems irrelevant to the rule.

97. In *Myers* the defendant pled guilty based on assurances from the prosecutor, relayed by the sheriff, that "if he pleaded guilty his punishment should not exceed two years imprisonment" (*Myers*, 18 N.E. at 42). The defendant pled guilty and was promptly sentenced to ten years in state prison (ibid., 43). The high court held that the trial judge abused his discretion in refusing to allow the defendant to withdraw his guilty plea (ibid., 44).

In *Kring* the Missouri court considered a defendant's claim that he had pled guilty to second-degree murder based on his agreement with the prosecutor, "apparently sanctioned by the judge of the criminal court, that the sentence should not exceed ten years imprisonment" (*Kring*, 71 Mo. at 552). The judge imposed a twenty-five-year term. The apparent participation of the court in the bargaining process of course makes this case very much unlike the ideal type envisioned by the rule—and exemplified in *Myers*—and would seem to give the defendant a plausible claim of fraudulent inducement. In fact, the court announced that this case was "precisely similar" to *Stephens*, in which the judge clearly had misled the defendant as to the consequences of his guilty plea, thereby justifying the defendant in seeking to withdraw the plea (see Hopkins, "Withdrawal," 480, which cites *Stephens*, 71 Mo. at 535).

98. Alexis Haller, one of my research assistants, devoted particular energy to this task.

99. Appeals courts in California, Louisiana, Mississippi, and New York all observed in similar fashion that "[t]he law . . . will permit a plea of guilty to be withdrawn if it fairly appears that defendant was in ignorance of his rights and of the consequences of his act, or was unduly and improperly influenced either by hope or fear in the making of it" (*People v. Miller*, 114 Cal. 10, 16 [1896]); "[t]he withdrawal of the plea of guilty should not be denied in any case, where it is in the least evident that the ends of justice will be subserved by permitting not guilty to be pleaded in its place" (*State v. Williams*, 14 So. 32, 32 [La. 1893]); "the defendant should be permitted to withdraw his plea of guilty, when unadvisedly given, where any reasonable ground is offered for going to the jury" (*Deloach v. State*, 77 Miss. 691, 692 [1900]); and "[w]here a person accused of crime may, inadvertently or unadvisedly, plead guilty to an indictment, and afterwards apply for the privilege to withdraw that plea and plead not guilty, the leave is commonly granted" (*People v. Joyce*, 4 N.Y. Crim. 341, 345 [Sup. Ct. 1886]).

100. See *Griffin v. State*, 12 Ga. App. 615, 624–25, 630–31 (1913); *State v. Walker*, 250 Ill. 427, 432 (1911); *Mounts v. Commonwealth*, 89 Ky. 274, 277–78 (1889) (dictum).

NOTES TO CHAPTER 6

1. See Chapter 5, Note 29, and accompanying text.

2. See Heumann, "Note," 515 n.1; Langbein, "Torture," 9 n.11.

3. Vogel identifies the Boston Police Court as the source of her data on guilty plea rates through 1866 in *Courts of Trade*, at 59, fig.1. See also "Social Origins," 170–72. She notes that prosecutors rarely appeared in the police court before 1850 (ibid., 218). Ferdinand (*Boston's Courts*, 46) notes the absence of a jury in police court.

4. Vogel, "Social Origins," 168.

5. Ibid., 165.

6. Ibid., 165–66.

7. Ibid., 200.

8. Ibid., 232–33.

9. Ibid., 208, 211.

10. See Chapter 5, Notes 32–47, and accompanying text. See also Chapter 8, where I discuss how social reformers with a charitable agenda advanced the cause of public defenders' offices by arguing that these offices would advance plea bargaining—and how these predictions had a self-fulfilling quality.

11. I encountered relatively few drunkenness or common-drunkard cases in the courts of the middle tier. I saw none at all between 1789 and 1843. Only during 1900 and 1910 did drunkenness and common-drunkard cases together account for as much as ten percent of the total.

12. Vogel, "Social Origins," 179.

13. Ibid., 185, 190–91. The lack of concessions is perhaps not surprising given the hopeless position of the typical accused drunk. Vogel reports that virtually all who refused to plead guilty and chose trial were convicted. Indeed, she found a one-hundred-percent conviction rate in her samples ("Social Origins," 181; *Courts of Trade*, 80). Ferdinand notes that in the twelve years of Boston Police Court records he studied between 1826 and 1850, the rate of not-guilty findings in drunkenness cases only once approached four percent of all cases and otherwise ranged between zero and two percent (Ferdinand, *Boston's Courts*, 63). A newspaper's comment decades later that drunkenness trials "take[], on an average, just one minute to try each" suggests how perfunctory the proceedings were ("Municipal Court—Judge May," *Boston Daily Globe*, January 9, 1879, 1).

Nursing no fond hope of acquittal after trial, and down and out and often without the means for a lawyer, those accused of drunkenness might well have pled guilty without any inducement from the magistrate. Vogel writes that "[t]hese acquittal rates appear very likely an important contributor to the high guilty plea rates for drunkenness" (*Courts of Trade*, 81). Recall that Vogel was studying a nonjury court, in which the defendant could better assess the likelihood of acquittal based on the court's past behavior.

A highly anecdotal account of court goings-on in Boston supplied this description of a drunkenness guilty plea in the police court in the early 1850s:

[S]ometimes the clerk will read the complaint to [the defendants], and sometimes he will omit it, simply holding the document in his hand, and saying to the prisoner:

"You was brought here for being drunk, last night! Was you drunk?"

If the prisoner says "Yes," the Clerk immediately adds, "The court find you guilty, and sentence you to pay a fine of three dollars and costs, for want of which you stand committed." (Fenner, *Raising the Veil*, 27)

Robert Hampel's findings in the courts of Salem confirm some aspects of this account. He reports that the court tried 43.3 percent of drunkenness defendants on the day of arrest and notes that "drunks could not afford the legal machinations used by sellers to prevent conviction" (Hampel, *Temperance*, 152).

14. Vogel, "Social Origins," 206. "It is also true," Vogel writes, that drunkenness, common-drunkard, and nightwalking offenses "had fewer direct consequences for 'the people's welfare' that was being shaped by economic growth" (ibid., 191).

15. Ibid., 195.

16. Vogel claims a significant role for another form of concession—the decision to retain a case in the police court rather than transfer it to the municipal court, where penalties perhaps were greater (ibid., 193). But Vogel provides no evidence as to how the decision to transfer a case was reached—whether it was at the discretion of the court or of the defendant herself or was reached automatically based on the crime charged or the sentence awarded in the police court. The only evidence she provides on the question is Barbara Hobson's argument that prostitution defendants *preferred* resolution of their cases in the municipal court, where they thought they could strike more favorable deals (ibid., 191 n.42). Because Vogel conducted her research only in the police court, she cannot tell us if defendants whose cases were resolved before the municipal court indeed fared worse. Moreover, she provides no evidence that the public was aware of whatever significance such transfers had, and public awareness is essential to her theory of episodic leniency.

17. Ibid., 184, 189, 195.

18. Ibid., 185 n.34. Although Vogel refers here to the reluctance of repeat offenders to plead guilty, the point may apply to more serious offenders, whether or not they had a record.

19. Ibid., 234. See also pp. 235–36, where Vogel repeats the claim that plea bargaining was "cognoscible."

20. McConville and Mirsky, "Rise of Guilty Pleas," 466.

21. Vogel, "Social Origins," 194.

22. Ibid., 194–95.

23. In any event, Vogel's evidence of mirroring is both limited to two crimes—larceny and assault and battery—and rather hard to interpret and to evaluate. See ibid., 195, table 13.

24. Ibid., 194; see *Selections from the Court Reports.*

25. Vogel, "Social Origins," 194–95. Vogel twice notes Gill's use of this word, but neither time cites a page (ibid.; see also Vogel, *Courts of Trade*, 85).

26. See *Selections from the Court Reports*, 78, 171.

27. Ibid., 41.

28. Vogel, "Social Origins," 206.

29. *Order for Committee of Asahel Huntington: Report*, H. Doc. No. 1499, at 2 (Mass. 1844), on file with the Massachusetts Archives.

30. The committee's report identifies Washburn as an "Esquire" from Lynn, a town in Essex County, which was within Huntington's jurisdiction. See *Case of Asahel Huntington: Report*, H. Doc. No. 4, at 3 (Mass. 1845).

31. The *Courier* claimed to have the largest circulation of any paper printed in Lowell. See "The List of Letters," *Lowell Daily Courier*, September 30, 1845, 2.

32. "Letters from the Editor.—No. 7," *Lowell Daily Courier*, January 20, 1844, 2; see also "The District Attorney," *Lowell Daily Courier*, July 13, 1844, 2, which is a reprint of an article from the *Salem Register*; "District Attorney Huntington," *Lowell Daily Courier*, December 26, 1844, 2; "House," *Lowell Daily Courier*, January 9, 1845, 2; "In the House," *Lowell Daily Courier*, March 14, 1844, 2; "In the Senate," *Lowell Daily Courier*, January 20, 1844, 2; "Letters from the Editor.—No. 6," *Lowell Courier*, January 14, 1845, 2; "Massachusetts Legislature," *Lowell Daily Courier*, March 16, 1844, 2; "Singular Proceedings," *Lowell Daily Courier*, January 23, 1844, 2.

33. "Letters from the Editor.—No. 7," *Lowell Daily Courier*, January 20, 1844, 2.

34. "In the Senate," *Lowell Daily Courier*, January 20, 1844, 2.

35. "Singular Proceedings," *Lowell Daily Courier*, January 23, 1844, 2.

36. See "In the House," *Lowell Daily Courier*, March 14, 1844, 2; "Massachusetts Legislature," *Lowell Daily Courier*, March 16, 1844, 2.

37. "The District Attorney," *Lowell Daily Courier*, July 13, 1844, 2.

38. Ibid.

39. "District Attorney Huntington," *Lowell Daily Courier*, December 26, 1844, 2.

40. "Letters from the Editor.—No. 6," *Lowell Courier*, January 14, 1845, 2.

41. Nineteenth-century newspapers are not generally indexed, so the task of surveying the century's newspapers for signs of public awareness of plea bargaining was quite labor-intensive. Several of my research assistants scrolled through dozens of reels of microfilmed newspapers and made copies of all news items that touched on any of the topics relevant to this study. The search focused on Middlesex County, but included as well many newspapers from outside the county. As a survey of the entire century was impossible, students focused their efforts on time spans critical to different parts of this history. Their efforts produced about 2,200 photocopied pages, which I have read and incorporated here. The newspapers studied include:

Boston Commonwealth	1889 (whole year)
Boston Evening Transcript	Jan.–Oct. 1880
	Jan. 1885
	Jan.–Feb. 1890
	Jan.–Mar. 1895
Boston Globe	Jan.–May 1879
Cambridge Herald	Jan.–Mar. 1848
Cambridge Owl	Apr.–Oct. 1848
Cambridge Palladium	Jan.–May 1843
Cambridge Tribune	1882–early 1885 (whole years)
Lowell Courier / Daily	June 1835–1838; 1840–1842 (whole years);
Courier	1843–1845 (selected times)
Lowell Journal	1847 (whole year)
	1848 (most of year)
Salem Gazette	Jan.–Aug. 1837
Springfield Daily Republican	Jan. 1865–May 1866
Voice of Industry / New Era	May 1845–Aug. 1848
of Industry (Lowell)	

My research assistants conducted a similar page-by-page search of various nineteenth-century law journals.

42. See *Lowell Courier*, September 19, 1837, 2, which noted, "[w]e understand . . . that nearly all the individuals indicted at the June Term, for breach of the license law, have submitted, and paid their fines and costs." Likewise, the *Salem Gazette* (December 27, 1836, 3) reported that "[s]everal others . . . who were indicted for breaches of the License Law, came into Court, and pleaded that they would not contend with the Commonwealth; and agreed not to sell any more spirits."

43. Among these few are repeated references made by the *Boston Globe*'s court reporter during the last quarter of the century to plea bargaining in drunkenness cases. It appears that the regularity with which accused drunks pled guilty and paid a standard three-dollar fine had become somewhat of a public joke. See, e.g., "Municipal Court—Judge May," *Boston Daily Globe*, April 4, 1879, 1, which commented that "[a]ll the [drunkenness defendants] exhibited a commendable resignation, and took their little fine of $3 and costs in a beautiful and touching way"; and "Municipal Court—Parmenter, J.," *Boston Daily Globe*, March 19, 1879, 1, which observed that "[e]leven simple drunks compounded for their sins on the ordinary terms."

44. See "Coroner's Inquisition," *Lowell Journal*, March 24, 1848, 4; "Examination of Barney Goulding on the Charge of Murdering His Wife," *Lowell Journal*, March 31, 1848, 1; "Police Court," *Lowell Journal*, March 31, 1848, 1.

45. Between Monday, October 13, and Friday, October 17, 1845, the *Courier* printed at least five substantial items on temperance, two of which were a full column or almost that in length.

46. "Midnight Robber Arrested," *Lowell Courier*, April 3, 1841, 2. The newspaper added that the result "was not satisfactory to many people."

47. *Lowell Courier*, April 10, 1841, 2. The constable was fined fifty dollars and costs (*Lowell Courier*, July 3, 1841, 2). Roger Lane reports, on the basis of other sources, that "there was no outcry" about the constable's actions (Lane, *Policing the City*, 57). He adds that "[t]he commonwealth also offered rewards, several of which went to [the constable]" (ibid., 259 n.57). The statutes Lane cites for support, however, have no relation to the case.

48. See "Compromising Crime," Boston *Daily Evening Traveller*, April 12, 1866, 1.

49. "Crime and Criminals, Law and Justice in New-York," *New York Times*, January 7, 1865, 4.

50. The *Times* printed this unflattering notice of plea bargaining in 1869:
[The district attorney may] accept a plea from a prisoner guilty of an offence many degrees lower in grade than that charged in the indictment by the Grand Jury.

This latter course has been pursued in this City hundreds of times, and criminals who, before a jury, might have been doomed to prison for a long term of years, have often, upon the direct invitation of the District-Attorney, pleaded guilty to an offence which simply secured them in confinement for months. A power so absolute is liable to be abused. ("Concerning Crime," *New York Times*, February 12, 1869, 1)

The next month, complaining of "the great army of arrested criminals left totally unaccounted for by the records," the *Times* surmised that "[e]ither the Police are constantly making large numbers of the most unwarranted arrests, or they and the judicial authorities are continually and unblushingly engaged in compounding felonies" ("City Crime," *New York Times*, March 26, 1869, 8). Eric Monkkonen ("American State," 529) quotes a similar sentiment in a *New York Times* editorial of 1866. In "The O'Hara Tragedy" (*New York Times*, April 22, 1873, 5), the *Times* reported a charge bargain in a murder case without editorial comment.

51. Ramsey, "Discretionary Power." Later in the same article (still in draft form as this book goes to print), Ramsey also surveys negative press accounts of plea bargaining by the New York district attorney.

52. See Wilbur R. Miller, *Cops and Bobbies*, 79, which quotes from the *New York Times*. Justin Miller ("Compromise of Criminal Cases," 4–5 n.16) quoted from a 1924 Massachusetts government report: "It seems to be a customary practice of winning favor with constituents to save them from the consequences of their illegal acts" (quoting *The Report of the Governor's Committee on Motor Traffic*, H. Doc. No. 1737 [Mass. 1924], reprinted in *Mass. L.Q.* [July 1924], pp. 1, 10).

53. "Massachusetts Temperance Alliance," *Boston Evening Transcript*, January 7, 1885, 8.

54. Letter from John A. Fitch to Asahel Huntington (January 11, 1843), on file with the Massachusetts Archives, contained in *Commonwealth v. Moses Phipps & Benjamin Phipps*, Middlesex Ct. C.P. File Papers (June 1843).

55. *Phipps & Phipps*, Middlesex Ct. C.P. File Papers. Eight witnesses testified before the grand jury.

56. Sol Wachtler (*After the Madness*, 292) claims credit for one version of the famous quip.

57. Chaplin, "Reform," 191.

58. It is interesting that another of the very few cases I have noticed in which citizens asked the district attorney to take action against a local liquor dealer also ended in a failure of the grand jury to indict. See *Commonwealth v. Manley Richardson*, Middlesex Ct. C.P. File Papers (June 1843), on file with the Massachusetts Archives. The case files contain a letter of complaint and a list of witnesses bearing on the rum-selling activities of a local innkeeper as well as documents suggesting that six witnesses testified before the grand jury.

59. See Act of May 16, 1856, ch. 173, § 1, 1856 Mass. Acts 98, 98–99. The office of attorney general apparently became elective in 1855 (see Mass. Const. art. XVII [ratified May 23, 1855]), though William Davis put the date at 1858 (see Davis, *Bench and Bar*, vol. 1, 290).

60. See Act of June 19, 1869, ch. 415, § 60, 1869 Mass. Acts 706, 723, which stated that "the prosecuting officer . . . shall not enter a *nolle prosequi* [in any case arising under this act] except with the concurrence of the court." See also Act of April 20, 1855, ch. 215, § 35, 1855 Mass. Acts 623, 641, which provided that "a *nolle prosequi* shall not be entered by the prosecuting officer [in any case arising under this act], excepting with the concurrence of the court." The 1855 reenactment followed a decision by the Supreme Judicial Court in 1854 declaring unconstitutional certain search-and-seizure provisions of the 1852 prohibition law (see *Fisher v. McGirr*, 67 Mass. [1 Gray] 1, 21 [1854]).

61. See Chapter 3, Notes 43–45, and accompanying text.

62. Act of May 12, 1865, ch. 223, § 1, 1865 Mass. Acts 617, 617.

63. See Act of June 19, 1885, ch. 359, § 1, 1885 Mass. Acts 817, 817, which provided that "[n]o case in court for the violation of . . . any . . . act . . . relating to intoxicating liquors shall be placed on file or disposed of, except by trial," except with the court's concurrence. See also Act of June 19, 1869, ch. 415, § 60, 1869 Mass. Acts 706, 723–24, which provided that "[n]o case in court for the violation of . . . this act . . . shall be laid on file or disposed of except by trial," except with the concurrence of the court.

The 1852 ban on nol prosses, reenacted in 1855, as well as the 1865 ban on putting cases on file, remained in place until both were repealed when the legislature briefly replaced the prohibition law with a license law in 1868. See Act of April 30, 1868, ch. 141, § 26, 1868 Mass. Acts 107, 115. Both acts were reinstated in 1869, when the state returned to a prohibition regime. See this chapter, Notes 60, 63. In 1875 the state reverted to a license-law scheme, and both were repealed (see Act of April 5, 1875, ch. 99, §§ 1–6, 1875 Mass. Acts 664; Act of March 9, 1875, ch. 43, § 1, 1875 Mass. Acts 631, 631). When the legislature reinstated the ban on filing cases in 1885, it made no direct reference to the prosecutor's nol pros power, but it did provide that no liquor case "shall be placed on file *or disposed of, except by trial,*" without the court's concurrence, seemingly constraining the nol pros power as well (Act of June 19, 1885, ch. 359, § 1, 1885 Mass. Acts 817, 817; emphasis added).

Hence there were two periods between 1866 and the end of the century during which prosecutors apparently had the freedom to nol pros liquor cases or place them on file—from 1868 to 1869 and from 1875 to 1885. But in both these periods, the governing liquor law granted broad sentencing discretion to the judge. The 1868 law provided that "[a]ny person convicted of a violation of any of the provisions of this act, shall be punished by a fine not exceeding five hundred dollars, and confinement at hard labor in the house of correction not exceeding six months" (Act of April 30, 1868, ch. 141, § 18, 1868 Mass. Acts 107, 112). By giving judges such wide sentencing discretion, this law—like most penal provisions in Massachusetts—deprived prosecutors of the sentencing control that they needed to charge bargain effectively.

The 1875 law, however, arguably opened a window for prosecutorial charge bargaining. It provided for a punishment of "a fine not less than fifty nor more than five hundred dollars, or imprisonment not less than one nor more than six months, or by both such fine and imprisonment" (Act of April 5, 1875, ch. 99, § 13, 1875 Mass. Acts 664, 668). By establishing a minimum fine, this law might seem to have created an opportunity for prosecutors to bring multiple counts to gain leverage for a charge bargain. But it is unlikely the tactic would have worked without judicial participation. Most defendants would have been reluctant to plead guilty to a liquor offense that carried up to six months' imprisonment without some assurance from the judge that he would not impose time. During the October 1880 term of court—the only term of court I studied closely during the decade this statute was in effect—I observed no charge bargaining in liquor cases. I also observed none in the June 1885 term, when this law was just being abolished.

64. See this chapter, Note 59; Act of March 14, 1832, ch. 130, § 8, 1832 Mass. Acts 396, 403–04; Vogel, "Social Origins," 218–19; Vogel, *Courts of Trade*, 136.

65. S. Doc. No. 68, at 7, 9 (Mass. 1844), which reprints the letter of J. H. Clifford, January 20, 1843 [sic]. Clifford became attorney general in 1849 and governor in 1853 (see Davis, *Bench and Bar*, vol. 1, p. 290).

66. See Chapter 2, Note 46.

67. See Chapter 2, Note 47.

NOTES TO CHAPTER 7

1. See Chapter 2, Notes 67–70, and accompanying text.

2. See Feeley, "Transformation of the Criminal Process"; Feeley and Lester,

"Legal Complexity"; Langbein, "Understanding," 262–65. J. M. Beattie (*Crime and the Courts*, 336–37 and n.52) observes that only about 1.5 percent of larceny defendants pled guilty in the courts of Surrey between 1722 and 1802 and concludes that "[t]here was no plea bargaining in felony cases in the eighteenth century."

3. See Feeley, "Transformation of the Criminal Process," 190, 202–5; Langbein, "Understanding," 262–65. Feeley reports that through the first half of the nineteenth century, a single judge and jury in London's Old Bailey court could hear between two and a half and almost five trials per day. See Feeley, "Transformation of the Criminal Process," 203, figure 5.

4. See Feeley, "Transformation of the Criminal Process," 199, figure 3, 203, figure 5. Feeley, however, might object to setting his findings in this light. Even as he emphasizes the increasing length and complexity of the average trial, a trend that moved almost in step with the advance of plea bargaining (ibid., 199, figure 3, 202–18), he disclaims any role for "increased case load pressures" in the rise of plea bargaining (ibid., 204). But longer trials surely increased caseload pressure. Feeley's point is apparently that we should seek out the mechanisms and not merely the motives of plea bargaining's rise.

5. Even then, they appeared only in a limited form. See Prosecution of Offences Act, 1879, 42 and 43 Vict., ch. 22; Kurland and Waters, "Public Prosecutions in England," 550–62.

6. See Feeley, "Transformation of the Criminal Process," 195, figure 1. Feeley measured counsel representation at the Old Bailey at twenty-year intervals. Except for the anomalous year 1795, when lawyers appeared for the prosecution in over seventy percent of cases, the figure did not exceed (or often approach) twenty percent until 1855.

7. See *Regina v. Dunn*, 1 C. and K. N.P.R. 730, 731 (Q.B. 1843); *Rex v. Cranmer*, 88 Eng. Rep. 1578 (K.B. 1702); Chitty, *Practical Treatise*, *479.

8. In 1715 thirty-six percent of prosecutions ended in acquittals; in 1774 the rate was forty-three percent. See *Proceedings of the Sessions of the Peace* (OBSP). I am excluding from these figures cases that ended in acquittal because the prosecutor never appeared for trial. I have counted as guilty verdicts those cases in which the jury convicted the defendant of a lesser crime than that charged in the indictment. Figures cited for 1715 represent every case heard at the Old Bailey that year; those for 1774 represent only two of the eight sessions for that year (April and September).

These figures and others I cite throughout this section may differ from seemingly similar statistics of business at the Old Bailey that I presented in an earlier article. See George Fisher, "Jury's Rise," 638–50. Because my aim there was to focus on the decision making of juries, I excluded from consideration cases not decided by the jury either because the defendant pled guilty or because the judge directed a verdict of not guilty, or might have done so (see ibid., 640 n.295). In particular, the rate of acquittals cited in the text here is far higher than that I cited in the earlier article (ibid., 641 n.299), because in a good many cases that ended in acquittals, it is unclear whether the judge or jury decided the outcome. I therefore excluded these cases from my earlier study.

9. See, e.g., *Rex v. Jeremiah Stamford, Proceedings of the Sessions of the Peace,* 184 (February 23, 1780, No. 3, Pt. 3), which reports that "[t]he prosecutrixes were called but not appearing . . . . Not Guilty"; *Rex v. Sarah Jackson, Proceedings of the Sessions of the Peace,* 4 (January 14–17, 1715), in which the narrative states, "[b]ut there being no Prosecution, she was acquitted."

10. David D. Friedman ("Making Sense of English Law Enforcement," 486–92) discusses the significance of the practice of "compounding" felonies, by which prosecutor and defendant essentially settled their case out of court. Norma Landau recently published the results of her study of the prosecution of minor assault crimes at the Middlesex (England) quarter sessions in the mid- and late eighteenth century (see Landau, "Indictment for Fun and Profit"). She found clear evidence that in the great majority of assault cases, the defendant paid cash to "satisfy" the prosecutor, who was the private crime victim. The justices used various means to persuade reluctant defendants to reach private financial settlements with the prosecutor. After settling with the prosecutor, most defendants pled guilty, and the court then assessed (but did not always collect) a token fine (ibid., 515–29).

11. See Blackstone, *Commentaries,* vol. 4, *363–64; Fisher, "Making Sense of English Law Enforcement," 510–11.

12. See Blackstone, *Commentaries,* vol. 4, *133–34.

13. Cottu, *L'Administration de la Justice Criminelle,* 99. I thank Al Alschuler for pointing me to this account.

14. See *Proceedings of the Sessions of the Peace* (OBSP). On the *Sessions Paper,* see generally Devereaux, "City and the Sessions Paper"; and Langbein, "Understanding," 267–72. Both Feeley and Langbein based their research on case accounts in the *Sessions Paper.*

15. Feeley, "Transformation of the Criminal Process," 203 figure 5.

16. Such an explosion came later—in the 1810s and 1820s. There seems to be little evidence of sharp growth in civil caseloads before 1800. See Brooks, "Interpersonal Conflict and Social Tension," 364.

17. See Fisher, "Birth of the Prison," 1252 n.62 table 5.

18. Ibid., 1276.

19. Ibid., 1265, table 7.

20. See, e.g., *Manchester Mercury,* January 25, 1791, 4, which reported in summary fashion on the results of cases heard at a recent sitting of the court of quarter sessions.

21. See Fisher, "Birth of the Prison," 1258–67, 1271–76.

22. Ibid., 1260–66.

23. See Friedman and Percival, *Roots of Justice.*

24. As I explained in Chapter 5, Note 29, the surviving records do not permit a complete analysis in 1910.

25. Friedman and Percival, *Roots of Justice,* 179.

26. See Act of May 1, 1851, ch. 29, § 598, 1851 Cal. Stat. 212, 279, which states that "[n]either the Attorney General [n]or the District attorney shall hereafter discontinue or abandon a prosecution for a public offence, except as provided in the last section." The previous section provided that "[t]he Court may, either of its own motion or upon the application of the District attorney, and in furtherance of justice, order any action or indictment to be dismissed; but in such case the reasons of the dismissal shall be set forth in the order, which must be entered on the minutes" (ibid., § 597).

27. Friedman and Percival, *Roots of Justice*, 177–78.

28. Ibid., 178.

29. The Middlesex figures for 1880 are projected from a study of one of the three terms of the court.

30. The *Massachusetts Lawyer's Diary* for 1898 (p. 15) identified Frederick N. Wier as the Middlesex district attorney and George A. Sanderson as his only assistant. The records of the Middlesex Superior Court for 1910 noted the appointment of Henry C. Sawyer as "Second Assistant District attorney" of Middlesex, but gave no hint whether the office was newly created or whether there might also have been a third assistant district attorney (Middlesex Super. Ct. R. Book, 325 [1910]).

31. Friedman and Percival, *Roots of Justice*, 50.

32. Ibid., 50–51.

33. See Chapter 2, Notes 14–19, and accompanying text.

34. See Table 7.3, p. 163.

35. See Table 5.2, p. 117.

36. See Figure 5.1 at page 122.

37. See Friedman and Percival, *Roots of Justice*, 46–48.

38. See Friedman, "Civil Wrongs," 359.

39. See Chapter 4, Note 28.

40. See Chapter 4, Note 16, and accompanying text.

41. See Friedman and Percival, *Roots of Justice*, 170.

42. Ibid., 171. Friedman and Percival report that at least one-quarter of the defendants in their sample had appointed counsel, but they cannot fix the proportion precisely.

43. See Table 4.1 (p. 97) and accompanying text.

44. See Tables 4.2 and 4.3 (pp. 98 and 99) and accompanying text.

45. See Friedman and Percival, *Roots of Justice*, 172 and 171 n.60, which quotes a 1926 study concluding that most assigned lawyers were either young and inexperienced or older but unable to attract better-paying business. Although it is difficult to compare my figures directly with Friedman and Percival's, it appears that at the beginning of their period, the rate of acquittal at trial was considerably higher in Alameda than in Middlesex, but that by the end of their period, Middlesex defendants fared better:

Verdicts at Trial

	ALAMEDA COUNTY				MIDDLESEX COUNTY		
YEARS	GUILTY OF CHARGED OFFENSE	GUILTY OF LESSER OFFENSE	NOT GUILTY	YEAR	GUILTY OF CHARGED OFFENSE	GUILTY OF LESSER OFFENSE	NOT GUILTY
1880–1889	36%	15%	39%	1880	64%	5%	23%
1890–1899	33%	17%	40%	1890	60%	5%	33%
1900–1910	42%	16%	30%	1900	44%	8%	45%
				1910	44%	9%	47%

SOURCES: Friedman and Percival, *Roots of Justice*, 182; Middlesex Super. Ct. R. Books; Middlesex Super. Ct. Docket Books.

Percentages may not add up to one hundred, because some trials ended in hung juries. My figures for 1880 represent only the October session of the court, and those for 1890 only the February session.

46. See Table 7.2 (p. 162) and accompanying text.

47. See Friedman and Percival, *Roots of Justice*, 43–44. Between 1880 and 1910, only about eight percent of cases began by way of indictment by a grand jury.

48. Ibid., 158.

49. See Mather, *Plea Bargaining or Trial?*, 50, which cites the Bureau of Criminal Statistics, *Felony Defendants Disposed of in California Courts: References Tables* (1970) and Carter, *Limits of Order*. Mather notes that at the time of her own study in the early 1970s, such deals were not common in Los Angeles.

50. See *Cal. Penal Code* §§ 666, 667 (Bancroft, 1885); *Ex parte* Gutierrez, 45 Cal. 429, 430 (1873).

51. See *Cal. Penal Code* § 666(1).

52. Ibid. § 667(2).

53. Friedman and Percival make it clear that the prosecutor had the discretion to charge or not to charge prior offenses (Friedman and Percival, *Roots of Justice*, 170).

54. See Moley, "Vanishing Jury"; and McConville and Mirsky, "Rise of Guilty Pleas." McConville and Mirsky are in the process of expanding their research into a book-length study.

55. See McConville and Mirsky, "Rise of Guilty Pleas," 466. The authors do not report the corresponding figures for other years.

56. See Moley, "Vanishing Jury," 111. Moley's categories are "Guilty to offense charged" and "Guilty to other offense." It is reasonable to suppose that "other offense" refers to a lesser offense. Moley did not clearly separate statistics for New York City from those for the rest of the state. In a table on p. 111 of the article, under

a column labeled "total for state," he noted that fifty-eight percent of guilty pleas statewide were to an offense other than that charged. New York City probably dominates this statistic, however, as in three other categories—"large upstate cities," "small cities," and "rural"—the proportion of guilty pleas made to an offense other than that charged was thirty-two percent, twenty-seven percent, and twenty-two percent respectively.

57. See Table 7.2 (page 162) and accompanying text.

58. The highest figure I found was a little over eight percent in 1859.

59. See Chapter 1, Notes 81–95, and accompanying text.

60. See McConville and Mirsky, "Rise of Guilty Pleas," 466.

61. See Moley, "Vanishing Jury," 108.

62. McConville and Mirsky do report that the annual caseload of the Court of General Sessions, New York City's major criminal court, increased from 268 indictments in 1839 to 1,323 in 1865 (McConville and Mirsky, "Rise of Guilty Pleas," 463). But they do not specify the size of the district attorney's staff and do not say whether prosecutors worked full- or part-time.

63. Moley, "Vanishing Jury," 108, 111.

64. Act of March 21, 1801, ch. 58, §§ 1, 2, 1801 *N.Y. Stat.* 97, 97. A penalty statute of 1813 (Act of March 19, 1813, ch. 29, § 3, 1813 *N.Y. Stat.* 407) left intact most of the scheme laid out in the 1801 law. The 1813 law complicated the penalties for arson, establishing death as the penalty for burning an inhabited dwelling house (ibid. § 3, at 407), and imprisonment for not more than fourteen years as the penalty for burning any other house, barn, public building, or mill (ibid. § 3, at 407). And it established differing penalties for several forms of forgery (ibid. § 3, at 408–9).

65. § 5, 1813 *N.Y. Stat.* at 409; § 4, 1801 *N.Y. Laws* at 97.

66. See *People v. Porter*, 4 Park. 524, 526 (N.Y. Oyer & Terminer 1860), which reports the opinion of a single judge of a court of oyer and terminer that, "[a]s I have before said, a nolle prosequi may be to the whole indictment, or to the whole of any one or more of several counts, but cannot be to a part of any one count."

67. See § 5, 1813 *N.Y. Stat.* at 409; § 4, 1801 *N.Y. Stat.* at 97.

68. See 2 *N.Y. Rev. Stat.* pt. 4, ch. 1, tit. 3, § 1, at 655 (Packard and Van Benthuysen 1829).

69. McConville and Mirsky, "Rise of Guilty Pleas," 466; Moley, "Vanishing Jury," 108.

70. See 2 *N.Y. Rev. Stat.* pt. 4, ch. 1, tit. 3, § 21, at 669.

71. See 2 *N.Y. Rev. Stat.* pt. 4, ch. 2, tit. 4, § 51, at 728, which states, "[w]hen by law an offence comprises different degrees, an indictment may contain counts for the different degrees of the same offence, or for any of such degrees"; cf. *People v. Adler*, 140 N.Y. 331, 333–37 (1893); *Hawker v. People*, 30 N.Y. 487, 489–90 (1878); *People v. Rynders*, 12 Wend. 425, 429–30 (N.Y. Sup. Ct. 1834); and *Kane v. People*, 8 Wend. 203, 210–11 (N.Y. 1831).

72. *People v. Porter*, 4 Park. 524, 526 (N.Y. Oyer & Terminer 1860).

73. See 2 *N.Y. Rev. Stat.* pt. 4, ch. 1, tit. 1, § 1, at 656; tit. 3, § 9, at 668; § 21, at 669; § 57, at 678; § 42, at 675; § 20, at 662–63.

74. "Drafting a New Penal Law in New York: An Interview with Richard Denzer," *Buff. L. Rev.* 18 (1969), 258.

75. See 2 *N.Y. Rev. Stat.* pt. 4, ch. 1, tit. 3, § 21, at 669; tit. 7, § 3(2), at 698.

76. The code provided that "[u]pon an indictment for [a broad category of offenses], the jury may find the accused not guilty of the offence . . . charged in the indictment, and may find such accused person guilty of . . . an attempt to commit such offence" (ibid. tit. 7, § 27, at 702). The jury's freedom to find the defendant guilty of attempt even though attempt was not charged is a strong indication that attempt is to be deemed a lesser-included offense of the crime charged.

77. See McConville and Mirsky, "Rise of Guilty Pleas," 466–67.

78. The first of these provisions imposed a minimum ten-year term on any person who, having been convicted in the past of a crime punishable by state prison time, was later convicted of a crime punishable by more than five years in state prison (see 2 *N.Y. Rev. Stat.* pt. 4, ch. 1, tit. 7, § 8(1), at 699). The second provided that any person who once was convicted of either petty larceny or an attempt to commit any crime punishable by state prison and who then was convicted of any crime punishable by a term in state prison less than life "shall be sentenced to imprisonment in such prison, for the longest term prescribed" by statute (ibid. § 9(2), at 699–700). The reference to those once convicted of an attempt is particularly significant given the use prosecutors made of attempt convictions in the course of charge bargaining.

79. *California Penal Code* §§ 666, 667; *Ex parte Gutierrez,* 45 Cal. 429, 430 (1873).

80. See *Commonwealth v. Gosselin,* 365 Mass. 116, 120–21 (1974), which relies on holdings of courts of other states and on analogous Massachusetts cases; see also this chapter, Note 76 and accompanying text.

81. A habitual-offender law of that year imposed a twenty-five-year term for offenders who twice previously served prison terms of three or more years (see Act of June 16, 1887, ch. 435, § 1, 1887 Mass. Acts 1098, 1098). In 1890 one of the proponents of the law complained that prosecutors had used it only three times (see "Twenty-Years' Sentence," *Boston Evening Transcript,* January 18, 1890, 9, letter of Clement K. Fay).

82. See Act of March 16, 1805, ch. 143, § 3, 1804 Mass. Acts 240, 241–42.

83. 2 *N.Y. Rev. Stat.* pt. 4, ch. 2, tit. 4, § 54, at 728.

84. 1 Hill 377 (N.Y. Sup. Ct. 1841).

85. Ibid., 405.

86. See Chapter 2, Notes 59–66, and accompanying text.

87. Act of May 22, 1852, ch. 322, § 13, 1852 Mass. Acts 257, 257.

88. See *Fourth Report of the Commissioners.* The proposed code of criminal procedure apparently was primarily Graham's work and became known as the Graham Code. See *People v. Willis,* 52 N.Y.S. 808, 809 (Sup. Ct. 1898).

89. *Fourth Report of the Commissioners* § 754, at 196; § 753, at 196.

90. Ibid., lxix.

91. *Code of Criminal Procedure*, 343.

92. Ibid.; see also *People v. McLeod*, 1 Hill 377, 405–06 (N.Y. Sup. Ct. 1841), which announced the holding to which the code authors referred.

93. *Code of Criminal Procedure*, 343.

94. "Concerning Crime," *New York Times*, February 12, 1869, 1. Alexis Haller, one of my research assistants, found this important evidence.

95. Ibid.

96. *Twenty-First Annual Report of the Prison Association of New York*, 134.

97. See Moley, "Vanishing Jury," 108.

98. McConville and Mirsky, "Rise of Guilty Pleas," 466; Moley, "Vanishing Jury," 111.

99. The legislature made only minor modifications to the Graham Code, and they are not important here. See Act of June 14, 1881, ch. 504, §§ 671–672, 1881 N.Y. Laws 164, 164–65; *People v. Willis*, 52 N.Y.S. 808, 809 (Sup. Ct. 1898).

100. Moley, "Vanishing Jury," 111.

101. Ibid., 108.

102. Ibid., 100–101.

NOTES TO CHAPTER 8

1. As Milton Heumann writes, "it is certainly not the most pleasurable of experiences to have a higher body produce a publicly available, written reversal of one's decisions (Heumann, *Plea Bargaining*, 144). Friedman and Percival break down the grounds for appeal of Alameda County cases between 1870 and 1910. Two-thirds of claimed errors can be traced to judicial rulings on evidence or law or to the judge's jury instructions (Friedman and Percival, *Roots of Justice*, 265 table 8.4).

2. See Chapter 6, Notes 65–66, and accompanying text.

3. See Ferdinand, *Boston's Courts*, 128, 130.

4. See Bolster, "Criminal Appeals," 16, unnumbered page opposite page 16.

5. See Friedman and Percival, *Roots of Justice*, 262, table 8.2.

6. Ibid.

7. *O'Hara v. People*, 3 N.W. 161, 161 (Mich. 1879) (emphasis added). The only similar case I have seen arose in the Lowell, Massachusetts, police court in 1841. Catherine Fitzgerald, charged with liquor-selling, objected that she could not be held responsible for a misdemeanor committed in her husband's presence. "Of this His Honor was not quite certain," the *Lowell Courier* reported, "but would not pass sentence till she would agree *not to appeal* . . . but would hold her to answer further, and her liege lord also. Kate paid the fine, rather than her 'man' should go to the Grand Jury" ("Lowell Police Court," *Lowell Courier*, May 11, 1841, 2). That is, the magis-

trate gave the defendant the option of paying a fine on the charged offense and forgoing her right to appeal or being bound over together with her husband to face higher charges before a grand jury. True, this was a proceeding in police court, and the defendant's appeal right consisted of a de novo proceeding in superior court rather than an appeal on questions of law. But as the magistrate apparently was worried that a higher tribunal would spy his mistake on a legal question, this case perhaps is an example of judges' general aversion to reversals.

    8. O'Brien, "Crime and Criminal Law," 33, 34, which states, "[f]ear of reversal in the Supreme Court compels trial judges to resolve doubtful questions as to the admission of testimony and instructions to the jury in favor of the defendant, for the Government has no right of appeal."

    9. Moley, "Vanishing Jury," 103.

    10. See Alschuler, "Plea Bargaining History," 38–39. The defendants' new procedural protections fell into two categories: those that expanded the substantive rights that may become the basis for appeal, including cases that required state courts to exclude illegally seized evidence; and those that directly expanded the opportunity for appeal by guaranteeing indigent defendants appellate counsel.

    11. Albert Alschuler (ibid., 38–39) writes that "[b]y increasing the likelihood of appeal, these decisions [granting defendants greater procedural protections] encouraged prosecutors to magnify the concessions granted to defendants in exchange for guilty pleas that would effectively foreclose appellate review of most issues."

    12. Ibid., 40. The most important of the Supreme Court's early decisions on plea bargaining appeared in 1970 and 1971. See *Santobello v. New York*, 404 U.S. 257 (1971); *North Carolina v. Alford*, 400 U.S. 25 (1970); *Parker v. North Carolina*, 397 U.S. 790 (1970); *McMann v. Richardson*, 397 U.S. 759 (1970); *Brady v. United States*, 397 U.S. 742 (1970).

    13. See Galanter, "Reading the Landscape," 38.

    14. See Chapter 5, Notes 39–41, and accompanying text.

    15. Pound, "The Judicial Office Today," 732.

    16. Of course, an *Alford* plea, in which the defendant adheres to her claim of innocence even while allowing that the government has enough evidence to prove her guilt beyond a reasonable doubt (*Alford*, 400 U.S. at 38), does not meet this condition. But *Alford* pleas represent a tiny proportion of all plea bargains.

    17. By the system's "legitimacy," I mean the public's perception that the system is, on the whole, doing justice.

    18. Kalven and Zeisel, *American Jury*, 30–31; see also 20–22, where they present data to support the quoted conclusions.

    19. Ibid., 21–22. Kalven and Zeisel based their work on close empirical study. A more abstract economist might object that a defendant's likelihood to plead guilty is largely a function of two variables—the chances of winning at trial and the size of the concession offered the defendant in exchange for his plea. In a world with equal access to information and untethered bargaining freedom, the prosecutor's offered

concession would expand with the likelihood of acquittal. The defendant's willingness to plead guilty therefore would remain about the same no matter how good or bad his case. See Sanchirico, "Character Evidence," 1255, n.70.

But bargaining freedom is probably not untethered. Assume, for example, that the defendant stands charged with a serious crime, but that the evidence against him is weak—so weak that he will refuse to plead guilty unless offered a sentence only one-third of that usually imposed for such crimes. The prosecutor may very well understand all this and yet feel unable, as a political matter, to reduce the sentencing recommendation to that degree. That is, prosecutors might prefer to risk losing a case after a hard-fought trial than to let the public perceive them as soft on crime.

20. Heumann, *Plea Bargaining*, 140.

21. The officers' actions in the King case so outraged the public, and particularly the African-American community, that any perceived compromise by the prosecution would have raised a political firestorm. Nor could the Los Angeles district attorney, who would soon face a reelection battle, have shown weakness in the Simpson case, in which his deputies claimed to have a "mountain of evidence." See David Margolick, "Judge Ito to Open Files on 10 Dismissed Jurors," *New York Times*, June 24, 1995, 6, which quotes deputy prosecutor Lisa Kahn. One of Simpson's defense lawyers later said the district attorney did offer a deal (Johnnie L. Cochran Jr. with Tim Rutten, *Journey to Justice* [1996], p. 253), but the district attorney denied the claim (Randall Kennedy, "Playing to the Crowd: Journey to Justice," *Los Angeles Times*, October 13, 1996, 4). These cases went to trial because the plea-bargaining system failed. As a result, the system was exposed to humiliation when the juries got such clear cases "wrong."

It is true that by withdrawing easy cases from the jury's consideration, plea bargaining (when working normally) both protects the jury from getting a clear case wrong *and* deprives it of the chance to get a clear case right. My argument assumes what to me (but perhaps not others) seems obvious: The damage done to the jury's legitimacy when it delivers a clearly mistaken verdict overwhelms the benefits of getting an easy case (or even many easy cases) right.

22. Kalven and Zeisel, *American Jury*, 31.

23. Charles Nesson, "Evidence or the Event?," 1369–70. Nesson was writing of the practice of granting a motion for a directed verdict: "The directed verdict permits the court to withhold from the jury those cases in which a finding of guilt or liability would be patently untenable in light of the case presented by the plaintiff. The trial judge allows a case to go to the jury only if the evidence suffices to support a verdict either way. Giving a case to the jury is tantamount to making a judgment that the jury cannot make an obvious error."

24. Not all lawyers for poor defendants were "public" defenders when these officials first appeared in the early twentieth century. I use the term because it is more familiar to modern ears than the arguably more accurate "institutional defenders."

25. For example, Samuel Barrows ("Introduction," in Follett, *Indeterminate*

Sentence, 5) wrote that "[t]he value of the indeterminate sentence as a protection to society lies in the fact that the prisoner is not released until it is deemed safe to discharge him." Charlton Lewis ("Indeterminate Sentence," 17) made a similar point in similar language. Seth Cary ("Prison Reform," 2) made the point more rhetorically: "if it be right to restrain one class [such as the idiotic or insane] so long as the disability continues, it must also be legitimate *to restrain all dangerous classes while the disability remains*. Therefore, it is the *right* and also the *duty* of the State to confine the criminal so long as he remains vicious."

26. The passing years brought the same verdict: Hence in 1899 the "Report of the Committee of the American Bar Association" (in Follett, *Indeterminate Sentence and the Parole Law*, 24, 26) concluded that "[s]trictly speaking, the right to impose [indeterminate] sentences does not exist in any State. Statutes permitting what are commonly called indeterminate sentences are such only in degree." In 1927 Clair Wilcox (*Parole of Adults*, 11) reached the same verdict: "[A]n absolutely indeterminate sentence . . . has never anywhere been enacted into law." And in 1937 the Harvard Law Review ("Legislation—Indeterminate Sentence Laws," 678) still could write: "The titles of [today's indeterminate sentence laws] are somewhat misleading because none of them provides for a truly indefinite sentence."

27. See Act of June 24, 1886, ch. 323, §§ 1–3, 1886 Mass. Acts 296, 296. New York's indeterminate sentencing law of 1877 was the nation's first substantial experiment with the concept, though Michigan had attempted a small-scale experiment in 1869. See Act of April 3, 1869, No. 145, §§ 4–5, 1869 Mich. Acts 264, 265–66, which provided that convicted adult prostitutes shall be punished by three years' imprisonment, but that they may be released "upon reformation, or marked good behavior" by the inspectors of the house of correction; see also Note 32 in this chapter.

28. To avoid this parenthetical in the future, and to avoid always putting "indeterminate sentence" in quotes, I will simply use the term indeterminate sentence with the understood qualification that there was no such thing in its pure form in American law.

29. § 1, 1886 Mass. Acts at 296.

30. "Indefinite Commitments," *Boston Evening Transcript*, January 30, 1890, 4.

31. In 1898 the legislature extended the reformatory's indeterminate sentencing structure to the Bridgewater State Farm (see Act of May 20, 1898, ch. 443, § 1, 1898 Mass. Acts 395, 395). In 1900 the state farm accounted for an additional six percent of all incarcerations and in 1910 for an additional ten percent. As virtually every sentence I saw to the state farm was for drunkenness, defendants sent there perhaps fell into a special class. Judges may have seen more sense in the ideal of the indeterminate sentence when the point of confinement was to cure the convict of an addiction.

32. In 1877 the New York legislature provided that judges would not set the length of sentences to the new reformatory at Elmira, but that convicts could not be

held beyond the maximum term specified by law for their crime (see Act of April 24, 1877, ch. 173, § 2, 1877 N.Y. Laws 186, 186).

33. Train, *Prisoner*, 165.

34. Ibid., 173. Train wrote: "Court officers . . . anxious that the particular [courtroom] to which they are assigned shall make as good a showing as possible in the number of cases disposed of . . . [contrast the] joys of Elmira . . . with other places of confinement."

35. In 1890 forty-six percent of those sent to the house of correction and forty-four percent of those sent to state prison had lost at trial. In 1896 these figures stood at thirty-four and eighty-six percent, respectively; in 1900, at sixteen and nineteen percent, respectively; and in 1910, at sixteen and twenty-six percent (see Middlesex Super. Ct. R. Books [February 1890, 1900]). The numbers in all categories declined between 1896 and 1900 as trials became rarer and guilty pleas more completely dominated dispositions (see Figure 4.1, p. 93).

36. See Act of May 26, 1894, ch. 440, § 1, 1894 Mass. Acts 492, 492.

37. See Lindsey, "Historical Sketch," 40.

38. Act of June 5, 1895, ch. 504, § 1, 1895 Mass. Acts 624, 624.

39. Ibid., § 2.

40. Ibid., § 1.

41. See Lindsey, "Historical Sketch," 102–5. In what seems to be a comprehensive review of indeterminate sentence laws, Edward Lindsey listed twenty-three states in which the judge determined a sentencing range (subject to a statutory maximum) within which the convict could receive parole. Although the range of discretion given the judge varied from state to state, I have excluded from my count one state (Indiana) that required the judge to set minimum and maximum sentences at the minimum and maximum defined by statute.

42. Even in absolute terms, the number of convicts sent to the state prison fell sharply between 1890 and 1900. For both 1890 and 1896, I studied only one term of court (of three). In the February 1890 term, the Middlesex Superior Court handed down sixteen state prison sentences. In October 1896, it imposed only seven. There were sixteen such sentences in all of 1900 and nineteen in all of 1910.

43. See Ruggles-Brise, *Some Observations*, 16; Lindsey, "Historical Sketch," 36.

44. See Figure 4.1, p. 93.

45. Act of April 25, 1898, ch. 371, 1898 Mass. Acts 312, 312.

46. See Act of April 6, 1909, ch. 120, § 2, 1909 N.H. Laws 460, 460.

47. Act of June 19, 1911, § 11, 1911 Pa. Laws 1055, 1058.

48. State of New Jersey, *Report of the Prison Inquiry Commission*, vol. 1, 62–63.

49. Train, *Prisoner*, 165; Train also noted that at Elmira, a convict "may reasonably expect to be discharged in fourteen months" (p. 179).

50. See Prison Association of New York, *Seventy-Second Annual Report*, 79.

51. "Topics of the Times," *New York Times*, June 9, 1923, 10. The previous year, the *Times* quoted the governor as saying, "Under the present law most prisoners

serving indeterminate sentences are now paroled on the expiration of their minimum term" ("Parole Bill Vetoed by Governor Miller," *New York Times* [April 16, 1922], 13). In 1924 it printed a letter in which the superintendent of the Institution for Defective Delinquents charged that "the Parole Boards seem to feel where the criminal has made a good institutional record, and has satisfactory arrangements as to work, &c., that he is entitled to receive parole at the expiration of his minimum sentence" ("Our Care of Criminals," *New York Times* [November 16, 1924], part 9, 12). And in 1926 the paper quoted Judge Charles C. Nott Jr. as saying that every prisoner is "'liberated almost as a matter of course on his minimum, without regard to the nature and gravity of his offense'" ("Darlings of Society," *New York Times* [April 29, 1926], 22).

52. "State Board Tells of Parole System," *New York Times* (June 12, 1926), 7 (emphasis added). The article paraphrases Board Chairman George W. Benham and Board Member Alexander Konta.

53. "Parole Board Hits Critics and Courts," *New York Times*, August 20, 1926, 8.

54. "The Parole Report," *New York Times*, December 14, 1926, 26.

55. 2 *New York Ann. Consolidated Laws*, Prison Law § 214, at 1664 (Banks, 2d ed., 1923).

56. *Report of the Crime Commission of New York State* (advance copy), 22 (1927).

57. "Legislation—Indeterminate Sentencing Laws," 683.

58. Newman, *Sourcebook*, 37.

59. As one observer wrote in 1925, "If prison and parole authorities tend to regard an indeterminate sentence with maximum and minimum expressed as practically equivalent to a definite sentence for the minimum period, it is not surprising that the prisoner should take it that way" (Lindsey, "Historical Sketch," 77).

During my time as an assistant district attorney in Middlesex County between 1987 and 1991, all parties understood that the defendant's release at the earliest eligibility date was a near certainty. A typical part of the plea negotiation process was therefore to calculate that date—often a difficult process given the various complicated and overlapping parole provisions. I recall one bargaining session that took place among the lawyers and the judge in the judge's chambers during which the judge phoned an official of the parole board to confirm our understanding of the defendant's first eligibility date if a contemplated sentence was imposed. Our doubts settled, the case quickly pled out.

60. In Massachusetts, before the "truth-in-sentencing" reform movement of the early 1990s, the disparity between a sentence's "face value" and its true meaning often was enormous. The most extreme examples were sentences to the reformatory at Concord, which remains in operation today. What was then known as a "Concord 20"— a sentence officially expressed as "twenty years' confinement, to be served at the Massachusetts reformatory at Concord"—provided for parole eligibility and almost certain release after two years (*Mass. Regs. Code* tit. 120, § 202.01, at 27 [1990]).

61. Alschuler, "Prosecutor's Role," 109.

62. Warner, "Factors Determining Parole," 172, 174 n.1.

63. Harno, "Workings of the Parole Board," 67.

64. See *Report of the Prison Survey Committee* (1920), 248. The committee concluded that "[t]here is obviously a defect in the system of reporting to this board adequately the conduct and working history of these inmates, or it would be impossible for any such number of applications to be heard in any such time."

The situation at the New York City Parole Commission (a separate body from the state parole board) was no better. The commission's secretary reported in 1924 that it "passed on the cases of about 2,500 penitentiary prisoners a year, making 'time allotments' to about fifty prisoners in two or three hours every Thursday" ("Hirshfield Favors Parole's Abolition," *New York Times*, May 29, 1924, 20).

65. See "2 Bills To Change the Parole System," *New York Times*, January 25, 1925, 31, which quotes an official of the New York Prison Association as saying that the board's sittings "consume usually less than a day—three or four Hours"; and "Haste in Paroles Assailed at Inquiry," *New York Times*, June 19, 1926, 17, which cites an observer's estimate of the average length of the board's sittings at each of the state's four prisons.

66. "Haste in Paroles Assailed at Inquiry," *New York Times*, June 19, 1926, 17, quoting E. R. Cass.

67. This defense appeared in a letter to the *Times* from Alexander Konta ("Defending Parole Board," *New York Times*, July 1, 1926, 22). See also "Parole Board Hits Critics and Courts," *New York Times*, August 20, 1926, 8, which reports the board's claim that "it frequently devotes hours and days to cases before they come up for public hearing."

68. "State Prisons Reach Capacity," *New York Times*, April 10, 1927, part 9, 13.

69. See Warren F. Spalding, *Indeterminate Sentences for Penitentiary Prisoners*, 10. Spalding wrote:

> The maximum should be enough longer than the minimum to induce the prisoner to make a hard struggle for his liberty. The pressure of the reformatory system cannot be brought to bear upon him, successfully, unless he has this inducement. There should certainly be a margin of three years upon the shorter sentences, and of five years on the longer ones, to enable the administration to make a successful appeal to the prisoner for his co-operation. (ibid.)

See also Conlon's Case, 148 Mass. 168, 169 (1889), which identifies Spalding as secretary of the Board of Commissioners of Prisons.

70. Henry Elmer Barnes (*Evolution of Penology*, 322–23) advocated more broadly spaced minimum and maximum sentences in Pennsylvania. Next door in New Jersey, the parole director declared that "[s]entences should be indeterminate . . . [with] real differences between the minimum and maximum" (see Lane, "New Day," 88, 107). Clair Wilcox (*Parole of Adults*, 18) noted that "[a]t times the spread between the maximum and minimum limits of the sentence imposed is so small that boards of

parole are given little discretion with regard to the time at which prisoners may be released"—though at other times, the spread was sufficiently generous.

71. "Legislation—Indeterminate Sentencing," 681. A few years earlier, Edwin Sutherland (*Principles of Criminology*, 482) observed that "[w]hen the court was given authority to fix limits within the limits fixed by the legislature some judges who were opposed to indeterminate sentences abused their authority by making the minimum almost identical with the maximum."

72. Several states required that the minimum term not exceed one-half of the statutory maximum term (e.g., Act of March 9, 1911, ch. 200, § 1, 1911 Idaho Sess. Laws 664, 664; Act of June 7, 1905, ch. 184, § 2, 1905 Mich. Acts 268, 268; Act of April 21, 1911, ch. 191, § 2, 1911 N.J. Laws 356, 356). Several others required that the minimum term not exceed one-half of the maximum imposed. See, for example, Act of February 10, 1917, ch. 16, § 1, 1917 Mont. Laws 16, 16; Act of May 4, 1909, ch. 282, § 1, 1909 New York Laws 511, 512; Act of June 29, 1923, ch. 397, § 6, 1923 Pa. Laws 975, 976.

73. Friedman and Percival report that Alameda County judges imposed longer prison terms after the legislature enacted a good-time law and a parole law. The judges apparently wanted to keep sentences at their old length (Friedman and Percival, *Roots of Justice*, 215–16).

74. See "Against Extension of the Parole Law," *New York Times*, February 10, 1918, 5, which quoted from the report of a subcommittee of the New York Lawyers' Association. See also "Court Hits Parole Board," *New York Times*, October 20, 1925, 10, which quoted a trial judge who assailed the state parole board as "a useless appendage to the criminal law" and who said, "The burden and responsibility of sentencing should be upon the judges, and sentences should be fixed and not indeterminate." For similar examples, see sources quoted in Ch. 5, n. 63.

75. The Massachusetts Department of Correction commissioned the study. See Sanford Bates, "Preface" to Warner, "Factors," 172.

76. Ibid., 174 & n.1.

77. See above, Notes 27, 29, and accompanying text; 2 Mass. Gen. Laws ch. 279, §§ 32–33, at 2840–41 (1921).

78. See Warner, "Factors," 202.

79. See Harno,"Workings of the Parole Board."

80. Ibid., 89.

81. Ibid.

82. Ibid., quoting a letter without attribution by name (ellipsis in original).

83. Ibid., 89–90.

84. Ibid., 90, which quotes an unnamed lawyer.

85. Ibid.

86. Ibid., quoting an unnamed lawyer.

87. In Moley's sampling of twenty-four American urban jurisdictions, all but three had guilty plea rates of seventy percent or more (Moley, "Vanishing Jury," 105).

Edward Lindsey reported that in 1922, forty-four states had some form of parole law (Lindsey, "Historical Sketch," 69).

88. See Act of May 18, 1917, ch. 527, § 1, 1917 Cal. Stat. 665, 665–66; Act of June 28, 1919, § 3, 1919 Ill. Laws 436, 437; Act of March 15, 1897, ch. 143, §§ 1, 3, 5, 1897 Ind. Laws 219, 219–221; Act of March 13, 1903, ch. 375, § 1, 1903 Kan. Sess. Laws 571, 571–75; Act of March 3, 1911, ch. 169, § 1, 1911 S.D. Laws 209, 209; Act of February 11, 1903, ch. 45, § 46, 1903 W. Va. Acts 138, 149–50.

89. See Mather, *Plea Bargaining or Trial*, 5, 28, 30.

90. Ibid., 30. Mather reports a toothless policy put in place by the district attorney in 1974, purportedly to limit plea bargaining: "Interestingly, in the one exception allowed by the new policy, district attorneys could still agree (with prior written approval from their superior) to a sentence bargain of 'no state prison.' This particular sentence commitment . . . was crucial in 'serious' cases and was one of the most common bargains *before* the policy change" (ibid., 153 n.4).

91. Ibid., 31–33.

92. See Alschuler, "Prosecutor's Role," 101–03 and n.126.

93. See Act of September 20, 1976, ch. 1139, § 271, 1976 Cal. Stat. 5061, 5139, which amended § 1168 of the Penal Code and greatly shrank the reach of the old indeterminate sentencing provision.

94. See this chapter, Notes 111–15 and accompanying text.

95. See Goldman, *Public Defender*, vii–viii.

96. Ibid.

97. "[A]ssigned counsel, whose retained clients are his chief concern, easily convinces himself that he has done his duty to his pauper client if the prosecutor will accept a plea of guilty to a lesser form of crime or be content to recommend a moderate sentence. . . . That such a system results in innocent men being branded and punished as criminals admits of no doubt" (ibid., 21–22, quoting from an address of Samuel Untermeyer). Later, Goldman added (ibid., 70): "How many innocent men have pleaded 'guilty' at the suggestion of assigned counsel, because of the latter's indifference or desire to escape the burden of trial, it is impossible to state; their number must be legion." Similarly, in *Justice and the Poor* (p. 114), Reginald Heber Smith wrote, "If not paid, [the professional assigned counsel] is perfectly willing to betray his client by neglecting the case, or forcing him to plead guilty, or deserting him altogether."

98. Goldman, *Public Defender*, 35, 49.

99. Ibid., 8.

100. Ibid., 40. Goldman repeated this view at least twice more: See ibid., 45–46 ("The indigent defendant, who is *innocent*, would be the only one really benefited by the services of the public defender—except that the guilty would be saved from over-punishment."); ibid. at 67 ("A district attorney is not expected to, nor should he, prosecute a person whom he knows or believes to be innocent. Why, therefore, should a public defender be criticized for a failure to defend one whom he believes to be guilty?").

101. Ibid., 41, quoting Judge Charles C. Nott. It is possible that Judge Nott

was a former prosecutor, which perhaps would make his views on the proper role of the public defender somewhat suspect. See Train, *Prisoner*, 155 n.*, which identifies Charles Cooper Nott, Jr., as a New York prosecutor as of 1905.

102. Walton J. Wood, "Los Angeles County Public Defender," 289–90 (emphasis added).

103. Aggeler, "Public Defense."

104. "Notes and Abstracts," 282. The Voluntary Defenders' Committee was founded in 1917 and soon became part of the Legal Aid Society of New York, a private organization that provided legal services to the poor (see Michael McConville and Chester L. Mirsky, "Criminal Defense of the Poor in New York City," *N.Y.U. Rev. L. & Soc. Change* 15 (1986–1987), 614, 617–18).

105. "Notes and Abstracts," p. 282.

106. Legal Aid Society, *45th Annual Report*, 69.

107. Goldman, *Public Defender*, 53, quoting an Omaha public defender.

108. In New York the Legal Aid Society in its 1926 annual report (*51st Annual Report*, 64) bragged that "[i]f the Committee had not been so successful in arriving at dispositions without trials, it might have been necessary to try several hundred cases, at an enormous expense to the community." A few years earlier the Los Angeles defender (Wood, "Necessity for Public Defender," 230) argued that because the public defender raises fewer technical obstacles than private counsel, trials are quicker and therefore cheaper.

109. McConville and Mirsky, "Criminal Defense," 877; see also ibid., 631.

110. See Foltz, "Public Defenders," 401 and n.2.

111. See McConville and Mirsky, "Criminal Defense," 596.

112. Smith (*Justice*, 121) wrote that "[i]t is the strongly prevailing present opinion of the bar that [when a client who has confessed guilt to her lawyer refuses to plead guilty] it is the lawyer's duty to defend, . . . requiring the state to prove fairly the truth of its charges."

113. Ibid. Smith noted that "[i]n practice this issue [of defending the guilty at trial] has not presented itself" because "[i]n New York, all defendants who have admitted guilt have been persuaded to be honest with the court and plead guilty." Earlier (ibid., p. 119) he reported that the Los Angeles public defender "instructs more of his clients to plead guilty than did assigned counsel under the former régime, and . . . tries only cases where he has faith in the defendant."

114. Foltz ("Public Defenders," 393, 399) wrote:

Innumerable innocent boys and girls and men and women are recorded as pleading guilty and railroaded into jail because too dazed to understand their rights and legal position. Hundreds of men and women plead guilty because advised to do so by some court or police officer and fear makes them obey. Others plead guilty and suffer punishment by fine because it is cheaper than counsel and they can better stand the disgrace than the money loss. . . .

. . .

[Assigned lawyers] are often caught up without a moment's notice and compelled to go to trial without adequate time to prepare on the law or to secure
testimony. The defense is almost of necessity inadequate, and about the wisest
course for a pauper prisoner caught in the mesh of misunderstanding or circumstantial evidence is to plead guilty, earn consideration by "saving the
county expense," and throw himself on the "mercy of the court."

115. Ibid., 402 (footnote omitted).

116. Goldman reported that Oklahoma established the nation's first public
defender in 1912, but that the first of the sort he envisioned took office in Los Angeles in 1914 (see Goldman, *Public Defender*, 81–82).

117. The four authors and editors of the three most prominent studies of the
1920s all were law professors—Roscoe Pound and Felix Frankfurter at Harvard
(*Criminal Justice in Cleveland*), Raymond Moley at Columbia ("Vanishing Jury"), and
Justin Miller at the University of Southern California ("Compromise"). Miller was
formerly a district attorney of Kings County, California.

118. See Wood, "Necessity," 230.

119. See Legal Aid Society, *Report of Voluntary Defenders' Committee*, 3;
Clary, "Public Defender," 56.

120. Legal Aid Society, *48th Annual Report*, 73.

121. Hence in 1926 it wrote that "[i]f the Committee had not been so successful in arriving at dispositions without trials, it might have been necessary to try several
hundred cases, at an enormous expense to the community" (Legal Aid Society, *51st
Annual Report*, 64). A year later, the society reported that 283 defendants pled guilty
in 1927 and claimed that "[b]y so doing they secured material advantages to themselves, and the community was saved enormous expense" (Legal Aid Society, *52d
Annual Report*, 70). See also Legal Aid Society, *53d Annual Report*, 83; and Legal Aid
Society, *55th Annual Report*, 66.

122. See Alschuler, "Defense Attorney's Role," 1207, who quotes the California public defender, who was quoting the judge.

123. Aggeler, "Public Defense," 4.

124. Embree, "Voluntary Defenders," 4.

125. The New York Legal Aid Society (*45th Annual Report*, 69) reported in
1920 that the committee's policy of refusing to take cases to trial when defendants
admitted their guilt "had the approval of judges in the Court of General Sessions." Six
years later the society's chief attorney (Fabricant, "Voluntary Defender," 77) wrote
"[w]e never try to dodge the facts of a case. Pleas of guilty are not withheld where the
facts given us by our clients warrant such a plea. Confidence is thus inspired both in
the court and the prosecutor."

126. See McConville and Mirsky, "Criminal Defense," 627.

127. See, e.g., *Cooper v. Fitzharris*, 551 F.2d 1162, 1163 n.1 (9th Cir. 1977),
which relates a public defender's account of her collapse under the weight of 2,000

cases per year, in a case alleging ineffective assistance of counsel (*modified en banc*, 586 F.2d 1325 [9th Cir. 1978]).

128. Albert Alschuler speculates that the due-process revolution contributed to greater trial lengths. In Los Angeles the average felony trial grew from 3.5 days in 1964 to 7.2 days in 1968 (Alschuler, "Plea Bargaining History," 38). In contrast to those who have claimed that the increasing procedural complexity of our modern trials made plea bargaining inevitable by making trials too cumbersome and expensive (see ibid., 40–41; Langbein, "Torture," 3, 9–11), one could argue that the causal chain ran largely the other way. That is, the Supreme Court might not have dared lavish time-consuming trial rights on criminal defendants if plea bargaining had not already eliminated all but a tiny proportion of trials.

129. See Alschuler, "Plea Bargaining History," 39.

130. Alschuler (ibid., 38) writes, "In the words of an Oakland public defender, 'rights are tools to work with,' and rather than insist on a hearing on a motion to suppress illegally obtained evidence, a defense attorney was likely to use a claim of illegality to exact prosecutorial concessions in plea bargaining."

131. See *Bordenkircher v. Hayes*, 434 U.S. 357, 363–65 (1978); *North Carolina v. Alford*, 400 U.S. 25 (1970); *Parker v. North Carolina*, 397 U.S. 790 (1970); *McMann v. Richardson*, 397 U.S. 759 (1970); and *Brady v. United States*, 397 U.S. 742 (1970).

132. State legislatures immediately recognized the risk of burdening defendants' exercise of their right against self-incrimination, and many of the earliest defendant-testimony laws banned comment on defendants' silence. The Massachusetts law, for example (Act of May 26, 1866, ch. 260, 1866 Mass. Acts 245, 245), stated, "nor shall the neglect or refusal to testify create any presumption against the defendant." Many states imposed no such ban. See, e.g., Act of March 25, 1864, ch. 280, 1864 Me. Acts 214, 214.

133. See *Griffin v. California*, 380 U.S. 609, 613 (1965). I thank Don Klerman for pointing out the significance of *Griffin*.

134. See Chapter 4, Note 42, and accompanying text.

135. See Act of May 7, 1869, ch. 678, § 1, 1869 N.Y. Laws 1597, 1597, which stated that "the neglect or refusal of any such person to testify shall not create any presumption against him."

136. Train, *Prisoner*, 161.

137. Seth Ames, "Testimony of Persons Accused of Crime," *American Law Review* 1 (1866–67): 443, 445.

NOTES TO CHAPTER 9

1. Of the several thousand cases I reviewed, exactly one appeared to me to involve a nonjury trial—and even in that case the record was ambiguous. See *Com-*

monwealth v. Artemas G. Upham, Middlesex Ct. C.P. R. Book 18 (February 1853). The clerk wrote that "after hearing the witnesses (duly sworn) and fully hearing and understanding the defence, it appeared to the said Court that the said Upham was guilty." This case concerned the misdemeanor of selling milk by an unapproved measure.

2. See Prologue, Note 8, and accompanying text.

3. Between 1846 and 1893, at least twelve states (not including Massachusetts) acted to permit nonjury trial in misdemeanor cases. See Towne, "Historical Origins of Bench Trial," 149 and n.131.

4. Although fairly common in some American colonies, nonjury trials in felony cases virtually died out by the end of the eighteenth century. They persisted in Maryland, but did not emerge elsewhere except in scattered instances until the late nineteenth century, when Connecticut, Louisiana, and Indiana acted to permit nonjury felony trials (see ibid., 145–50). Only in the twentieth century did the practice spread more broadly (ibid., 123–24).

5. At nonjury trials there is of course no need to choose a jury, a process that can consume days or even weeks. Even typical examinations of witnesses go more quickly, because judges require less background information than do juries and because they are less impressed by fiery (and often dragged-out) courtroom theater.

6. Moley, "Vanishing Jury," 127.

7. Ibid. Moley also wrote that "[t]he fundamental treatment for the tendency which we have discussed in this article is not a direct attack upon the practice of prosecutors. Their range of methods by which criminal charges can be disposed of is so great that merely to shut off one practice will open up others."

8. See Alschuler, "Plea Bargaining History," 33.

9. See Kalven and Zeisel, *American Jury*, 22 and n.18.

10. See Alschuler, "Plea Bargaining History," 33. Alschuler suggests that the nonjury trial may have depressed the proportion of plea bargains, though only for a short time. He reports that in 1936, after many states had acted to permit nonjury trials, the proportion of plea bargains was lower than in the 1920s, but then resumed its upward trend and had recovered any loss by 1940. Alschuler's figures reflect state court practice. As many states aided in enforcing federal prohibition, the end of prohibition perhaps provides an alternative explanation for the decline in pleas between the 1920s and 1936.

11. To keep this illustration simple, I will assume the chance of reversal on appeal is subsumed in the chance of acquittal after trial.

12. Lynn Mather reports that when the Los Angeles district attorney took up a campaign to become California's attorney general in 1970, his office forbade prosecutors to engage in a form of charge bargaining that had been routine in cases of marijuana possession (Mather, *Plea Bargaining or Trial?*, 17–18). "After all, the district attorney is a political animal," one prosecutor explained to Mather. "Drugs are a very controversial issue right now." (Ibid., 18.)

13. During my tenure as a Middlesex County prosecutor, this situation arose most often in cocaine distribution cases. Massachusetts law imposes an escalating series of mandatory-minimum prison terms according to the quantity of cocaine found in the defendant's possession: three years for fourteen grams (one-half ounce), five years for twenty-eight grams, ten years for one hundred grams, and fifteen years for two hundred grams (see *Mass. Gen. Laws Ann.* ch. 94C, § 32E(b)(1)–(4) [West 1997]). Many judges regarded these sentences as unjustifiably harsh and pressured prosecutors to consider reducing the charged offense in exchange for a plea, especially when the defendant had no other criminal record. Our office rigidly enforced a policy against any such reduction. Judges therefore advised or hinted to defense counsel that they would, in a nonjury trial, find reasonable doubt as to the weight of the cocaine and find the defendant guilty of possessing a smaller quantity than that charged.

14. Lynn Mather describes a California adaptation of the nonjury trial that, although not resulting in a plea bargain, substitutes for a plea bargain in a procedurally ingenious way. I noted earlier that until California effectively ended its indeterminate sentence regime in 1976, judges had no power to dictate the length of state prison sentences, and so plea bargains often turned on the distinction between a sentence to the state prison and one to a lesser institution. See Chapter 8, Notes 88–93, and accompanying text. The judge often could not avoid imposing a state prison sentence, however, unless the prosecutor first reduced the charged offense.

Mather reports that in Los Angeles County, the district attorney often forbade courtroom prosecutors to reduce charges without clearance from their superiors. To achieve the same end as the plea bargain without any reduction in charge, the lawyers would agree to a "submission on the transcript." This was a nonjury trial in which the only evidence presented to the judge was the transcript of the preliminary hearing. The parties understood that the judge typically would find the defendant guilty of a lesser offense and avoid sending the defendant to state prison. Afterward, the courtroom prosecutor could report to superiors that the *judge* had reduced the charge (see Mather, *Plea Bargaining or Trial?*, 19–20, 55–58).

15. Adam Kurland reports that prosecutors can veto a defendant's request for a nonjury trial in twenty-seven states and the District of Columbia. In one state (North Carolina), nonjury trials are not available in felony trials. And in one other (Colorado), the prosecutor may not veto a nonjury trial if being subjected to a jury trial would violate the defendant's right to due process. That leaves twenty-one states in which the defendant may elect a nonjury trial either unilaterally or with the judge's consent. See Kurland, "Providing a Federal Criminal Defendant," 321–23 & nn.39, 40, 42, 43 & 45; *People v. District Court*, 843 P.2d 6, 11 (Colo. 1992).

16. See, e.g., 18 U.S.C. § 113 (1982), which punished various assault crimes with terms of zero to twenty years, zero to ten years, and zero to five years; 18 U.S.C. § 1963 (1982), which punished racketeering crimes (RICO violations) with terms of zero to twenty years and/or a fine; 18 U.S.C. § 923 (1982), which punished unlicensed

gun dealing with terms of zero to five years and/or a fine; 18 U.S.C. § 3651 (1985), which granted judges discretion to impose probation rather than prison time for any offense not punishable by death or life imprisonment. This last statute was repealed, effective November 1, 1987, by Pub. L. No. 98–473, Tit. II, §§ 212(a)(1), (2), 235(a)(1), 98 Stat. 1987, 2031 (October 12, 1984).

17. In the introduction to the Guidelines, the Commission noted that one of Congress's chief aims in enacting the Sentencing Reform Act of 1984, which gave rise to the Guidelines, was to achieve "*uniformity* in sentencing by narrowing the wide disparity in sentences imposed by different federal courts for similar criminal conduct by similar offenders." See U.S. Sentencing Commission, *Sentencing Guidelines* (1987), Intro., 3, at 1.2. The Commission added that "[t]he overriding, more broad-based concern with the existing system . . . [was] the apparent unwarranted disparity and inequality of treatment in sentencing" (U.S. Sentencing Commission, *Supplementary Report*, 8).

18. The Sentencing Reform Act of 1984 influenced the fundamental architecture of the Guidelines by imposing certain constraints on whatever sentencing mechanism the Commission might devise (see 28 U.S.C. § 994[b]–[d]). The twenty-five percent rule, detailed in the next note, was the most important of these. The sentencing table itself, as created and later revised by the Commission, appears in chapter 5, part A, of the *Guidelines Manual*. On the table's development, see Marc Miller, "True Grid," 587, 590–604.

19. See 28 U.S.C. § 994(b)(2) (1994 & Supp. 1996), which provides that the maximum term may not exceed the minimum term by more than twenty-five percent or six months, whichever is greater, but allowing for a maximum term of life imprisonment if the minimum term is thirty years or more.

20. Jeffrey Standen succinctly compares judges' largely wide-open sentencing authority before the Guidelines and their constrained discretion under the Guidelines; see Standen, "End of the Era," 788–89.

21. The Commission wrote that it "recognizes that a charge offense system has drawbacks of its own. One of the most important is its potential to turn over to the prosecutor the power to determine the sentence by increasing or decreasing the number (or content) of the counts in an indictment" (*Sentencing Guidelines* [1987], Intro., 4(a), at 1.6).

The Commission wrote that it "ultimately decided on a multi-pronged strategy designed to minimize the likelihood that charging and plea practices would circumvent the guidelines and thereby impede the objectives of the Act." It outlined its five steps at pages 162–66 of this report (U.S. Sentencing Commission, *Federal Sentencing Guidelines: Report*, vol. 1 [1991]).

22. Ibid., 165–66.

23. For example, research funding supported joint efforts by Ilene H. Nagel and Stephen J. Schulhofer to investigate the early operation of the Guidelines and to

suggest ways to increase fidelity to their terms. See, e.g., Schulhofer and Nagel, "Negotiated Pleas."

24. U.S. Sentencing Commission, *Federal Sentencing Guidelines: Report,* vol. 1 (1991), 164.

25. See ibid., 162; U.S. Sentencing Commission, *Sentencing Guidelines Manual* (1999), § 1B1.3(a). In 2000 the Commission further provided for an upward departure from the guideline sentencing range to reflect conduct underlying a charge that was dismissed or not pursued as part of a plea agreement. See U.S. Sentencing Commission, *Sentencing Guidelines Manual* § 5K2.21 (added by Amendment No. 604, effective November 1, 2000).

26. The U.S. Supreme Court held in 1997 that relevant conduct need be proved only by a preponderance of the evidence at sentencing (*United States v. Watts,* 519 U.S. 148, 157 [1997]). And the Commission has noted that it "believes that use of a preponderance of the evidence standard is appropriate" (see U.S. Sentencing Commission, *Sentencing Guidelines Manual* [1999], § 6A1.3 [commentary]).

In the Ninth Circuit, proof of relevant conduct must be by clear and convincing evidence if the resulting sentence enhancement will have an "extremely disproportionate impact" on the overall sentence. See *United States v. Jordan,* 256 F.3d 922, 927–29 (9th Cir. 2001). See also *United States v. Kikumura,* 918 F.2d 1084, 1100–1102 (3d Cir. 1990), which holds that the facts justifying an upward departure from the guideline range must be proved "at least by clear and convincing evidence" if the resulting increase in sentence "is sufficiently great that the sentencing hearing can fairly be characterized as 'a tail which wags the dog of the substantive offense.'" The U.S. Supreme Court ruled recently in a non-Guidelines case that except for "the fact of a prior conviction, any fact that increases the penalty for a crime beyond the prescribed statutory maximum must be submitted to a jury, and proved beyond a reasonable doubt" (*Apprendi v. New Jersey,* 530 U.S. 466, 490 [2000]).

27. Congress provided that "[a] United States probation officer shall make a presentence investigation of a defendant that is required [by] . . . the Federal Rules of Criminal Procedure, and shall, before the imposition of sentence, report the results of the investigation to the court" (18 U.S.C. § 3552(a)). Federal Rule of Criminal Procedure 32(b)(4)(B) requires the "Presentence Report" prepared by the probation officer to state "the classification of the offense and of the defendant under the categories established by the Sentencing Commission . . . as the probation officer believes to be applicable to the defendant's case . . . ." A pending amendment to this rule, recodified as Rule 32(d)(1)(A)–(E), will change the language but not the substance. Moreover, probation authorities at the Administrative Office of the U.S. Court require that probation officers disclose all "reliable information" to the court and refer to the probation officer as "the court's independent investigator" (Administrative Office of the U.S. Courts, Division of Probation, *Presentence Investigation Reports Under the Sentencing Reform Act of 1984,* 4–5 [1987], cited in Stith and Cabranes, *Fear of Judging,* 86, 222 nn.26–27).

On the connivance sometimes engaged in by prosecutors and defense counsel to conceal relevant conduct from the judge, see this chapter, Notes 95–96, and accompanying text.

28. U.S. Sentencing Commission, *Federal Sentencing Guidelines: Report*, vol. 1 (1991), 162. In a co-authored article, the original chair of the Commission wrote in 1990 that the real-offense provision of the Guidelines "significantly reduces the impact of prosecutorial charge selection and plea bargaining by ensuring that the court will be able to consider the defendant's real offense behavior in imposing a guideline sentence" (Wilkins and Steer, "Relevant Conduct," 499 n.27). See also Zipperstein, "Certain Uncertainty," 649–50 nn. 93, 97, and cases cited, which discusses approval by appeals courts, in certain circumstances, of decisions by sentencing judges to consider the conduct underlying dismissed charges as "relevant conduct" in sentencing.

29. See U.S. Sentencing Commission, *Federal Sentencing Guidelines: Report*, vol. 1 (1991), 162–64; U.S. Sentencing Commission, *Sentencing Guidelines Manual* (1999), § 6B1.2, cmt.

30. See Dick, Note, "Sentence Bargains," 1046–50 and cases cited.

31. Among the foremost critics is District Judge Jack B. Weinstein ("Trial Judge's First Impression," 15, 30), who complains of the Commission's "vindictiveness" and of its capture "by the desire of some to employ the most punitive devices" and suggests that the Guidelines "callously mandate incarceration across the board no matter how costly or destructive the result." For a partial list of the mandatory-minimum sentencing provisions enacted in the 1980s, see Stith and Cabranes, *Fear of Judging*, 210 n.38. The laws targeted mainly drug offenses and the use of firearms during drug crimes.

32. As one judge recently complained, when prosecutors and defense counsel hide facts relevant to sentencing from the court, judges "tacitly acquiesce when satisfied with the negotiated plea" (*Berthoff v. United States*, 140 F. Supp. 2d 50, 63 [D. Mass. 2001]).

33. Judge Gerald Heaney ("Reality of Guidelines Sentencing," 172) observes: "Typically, the probation officer's investigation ends after the review of the government files and interview of the [investigating] agents. Indeed, the government's files constitute the primary source of information . . . . The probation officer ordinarily undertakes no independent investigation of the facts and interviews no witnesses." Assistant Federal Defender Felicia Sarner ("'Fact Bargaining,'" 329) agrees: "I have never heard of a probation officer actively investigating the disputed facts of a case by interviewing defense witnesses, requesting defense investigation reports, or otherwise uncovering evidence that contradicts the prosecutor's version of the offense." Likewise, Judge William Stafford ("Settling Sentencing Facts," 30): "Let's not forget where the probation officer goes to get 'the facts'—to the government's counsel or the case agent."

34. Stephen Schulhofer and Ilene Nagel ("Plea Negotiations," 1300–1301) write that "[m]any judges . . . would prefer to rely on the parties to settle the facts

before sentencing." Likewise, Felicia Sarner ("'Fact Bargaining,'" 329) notes: "My experience [is] that most judges accept fact stipulations in any event." See also Stafford ("Settling Sentencing Facts," 29–30), who argues that it is inappropriate to "thrust the . . . probation officer into the role of criminal investigator" by asking her "to divine the facts, when the prosecution and the defense are unable to agree."

35. Susan Klein called my attention to a few other mechanisms by which judges could undercut prosecutors' sentencing deals. In certain (unusual) circumstances, a judge may dismiss an indictment or a single charge within an indictment. Or a judge may recognize new substantive defenses, such as "sentencing entrapment." In *United States v. Searcy*, 233 F.3d 1096, 1099 (8th Cir. 2000), the Eighth Circuit held (citing *Guidelines* § 2D1.1, cmt. nn.12, 15) that the Guidelines "recognize sentencing entrapment as a viable basis for a downward departure." Or a judge may require the prosecutor to move for a substantial-assistance departure if the judge determines that the prosecutor's refusal to do so was motivated by the defendant's race, ethnicity, or religion. The Supreme Court held in *Wade v. United States*, 504 U.S. 181, 185–86 (1992), that a district court has the power to grant a remedy if it finds that the government's refusal to move for a substantial-assistance departure "was based on an unconstitutional motive." A judge could not deploy such extraordinary powers, however, unless particular facts warranted them—a determination that could be reviewed and reversed on appeal.

36. U.S. Sentencing Commission, *Sentencing Guidelines* (1987), Intro., 4(g), at 1.11.

37. Ibid. § 3E1.1(a), at 3.12; Ch. 5, Pt. A, at 5.2 (sentencing table).

38. See U.S. Sentencing Commission, *Sentencing Guidelines Manual* (1999), app. C, amend. 459, at 879–82. To win the three-step reduction, the defendant must "timely provid[e] complete information . . . concerning his own involvement in the offense" or "timely notify[] authorities of his intention to enter a plea of guilty," hence saving both prosecution and judicial resources (p. 880).

39. The department signaled its acquiescence to acceptance-of-responsibility discounts in the course of plea bargains on the day the Guidelines took effect. See Nagel and Schulhofer, "Tale of Three Cities," 506, which discusses the department's *Prosecutor's Handbook on Sentencing Guidelines*, known as the "Redbook."

40. See this chapter, Note 26, and accompanying text.

41. Drug quantity, money stolen, and victim's injuries are all among the examples discussed in illustrations following the relevant section of the *Guidelines Manual*. See U.S. Sentencing Commission, *Sentencing Guidelines Manual* (1999), § 1B1.3, "Illustrations of Conduct for Which the Defendant Is Accountable."

42. Judge Heaney ("Reality," 190) notes that "[a] district court *must* consider the relevant conduct and the sentencing facts as presented to it and must impose a sentence within a given range if the appropriate facts are established by reliable evidence."

43. See U.S. Sentencing Commission, *Federal Sentencing Guidelines: Report*, vol. 1 (1991), 127–28. For example, in an appropriate case, the prosecutor could file

a weapon count under 18 U.S.C. § 924(c), which would add a mandatory five-year term to the defendant's sentence, or could seek to double the defendant's sentence for drug distribution by prosecuting the same conduct as a second offense; see, e.g., 21 U.S.C. § 841(b)(1)(A), (B).

44. 18 U.S.C. § 3553(b) (1994 & Supp. 1996); *Guidelines* (1999) § 5K2.0 (Policy Statement).

45. See U.S. Sentencing Commission, *Sentencing Guidelines Manual* (1999), §§ 5H1.1 (Age); 5H1.3 (Mental and Emotional Conditions); 5H1.5 (Employment Record); 5H1.6 (Family Ties and Responsibilities, and Community Ties). The Supreme Court has held that the Commission's designation of a factor as "not ordinarily relevant" does not altogether bar district judges from considering the factor in determining whether to depart from the guideline range. Rather, "the court should depart only if the factor is present to an exceptional degree or in some other way makes the case different from the ordinary case where the factor is present" (*Koon v. United States*, 518 U.S. 81, 96 [1996]).

46. See U.S. Sentencing Commission, *Federal Sentencing Guidelines: Report*, vol. 1 (1991), 218.

47. See U.S. Sentencing Commission, *Sentencing Guidelines Manual* (1999), §§ 5H1.11 (Military, Civic, Charitable or Public Service); 5H1.12 (Lack of Guidance as a Youth and Similar Circumstances).

48. See 18 U.S.C. § 3742(b)(3).

49. See U.S. Sentencing Commission, *Sourcebook* (2001), 109 table 58, *available at* http://www.ussc.gov/research.htm; U.S. Sentencing Commission, *Sourcebook* (2000), 109 table 58; U.S. Sentencing Commission, *Sourcebook* (1999), 109 table 58; U.S. Sentencing Commission, *Sourcebook* (1998), 107 table 56; U.S. Sentencing Commission, *Sourcebook* (1997), 107 table 56; U.S. Sentencing Commission, *Sourcebook* (1996), 79 table 51.

The Commission reports these results in terms of the "affirmance rate"—the rate at which appeals courts upheld the sentences imposed by district judges. It explains that the "Affirmance Rate includes all appeals cases not reversed by the circuit court" (U.S. Sentencing Commission, *Sourcebook* [2001], 109 table 58 and n.2). When prosecutors have appealed a judge's decision to depart downward, an "affirmance" must be counted as a loss.

I thank Stephanos Bibas for pointing out that prosecutors are probably less likely to appeal modest departures. And my thanks to Lou Reedt of the U.S. Sentencing Commission for supplying me with fiscal year 2001 data in advance of publication.

50. Congress authorized appeals only when the trial judge imposes sentence "in violation of law"; "as a result of an incorrect application of the sentencing guidelines"; or "for an offense for which there is no sentencing guideline and [the sentence is] plainly unreasonable"; or when she departs above or below the guideline range. See 18 U.S.C. § 3742(a), (b). All of the federal appeals courts have held that absent a mistake of law, a court's decision not to depart is unappealable (see Stith and Cabranes, *Fear of Judg-*

ing, 73; Hutchison et al., *Federal Sentencing Law*, 1606–7, 1608 n.8). A defendant can appeal a court's decision not to depart downward if the court wrongly thought it lacked discretion to do so. See *United States v. Pinnick*, 47 F.3d 434, 439 (D.C. Cir. 1995), which noted that "[a] sentencing court's refusal [to depart] is reviewable . . . if it rests on a 'misconstruction of its authority to depart.' A court's discretionary decision that the particular circumstances of a given case do not warrant a departure, however, is not reviewable." See also Zipperstein, "Certain Uncertainty," 633.

51. Stith and Cabranes, *Fear of Judging*, 73.

52. See U.S. Sentencing Commission, *Sourcebook* (1998), figure G, 51; U.S. Sentencing Commission, *Sourcebook* (2001), figure G.

53. See U.S. Sentencing Commission, *Sourcebook* (2001), figure G.

54. Of all downward departures in 2001, 48.3 percent involved "substantial assistance" motions by the government resulting from cooperation arrangements, and another 9.1 percent were labeled, "Pursuant to plea agreement" (ibid., figure G, table 25).

55. When the departure in question would reduce the sentence beneath the statutory minimum, Congress required that the prosecution initiate the departure. See 18 U.S.C. § 3553(e), which provides that "[u]pon motion of the Government, the court shall have the authority to impose a sentence below a level established by statute as [the] minimum sentence so as to reflect a defendant's substantial assistance in the investigation or prosecution of another person." In *Melendez v. United States*, 518 U.S. 120, 125–26 (1996), the Supreme Court held that a sentencing judge may not depart below the minimum penalty prescribed by law absent a specific motion by the government to do so.

When the departure merely would reduce the sentence beneath the guideline range (but not beneath the statutory minimum), Congress did not require that the prosecution initiate the departure, but the Commission did so. See 28 U.S.C. § 994(n), which directs the Commission to provide for departures beneath the guideline range, even "including a sentence that is lower than that established by statute as a minimum sentence, to take into account a defendant's substantial assistance in the investigation or prosecution of another person who has committed an offense." The Commission (*Sentencing Guidelines Manual* [1999] § 5K1.1) provided that "upon motion of the government stating that the defendant has provided substantial assistance in the investigation or prosecution of another person who has committed an offense, the court may depart from the guidelines." In *Wade v. United States*, 504 U.S. 181, 185 (1992), the Supreme Court assumed that a government motion is a "condition limiting the court's authority" to depart under § 5K1.1. And the District of Columbia Circuit held in *In re Sealed Case*, 181 F.3d 128, 130, 142 (D.C. Cir. 1999) that a district court has no authority under § 5K1.1 to depart from the guideline range if the government declines to file a motion.

A district court can remedy the government's refusal to bring a motion under § 5K1.1 if the refusal "was based on an unconstitutional motive," such as the defendant's race or religion. See *Wade*, 504 U.S. at 185–86.

56. Indeed, at least one federal appeals court has held that absent a government request, district judges have no power to depart downward on grounds of the defendant's consent to deportation (see *United States v. Marin-Castaneda*, 134 F.3d 551, 555–56 [3d. Cir.], *cert. denied*, 523 U.S. 1144 [1998]). But at least three other appeals courts have held district judges may depart on this basis without a government request: See *United States v. Sera*, 256 F.3d 778, 780 (8th Cir. 2001); *United States v. Rodriguez-Lopez*, 198 F.3d 773, 777 (9th Cir. 1999); and *United States v. Galvez-Falconi*, 174 F.3d 255, 256–58, 260 (2d Cir. 1999). Some circuit courts have held that with or without a government motion, district judges lack authority to depart based on the defendant's consent to be deported unless the defendant had a "nonfrivolous defense" to deportation. See, for example, *United States v. Marin-Castaneda*, 134 F.3d at 555–56; and *United States v. Clase-Espinal*, 115 F.3d 1054, 1059 (1st Cir. 1997).

The best evidence of the importance of a government request in granting deportation departures emerges from Commission statistics. Between 1988 and 1994, deportation departures never amounted to 1 percent of all downward departures. Then, in April 1995 the attorney general authorized federal prosecutors to recommend such departures (see *Galvez-Falconi*, 174 F.3d at 259). The rate of deportation departures promptly began to rise—to 2.1 percent of all downward departures in 1995; 6.7 percent in 1996; and 10.3 percent in 1997 (see U.S. Sentencing Commission, *Annual Report* [1995], figure H, at 86; ibid., table 30; U.S. Sentencing Commission, *Sourcebook* [1996], figure G, at 39; ibid., table 25; U.S. Sentencing Commission, *Sourcebook* [1997], figure G, at 51; ibid., 52, table 25).

In November 1997 the Justice Department advised that recent immigration law changes "had cast doubt on whether such departures remained appropriate" (see *Galvez-Falconi*, 174 F.3d at 259). Some U.S. attorneys apparently waited until the following summer before ending their past support of deportation departures (ibid.). Again, the Commission's statistics reflect this policy change. Deportation departures fell to 7.9 percent of all downward departures in 1998; 4.0 percent in 1999; 3.4 percent in 2000; and 2.5 percent in 2001; see U.S. Sentencing Commission, *Sourcebook*, (1998), 51, figure G; ibid., 52, table 25; U.S. Sentencing Commission, *Sourcebook* (1999), figure G, table 25; U.S. Sentencing Commission, *Sourcebook* (2000), figure G, table 25; U.S. Sentencing Commission, *Sourcebook* (2001), figure G, table 25.

Stephanos Bibas, a former federal prosecutor in the Southern District of New York, confirms much of this account from personal experience. Until 1998, he reports, prosecutors in that district routinely assented to or failed to oppose motions for deportation departures. Sometime in late 1998 the office policy changed, and such departures ceased to be automatic.

Bibas also called my attention to "fast-track" departures, initiated in the late 1990s by federal prosecutors in jurisdictions along the American border with Mexico. The government recommends such departures for low-level drug dealers and immigration defendants who offer quick guilty pleas and who agree to deportation or waive other procedural protections (see Bowman and Heise, "Quiet Rebellion II," 547, 550).

The category of "Fast track" departures appeared for the first time in the Commission's 1999 annual report. It accounted that year for 4.4 percent of all downward departures (see U.S. Sentencing Commission, *Sourcebook*, [1999], figure G, table 25). In 2001 the "Fast track" category made up 4.0 percent of all downward departures (see U.S. Sentencing Commission, *Sourcebook* [2001], figure G; ibid., table 25). Although the Ninth Circuit has held that district judges have the power to grant fast-track departures even without the government's consent, it also has noted that "consent is relevant to a sentencing court's decision whether to depart" (*United States v. Rodriguez-Lopez*, 198 F.3d 773, 777–78 [9th Cir. 1999]). I have included fast-track departures within the general category of deportation departures noted in the text.

57. This is the figure for 2001. See U.S. Sentencing Commission, *Sourcebook* (2001), figure G, table 25.

58. To arrive at this figure, I have performed the calculations described in the text for every year from 1988 through 2001—the first and last for which data are available—and then have averaged the figures achieved for each year. Therefore I have weighted the various years equally, though of course total annual cases have increased substantially over time.

59. Judge Heaney ("Reality," 171) reports that in the districts he studied, "negotiations usually involve [as one possibility among several] . . . an agreement that the government will . . . not object to downward departure by the court for other reasons."

60. Stith and Cabranes, *Fear of Judging*, 90, quoting Judge Wayne R. Anderson.

61. When the Guidelines came in force, Connecticut probation officers eliminated that portion of their presentence reports to the court that examined the characteristics of individual offenders. This step conformed with national recommendations and with the Commission's judgment deeming such characteristics not ordinarily relevant. At the request of the federal bench in Connecticut, however, the district's probation officers restored this section of their reports (see Lisa M. Farabee, "Disparate Departures," 603–5).

62. See U.S. Sentencing Commission, *Sourcebook* (2001), 53, table 26.

63. Ibid., 53–55. According to the most recent figures available, the rate of "other downward departures" and the proportion of immigration offenses in these four districts (and in Connecticut and nationally for comparison) are as follows:

Rates of "Other Downward Departures" and Proportion of Immigration Offenses in Selected Federal Judicial Districts

DISTRICT	OTHER DOWNWARD DEPARTURES (2001)*	IMMIGRATION OFFENSES (2000)*
Arizona	62.8	53.8
California, Southern	50.5	43.6
Connecticut	33.8	4.2

(table continued on next page)

DISTRICT	OTHER DOWNWARD DEPARTURES (2001)*	IMMIGRATION OFFENSES (2000)*
New Mexico	38.7	36.2
Washington, Eastern	51.8	38.5
National Totals	18.3	17.5

SOURCES: U.S. Sentencing Commission, *Sourcebook* (2001), 53–55, table 26; App. B.
*Percentage of all cases sentenced.

In Connecticut, as I mentioned, the high rate of downward departures is apparently owing to judges who pointedly seek out ways to reduce sentences. In the other districts listed, the high rate of immigration cases supplies an alternate explanation. It is true that in the Eastern District of Washington, the rate of immigration offenses, though high, cannot alone explain the very high rate of downward departures. I asked Steven Hormel, the Chief Trial Attorney of the Federal Defender's Office in Spokane, why his district had so high a rate of downward departures. He mentioned the many illegal-entry cases and the great number of immigrant farmworkers in Washington's Yakima Valley. But he also said that the district's judges are unusually independent and more willing than most to depart downward even in the face of government objections. (Conversation with the author, July 12, 2002.) That the district has a comparatively small caseload—slightly larger than Connecticut's but only one-fifteenth as large as the Southern District of California's—perhaps permits a small number of judges to have a disproportionate impact on case outcomes.

64. I have discussed the fast-track program in some detail in Note 56 of this chapter.

65. One example of a liberal Second Circuit decision is *United States v. Johnson*, 964 F.2d 124 (2d Cir. 1992), which held that a district judge could depart downward based on the defendant's "extraordinary parental responsibilities," despite the Commission's injunction that "[f]amily ties and responsibilities . . . are not ordinarily relevant in determining whether a sentence should be outside the applicable guideline range" (pp. 128–30). See also U.S. Sentencing Commission, *Sentencing Guidelines Manual* (1999), § 5H1.6. In a study comparing sentencing under the guidelines in Connecticut and Massachusetts, Lisa Farabee argues that one explanation for the higher rate of downward departures (other than those for substantial assistance) in Connecticut is that the case law of the Second Circuit is far more liberal toward downward departures than that of the First Circuit, which includes Massachusetts (see Farabee, "Disparate Departures," 588–89, 591–93).

66. As Daniel Freed ("Federal Sentencing," 1697) writes: "The guidelines do not explicitly confer new power on the prosecutor, nor do they, in a technical sense, 'transfer' power from the judge to the Assistant U.S. Attorney (AUSA). But to the extent that the guideline parameters diminish the power of the judge, they correspondingly enhance the power of the prosecutor."

67. One U.S. District Judge asked in 1990, "Are prosecutors, some just out of

law school, to be given totally unfettered discretion?" (See, e.g., *United States v. Redondo-Lemos*, 754 F. Supp. 1401, 1403–06 [D. Ariz. 1990], *rev'd* 955 F.2d 1296 [9th Cir. 1992].) Judge Heaney ("Reality," 226) reported the following year that many participants in the system believe "[t]he guidelines result in a massive though unintended transfer of discretion and authority from the court to the prosecutor." Defense lawyer Daniel J. Sears ("Practice Under the Guidelines," 488) agreed: "[U]nder the guideline scheme, a prosecutor's sentencing discretion has been greatly expanded and enhanced while, at the same time, the sentencing judge's has been almost entirely eliminated."

68. See Bowman and Heise, "Quiet Rebellion?," 1046.

69. In the 2001 study, Bowman and Heise argued that a pattern of more lenient sentencing in federal drug cases in recent years suggests a greater exercise of discretion by court actors than in the earlier years of the Guidelines' operation. Despite sustained and intelligent analysis, however, Bowman and Heise did little to disturb the old articles of faith. Little of what they said was inconsistent with the standard view that prosecutors now hold far more sentencing discretion than before, while judges hold less.

One difficulty is that Bowman and Heise rarely attempted to disaggregate exercises of judicial discretion from exercises of prosecutorial discretion. They often lumped the two together and claimed simply that *someone*, whether prosecutor or judge, was exercising more discretion. For example, they argued that increased leniency in applying certain "safety valve" provisions, which permit lower sentences in some drug cases, "could represent a shift in the exercise of discretion by prosecutors and judges" (Bowman and Heise, "Quiet Rebellion?," 1072–74 and n.118); that more lenient trends in awarding certain adjustments under the Guidelines may "reflect a progressive change in the way judges and prosecutors make the partly discretionary choices about who deserves aggravating or mitigating role adjustments" (ibid., 1096); and that "judges and prosecutors are using the discretionary powers granted by the departure provisions of the [Sentencing Reform Act] and the Guidelines for purposes other than those for which those departure provisions were intended" (ibid., 1117).

A second difficulty is that, while attributing much of the downturn in drug sentences to plea bargaining, Bowman and Heise assigned judges too much responsibility for the practice. Although they noted that plea bargaining involves a great deal of prosecutorial discretion (see ibid., 1103–4), they also suggested that it is an exercise in shared discretion: "The decision by the parties to enter into a plea agreement and the judge's acceptance of such an agreement are discretionary choices" (ibid., 1105). But the judge's "discretion" generally is limited either to acquiescing in the lawyers' agreement or to frustrating it—and thereby forcing the case to jury trial. Given judges' strong desire to avoid jury trials, this option affords no effective discretion at all.

Meanwhile, Bowman and Heise noted several ways in which declining drug sentences result from exercises of exclusively prosecutorial discretion. For example, they wrote that "there is a substantial element of prosecutorial discretion involved in whether a defendant will receive" either a statutorily imposed five-year penalty or a two-level increase under the Guidelines for using, carrying, or possessing a firearm in connection with a drug crime (ibid., 1084–86). They noted that in determining whether the defendant has made sufficiently "timely" disclosures to the government to justify an enhanced sentence reduction for acceptance of responsibility, "the sentencing judge necessarily relies heavily on the assessment of government counsel"—an assessment that "has a significant discretionary element" (ibid., 1106–7). And they remarked on the prosecutor's discretion to choose whether to pursue a mandatory sentence increase based on an offender's previous drug offense or to permit a drug trafficking defendant to plead to a far less serious drug offense (ibid., 1120–21).

70. See Bowman and Heise, "Quiet Rebellion II," 528–29, 531, 538–39, 542–44, 552, 554–55.

71. Ibid., 556. One reason Bowman and Heise were reluctant to conclude that caseload pressure played a prominent role in prompting prosecutorial plea bargaining was that "[a]verage caseloads of Assistant U.S. Attorneys are just not very high . . . ." (ibid.). But *average* caseloads are surely not the point. If, as Bowman and Heise found, disparate sentence length (and therefore, presumably, disparate plea-bargaining practices) correlate with disparate prosecutorial caseloads, then we should look at the caseloads of those prosecutors in the high-caseload districts. Yet Bowman and Heise do not supply these figures. Moreover, even average caseloads may be much higher than Bowman and Heise's calculations showed. To determine caseload, they divided the number of cases by the number of assistant U.S. attorneys. They made no deduction for AUSAs who held purely administrative positions or conducted only appellate work and who therefore carried no trial caseload at all. More critically, they apparently made no attempt to exclude those AUSAs assigned to handle civil matters only. See ibid., 556–57 and n.310, where they discuss how they calculated workload.

72. Ibid., 552–53.

73. According to one study, the average time to be served by federal convicts was 20.7 months for those entering prison in 1986 and 46.9 months for those entering in 1997 (see Sabol and McGready, *Time Served in Prison*, 4, table 1, *available at* http://www.ojp.usdoj.gov/bjs/pub/pdf/tspfo97.pdf). These figures represent a projection of actual time served and therefore take into account the abolition of parole in the 1980s (see ibid., 3–4; this chapter, Notes 81–82, and accompanying text). Much or most of the increase in term length resulted from harsher sentences in drug and weapons offenses, which often are subject to mandatory-minimum sentencing provisions (see ibid., 5, table 2). But sentences for violent crimes, which generally are not subject to mandatory sentencing provisions, also grew by about fifty percent in terms of time to be served between 1984 and 1993 (see Hofer and Semisch, "Examining Changes," 16–17).

All these figures actually *understate* the real increase in sentence severity. That is because between 1984 and 2001, the proportion of federal offenders sentenced to prison, as opposed to probation or other intermediate sanction, grew steadily. In the five years before the Guidelines took effect, prison sentences accounted for a nearly

constant (if slightly rising) proportion of all sentences of either imprisonment or probation—varying only from 45.6 to 49.6 percent. In the first fourteen years after the
Guidelines took effect, that proportion grew progressively larger, from 52.3 percent in
1988 to 81.8 percent in 2001 (see Bureau of Justice Statistics, *Sourcebook* [2001],
table 5.22).

74. At the time the Guidelines were issued, the Commission reported that
"[g]uideline sentences in many instances will approximate existing practice" (see U.S.
Sentencing Commission, *Sentencing Guidelines* [1987], Introduction, 4(g), at 1.11).
The commission acknowledged, however, that its sentences would exceed past practice
in cases involving white-collar crimes and would do so "substantially" in cases involving certain violent crimes (see U.S. Sentencing Commission, *Supplementary Report*,
18–19 and n.61). Even in cases governed by the new mandatory-minimum sentencing
laws, the guideline range often called for sentences well above the statutory minimum
(see Stith and Cabranes, *Fear of Judging*, 60–61).

75. See *Mistretta v. United States*, 488 U.S. 361, 412 (1989). Before *Mistretta*,
more than 200 district judges had invalidated the Guidelines (see U.S. Sentencing
Commission, *Report* [1991], 8). The most prominent constitutional challenge alleged
that service of Article III judges on the Commission and its placement within the judicial branch violated the principle of separation of powers. See, for example, *Gubiensio-Ortiz v. Kanahele*, 857 F.2d 1245, 1266 (9th Cir. 1988); *United States v. Bogle*, 689
F. Supp. 1121, 1124–25 (S.D. Fla. 1988) (*en banc*); and *United States v. Arnold*, 678
F. Supp. 1463, 1465 (S.D. Cal. 1988).

76. Where possible, I have presented guilty plea rates as a proportion of all
adjudicated cases—those cases ending in either a trial or a plea of guilty or nolo contendere. Because the denominator includes cases that ended in acquittals after trial,
my guilty plea rates appear lower than they would if presented as a proportion of all
convictions. Almost all studies of the Guidelines, including the Commission's own
publications, use the latter measure. See, for example, U.S. Sentencing Commission,
Sourcebook (2001), 24, table 11, which reports a guilty plea rate in 2001 of 96.6 percent, measured as a proportion of all convictions. Because my focus is on the dynamics that drive the decision to strike a deal rather than go to trial, there is no reason to
let juries' decisions to acquit or convict after trial affect the measure of plea-bargaining frequency.

77. In 1995 the Commission noted that this increase was under way, but
attributed it, in part, to a differing mix of cases: The proportion of immigration and
fraud cases had grown while that of drug trafficking cases, in which pleas were relatively less common, had shrunk (see U.S. Sentencing Commission, *Annual Report*
[1995], 51).

It is true there was a shift in case mix. Between 1991 and 1995, the proportion
of immigration cases had increased slightly from 7.0 percent of the total to 8.3 percent,
and that of fraud cases from 10.5 percent to 15.4 percent. At the same time, the proportion of drug-trafficking cases had declined slightly from 40.7 percent to 37.0 per-

cent. But across all three crime categories, the proportion of convictions resulting from a plea had increased—in immigration cases from 96.1 percent to 98.1 percent, in fraud cases from 92.5 percent to 94.1 percent, and in trafficking cases from 78.6 percent to 89.3 percent. See U.S. Sentencing Commission, *Annual Report* (1991), 63, table 22, 53, table 15; U.S. Sentencing Commission, *Annual Report* (1995), 56, table 17. A glance at these numbers makes it plain that the dominant force in bringing about the overall rise in guilty pleas was the increased pleading rate in trafficking cases.

By 2001 the story had grown even clearer. True, the proportion of immigration cases had risen sharply to 17.5 percent. But that of trafficking cases had recovered to 40.3 percent, and the proportion of fraud cases had retreated to 11.2 percent. And across all three crimes, the rate of convictions resulting from pleas had continued to rise—to 99.0 percent in immigration cases, to 96.5 percent in fraud cases, and to a striking 96.9 percent in trafficking cases (see U.S. Sentencing Commission, *Sourcebook* (2001), 12, table 3, 24, table 11). It is apparent that the changing mix of cases, though important, has been a relatively small factor in generating the overall increase in guilty pleas.

78. Bureau of Justice Statistics, *Sourcebook* (2001), table 5.21.

79. Those judges who entertained pleas offered under Fed. R. Crim. P. 11(e)(1)(C) and 11(e)(4) effectively promised the defendant that they would either follow the parties' sentencing recommendation or give the defendant a chance to withdraw his plea. These rules are slated to be recodified as Rule 11(c)(1)(C) and 11(c)(5)(B).

80. See Fed. R. Crim. P. 11(e)(1), which forbids courts to participate in plea negotiations (slated to be recodified as Rule 11(c)(1)); *Longval v. Meachum*, 651 F.2d 818, 820–21 (1st Cir. 1981), which disapproved of a trial judge's threat of "a substantial prison sentence" should the defendant choose trial and lose; *Scott v. United States*, 419 F.2d 264, 273–74 (D.C. Cir. 1969), which disapproved of direct judicial participation in plea bargaining.

81. In pre-Guidelines days, defendants sentenced to more than a year in prison became parole eligible after serving one-third of their term (see Heaney, "Reality," 177 n.51). The actual time convicts served varied from an average of forty percent of their imposed terms for those sentenced to more than fifteen years to an average of seventy percent of their imposed terms for those sentenced to between one and five years (see Sabol and McGready, *Time Served*, 1).

82. See 18 U.S.C. § 4205(a) (1982) (providing for parole), *repealed* eff. November 1, 1987, by Pub. L. No. 98–473, Tit. II, Ch. II, §§ 218(a)(4), 235, 98 Stat. 2027, 2031 (October 12, 1984).

83. See 18 U.S.C. § 3624(a), (b), which provides that prisoners shall serve their whole terms except for an allowance of up to 15 percent off for good behavior. William J. Sabol and John McGready (*Time Served*, 4) report that under the Guidelines, federal prisoners now serve an average of 86.7 percent of their imposed terms.

84. U.S. Sentencing Commission, *Sentencing Guidelines Manual* (1987), Intro., 4(c), at 1.8.

85. It is no easy matter to prove whether the gap between post-plea and post-trial sentences has widened since the Guidelines took effect. There is good evidence that the gap between the *average* sentence imposed after trial and that awarded after a plea has grown. The U.S. Probation Department in the District of Massachusetts reported that in 1990, the average defendant who pled guilty received a sentence fifty-eight percent smaller than the average defendant who lost after trial. By 1999 that discount had grown to seventy-two percent (see *Berthoff*, 140 F. Supp. 2d at 67–68 [citing Report from U.S. Probation Department, District of Massachusetts, December 2, 1999]).

Such composite statistics cannot tell us, however, whether Jennifer Reinganum is right in concluding that "cases involving more serious crimes are more likely to go to trial" (Jennifer F. Reinganum, "Sentencing Guidelines," 68). See also U.S. Sentencing Commission, *Supplementary Report*, 50 n.85, which noted that "research has shown that lower sentences for guilty pleas result in part from the circumstance that the cases that go to trial tend to be more aggravated." If that is true, then as the pool of cases going to trial shrinks—as it has done since 1991—the average seriousness of those cases may increase relative to cases ending in pleas. In that event we would expect a growing gap between average post-trial and post-plea sentences even absent a change in the size of the discount that an average defendant wins from his post-trial sentence by pleading guilty.

86. See this chapter, Note 31, and accompanying text.

87. See 18 U.S.C. § 3553(e), which permits the government to move for a sentence below the statutory minimum. As Stephanos Bibas points out to me, a judge can exercise a modicum of mercy in certain drug cases by granting the two-level "safety valve" reduction permitted by guideline section 2D1.1(b)(6). But the five stated criteria for earning this reduction—which involve such matters as the seriousness of the defendant's record and whether he possessed a weapon, inflicted injury, organized others in the offense, or supplied the government with whatever information he has—are sufficiently rigid and demanding to deny judges broad discretion to reduce sentences. Moreover, the permitted reduction is fixed at two levels. A well-informed defense lawyer therefore is likely to factor in the safety valve reduction when counseling her client on the consequences of trial and conviction—leaving the defendant without realistic hope of a lesser sentence.

88. See this chapter, Note 73.

89. My thanks to Marc Miller for offering this point.

90. I figured these percentages from data supplied by the Federal Justice Statistics Database, *available at* http://fjsrc.urban.org. Michael M. O'Hear ("Remorse," 1534) reports that in the District of Connecticut, a reduction for acceptance of responsibility "has effectively become an automatic discount for guilty pleas."

91. See U.S. Sentencing Commission, *Sentencing Guidelines Manual* (1999), § 3E1.1, cmt. n.2, which suggests that it might be appropriate for a judge to award a discount for acceptance of responsibility even after trial if "a defendant goes to trial to assert and preserve issues that do not relate to factual guilt (e.g., to make a constitu-

tional challenge to a statute . . .)." O'Hear ("Remorse," 1539–40) reports findings of a study suggesting that in the great majority of cases in which defendants receive this discount after trial, "the defendant made at least a partial admission of guilt to a probation officer or the government."

92. U.S. Sentencing Commission, *Sentencing Guidelines* (1987), § 3E1.1, cmt., at 3.13.

93. U.S. Sentencing Commission, *Sentencing Guidelines Manual* (1999), § 3E1.1, cmt. n.2 (added by Amendment No. 351, effective November 1, 1990). In *United States v. Dia*, 69 F.3d 291, 293 (9th Cir. 1995), the Ninth Circuit upheld a district judge's refusal to grant an acceptance-of-responsibility discount where "there was no evidence that [the defendant] accepted responsibility before responsibility was forced on him by trial and conviction." The Tenth Circuit declared more generally in *United States v. Portillo-Valenzuela*, 20 F.3d 393, 395 (10th Cir.), *cert. denied*, 513 U.S. 886 (1994), that "in all but rare cases going to trial will preclude reduction for acceptance of responsibility." I thank Stephanos Bibas for calling my attention to the Commission's change of views on this score.

94. Nagel and Schulhofer, "Tale of Three Cities," 529–30, paraphrasing one public defender.

95. In a recent, rather bitter opinion, Massachusetts District Judge William G. Young castigated fact bargaining even as he conceded its legality in the First Circuit:

[B]ecause certain material 'facts,' so called, now mathematically drive every sentencing decision, fact bargaining is today central to plea negotiation in federal court. Everyone involved knows it. Prosecutors and defense counsel are knowingly involved in this fraud and courts—now largely stripped of the powers to make fully informed sentencing decisions—tacitly acquiesce when satisfied with the negotiated plea. As a result, sentencing under the Sentencing Guidelines today is, as one of my colleagues so aptly puts it, "a massive exercise in hypocrisy." (*Berthoff v. United States*, 140 F. Supp. 2d 50, 62–64, 66 [D. Mass. 2001])

Young added that "beyond being a fraud on the courts, fact bargaining brings with it . . . unfettered prosecutorial discretion in that the judgment of offense-seriousness is placed in the hands of the prosecutor with little possibility of judicial oversight" (ibid., 63 n.23). See also Matt Kelly, "Chief Judge Chastises Criminal Bar Over 'Fact-Bargaining,' " *Boston Law Tribune*, November 19, 2001, 1, which quotes Judge Young in an address to prosecutors and defense lawyers: "The guidelines say you can't fact-bargain, and you all do it, and it's a fraud."

96. U.S. Sentencing Commission, *Sentencing Guidelines Manual* (1999), § 6B1.4, cmt.; Nagel and Schulhofer, "Tale of Three Cities," 547.

97. See U.S. Sentencing Commission, Sentencing Guildelines Manual (1999), § 3B1.2; Schulhofer and Nagel, "Plea Negotiations," 1293.

98. See this chapter, Notes 54–55 and accompanying text.

99. In a statistical study of three Northeastern jurisdictions, Abigail Payne

found the same striking pattern in all three. After the guidelines took hold, the proportion of defendants who switched initial not-guilty pleas to guilty pleas fell substantially. At the same time, the proportion who pled guilty in the first instance rose by an even larger margin (Abigail Payne, "Inter-Judge Disparity," 345, table 1). These changes suggest falling rates of regular charge bargaining and rising rates of pre-charge bargaining.

Ahmed Taha likewise found evidence of increased pre-charge bargaining after the Guidelines took effect. In the year after the Supreme Court declared the Guidelines constitutional, the proportion of defendants convicted of the same charges initially filed increased 7.6 percent over a sample of cases resolved before the Guidelines took effect. This result was statistically significant at the five- percent level. See Taha, "Equilibrium Effect," 255, 257 and n.27, 259 and table 3, 260. It is likely, I believe, that similar research conducted for a later period, after all parties had learned how to bargain under the Guidelines, would show larger increases. Larger increases might also appear if the data permitted (as Taha's did not) segregation of cases in which defendants pled guilty to the charges filed from those in which defendants were convicted after trial of the charges filed. See ibid., 256.

The commission reported in 1991 that prosecutors from one office said as many as seventy percent of fraud and white-collar cases in their office involved pre-charge bargains (see U.S. Sentencing Commission, *Report* [1991], 174).

100. Nagel and Schulhofer ("Tale of Three Cities," 516, 540) report that pre-charge bargaining permits prosecutors to strike deals with less oversight from their superiors and with less risk that the court will enhance the defendant's sentence based on his or her relevant conduct.

101. See Chapter 7, Notes 46–53, and accompanying text.

NOTES TO APPENDIX A

1. See Prologue, Notes 5–8, and accompanying text describing the middle-tier courts.

2. See Prologue, Note 10, and Chapter 2, Note 6, and accompanying text describing this jurisdictional shift.

3. See Chapter 1, Note 86.

4. See Chapter 1, Note 91 and Table 1.2.

5. See Chapter 1, Notes 30–38, and Chapter 3, Notes 15–23, and accompanying text.

6. See Chapter 2, Notes 59–65 and accompanying text; Chapter 6, Notes 59–63 and accompanying text; Chapter 3, Notes 33–36 and 83–90, and accompanying text.

7. See, e.g., Chapter 5, Table 5.1, which includes liquor cases.

8. See Chapter 1, Notes 30–38 and accompanying text.

9. See Chapter 1, Notes 30–33 and 54, and Chapter 3, Note 1, and accompanying text, which describe various incarnations of the liquor license and prohibition laws.

10. See *Mass. Rev. Stat.* ch. 130, § 18 (Dutton and Wentworth 1836), which provided for a fine "not exceeding five dollars" for a first offense of drunkenness; Act of March 29, 1834, ch. 61, § 2, 1834 Mass. Acts 189, 190–91, which provided for commitment of an unspecified length to a house of correction for being a common drunkard.

11. See Act of May 19, 1855, ch. 405, 1855 Mass. Acts 803, and table 5.1, note b, which cites the statutes.

12. One of the penalty provisions of the 1855 act gave the judge a good deal of sentencing discretion. See ibid., §§ 1, 2, at 803–4, which provided for a "fine not exceeding one thousand dollars, or . . . imprisonment . . . not more than one year" for maintaining a liquor nuisance. Another gave the prosecutor substantial sentencing power by imposing a minimum sentence. See ibid., § 4, at 804, which called for "a fine of not less than one hundred, nor more than one thousand dollars, or . . . imprisonment in the county jail not less than thirty days, nor more than six months." Even this latter provision, however, probably could not have supported a successful charge-bargaining regime. Although it assured the prosecutor a substantial minimum sentence, it did not protect the defendant against an unreasonable maximum. That is, even if the prosecutor and defendant agreed that the defendant would plead guilty to one count and be fined $100, the judge could imprison the defendant for six months.

13. See, e.g., Chapter 3, Note 47, and accompanying text.

14. See Chapter 1, Note 28.

NOTES TO APPENDIX B

1. Ferdinand, *Boston's Courts*, 59, table 2.3.

2. Ibid., 75, table 3.3.

3. See Act of March 24, 1832, ch. 166, § 5, 1832 Mass. Acts 474, 474–75; see also Act of April 20, 1837, ch. 242, § 1, 1837 Mass. Acts 279, 279, which raised the statutory penalty for Sunday sales to twenty dollars per offense.

4. See Chapter 1, Notes 27–38, 50–57, and 75 and accompanying text.

5. See, e.g., *Commonwealth v. Thomas Barber*, Middlesex Ct. C.P. R. Book 158 (October 1842), copy on file with the author, which charged four Sunday sales; *Commonwealth v. Thomas Barber*, Middlesex Ct. C.P. File Papers (October 1842), copy on file with the author, which contains the preprinted indictment form for the previous case.

6. Ferdinand, *Boston's Courts*, 150.

7. Ibid., 59, table 2.3.

8. § 11, 1832 Mass. Acts at 478–79; see also Act of February 28, 1787, ch. 68,

1786 Mass. Acts 210, 210, an earlier version of the same act, which provided for a fine of forty shillings for permitting gaming and a fine of twenty shillings for taking part.

9. See *Mass. Rev. Stat.* ch. 50, § 18 (Dutton & Wentworth 1836), which prescribed the punishment for playing at billiards.

10. See ibid., § 17, which called for fines of up to one hundred dollars for persons not licensed as innholders who are convicted of keeping gaming apparatus or related offenses; ibid., ch. 132, §§ 1–2, 4–5, which punished various "lottery" offenses with fines of up to two thousand dollars or prison terms of up to three years.

11. Ibid., ch. 143, §§ 5, 6.

12. Ibid., ch. 130, § 8.

13. Ferdinand finds it significant that the practice of switching an initial not-guilty plea to a guilty plea developed earlier in prostitution cases than in others (see *Boston's Courts*, 75, table 3.3, 77, 81, 94). Moreover, he reports a striking drop in the rate of not-guilty pleas in prostitution cases in the mid- and late 1840s (ibid., 75, table 3.3) and presents evidence that those prostitution defendants who pled guilty got shorter prison terms than those who went to trial and lost (ibid., 78, table 3.5).

14. See ibid., 50, table 2.2. He reports "little evidence" of plea bargaining among common law crimes (ibid., 92).

15. See Chapter 6, Note 13.

16. See Ferdinand, *Boston's Courts*, 59, table 2.3.

17. See Chapter 3, Notes 9–10 and 71–74, and accompanying text.

18. See Augustus, *Report of the Labors*, 33–37; see also ibid., 78–79, which reprints an 1848 newspaper item accusing Augustus of keeping "a sort of Magdalen Asylum."

19. See Ferdinand, *Boston's Courts*, 74, table 3.2.

Bibliography

BOOKS, ARTICLES, DISSERTATIONS,
AND UNPUBLISHED DOCUMENTS

Act To Prohibit the Justices of the Court of Common Pleas from Practising as Attornies or Counsellors. Unpublished document on file with the Harvard Law School Library, proposed 1811.

Aggeler, William T. "Public Defense of Accused Upheld as Duty to Society." *New York Times*, October 22, 1922, part 9, 4.

Allen, Frederick B. *Prison Reform in Massachusetts*. Boston: Christian Soc. Union, 1898.

Alschuler, Albert W. "The Defense Attorney's Role in Plea Bargaining." *Yale Law Journal* 84 (1975): 1179.

———. "Foreword: The Vanishing Civil Jury." *University of Chicago Legal Forum* 1990 (1990): 1.

———. "Plea Bargaining and Its History." *Columbia Law Review* 79 (1979): 1.

———. "The Prosecutor's Role in Plea Bargaining." *University of Chicago Law Review* 36 (1968): 50.

———. "The Trial Judge's Role in Plea Bargaining." *Columbia Law Review* 76 (1976): 1059.

American Law Institute. *A Study of the Business of the Federal Courts*, vol. 1. Philadelphia: Executive Office, American Law Inst., 1934.

[Ames, Seth]. "Testimony of Persons Accused of Crime." *American Law Review* 1 (1866–1867): 443.

Augustus, John. *A Report of the Labors of John Augustus, for the Last Ten Years, in Aid of the Unfortunate*. Boston: Wright and Hasty, 1852.

Barnes, Harry Elmer. *The Evolution of Penology in Pennsylvania*. Montclair, N.J.: Patterson Smith, 1927.

Barney, Edwin L. Diaries of Edwin L. Barney, vols. 1–3 (1858–1896). Unpublished documents on file with the Massachusetts Historical Society.

Beattie, J. M. *Crime and the Courts in England, 1660–1800*. Princeton: Princeton University Press, 1986.

Bergstrom, Randolph E. *Courting Danger: Injury and Law in New York City, 1870–1910*. Ithaca: Cornell University Press, 1992.

Blackstone, William. *Commentaries on the Laws of England*, vol. 4. Boston: T. B. Wait and Sons, 1818.

Bolster, Wilfred. "Criminal Appeals." *Massachusetts Law Quarterly* (August 1922).

Bowman, III, Frank O., and Michael Heise. "Quiet Rebellion? Explaining Nearly a Decade of Declining Federal Drug Sentences." *Iowa Law Review* 86 (2001): 1043.

———. "Quiet Rebellion II: An Empirical Analysis of Declining Federal Drug Sentences Including Data from the District Level." *Iowa Law Review* 87 (2002): 477.

Brooks, C. W. "Interpersonal Conflict and Social Tension: Civil Litigation in England, 1640–1830." In *The First Modern Society: Essays in English History in Honour of Lawrence Stone*, edited by A. L. Beier, et al., 357. New York: Cambridge University Press, 1989.

Bureau of Criminal Statistics. *Felony Defendants Disposed of in California Courts: References Tables.* Washington, D.C., 1970.

Bureau of Justice Statistics. *Sourcebook of Criminal Justice Statistics—1997.* Washington, D.C.: U.S. Department of Justice, 1998.

———. *Sourcebook of Criminal Justice Statistics—1998.* Washington, D.C.: U.S. Department of Justice, 1999.

———. *Sourcebook of Criminal Justice Statistics—1999.* Washington, D.C.: U.S. Department of Justice, 2000.

———. *Sourcebook of Criminal Justice Statistics—2000.* Washington, D.C.: U.S. Department of Justice, 2001.

———. *Sourcebook of Criminal Justice Statistics—2001.* Washington, D.C.: U.S. Department of Justice, 2002.

Callagy, Martin V. "Legal Aid in Criminal Cases." *Journal of Criminal Law, Criminology and Police Sciences* 42 (1952): 589.

Carter, Lief H. *The Limits of Order.* Lexington: Lexington Books, 1974.

Cary, Seth Cooley. "Prison Reform—The Indeterminate Sentence." *Alpha* 8 (1889–1890): 1.

Case of Asahel Huntington: Report. Mass. House Doc. No. 4 (1845).

Chaplin, Heman W. "Reform in Criminal Procedure." *Harvard Law Review* 7 (1893): 189.

Chitty, Joseph. *A Practical Treatise on the Criminal Law*, vol. 1. Philadelphia: Isaac Riley, 1819.

Clary, William W. "The Public Defender." *Pomona College Quarterly Magazine* 7 (1918): 49.

Clifford, John Henry. John Henry Clifford Papers (1840–1875). Unpublished documents on file with the Massachusetts Historical Society.

Cochran, Jr., Johnnie L., with Tim Rutten. *Journey to Justice.* New York: Ballantine Books, 1996.

Cockburn, J. S. "Trial by the Book? Fact and Theory in the Criminal Process, 1558–1625." In *Legal Records and the Historian*, edited by J. H. Baker. London: Royal Historical Society, 1978.

The Code of Criminal Procedure of the State of New-York: Reported Complete by the

Commissioners on Practice and Pleadings. New York: Albany, Weed, Parsons and Co., 1850.

Commonwealth of Massachusetts. *Probation Manual.* Boston: Wright and Potter, 1916.

A Compendium of the Ninth Census. Washington, D.C.: Government Printing Office, 1872.

Compendium of the Tenth Census. Part 1. Washington, D.C.: Government Printing Office, 1883.

Cottu, Charles. *De L'Administration de la Justice Criminelle en Angleterre, et de L'Esprit du Gouvernement Anglais* (1822). New York: Arno Press, 1979.

Crime Commission of New York State. "Report of the Crime Commission." In *New York Legislative Documents*, vol. 6, no. 23, 1 (151st. Sess., 1928).

Dana, James. *Memoir of the Late Hon. Samuel Dana.* Cambridge: John Wilson and Son, 1877.

Dana, Samuel. Mr. Dana's Answer to the Report of the Committee of the House of Representatives (Feb. 28, 1808). Unpublished document on file with the Massachusetts Historical Society.

D'Anca, Alfred R. "The Role of the Federal Probation Officer in the Guidelines Sentencing System." *Probation* 65 (2001): 20.

Davis, William T. *Bench and Bar of the Commonwealth of Massachusetts*, vols. 1, 2. Boston: Boston History Company, 1895.

———. *History of the Judiciary of Massachusetts.* New York: Da Capo Press, 1900.

Devens, Charles. Charles Devens Notebooks (1867–1875). Unpublished documents on file with the Massachusetts Historical Society.

Devereaux, Simon. "The City and the Sessions Paper: 'Public Justice' in London, 1770–1800." *Journal of British Studies* 35 (1966): 466.

Dick, John M., Note, "Allowing Sentence Bargains To Fall Outside of the Guidelines Without Valid Departures: It Is Time for the Commission To Act." *Hastings Law Journal* 48 (1997): 1017.

Dimond, Alan J. *The Superior Court of Massachusetts.* Boston: Little, Brown, 1960.

"Drafting a New Penal Law in New York: An Interview with Richard Denzer." *Buffalo Law Review* 18 (1969): 251.

Embree, William Dean. "The Voluntary Defenders." *Legal Aid Review* 28 (1928): 1.

Emery, Ex–Chief Justice. "The Nolle Prosequi in Criminal Cases." *Maine Law Review* 6 (1913): 199.

Fabricant, Louis. "The Voluntary Defender in Criminal Cases." *Annals* 124 (1926): 74.

Farabee, Lisa M. "Disparate Departures Under the Federal Sentencing Guidelines: A Tale of Two Districts." *Connecticut Law Review* 30 (1998): 569.

Federal Justice Statistics Database. Available at http://fjsrc.urban.org.

Feeley, Malcolm M. "Legal Complexity and the Transformation of the Criminal Process: The Origins of Plea Bargaining." *Israel Law Review* 31 (1997): 183.

Feeley, Malcolm M., and Charles Lester. "Legal Complexity and the Transformation of the Criminal Process." In *Subjektivierung des justiziellen Beweisverfahrens*, edited by André Gouron et al., 337. Frankfurt: Vittorio Klosterman, 1994.

Fenner, Ball. *Raising the Veil; or, Scenes in the Courts.* Boston: James French, 1856.

Ferdinand, Theodore. *Boston's Lower Criminal Courts, 1814–1850.* Newark: University of Delaware Press, 1992.

Fisher, Barry J. "Judicial Suicide or Constitutional Autonomy? A Capital Defendant's Right to Plead Guilty." *Albany Law Review* 65 (2001): 181.

Fisher, George. "The Birth of the Prison Retold." *Yale Law Journal* 104 (1995): 1235.

———. "The Jury's Rise as Lie Detector." *Yale Law Journal* 107 (1997): 575.

———. "Making Sense of English Law Enforcement in the Eighteenth Century: A Response." *University of Chicago Law School Roundtable* 2 (1995): 507.

Fitch, John A. Letter from John A. Fitch to Asahel Huntington (Jan. 11, 1843). Unpublished document on file with the Massachusetts Archives, contained in *Commonwealth v. Moses Phipps and Benjamin Phipps*, Middlesex Court of Common Pleas File Papers (June 1843).

Flaherty, David H. "Criminal Practice in Provincial Massachusetts." In *Law in Colonial Massachusetts 1630–1800.* Conference held by The Colonial Society of Massachusetts, Nov. 7, 1981. Charlottesville: University Press of Virginia, 1984.

Follett, Martin Dewey. "Aims of the Indeterminate Sentence." In *The Indeterminate Sentence and the Parole Law: Reports Prepared for the International Prison Commission.* Mass. Sen. Doc. No. 55–159 (1899).

Foltz, Clara. "Public Defenders." *American Law Review* 31 (1897): 393.

Fosdick, Raymond, et al. *Criminal Justice in Cleveland.* Roscoe Pound and Felix Frankfurter, eds. Cleveland: The Foundation, 1922.

Fourth Report of the Commissioners on Practice and Pleadings: Code of Criminal Procedure. New York: Albany, Weed, Parsons, 1849.

Freed, Daniel J. "Federal Sentencing in the Wake of Guidelines, Unacceptable Limits on the Discretion of Sentencers." *Yale Law Journal* 101 (1992): 1681.

Friedman, David D. "Making Sense of English Law Enforcement in the Eighteenth Century." *University of Chicago Law School Roundtable* 2 (1995): 475.

Friedman, Lawrence M. "Civil Wrongs: Personal Injury Law in the Late 19th Century." *American Bar Foundation Research Journal* (1987): 351.

———. "Courts over Time: A Survey of Theories and Research." In *Empirical Theories About Courts*, edited by Keith O. Boyum and Lynn Mather, 9. New York: Longman, 1983.

———. *A History of American Law.* New York: Simon and Schuster, 1973.

Friedman, Lawrence M., and Robert V. Percival. *The Roots of Justice: Crime and Punishment in Alameda County, California 1870–1910.* Chapel Hill: University of North Carolina Press, 1981.

Fuller, Hugh N. *Criminal Justice in Virginia.* New York: Century, 1931.

Galanter, Marc. "Reading the Landscape of Disputes: What We Know and Don't Know (and Think We Know) About Our Allegedly Contentious and Litigious Society." *UCLA Law Review* 31 (1983): 4.

Georgia Department of Public Welfare. "Crime and the Georgia Courts, a Statistical Analysis." *Journal of Criminal Law and Criminology* 16 (1925): 169.

Gold, David M. *The Shaping of Nineteenth-Century Law*. New York: Greenwood, 1990.

Goldman, Mayer C. *The Public Defender: A Necessary Factor in the Administration of Justice*. New York: G. P. Putnam's Sons, 1917.

Goodwin, Frank A. "Community vs. Criminal," *Massachusetts Law Quarterly* 11 (May 1926): 16.

Gould, John Stanton, et al. "Report on Common Jails and the Administration of Criminal Justice." In *Twenty-First Annual Report of the Executive Committee of the Prison Association of New York* (1866), 137. Reprinted in N.Y. Assembly Doc. No. 50 (1866).

Grinnell, Frank W. "Courts and Lawyers in Metropolitan Boston." In *Metropolitan Boston: A Modern History*, vol. 1, edited by Albert P. Langtry, 243. New York: Lewis Historical, 1929.

———. "Probation as an Orthodox Common Law Practice in Massachusetts Prior to the Statutory System." *Massachusetts Law Quarterly* 2 (Aug. 1917): 591.

G[rinnell], F. W. "Legislative Problems in Regard to the Administration of the Criminal Law and Legislative Progress During the Session of 1923." *Massachusetts Law Quarterly* (May 1923): 7.

Haines, Jr., Roger W., Kevin Cole, and Jeniffer C. Woll. *Federal Sentencing Guide*. Costa Mesa (Cal.): James Publishing, 1997.

Hale, Matthew. *History of the Pleas of the Crown*, vol. 2. Philadelphia: Robert H. Small, 1847.

Hampel, Robert L. *Temperance and Prohibition in Massachusetts, 1813–1852*. Ann Arbor: UMI Research Press, 1982.

Handlin, Oscar. *Boston's Immigrants*. Cambridge: Belknap Press, 1959.

Harno, Albert J. "The Workings of the Parole Board and Its Relation to the Court (1928)." Photo reprinted in *The Workings of the Indeterminate-Sentence Law and the Parole System in Illinois*, edited by Andrew Bruce, et al. Montclair: Patterson Smith, 1979.

Harris, Robert O. *Report of District Attorney* (1898). In *Report of the County Commissioners of the County of Plymouth*. Plymouth: Avery Printing, 1899.

Heaney, Gerald W. "The Reality of Guidelines Sentencing: No End to Disparity." *American Criminal Law Review* 28 (1991): 161.

Heumann, Milton. "A Note on Plea Bargaining and Case Pressure." *Law and Society Review* 9 (1975): 515.

———. *Plea Bargaining: The Experiences of Prosecutors, Judges, and Defense Attorneys*. Boston: G. K. Hall, 1977.

Hindus, Michael Stephen. *Prison and Plantation: Crime, Justice, and Authority in Massachusetts and South Carolina, 1767–1878.* Chapel Hill: University of North Carolina Press, 1980.

Hindus, Michael Stephen, et al. *The Files of the Massachusetts Superior Court, 1859–1959.* Boston: G. K. Hall, 1980.

Hirsch, Adam Jay. *The Rise of the Penitentiary: Prisons and Punishment in Early America.* New Haven: Yale University Press, 1992.

Hofer, Paul J., and Courtney Semisch. "Examining Changes in Federal Sentence Severity: 1980–1998." *Federal Sentencing Reporter* 14 (2000): 12.

Hopkins, M. W. "Withdrawal of Plea of Guilty." *Criminal Law Magazine* 11 (1889): 479.

Hurst, James Willard. *The Growth of American Law: The Law Makers.* Boston: Little, Brown, 1950.

Hutchison, Thomas W., et al., *Federal Sentencing Law and Practice.* St. Paul: West Publishing, 2001.

Illinois Association for Criminal Justice. *The Illinois Crime Survey.* Chicago: Blakely, 1929.

The Indeterminate Sentence and the Parole Law: Reports Prepared for the International Prison Commission. Mass. Sen. Doc. No. 55–159 (1899).

Kalven, Jr., Harry, and Hans Zeisel. *The American Jury.* Boston: Little, Brown, 1966.

Kelly, Matt, "Chief Judge Chastises Criminal Bar Over 'Fact-Bargaining.'" *Boston Law Tribune* (Nov. 19, 2001): 1.

Kocourek, Albert. "An Unconsidered Element in the Probation of First Offenders." *Journal of Criminal Law and Criminology* 6 (1915–1916): 9.

Kuntz II, William Francis. *Criminal Sentencing in Three Nineteenth-Century Cities: Social History of Punishment in New York, Boston, and Philadelphia 1830–1880.* New York: Garland, 1988.

Kurland, Adam H. "Providing a Federal Criminal Defendant with a Unilateral Right to a Bench Trial: A Renewed Call to Amend Federal Rule of Criminal Procedure 23(a)." *U.C. Davis Law Review* 26 (1993): 309.

Kurland, Philip B., and D.W.M. Waters. "Public Prosecutions in England, 1854–79: An Essay in English Legislative History." *Duke Law Journal* 1959 (1959): 493.

Landau, Norma. "Indictment for Fun and Profit: A Prosecutor's Reward at Eighteenth-Century Quarter Sessions." *Legal and Historical Review* 17 (1999): 507.

Lane, Roger. *Policing the City: Boston 1822–1885.* Cambridge: Harvard University Press, 1967.

Lane, Winthrop D. "A New Day Opens for Parole." *Journal of Criminal Law and Criminology* 24 (1933): 88.

Langbein, John H. "Torture and Plea Bargaining." *University of Chicago Law Review* 46 (1978): 3.

———. "Understanding the Short History of Plea Bargaining." *Law and Society Review* 13 (1979): 261.

Legal Aid Society. *Report of Voluntary Defenders' Committee.* 1917. New York: Voluntary Defenders Committee.

———. *45th Annual Report, Voluntary Defenders' Committee.* 1920. New York: Voluntary Defenders Committee.

———. *48th Annual Report, Voluntary Defenders' Committee.* 1923. New York: Voluntary Defenders Committee.

———. *51st Annual Report, Voluntary Defenders' Committee.* 1926. New York: Voluntary Defenders Committee.

———. *52d Annual Report, Voluntary Defenders' Committee.* 1927. New York: Voluntary Defenders Committee.

———. *53d Annual Report, Voluntary Defenders' Committee.* 1928. New York: Voluntary Defenders Committee.

———. *55th Annual Report, Voluntary Defenders' Committee.* 1930. New York: Voluntary Defenders Committee.

"Legislation—Indeterminate Sentence Laws—The Adolescence of Penocorrectional Legislation," *Harvard Law Review* 50 (1937): 677.

Lettow, Renée B. "New Trial for Verdict Against Law: Judge-Jury Relations in Early Nineteenth-Century America." *Notre Dame Law Review* 71 (1996): 505.

Lewis, Charlton T. "The Indeterminate Sentence." *Yale Law Journal* 9 (1899): 17.

Lindsey, Edward. "Historical Sketch of the Indeterminate Sentence and Parole System." *Journal of Criminal Law and Criminology* 16 (1925): 9.

Massachusetts House of Representatives. *Report of the Committee Appointed on the Memorial of Samson Woods, Complaining of Certain Conduct of Samuel Dana, Esquire, in His Office of County Attorney for the County of Middlesex,* 1809.

Massachusetts Lawyer's Diary, 1898.

Mather, Lynn M. "Comments on the History of Plea Bargaining." *Law and Society Review* 13 (1979): 281.

———. *Plea Bargaining or Trial?: The Process of Criminal Case Disposition.* Lexington: Lexington Books, 1979.

Maury, William A. "Validity of Statutes Authorizing the Accused To Testify." *American Law Review* 14 (1880): 753.

McConville, Michael, and Chester L. Mirsky. "Criminal Defense of the Poor in New York City." *New York University Review of Law and Social Change* 15 (1986–1987): 581.

———. "The Rise of Guilty Pleas: New York, 1800–1865." *Journal of Law and Society* 22 (1995): 443.

Menand, Catherine S. *A Research Guide to the Massachusetts Courts and Their Records.* Boston: Massachusetts Supreme Judicial Court Archives and Records, 1987.

Middlesex County. *Statement of Receipts and Expenditures of the County of Middlesex for the Year Ending December 31, 1881.* (n.p., n.d.).

————. *Statement of Receipts and Expenditures of the County of Middlesex for the Year Ending December 31, 1882.* (n.p., n.d.).

Millender, Michael Jonathan. *The Transformation of the American Criminal Trial, 1790–1875.* Ph.D. dissertation, Princeton University, Princeton, 1996.

Miller, Justin. "The Compromise of Criminal Cases." *Southern California Law Review* 1 (1927): 1.

Miller, Marc. "True Grid: Revealing Sentencing Policy." *U.C. Davis L. Review* 25 (1992): 587.

Miller, Wilbur R. *Cops and Bobbies: Police Authority in New York and London, 1830–1870.* Chicago: University of Chicago Press, 1977.

Missouri Association for Criminal Justice. *The Missouri Crime Survey.* New York: Macmillan, 1926.

Moley, Raymond. "The Vanishing Jury." *Southern California Law Review* 2 (1928): 97.

Monkkonen, Eric. H. "The American State from the Bottom Up: Of Homicides and Courts." *Law and Society Review* 24 (1990): 521.

Morse, Lewis W. "Historical Outline and Bibliography of Attorneys General Reports and Opinions from Their Beginning Through 1936." *Law Library Journal* 30 (1937): 39.

Morse, Wayne L., and Ronald H. Beattie. *Survey of the Administration of Criminal Justice in Oregon: Final Report on 1771 Felony Cases in Multnomah County.* Eugene (Ore.): University Press, 1932.

Nagel, Ilene H., and Stephen J. Schulhofer. "A Tale of Three Cities: An Empirical Study of Charging and Bargaining Practices Under the Federal Sentencing Guidelines." *Southern California Law Review* 66 (1992): 501.

National Commission on Law Observance and Enforcement. *Report on the Enforcement of the Prohibition Laws of the United States.* Washington, D.C.: U.S. Government Printing Office, 1931.

National Cyclopedia of American Biography, vol. 14. New York: J.T. White, 1910.

Nesson, Charles. "The Evidence or the Event? On Judicial Proof and the Acceptability of Verdicts." *Harvard Law Review* 98 (1985): 1357.

Newman, Charles L. *Sourcebook on Probation, Parole and Pardons.* Springfield, Ill.: Thomas, 1968.

"Notes and Abstracts: The Voluntary Defenders Committee." *Journal of Criminal Law and Criminology* 8 (1917–1918): 278.

O'Brien, Thomas C. "Crime and Criminal Law." *Massachusetts Law Quarterly* (May 1926): 33.

O'Hear, Michael M. "Remorse, Cooperation, and 'Acceptance of Responsibility': The Structure, Implementation, and Reform of Section 3E1.1 of the Federal Sentencing Guidelines." *Northwestern University Law Review* 91 (1997): 1507.

Old Bailey Sessions Paper (OBSP). See *The Proceedings of the Sessions of the Peace and . . .*

Order for Committee of Asahel Huntington: Report. Mass. House Doc. No. 1499 (1844). Unpublished document on file with the Massachusetts Archives.

Payne, Abigail A. "Does Inter-Judge Disparity Really Matter? An Analysis of the Effects of Sentencing Reforms in Three Federal District Courts." *International Review of Law and Economics* 17 (1997): 337.

Pound, Roscoe. *Criminal Justice in America.* New York: H. Holt, 1930.

———. "The Judicial Office Today." *American Bar Association Journal* 25 (1939): 731.

———. *Organization of Courts.* Boston: Little, Brown, 1940.

Pound, Roscoe, and Felix Frankfurter, eds. *Criminal Justice in Cleveland.* Cleveland: The Foundation, 1922.

Prison Association of New York. *Seventy-Second Annual Report of the Prison Association of New York: Prison Progress in 1916.* Albany: J. B. Lyon, 1917.

The Proceedings of the Sessions of the Peace, and Oyer and Terminer, for the City of London, and County of Middlesex. London: Joseph Gurney, 1758 (and others).

Purdy, Jr., Donald A. "Plea Bargaining: What Is the Problem and Who Is Responsible?" *Federal Sentencing Reporter* 8 (1996): 331.

Radzinowicz, Sir Leon, and Roger Hood. *A History of English Criminal Law and Its Administration from 1750: The Emergence of Penal Policy,* vol. 5. New York: Macmillan, 1986.

Ramsey, Carolyn B. "The Discretionary Power of 'Public' Prosecutors in Historical Perspective." *American Criminal Law Review* 39 (forthcoming, 2002): 1309.

Reinganum, Jennifer F. "Sentencing Guidelines, Judicial Discretion, and Plea Bargaining." *Rand Journal of Economics* 31 (2000): 62.

Report of the Crime Commission of New York State. Albany: Crime Commission of New York State, 1927 (advance copy).

"Report of the Minnesota Crime Commission." *Minnesota Law Review Supplement* 11 (1927): 1.

Report of the Prison Survey Committee. 1920.

Ruggles-Brise, Evelyn. *Some Observations on the Treatment of Crime in America.* London: Darling and Son, 1899.

Rush, Benjamin. *An Enquiry into the Effects of Public Punishments upon Criminals and upon Society.* Philadelphia: Joseph James, 1787.

Sabol, William J., and John McGready, "Time Served in Prison by Federal Offenders, 1986–97. Washington, D.C.: Bureau of Justice Statistics, U.S. Department of Justice, 1999.

Sanchirico, Chris William. "Character Evidence and the Object of Trial." *Columbia Law Review* 101 (2001): 1227.

Sarner, Felicia. "'Fact Bargaining' Under the Sentencing Guidelines: The Role of the Probation Department." *Federal Sentencing Reporter* 8 (1996): 328.

Savage, Edward H. *Annual Report of the Probation Officer for Suffolk County, for the Year 1880.* Boston: Rockwell and Churchill, 1881.

——. *Police Records and Recollections, or Boston by Daylight and Gaslight for Two Hundred and Forty Years* (1873). Montclair, N.J.: Patterson Smith, 1971.

——. *Probation Work for the County of Suffolk: The Tenth Annual Report for the Central Probation District.* Boston: Rockwell and Churchill, 1889.

Schulhofer, Stephen J., and Ilene H. Nagel. "Negotiated Pleas Under the Federal Sentencing Guidelines: The First Fifteen Months," *American Criminal Law Review* 27 (1989), 231.

——. "Plea Negotiations Under the Federal Sentencing Guidelines: Guideline Circumvention and Its Dynamics in the Post-*Mistretta* Period." *Northwestern University Law Review* 91 (1997): 1284.

Sears, Daniel J. "Practice Under the Federal Sentencing Guidelines: Bargaining for Freedom." *Colorado Lawyer* 22 (1993): 485.

Selections from the Court Reports Originally Published in the Boston Morning Post, *from 1834 to 1837* (1837). Arno Press Reprint, 1974.

Silverman, Robert A. *Law and Urban Growth: Civil Litigation in the Boston Trial Courts, 1880–1900.* Princeton: Princeton University Press, 1981.

Smith, Reginald Heber. *Justice and the Poor.* New York: Carnegie Foundation for the Advancement of Teaching, 1924.

Spalding, Warren F. "The Indeterminate Sentence: Its History and Development in the United States." In *The Indeterminate Sentence and the Parole Law: Reports Prepared for the International Prison Commission.* Mass. Sen. Doc. No. 55–159 (1899).

——. *Indeterminate Sentences for Penitentiary Prisoners: A Paper Prepared for the National Prison Congress, 1895.* n.p., 1895.

Stafford, William. "Settling Sentencing Facts at the Guilty Plea Hearing: A Time-Saver for the Trial Court." *Federal Sentencing Reporter* 10 (1997): 29.

Standen, Jeffrey. "The End of the Era of Sentencing Guidelines: *Apprendi v. New Jersey.*" *Iowa Law Review* 87 (2002): 775.

The State Board of Prison Directors of the State of California. *Eighth Annual Report.* Sacramento: J.D. Young, 1887.

State of New Jersey. *Report of the Prison Inquiry Commission,* vol. 1. 1917.

Stith, Kate, and José A. Cabranes. *Fear of Judging: Sentencing Guidelines in the Federal Courts.* Chicago: University of Chicago Press, 1998.

Storey, Moorfield. *The Reform of Legal Procedure.* New Haven: Yale University Press, 1911.

Sutherland, Edwin H. *Principles of Criminology.* Chicago: J. P. Lippincott, 1934.

Taha, Ahmed E. "The Equilibrium Effect of Legal Rule Changes: Are the Federal Sentencing Guidelines Being Circumvented?" *International Review of Law and Economics* 21 (2001): 251.

Thompson, Charles. Diaries and Lawyer's Daybooks of Charles Thompson, vols. 1–13 (1857–1888). Unpublished documents on file with the Harvard Law School.

Timasheff, N. S. *One Hundred Years of Probation, 1841–1941*, vol. 1. New York: Fordham University Press, 1941.

Towne, Susan C. "The Historical Origins of Bench Trial for Serious Crime." *American Journal of Legal History* 26 (1982): 123.

Train, Arthur. *The Prisoner at the Bar*. New York: Charles Scribner's Sons, 1906.

Twenty-First Annual Report of the Executive Committee of the Prison Association of New York (1866). Reprinted in New York Assembly Doc. No. 50 (1866).

U.S. Census Office. *Census Reports: Twelfth Census of the United States*, vol. 1., Washington, D.C., 1901.

U.S. Sentencing Commission. *Annual Report, 1988*. Washington, D.C., 1988.

———. *Annual Report, 1989*. Washington. D.C., 1989.

———. *Annual Report, 1990*. Washington, D.C., 1990.

———. *Annual Report, 1991*. Washington, D.C., 1991.

———. *Annual Report, 1992*. Washington, D.C., 1992.

———. *Annual Report, 1993*. Washington, D.C., 1993.

———. *Annual Report, 1994*. Washington, D.C., 1994.

———. *Annual Report, 1995*. Washington, D.C., 1995.

———. *The Federal Sentencing Guidelines: A Report on the Operation of the Guidelines System and Short-Term Impacts on Disparity in Sentencing, Use of Incarceration, and Prosecutorial Discretion and Plea Bargaining*. 3 vols. Washington, D.C., 1991.

———. *1996 Sourcebook of Federal Sentencing Statistics*. Washington, D.C., 1996.

———. *1997 Sourcebook of Federal Sentencing Statistics*. Washington, D.C., 1997.

———. *1998 Sourcebook of Federal Sentencing Statistics*. Washington, D.C., 1998.

———. *1999 Sourcebook of Federal Sentencing Statistics*. Washington, D.C., 1999.

———. *2000 Sourcebook of Federal Sentencing Statistics*. Washington, D.C., 2000.

———. *2001 Sourcebook of Federal Sentencing Statistics*. Washington, D.C., 2001. (Available at: *http://www.ussc.gov/research.htm.*)

———. *Sentencing Guidelines and Policy Statements*. Washington, D.C., 1987.

———. *Supplementary Report on the Initial Sentencing Guidelines and Policy Statements*. Washington, D.C., 1987.

———. *Guidelines Manual*. Washington, D.C., 1998.

Vogel, Mary Elizabeth. *Courts of Trade: Social Conflict and the Emergence of Plea Bargaining in Boston, Massachusetts, 1830–1890*. Ph.D. dissertation, Harvard University, Cambridge, 1988.

———. "The Social Origins of Plea Bargaining: Conflict and the Law in the Process of State Formation, 1830–1860." *Law and Society Review* 33 (April 1999): 161.

Wachtler, Sol. *After the Madness: A Judge's Own Prison Memoir*. New York: Random House, 1997.

Warner, Sam B. "Factors Determining Parole from the Massachusetts Reformatory." *Journal of Criminal Law and Criminology* 14 (1923–1924): 172.

Warren, Charles. *History of the Harvard Law School and of Early Legal Conditions in America*, vol. 1. New York: Lewis, 1908.

Washburn, Emory. *A Manual of Criminal Law* (3d ed.). Chicago: Callaghan, 1900.

Weinstein, Jack B. "A Trial Judge's First Impression of the Federal Sentencing Guidelines." *Albany Law Review* 52 (1988): 1.

White, Peregrine. *John A. Peters: A Memoir.* Bangor: n.p., on file, University of Maine, Orono, 1906.

Wigmore, John Henry. *A Treatise on the Anglo-American System of Evidence in Trials at Common Law*, vol. 3 (3rd ed.). Boston: Little, Brown, 1940.

Wilcox, Clair. *The Parole of Adults from State Penal Institutions in Pennsylvania and in Other Commonwealths.* Ph.D. dissertation, University of Pennsylvania, 1927.

Wilkins, Jr., William W., and John R. Steer. "Relevant Conduct: The Cornerstone of the Federal Sentencing Guidelines." *Southern California Law Review* 41 (1990): 495.

Wines, Frederick Howard. *Monograph on Sentences for Crime.* Springfield (Ill.): H. W. Rokker, 1885.

Wood, Walton J. "The Annual Report of the Los Angeles County Public Defender," *Journal of Criminal Law and Criminology* 9 (1918): 289.

———. "Necessity for Public Defender Established by Statistics." *Journal of Criminal Law and Criminology* 7 (1916–1917): 230.

Woodman, Horatio, editor. *Reports of Criminal Cases, Tried in the Municipal Court of the City of Boston, Before Peter Oxenbridge Thacher.* Boston: Little, Brown, 1845.

Zipperstein, Steven E. "Certain Uncertainty: Appellate Review and the Sentencing Guidelines." *Southern California Law Review* 66 (1992): 621.

CASES

U.S. Supreme Court

Apprendi v. New Jersey, 530 U.S. 466 (2000).

Bordenkircher v. Hayes, 434 U.S. 357 (1978).

Brady v. United States, 397 U.S. 742 (1970).

Ferguson v. Georgia, 365 U.S. 570 (1961).

Griffin v. California, 380 U.S. 609 (1965).

McMann v. Richardson, 397 U.S. 759 (1970).

Melendez v. United States, 518 U.S. 120 (1996)

Mistretta v. United States, 488 U.S. 361 (1989).

North Carolina v. Alford, 400 U.S. 25 (1970).

Parker v. North Carolina, 397 U.S. 790 (1970).

Santobello v. New York, 404 U.S. 257 (1971).

Ex parte United States, 242 U.S. 27 (1916).
Wade v. United States, 504 U.S. 181 (1992).
Watts, United States v., 519 U.S. 148 (1997).

U.S. Appeals Court

Clase-Espinal, United States v., 115 F.3d 1054 (1st Cir. 1997).
Cooper v. Fitzharris, 551 F.2d 1162 (9th Cir. 1977).
Dia, United States v., 69 F.3d 291 (9th Cir. 1995).
Flores-Uribe, United States v., 106 F.3d 1485 (9th Cir. 1997).
Galvez-Falconi, United States v., 174 F.3d 255 (2d Cir. 1999).
Gubiensio-Ortiz v. Kanahele, 857 F.2d 1245 (9th Cir. 1988).
Johnson, United States v., 964 F.2d 124 (2d Cir. 1992).
Jordan, United States v., 256 F.3d 922 (9th Cir. 2001).
Kikumura, United States v., 918 F.2d 1084 (3d Cir. 1990).
Longval v. Meachum, 651 F.2d 818 (1st Cir. 1981).
Marin-Castaneda, United States v., 134 F.3d 551 (3d. Cir.), *cert. denied.*, 523 U.S. 1144 (1998).
Pinnick, United States v., 47 F.3d 434 (D.C. Cir. 1995).
Portillo-Valenzuela, United States v., 20 F.3d 393 (10th Cir. 1994).
Rodriguez-Lopez, United States v., 198 F.3d 773 (9th Cir. 1999).
Scott v. United States, 419 F.2d 264 (D.C. Cir. 1969).
In re Sealed Case, 181 F.3d 128 (D.C. Cir. 1999).
Searcy, United States v., 233 F.3d 1096 (8th Cir. 2000).
Sera, United States v., 256 F.3d 778 (8th Cir. 2001).

U.S. District Court

Arnold, United States v., 678 F. Supp. 1463 (S.D. Cal. 1988).
Berthoff v. United States, 140 F. Supp. 2d 50 (D. Mass. 2001).
Bogle, United States v., 689 F. Supp. 1121 (S.D. Fla. 1988).
Redondo-Lemos, United States v., 754 F. Supp. 1401 (D. Ariz. 1990).

Massachusetts

Andrews, Commonwealth v., 2 Mass. (1 Tyng) 408 (1807).
Battis, Commonwealth v., 1 Mass. (1 Will.) 94 (1804).
Bonner, Commonwealth v., 97 Mass. 587 (1867).
Briggs, Commonwealth v., 24 Mass. (7 Pick.) 177 (1828).
Carver, Commonwealth v., 224 Mass. 42 (1916).
Chase, Jerusha, Commonwealth v., (Boston Mun. Ct. 1831), in *Reports of Criminal Cases, Tried in the Municipal Court of the City of Boston, Before Peter Oxenbridge Thacher* (Horatio Woodman ed., Boston: Little and Brown, 1845).
Conlon's Case, 148 Mass. 168 (1889).

Dowdican's Bail, Commonwealth v., 115 Mass. 133 (1874).

Fano, Commonwealth v., 400 Mass. 296 (1987).

Fisher v. McGirr, 67 Mass. (1 Gray) 1 (1854).

Gorham, Commonwealth v., 99 Mass. 420 (1868).

Gosselin, Commonwealth v., 365 Mass. 116 (1974).

Green v. Commonwealth, 94 Mass. (12 Allen) 155 (1866).

Hagarman, Commonwealth v., 93 Mass. (10 Allen) 401 (1865).

Horton, Commonwealth v., 26 Mass. (9 Pick.) 206 (1829).

Ingersoll, Commonwealth v., 145 Mass. 381 (1888).

Jennings, Commonwealth v., 105 Mass. 586 (1870).

Kossowan, Commonwealth v., 265 Mass. 436 (1929).

Lewis, Commonwealth v., 1 Mass. (1 Will.) 517 (1805).

M'Monagle, Commonwealth v., 1 Mass. (1 Will.) 517 (1805).

Mahoney, Commonwealth v., 115 Mass. 151 (1874).

Maloney, Commonwealth v., 145 Mass. 205 (1887).

Marks v. Wentworth, 199 Mass. 44 (1908).

McGovern, Commonwealth v., 183 Mass. 238 (1903).

Murach v. Massachusetts Bonding and Ins. Co., 339 Mass. 184 (1959).

Shanahan v. Boston and N.S. Ry., 193 Mass. 412 (1907).

Sullivan, Commonwealth v., 150 Mass. 315 (1889).

Taunton Mfg. Co. v. Smith, 26 Mass. (9 Pick.) 11 (1829).

Taylor, Commonwealth v., 370 Mass. 141 (1976).

Tuck, Commonwealth v., 37 Mass. (20 Pick.) 356 (1838).

Uhrig, Commonwealth v., 167 Mass. 420 (1897).

Wakelin, Commonwealth v., 230 Mass. 567 (1918).

Wallace, Commonwealth v., 108 Mass. 12 (1871).

Wheeler, Commonwealth v., 2 Mass. (1 Tyng) 172 (1806).

Winton, Commonwealth v., 108 Mass. 485 (1871).

Other States

CALIFORNIA
People v. Miller, 114 Cal. 10 (1896).

GEORGIA
Griffin v. State, 12 Ga. App. 615 (1913).

ILLINOIS
State v. Walker, 250 Ill. 427 (1911).

INDIANA
Miller v. State, 149 Ind. 607 (1898).

Myers v. State, 115 Ind. 554 (1888).

Sanders v. State, 85 Ind. 318 (1882).

IOWA
Iowa v. Hortman, 122 Ia. 104 (1904).

KENTUCKY
Mounts v. Commonwealth, 89 Ky. 274 (1889).

LOUISIANA
State v. Williams, 14 So. 32 (La. 1893).

MICHIGAN
People v. Brown, 54 Mich. 15 (1884).
People v. Cummings, 88 Mich. 249 (1891).
People v. O'Hara, 41 Mich. 623 (1879).

MISSISSIPPI
Deloach v. State, 77 Miss. 691 (1900).

MISSOURI
State v. Kring, 71 Mo. 551 (1880).
State v. Stephens, 71 Mo. 535 (1880).

NEW YORK
Adler, People v., 140 N.Y. 331 (1893).
Hawker v. People, 30 N.Y. 487 (1878).
Joyce, People v., 4 N.Y. Crim. 341 (Sup. Ct. 1886).
Kane v. People, 8 Wend. 203 (Ct. Corr. Err. 1831).
McLeod, People v., 1 Hill 377 (N.Y. Sup. Ct. 1841).
Porter, People v., 4 Park. 524 (N.Y. Oyer and Terminer 1860).
Rynders, People v., 12 Wend. 425 (N.Y. Sup. Ct. 1834).
Willis, People v., 52 N.Y.S. 808 (Sup. Ct. 1898).

OHIO
Craig v. State, 49 Ohio St. 415 (1892).

RHODE ISLAND
State v. Conway, 20 R.I. 270 (1897).

ENGLAND
Cranmer, Rex v., 88 Eng. Rep. 1578 (K.B. 1702).
Dunn, Regina v., 1 C. and K. N.P.R. 730, 731 (Q.B. 1843).

CODES AND SESSIONS LAWS

Massachusetts

Massachusetts Revised Statutes. Dutton and Wentworth, 1836.

Massachusetts General Statutes. William White, 1860.

Massachusetts Public Statutes. Rand, Avery, 1882.

Massachusetts Revised Laws. Wright and Potter, 1902.

Massachusetts General Laws. Wright and Potter, 1921.

Act of May 25, 1715, 1 Geo. 2, at 253 (Mass.) ("An Act Against Burglary").

Act of Apr. 26, 1770, ch. 16, §§ 2–3, 5 Mass. Prov. Acts 43 ("An Act for Preventing and Punishing Burglary, and for Repealing One Act Intitled 'An Act Against Burglary'").

Act of July 3, 1782, ch. 15, 1782 Mass. Acts 157 ("An Act for Establishing Courts of General Sessions of the Peace").

Act of Feb. 28, 1787, ch. 68, 1786 Mass. Acts 210 ("An Act for the Due Regulation of Licensed Houses").

Act of Mar. 9, 1804, ch. 89, §§ 3–4, 1804 Mass. Acts 490 ("An Act for Enlarging the Jurisdiction of the Courts of Common Pleas, and Other Purposes").

Act of Mar. 9, 1804, ch. 154, §§ 3–4, 1803 Mass. Acts 788 ("An Act Fixing the Times and Places of Holding the Courts of Common Pleas, and Courts of General Sessions of the Peace in the County of Middlesex").

Act of Mar. 16, 1805, ch. 143, § 3, 1804 Mass. Acts 240 ("An Act Providing for the Punishment of the Crimes of Robbery and Other Larcenies, and for the Prevention Thereof").

Act of June 20, 1807, ch. 18, § 1, 1807 Mass. Acts 172 ("An Act Respecting the Offices and Duties of the Attorney-General, Solicitor-General, and County Attorneys").

Act of June 20, 1809, ch. 32, 1809 Mass. Acts 37 ("An Act Repealing the First Section of an Act, Entitled 'An Act Respecting the Offices and Duties of the Attorney General, Solicitor General, and County Attorneys'").

Act of June 18, 1811, ch. 10, § 1, 1811 Mass. Acts 279 ("An Act Respecting the Offices and Duties of the Attorney-General, Solicitor General, and County Attornies").

Act of June 21, 1811, ch. 33, § 2, 1811 Mass. Acts 424 ("An Act Establishing Circuit Courts of Common Pleas Within This Commonwealth").

Act of Feb. 14, 1821, ch. 79, §§ 2–12, 8 Mass. Laws 545 ("An Act to Establish a Court of Common Pleas for the Commonwealth of Massachusetts").

Act of June 16, 1821, ch. 23, § 4, 8 Mass. Laws 595 ("An Act in Further Addition to an Act, Entitled, 'An Act To Establish a Court of Common Pleas for the Commonwealth of Massachusetts'").

Act of Mar. 14, 1832, ch. 130, §§ 10, 11, 12, Mass. Laws 396 ("An Act Enlarging the

Jurisdiction of the Court of Common Pleas in Criminal Cases, and Regulating the Appointment and Duties of Prosecuting Officers").

Act of Mar. 24, 1832, ch. 166, §§ 5, 15, 1832 Mass. Acts 473 ("An Act for the Due Regulation of Licensed Houses").

Act of Mar. 29, 1834, ch. 61, § 2, 1834 Mass. Acts 189 ("An Act for the Regulation of Goals and Houses of Correction").

Act of Apr. 20, 1837, ch. 242, § 1, 1837 Mass. Acts 279 ("An Act Concerning Licensed Houses, and the Sale of Intoxicating Liquors").

Act of Apr. 17, 1838, ch. 123, 1838 Mass. Acts 421 ("An Act Concerning the Police of Boston").

Act of Mar. 7, 1843, ch. 9, § 1, 1843 Mass. Acts 6 ("An Act Establishing the Salaries of Certain Public Officers").

Act of Mar. 24, 1843, ch. 99, 1843 Mass. Acts 60 ("An Act Abolishing the Office of Attorney General").

Act of Jan. 29, 1845, ch. 14, 1845 Mass. Acts 401 ("An Act Establishing the Salary of the District Attorney for the Southern District of This Commonwealth").

Act of Feb. 10, 1845, ch. 36, 1845 Mass. Acts 412 ("An Act Establishing the Salary of the District Attorney for the Northern District").

Act of Feb. 16, 1848, ch. 16, 1848 Mass. Acts 605 ("An Act to Establish an Additional District, for the Administration of Criminal Law").

Act of May 1, 1849, ch. 186, 1849 Mass. Acts 117 ("An Act To Establish the Office of Attorney General").

Act of May 15, 1851, ch. 162, 1851 Mass. Acts 657 ("An Act Providing for the Appointment of Police Officers").

Act of May 22, 1852, ch. 312, § 60, 1852 Mass. Acts 235 ("An Act Relating to the Proceedings, Practice, and Rules of Evidence in Actions at Law").

Act of May 22, 1852, ch. 322, § 13, 1852 Mass. Acts 257 ("An Act Concerning the Manufacture and Sale of Spirituous or Intoxicating Liquors").

Act of Apr. 20, 1855, ch. 215, §§ 15, 17, 24, 35, 1855 Mass. Acts 623 ("An Act Concerning the Manufacture and Sale of Spirituous and Intoxicating Liquors").

Act of May 19, 1855, ch. 405, §§ 1, 2, 1855 Mass. Acts 803 ("An Act for the Suppression of Certain Common Nuisances").

Act of May 16, 1856, ch. 173, §§ 1, 1856 Mass. Acts 98 ("An Act Concerning the Election of Clerks of Courts and Other County Officers").

Act of May 30, 1857, ch. 284, § 1, 1857 Mass. Acts 72 ("An Act Concerning the Discipline of the State Prison").

Act of Mar. 24, 1858, ch. 77, 1858 Mass. Acts 58 ("An Act Concerning the Discipline of Jails and Houses of Correction").

Act of Mar. 27, 1858, ch. 154, 1858 Mass. Acts 126 ("An Act in Relation to the Crime of Murder").

Act of Apr. 5, 1859, ch. 196, 1859 Mass. Acts 339 ("An Act Establishing the Superior Court").

Act of Apr. 6, 1859, ch. 216, § 1, 1859 Mass. Acts 371 ("An Act Fixing the Salaries of District-Attorneys").

Act of Oct. 17, 1859, ch. 282, § 1, 1859 Mass. Acts 632 ("An Act Relating to the Jurisdiction in Criminal Cases").

Act of Mar. 22, 1862, ch. 84, § 1, 1862 Mass. Acts 64 ("An Act Relating to the Challenging of Jurors in Civil and Criminal Cases").

Act of May 12, 1865, ch. 223, § 1, 1865 Mass. Acts 617 ("An Act To Prevent Evasions of the Provisions of Section Fifty-Eight of the Eighty-Sixth Chapter of the General Statutes").

Act of May 26, 1866, ch. 260, 1866 Mass. Acts 245 ("An Act in Relation to Evidence in Criminal Prosecutions").

Act of Apr. 30, 1868, ch. 141, §§ 18, 26, 1868 Mass. Acts 107 ("An Act To Regulate the Sale of Intoxicating Liquors").

Act of June 19, 1869, ch. 415, § 60, 1869 Mass. Acts 706 ("An Act Concerning the Manufacture and Sale of Intoxicating Liquors").

Act of May 6, 1872, ch. 352, § 1, 1872 Mass. Acts 320 ("An Act To Establish the Salaries of District Attorneys, and of the Assistant District Attorney for the Suffolk District").

Act of May 12, 1873, ch. 278, § 1, 1873 Mass. Acts 707 ("An Act Relating to Clerical Assistance for District Attorneys").

Act of Feb. 11, 1875, ch. 12, § 1, 1875 Mass. Acts 602 ("An Act Relating to Assistance for District-Attorneys in Certain Districts . . .").

Act of Mar. 9, 1875, ch. 43, § 1, 1875 Mass. Acts 631 ("An Act To Repeal Section Sixty of Chapter Four Hundred and Fifteen of the Acts of the Year Eighteen Hundred and Sixty-Nine Concerning the Precedents and Continuance of Liquor Cases").

Act of Apr. 5, 1875, ch. 99, §§ 1–6, 13, 1875 Mass. Acts 664 ("An Act To Regulate the Sale of Intoxicating Liquors").

Act of May 11, 1877, ch. 211, § 3, 1877 Mass. Acts 595 ("An Act Concerning Justices of the Peace and Trial Justices").

Act of Apr. 26, 1878, ch. 198, § 1, 1878 Mass. Acts 146 ("An Act Relative to Placing on Probation Persons Accused or Convicted of Crimes and Misdemeanors in the County of Suffolk").

Act of Feb. 20, 1880, ch. 28, 1880 Mass. Acts 31 ("An Act in Reference to Jurisdiction over Actions of Tort").

Act of Mar. 22, 1880, ch. 129, §§ 3, 4, 6–9, 1880 Mass. Acts 87 ("An Act To Provide for the Appointment of Probation Officers").

Act of Apr. 12, 1881, ch. 199, § 1, 1881 Mass. Acts 521 ("An Act Providing for the Trial of Actions Against Railroad Corporations, Common Carriers and Towns for Loss of Life By Negligence").

Act of May 13, 1883, ch. 223, 1883 Mass. Acts 510 ("An Act Granting Jurisdiction in Equity to the Superior Court").

Act of June 16, 1883, ch. 243, § 1, 1883 Mass. Acts 532 ("An Act Fixing the Responsibility of Railroad Corporations for Negligently Causing Death of Employees").

Act of May 21, 1884, ch. 255, §§ 2, 3, 1884 Mass. Acts 220 ("An Act To Establish a Reformatory for Male Prisoners").

Act of June 19, 1885, ch. 359, § 1, 1885 Mass. Acts 817 ("An Act Relating to the Disposition of Cases for the Violation of the Laws Relating to the Sale of Intoxicating Liquors").

Act of June 24, 1886, ch. 323, §§ 1–3, 1886 Mass. Acts 296 ("An Act Concerning Sentences to the Massachusetts Reformatory and the Terms of Imprisonment Therein").

Act of May 14, 1887, ch. 270, § 2, 1887 Mass. Acts 899 ("An Act To Extend and Regulate the Liability of Employers To Make Compensation for Personal Injuries Suffered by Employees in Their Service").

Act of May 31, 1887, ch. 332, 1887 Mass. Acts 954 ("An Act To Enlarge the Jurisdiction of the Superior and Probate Courts").

Act of June 16, 1887, ch. 435, § 1, 1887 Mass. Acts 1098 ("An Act To Provide for the Punishment of Habitual Criminals").

Act of May 28, 1891, ch. 356, §§ 1, 3, 1891 Mass. Acts 920 ("An Act To Provide for the Appointment of Probation Officers").

Act of June 6, 1891, ch. 379, § 1, 1891 Mass. Acts 966 ("An Act Relating to Prosecutions for Capital Crimes").

Act of Apr. 5, 1894, ch. 204, 1894 Mass. Acts 186 ("An Act Relating to the Trial of Indictments for Capital Crimes").

Act of May 26, 1894, ch. 440, § 1, 1894 Mass. Acts 492 ("An Act Relative to the Release of Prisoners from the State Prisons on Parole").

Act of June 4, 1895, ch. 469, § 1, 1895 Mass. Acts 532 ("An Act Relative to Sentence in Criminal Cases").

Act of June 5, 1895, ch. 504, §§ 1–2, 1895 Mass. Acts 624 ("An Act Relative to Sentences to the State Prison").

Act of Apr. 25, 1898, ch. 371, 1898 Mass. Acts 312 ("An Act Relative to Sentences to the State Prison").

Act of May 20, 1898, ch. 443, § 1, 1898 Mass. Acts 395 ("An Act Relative to Sentences to the State Farm").

Act of June 8, 1898, ch. 511, § 1, 1898 Mass. Acts 474 ("Act To Provide for the Appointment of Probation Officers in the Superior Court").

Mass. Rev. Laws ch. 173, § 112, at 1569 (Wright and Potter, 1902) ("Of Pleading and Practice").

Mass. Gen. Laws ch. 279, §§ 32–33, at 2840–41 (1921) ("Of Judgment and Execution").

Act of Apr. 23, 1926, ch. 271, § 1, 1926 Mass. Acts 267 ("An Act Relative to Probation, Suspended Sentences, and Filing of Complaints in District Courts").

Act of July 10, 1945, ch. 578, § 1, 1945 Mass. Acts 590 ("An Act Regulating the Setting Aside of Verdicts, and the Granting of New Trials, when Damages Awarded Are Inadequate").

California

California Penal Code. Sumner Whitney, 1881.

California Penal Code. Bancroft, 1885.

California Penal Code. San Francisco, Sumner Whitney, 1885.

California Penal Code. Legal Book Corp., 1976.

Act of Apr. 20, 1850, ch. 119, § 480, 1850 Cal. Stat. 275, 310 ("An Act To Regulate Proceedings in Criminal Cases").

Act of May 1, 1851, ch. 29, § 598, 1851 Cal. Stat. 212 ("An Act To Regulate Proceedings in Criminal Cases").

Act of Apr. 2, 1866, ch. 644, § 1, 1866 Cal. Stat. 865 ("An Act Relating to Criminal Prosecutions").

Act of Feb. 23, 1903, ch. 34, 1903 Cal. Stat. 34, 34 ("An Act To Amend an Act Entitled 'An Act To Establish a Penal Code'").

Act of Sept. 20, 1976, ch. 1139, § 271, 1976 Cal. Stat. 5061, 5139–40 ("An Act To Amend [Various] Sections . . .").

Idaho

Act of Mar. 9, 1911, ch. 200, § 1, 1911 Idaho Sess. Laws 664 ("An Act To Amend Sections 1 and 5 of an Act Entitled, 'An Act To Provide for the Indeterminate Sentence of Persons Convicted of Certain Felonies . . .'").

Illinois

Act of Mar. 3, 1845, ch. 300, § 183, 1845 Ill. Rev. Stat. 185 ("Of Process, Indictment, Arraignment, Trial, Judgment, Execution, and Writ of Error").

Act of June 28, 1919, § 3, 1919 Ill. Laws 436 ("An Act To Amend an Act Entitled, 'An Act To Revise the Law in Relation to the Sentence and Commitment of Persons Convicted of Crime . . .'".

Indiana

Act of Mar. 15, 1897, ch. 143, §§ 1, 3, 5, 1897 Ind. Laws 219 ("An Act Concerning the Manner of Procedure in the Trial of Certain Felonies, and Prescribing Punishment Therefor, and Appointing a Commission on Parole . . .").

Kansas

Act of Mar. 13, 1903, ch. 375, § 1, 1903 Kan. Sess. Laws 571 ("An Act To Provide for Indeterminate Sentence of Persons Convicted of Certain Felonies . . .").

Maine

Act of Mar. 25, 1864, ch. 280, § 1, 1864 Me. Laws 214 ("An Act Relating to Evidence in Criminal Prosecutions").

Maryland

Act of Apr. 6, 1894, ch. 402, § 1, 1894 Md. Stat. 583 ("An Act To Add an Additional Section to Article 27 of the Code of Public General Laws, Title 'Crimes and Punishments,' sub-title 'Sentence' ").

Michigan

Act of Apr. 3, 1869, No. 145, §§ 4–5, 1869 Mich. Acts 264 ("An Act To Provide for the Imprisonment and Detention of Convicted Persons in the Detroit House of Correction").

Act of June 7, 1905, ch. 184, § 2, 1905 Mich. Acts 268 ("An Act To Provide for the Indeterminate Sentence as a Punishment for Crime . . .").

Montana

Act of Feb. 10, 1917, ch. 16, § 1, 1917 Mont. Laws 16 ("A Bill for an Act Entitled: 'An Act To Amend Chapter 14 of the Laws of the Fourteenth Legislative Assembly, Entitled, "An Act Providing for Indeterminate Sentences . . ."'").

New Hampshire

Act of Apr. 6, 1909, ch. 120, § 2, 1909 N.H. Laws 460 ("An Act Relative to Sentences to the State Prison").

New Jersey

Act of Apr. 21, 1911, ch. 191, § 2, 1911 N.J. Laws 356 ("A Supplement to an Act Entitled 'An Act Relating to Courts Having Criminal Jurisdiction and Regulating Proceedings in Criminal Cases . . .' ").

New York

New York Revised Statutes, vol. 2. Packard and Van Benthuysen, 1829.

Annotated Consolidated Laws of the State of New York, vol. 2 (2d ed.). Banks Law, 1923.

Act of Mar. 21, 1801, ch. 58, §§ 1, 2, 1801 N.Y. *Stat.* 97 ("An Act Declaring the Crimes Punishable with Death or with Imprisonment in the State-Prison").

Act of Mar. 19, 1813, ch. 29, §§ 3, 4, 1813 N.Y. *Stat.* 407 ("An Act Declaring the Punishment of Certain Crimes").

Act of Apr. 15, 1817, ch. 269, §§ 5, 19, 1817 N.Y. Laws 310 ("An Act To Amend an Act Entitled, 'An Act Concerning the State Prisons'").

Act of May 7, 1869, ch. 678, § 1, 1869 N.Y. Laws 1597 ("An Act in Relation to Evidence in Criminal Prosecutions, and in all Proceedings in the Nature of Criminal Proceedings").

Act of Apr. 24, 1877, ch. 173, § 2, 1877 N.Y. Laws 186 ("An Act in Relation to the Imprisonment of Convicts in the New York State Reformatory at Elmira, and the Government and Release of Such Convicts by the Managers").

Act of June 14, 1881, ch. 504, §§ 671–672, 1881 N.Y. Laws 164 ("An Act To Establish a Code of Criminal Procedure").

Act of June 6, 1889, ch. 384, § 1, 1889 N.Y. Laws 532 ("An Act To Amend Section Three Hundred and Thirty-Two of the Code of Criminal Procedure, Providing That No Conviction Shall Be Had upon a Plea of Guilty in Certain Cases").

Act of Apr. 4, 1893, ch. 279, § 1, 1893 N.Y. Laws 559 ("An Act To Amend Section Twelve of the Penal Code, Relating to Punishment for Crimes").

Act of May 29, 1905, ch. 655, § 1, 1905 N.Y. Laws 1664 ("An Act To Amend the Penal Code, Relative to Juvenile Offenders and the Suspension of Sentence").

Act of May 4, 1909, ch. 282, § 1, 1909 N.Y. Laws 511 ("An Act To Amend the Penal Law, in Relation to the Minimum Terms of Indeterminate Sentences").

Act of May 6, 1918, ch. 457, § 1, 1918 N.Y. Laws 1339 ("An Act To Amend the Penal Law, in Relation to Suspension of Sentence, Suspension of Execution of Judgment and Probation, and To Provide for Cases in which Execution of Judgment has Heretofore Been Suspended").

Ohio

Act of Apr. 8, 1856, § 17, 1856 Ohio Laws 126 ("An Act Providing for the Appointment of Officers of the Ohio Penitentiary . . .").

Pennsylvania

Act of June 19, 1911, § 11, 1911 Pa. Laws 1055 ("An Act Authorizing the Release on Probation of Certain Convicts, Instead of Imposing Sentences; the Appointment of Probation and Parole Officers . . .").

Act of June 29, 1923, ch. 397, § 6, 1923 Pa. Laws 975 ("An Act To Amend Section Six of the Act . . . Entitled, 'An Act Authorizing the Release on Probation of Certain Convicts, Instead of Imposing Sentences; the Appointment of Probation and Parole Officers . . .'").

South Dakota

Act of Mar. 3, 1911, ch. 169, § 1, 1911 S.D. Laws 209 ("An Act Providing for the Imposing of Indeterminate Sentences Upon Convicts and the Parole of Same").

Tennessee

Act of Feb. 20, 1836, ch. 63, § 4, 1835–1836 Tenn. Pub. Acts 171 ("An Act To Amend an Act, Entitled 'An Act Prescribing the Mode of Conveying Criminals to the Public Jail and Penitentiary House Established in this State, and for Their Government Therein,'").

West Virginia

Act of Feb. 11, 1903, ch. 45, § 46, 1903 W. Va. Acts 138, 149–50 ("An Act To Amend and Re-enact Chapter One Hundred and Sixty-Three of the Code of West Virginia").

England

Prosecution of Offences Act, 1879, 42 and 43 Vict., ch. 22.

NEWSPAPERS

Boston Commonwealth, 1889.
Boston Daily Globe, 1879.
Boston Evening Transcript, 1880–1895, intermittently.
Cambridge Herald, 1848.
Cambridge Owl, 1848.
Cambridge Palladium, 1843.
Cambridge Tribune, 1882–1885.
Daily Evening Traveller (Boston), 1866.
Los Angeles Times, 1996.
Lowell Courier/Daily Courier, 1835–1847.
Lowell Journal, 1847–1848.
Manchester Mercury, 1791.
New York Times, 1865–1995, intermittently.
Salem Gazette, 1836–1837.
Springfield Daily Republican, 1865–1866.
Voice of Industry/New Era of Industry (Lowell), 1845–1848.

Index